17.95

Economic Policies in Canada

Ingrid A. Bryan

Butterworths
Toronto

Economic Policies in Canada

Printed and bound in Canada
5 4 3 2 1   2 3 4 5 6 7 8 9/8

Canadian Cataloguing in Publication Data

Bryan, Ingrid A.
  Economic policies in Canada

Includes bibliographies and index.
ISBN 0−409−81640−X

1. Canada−Economic policy−1945−1971.*
2. Canada−Economic policy−1971−   *
I. Title.

HC115.B79   330.971'064   C82−094064−X

The Butterworth Group of Companies
Canada:
Butterworth & Co. (Canada) Ltd., Toronto and Vancouver

United Kingdom:
Butterworth & Co. (Publishers) Ltd., London

Australia:
Butterworths Pty. Ltd., Sydney

New Zealand:
Butterworths of New Zealand Ltd., Wellington

South Africa:
Butterworth & Co. (South Africa) Ltd., Durban

United States:
Butterworth (Publishers) Inc., Boston
Butterworth (Legal Publishers) Inc., Seattle
Mason Publishing Company, St. Paul

For my father, Arvid Eriksson,
and to the memory of my mother, Gunvor.

Abbreviations

ADA   Area Development Agency
ADIA   Area Development Incentives Act
CDC   Canada Development Corporation
CPI   Consumer Price Index
CTC   Canadian Transport Commission
DREE   Department of Regional Economic Expansion
ECC   Economic Council of Canada
EPF   Established Program Financing
FIRA   Foreign Investment Review Agency
FRED   Fund for Rural Economic Development
GATT   General Agreement on Tariffs and Trade
GDA   General Development Agreements
GDP   Gross Domestic Product
GNE   Gross National Expenditures
GNP   Gross National Product
ICNT   Informal Composite Negotiating Text
IMF   International Monetary Fund
LIFT   Lower Inventories for Tomorrow
LNG   Liquid Natural Gas
OECD   Organization for Economic Cooperation and Development
OPEC   Organization for Petroleum Exporting Countries
PAFTA   Pacific Free Trade Area
RDIA   Regional Development Incentives Act

Contents

Tables

Maps

Figures

Preface

The purpose of this book is to give students and the general reader an up-to-date survey of current economic problems and policies in Canada. There is a need for a book in this area, a book which integrates the vast literature available on Canadian economic issues. In the last few years, a number of excellent books have been published by organizations such as the Economic Council of Canada, the C.D. Howe Research Institute, the Fraser Institute, and the Institute for Research on Public Policy. It has become almost impossible for the student, the practising economist or, indeed, the teacher to keep abreast of the flow of information. This book is an attempt to integrate some of the information into a comprehensive look at the Canadian economy from three angles: the allocation of resources, the distribution of income, and stabilization.

This is not an introductory economics textbook. I have assumed that the reader has some knowledge of the basic principles of economics. The material was developed for a second-year course on economic policy, taught to business and journalism students at Ryerson Polytechnical Institute, Toronto. Most of this book was written while I was on leave from Ryerson at the Economic and Social Research Institute in Dublin, Ireland in 1979–80. I am grateful to the Institute for providing office space, excellent library facilities and many stimulating discussions on economic policies.

Credit should also go to all my colleagues at Ryerson who offered much useful information, and to Bruce Wilkinson who commented on an early draft of the manuscript. I am also indebted to my editor, Sonia Paine, whose diligent efforts substantially improved the book and to Gail Duffus who typed the manuscript. Finally, I would like to thank my husband and children for their patience during the time I was writing the book.

Economic Policy in Canada

This book is about economic policy in Canada. It includes not only traditional stabilization policies – monetary and fiscal – but also economic policies as they affect industry, services, agriculture, the balance of payments, distribution of income, and trade. The book follows the traditional classification of the economic functions of government: allocation, distribution and stabilization. Government policies as they pertain to the allocation of resources between various sectors in the Canadian economy are analysed in Part I, distribution policies as they affect people and the provinces in Part II, and stabilization policies in Part III. In each chapter the problems government policies aim to solve are analysed, criticized and possible solutions delineated. As much as possible, the consensus solution is presented, that is, the solution most economists advocate. In those areas where considerable controversy exists, both sides are given.

The well-read student will, of course, object that economists do not agree on anything, and therefore uncontested policy conclusions are impossible. This belief is widely held, but it has little factual basis. Lipsey (1981: 41-3) points out that there are several reasons for the public's impression that economists never agree. In the first place, demand for dissent creates its own supply of dissent. Most economists are against permanent wage and price controls, but a large part of the public, and therefore politicians, are in favour of controls. If the politicians can drag out an obscure economist from the Hairy Hills Bible College who is prepared to admit that he or she thinks that wage and price controls are a great idea, that economist is going to attract a lot of attention. A second reason is media coverage. On any issue, the media attempt to present a balanced view by submitting at least two opposing views. If, in a given case, 95 percent of economists are in favour of a policy, the common practice of the media of interviewing one in favour and one against will create the erroneous impression of a fifty-fifty split. A third reason is the information explosion. An economist cannot be expected to know the relevant theories and facts in all parts of a discipline. Unfortunately, some economists may have a tendency to pontificate on matters of which they know little. Lipsey (1981:43) points out that the experts in an area usually agree on matters of substance.

The Introduction sets the stage for the book. It begins with a discussion of the relations between economic theory, analysis, policy, and management, followed by a discussion of the goals of the Canadian economy and their achievement.

Economic Theory, Analysis, Policy, and Management

It is useful to make a distinction between economic theory, analysis, policy, and management. Economic theory can be defined as the generally accepted body of theory available to the economist at a point in time. The body of theory is not fixed, but changes continually as some theories are proven wrong in the light of new evidence, and others are added. For example, the ideas of Keynes radically changed economic theory in the fields of employment and national income analysis. Recently, however, Keynesian theories have come under attack from the monetarist school, and economic theory pertaining to these fields has been in a state of flux.

Without theory there can be no analysis, as economic analysis uses economic theory to analyse real-life situations. Similarly, without economic analysis good economic policy cannot be designed, as without an understanding of the scope and the causes of a problem, a solution cannot be found. Economic policy includes a set of objectives (goals) as well as the instruments necessary for their achievement. The goals are usually determined through the political process. The appropriate instruments can be derived from economic analysis, but they may also be politically determined. For example, let us assume that an economic analysis of a problem suggests that an increase in government expenditures is a better measure to combat unemployment than a cut in taxes. However, any government today would probably reject an increase in the size of the budget in favour of a cut in taxes in view of the mood of the electorate which perceives government spending as being the source of all evils. This type of conflict between economic efficiency and political expediency is not unusual in western democracies, but is in many cases ignored by economists who perceive governments as being irrational and ill-informed. The fact that "good economic policy" often entails political suicide for the government has been of little interest to most economists.

Economists have in general held extremely unrealistic views of governments. They assume that the prime motive of governments is the maximization of the welfare of its citizens, ignoring the facts that governments need to be re-elected and that for this reason they often have to bow to special interest groups. Economic policy-making is likely to be more effective when economists recognize these facts.

Economic management refers to the actual process of coordinating and controlling the instruments and goals of economic policy. The field of economic management belongs to the realm of political and organizational theory.[1] In the federal government, economic management rests with the cabinet, the department of Finance and the Treasury Board. Specific areas of management are delegated to the Bank of Canada, to the departments of Industry, Trade and Commerce, Regional Economic Expansion, Consumer and Corporate Affairs, and others. In keeping with the biases of most economists, the problems of economic management will not be discussed in this book. However, we should bear in mind that good economic policy cannot be implemented without good economic management.

Goals for Economic Policy and Their Achievements

Most western democracies have set full employment, price stability, a high rate of economic growth, a viable balance of payments, and an equitable distribution of income as primary goals for economic policies. These goals were first introduced by the Canadian government in 1963 by the Economic Council of Canada in its first annual review.[2]

Full Employment

The goal of full employment is understood and supported by most people and governments in the East and West for the simple reason that most people do not like to be unemployed. Unemployment, despite the availability of unemployment insurance, usually leads to a lower standard of living and, for most people, to considerable mental suffering.

An economist would argue that unemployment has two effects on the economy: one is in terms of lost output and the other in terms of distribution. When there is unemployment, some output will be lost in consumption simply because it will not be produced. This means that a country's standard of living will be affected, for people will not be able to consume as many goods and services as previously. The living standards of future generations will also be affected if unemployment leads to lower production of investment goods. Less investment today leads to less output in the future.

Unemployment will also have distributional effects, the size and direction of which will depend on the nature of unemployment. If unemployment is caused by a general recession, unskilled workers will be affected. If a recession hits only selective industries, the distributional effects may be complex.

In its first annual review, the Economic Council (ECC) set a target of

3 percent as a desirable unemployment figure to be reached by 1970. This was rather optimistic, as the average unemployment rate for the period 1958-62 was 6.2 percent. The rate dropped in 1965 and 1966 to a low of 3.6 percent, a level which has not been achieved since. In its fourth annual review, the ECC recognized that 3 percent could not be achieved by 1970 and therefore extended the deadline to 1975. In 1972, the ECC gave up the idea of fixed goals and instead adopted the concept of performance indicators. These were designed as three-year performance targets, revised annually to take account of changing circumstances. The target for unemployment was changed to 4.2 percent. Since then the situation has gone from bad to worse. In the fifteenth annual review, the Council set a target of 7.3 percent which the Council felt was realistic. Recently, the rate has been hovering between 7 and 8.5 percent.

Table 1 indicates how Canada's unemployment rate compares with that of other countries. A word of caution: international comparisons are fraught with pitfalls as the sampling procedure or statistical methods used in assembling the data differ between countries, and for this reason the resulting unemployment rates may not be comparable. For example, the Swedish figures, often regarded as too low, do not include unemployed people who are undergoing retraining programs because they are not in the labour force. Similarly, people who have given up looking for work (discouraged workers) are not included in the Canadian statistics. Despite these qualifications it is probably correct to say that our unemployment rate is higher than in most other countries in the West. In 1979, only Belgium, Italy and Spain had a higher unemployment rate among those OECD countries for which unemployment rates are published. Japan, Sweden and Norway all had rates of less than 3 percent.

Price Stability

The goal of price stability is at least as elusive as the goal of full employment. Stable prices are usually desired by the electorate since most people perceive rising prices as lowering their standard of living. However, wages increase at a faster rate than prices for many groups in society.

Inflation does, nevertheless, impose some real costs on the economy. Economic growth will be affected if businessmen shy away from long-term investments because of uncertainty as to the future path of prices. Inflation also increases the cost of information in that both consumers and businessmen have to keep abreast of constantly changing prices, which in turn may divert resources from productive activity to information search. Inflation can be the cause of the misallocation of resources if consumers favour certain industries during periods of inflation which will then need more labour and capital. An example is the housing industry: people have learned by experience that property is a

TABLE 1
Selected Economic Indicators
for Some OECD Countries, 1979

	Increases in GDP at 1975 prices (%)	GDP per capita (current prices) (U.S. dollars)	Unemployment rate (%)	Inflation rate (%)	Current account balance (billions of U.S. dollars)	GINI* Coefficient Pre-tax	GINI* Coefficient Post-tax
Canada	2.9	9581.70	7.5	9.17	−5.098	.382	.354 (1969)
United States	2.3	10662.15	5.8	11.39	−0.788	.404	.381 (1972)
Japan	5.9	8721.52	2.1	3.73	−8.754	.335	.316 (1969)
Australia	4.4	8372.75	6.2	9.08	−1.807	.313	.312 (1966-67)
Belgium	2.4	11262.19	10.9	4.5	−0.101	—	—
France	3.2	10683.08	—	10.7	+4.913	.416	.414 (1970)
Germany	4.6	12449.68	3.8	4.13	−10.142	.396	.383 (1973)
Italy	5.0	5688.37	7.7	15.74	+4.249	—	.398 (1969)
Spain	0.8	5309.91	9.2	15.74	−0.054	—	.355 (1973-74)
Sweden	3.8	12278.21	2.1	8.27	−11.195	.346	.302 (1972)
United Kingdom	0.9	7165.12	5.4	13.32	−1.863	.354	.307 (1970)
Norway	3.2	11357.38	1.3	4.65	−5.855	—	—
Denmark	3.5	12943.13	6.0	7.57	−15.505	—	—
The Netherlands	2.2	10623.66	—	4.23	−4.686	.385	.354 (1967)
Switzerland	2.2	14966.92	—	3.65	—	—	—

*The GINI coefficient measures income distribution. The more equal the distribution, the lower the coefficient. For a full explanation, see Chapter 10.

Sources: OECD, *Main Economic Indicators*, Dec. 1980; OECD, *Economic Outlook*, July 1976.

reasonable hedge against inflation and are therefore attracted to the housing markets in periods of rising prices. The operations of capital markets also tend to get disturbed as people switch from long-term to short-term securities, from paper to "real" assets such as gold.

If the inflation rate in a country is worse than that in other countries, the Balance of Payments will be affected. As export markets shrink because our goods are too expensive, and as imports increase because foreign goods are now cheap, the Balance of Trade will deteriorate. If there are no offsetting international capital movements, and if the exchange rate is free to move, the exchange rate will drop. This drop tends to correct the Balance of Payments disequilibrium by making exports cheaper and imports more expensive. If imports claim a large share of the gross domestic product (GDP), this in turn can set off another inflationary round, and the economy is plunged into a vicious cycle (the British disease).

Inflation will also have distributional effects. It redistributes incomes from people to government as well as from one group of people to another group of people. The first effect is caused by increases in wages accompanying inflation. This pushes income earners into higher tax brackets if the income tax system is reasonably progressive. The result is that people must pay a larger share of their income in taxes, and the government's share of the GNP increases. The federal government has introduced indexing of personal exemptions and tax brackets to counter this effect of inflation.

The second effect is caused by the fact that everybody's income is not affected equally by inflation. Debtors gain and creditors lose. Wages of workers belonging to strong unions tend to keep up with inflation, whereas people on fixed incomes (for example, pensioners) tend to suffer. The effects on people with fixed incomes can be reduced through indexation, a controversial topic which will be discussed later.

Inflation can be defined as a continuous increase in the general level of prices. This increase is measured by the rate of increase of an index of prices, most commonly the consumer price index. The ECC, in its first annual review, advocated a goal of 2 percent inflation as being desirable. This goal was actually achieved in the early 1960s, but the inflationary spurt which began in 1973 made this goal unrealistic. In 1972, in its new policy of performance indicators, the Economic Council advanced a new way of defining inflation: inflation becomes a serious problem only if the rate exceeds that of a number of industrialized countries. This new definition indicates that the council regards the effects of inflation on the Balance of Payments as the most serious. However, such an attitude is illogical under a fluctuating exchange rate and puts too little emphasis on the other effects of inflation discussed above.

Canada's inflation rate during the '70s was high—an average of 8.9

percent between 1972 and 1977 (see Table I). Yet compared with other countries, Canada did quite well; only six countries in the OECD (Organization for Economic Cooperation and Development) did better (Germany, Switzerland, USA, Luxemburg, Austria, and the Netherlands). In 1979 Canada's price performance was not quite as good, with over 9 percent inflation, compared with several other countries that experienced inflation rates in the 3 to 4 percent range.

Economic Growth

The economic growth rate is the rate at which real output (GNP) grows. The desirability of a high rate of growth is not as obvious as it used to be. A high growth rate was thought to be beneficial because it entails large increases in the amount of goods and services produced and a source of potential improvement in the standard of living of the population.

The debate on the desirability of economic growth has concentrated on the concept of GNP as a measure of well-being, for economic growth can lead to substantial environmental decay and unhappiness. The well-known book, *The Limits to Growth* (Meadows *et al.* 1972), predicts that unless all economic growth is immediately stopped, the industrialized world will collapse by the year 2040. The collapse will be caused by over-population, scarcity of raw materials and environmental pollution. The book has been widely criticized for extrapolating from present trends to predict the future without allowing for changes in technology and for substitution of raw materials. (Needless to say, it is impossible to predict the technological changes that might occur before the year 2040.) Some-body once said that if a similar study had been made in the 1890s, the study would have predicted that on the basis of the current technology and trends, the main problem of cities in the 1980s would be the disposal of horse manure.

A more recent analysis of the implications of continued growth has come from the late Fred Hirsch in a very thoughtful book on *The Social Limits to Growth* (1976). Hirsch argued that as society progressed, more of the goods consumed would be positional goods. An example of a positional good is dining in an exclusive restaurant. As more people dine in such restaurants, one's own potential for deriving satisfaction from dining in them will be substantially diminished. Positional goods cannot be acquired or used by all, at least not without spoiling them for others, and therefore the result will be frustration and unsatisfied consumers.

However, to use these arguments as a justification for stopping all economic growth immediately is ludicrous. In the first place, a policy of no growth would be a policy of constant technology; that is, a worn-out machine has to be replaced by the same machine, not by a better one, as a better one would presumably be more efficient and therefore lead to more output. Secondly, without an active redistribution policy, a no-growth world would condemn the disadvantaged in the world to the economic status to which they were born. Yet we should not be complacent: "We [Economists] really have no business of being so goddamn cheerful" (Rosenbluth 1976:238). The possibility of shortages of raw materials and serious environmental impacts of new technologies are real enough to be taken seriously. It could therefore be argued that the rate at which new technologies are introduced and material output expanded should be slowed down. The rate of population growth should be curtailed and resources should be transferred from rich to poor countries (*ibid.*). We could therefore conclude that the appropriate policy is not to maximize the growth rate of GNP, but to maximize the growth rate of a better measure of economic well-being, a measure which takes account of all the negative aspects of growth such as environmental deterioration and effects on income distribution.

Considerable work has been done recently on designing such an indicator, most of which has concentrated on incorporating changes in leisure and income distribution in GNP estimates.[3] If GNP remains constant but the amount of leisure people have at their disposal increases, most people would agree that there is an improvement in economic welfare. Similarly, people would also agree that if the poor have become poorer and the rich richer while the GNP remains constant, then the economic welfare has decreased.

Beckerman (1978), in a study for OECD countries, adjusted GNP for changes in these two variables. He found that the ranking of countries based on GNP adjusted for leisure and income distribution was not appreciably different from a ranking of countries based on the 'crude' GNP. He therefore concluded that GNP is not a bad measure of economic welfare after all.

Compared with other countries, Canada has experienced a relatively high growth rate. In the period 1972-77, our average growth rate was 4.2 percent, which placed us fifth among OECD countries after Turkey, Yugoslavia, Norway, and Japan. In 1979 Canada's performance was not as impressive. Table 1 shows that countries such as Germany, Australia, Italy, and Japan did far better.

An Equitable Distribution of Income

The distribution of income takes two dimensions: the variation in income between people (the size distribution of income), and the variation in income between regions (the regional distribution of income). What constitutes an equitable distribution of income has never been defined, not even by the Economic Council of Canada. The issue is controversial, at least with respect to the size distribution of income. In all probability few people would want an absolutely equal distribution of income wherein everyone earned the same amount. An equal distribution, according to Marxist ideology, means everyone would receive according to his needs (which does not necessarily imply perfect equality). Such a system would engender its own problems, stemming from the removal of one of the major incentives to hard work: more money. Some communist countries have seen the reintroduction of monetary incentives to boost productivity. Therefore the goal of an equitable size distribution of income can probably be taken to mean more equitable than at present: most people would want to see a narrowing of the gap between the rich and the poor, presumably by making the poor richer. Why? Partly for moral reasons. Our Judeo-Christian heritage teaches us to help people who are less fortunate in life.[4] Another reason is that poverty imposes a real cost on the economy. Poverty often leads to illness and low productivity because of inadequate nutrition, hygiene and medical care.

The goal of an equitable regional income distribution is less controversial, and the ultimate aim could be taken to be the elimination of regional income disparities. Some economists have treated the income distribution goal as secondary compared to the other four goals (Officer and Smith 1974:2). This is hardly realistic in the Canadian context, as regionalism is one of the most pervasive aspects of Canadian life. A decrease in regional disparities is probably one of the preconditions for achieving the political goal of national unity.

Recent government policies have not radically altered either the size distribution or the regional distribution of income. Poverty by any measure is still widespread in Canadian society. Do we have proportionately more poor people in Canada than in other countries? Again, measurement problems are horrendous. Table 1 indicates that countries such as Sweden and the United Kingdom have a more even income distribution than Canada, whereas the United States, Germany and France have a more uneven distribution (assuming the figures are comparable and stable over time).

A Viable Balance of Payments

The goal of a viable Balance of Payments is difficult to define. The Balance of Payments is the record of all the transactions between Canadians and foreigners. It is divided into two accounts: the goods and service account, and the capital account. The goods and service account is broken down into the import and export of goods that make up the merchandise trade account, and the import and export of services—such as travel, transportation, consulting, interest, and dividends—comprise the service account. The capital account records capital inflows and outflows, such as sales or purchases of stocks and bonds and various types of

IOU's. Anything that is a claim to Canadian resources is entered as a payment in the Balance of Payments. Anything that affects Canadians having a claim to foreign resources is a positive item (a receipt).

Under flexible exchange rates, the movement in the exchange rate reflects the external balance situation. If Canadians wish to acquire more foreign exchange (for example, to pay for imports and foreign travel) than foreigners are willing to supply at the going rate (foreigners supply foreign exchange to us when they demand Canadian dollars for purchases of Canadian goods, services or securities), the exchange rate, like any other price, will fall (depreciate) until the market is cleared. If the demand for Canadian dollars is greater than the supply, the exchange rate will appreciate.

A depreciating Canadian dollar makes our exports cheaper in foreign countries and imports more expensive in Canada, a situation which will tend to correct the imbalance. However, a falling currency can be inflationary, if trade constitutes a large share of the economy. The price of imports will have increased for domestic consumers; and an increased world demand for Canadian products will push up export prices as well. Inflation can lead to further depreciations. Speculators may reinforce the downward movement. Large variations in exchange rates increase information costs to consumers and producers, who have to keep abreast of the changes. These costs may in the end turn out so large that trade is discouraged and employment decreases.

What is a viable Balance of Payments under a flexible exchange rate regime? Perhaps it can be thought of as a situation where there are only minor fluctuations in the demand and supply for Canadian dollars and therefore smooth and gradual movements in the exchange rate.

During the last few years, Canada has hardly experienced a viable Balance of Payments by any definition. Traditionally, we have had a current account deficit which has been financed by long-term capital inflows, partly in the form of direct investments and partly in the form of borrowing. Recently the current account deficit has increased because of a large increase in the deficit of the interest and dividend account. Meanwhile direct investment has decreased in size; also, in the last few years, Canadians have invested more abroad than have foreigners in Canada.[5] These trends, combined with a weakening of the tendency to borrow abroad by large corporations and municipalities, has led to a persistent downward pressure on the Canadian dollar, which was probably reinforced by speculation. This happened despite the intervention of the Bank of Canada, both in the form of official purchases of Canadian dollars and frequent adjustments in short-term interest rates to encourage capital inflows into Canada.

Table 1 shows current account deficits of some OECD countries. As in the other areas of full employment, price stability, economic growth, and income distribution, Canada's performance is mediocre and could be greatly improved by more effective economic policies.

Policy Conflicts and Policy-Making

Economic policy-making is extremely hazardous as the goals are not necessarily independent; that is, a policy designed to lessen unemployment and increase growth may make inflation worse. An anti-inflationary policy may also conflict with the income distribution goals as such a policy may increase unemployment in some regions more than others, as well as affect some income groups more than others. Policies designed to stabilize the exchange rate (e.g., high interest rates) can adversely affect unemployment and economic growth just as it can discourage domestic investments.

Because of these policy conflicts, a choice between the goals may have to be made, and the choice will probably be made politically. Recent studies have shown that the electorate, at least in other countries, is more adverse to an increase in unemployment than to an increase in inflation.[6] For example, one study shows that an increase in the unemployment rate of 1 percent led to a decrease in electoral support for the government by 4.2 percent in the United States and 6 percent in the United Kingdom, whereas an increase in the inflation rate of 1 percent led to a decrease in support by 1 percent in the United States and 0.6 in the United Kingdom (Frey 1978). If these rates are an indication of the situation in other countries as well, then it follows that if a government is not certain about its re-election, it is more likely to put a priority on achieving full employment than price stability.

Other figures show a direct relation between income level, unemployment, inflation, and electoral support. For example, in the United States in the period 1969-75, a 1 percent increase in the unemployment rate lost 4.4 percent in electoral support among people earning less than $3,000 and only 1.8 percent among people earning over $15,000. The corresponding figures for a 1 percent increase in the inflation rate was a 1 percent loss of support among low-income earners and a 2.6 percent loss among high-income earners. These figures indicate that government policies may also depend on where the government feels its support lies: among low-income earners or others.

The conflict with the distribution goal, or rather, the effects of policies on income distribution have become a serious obstacle to any change in economic policies. Policy changes were easy to effect in the sixties when growth was rapid. Rapid growth made it possible for individuals to become better off without making others worse off. If a group consistently had to bear the burden of policy changes, the group was not sufficiently organized to block the changes. The slowing down of growth, and the organization of various minorities into effective pressure groups have changed the situation radically. According to Lester Thurow, in his book *Zero-Sum Growth* (1980), the whole of society today resembles a zero-sum game (the gains exactly equal the losses), and therefore most policy initiatives designed to deal with today's problems will be defeated. For example, the federal government has been unable to raise the price of oil to world levels because of the effects this would have on the auto industry in Ontario. No citizens want waste disposal sites or nuclear power plants near their residential areas. Any policy which harms somebody is going to be vigorously opposed, and most policies have distributional implications. Thurow (p. 10) tells a story of the time he was addressing a Harvard Alumni Union on the topic of economic growth. He was making the point that a higher level of growth would mean higher investments. Higher investments could only come from more savings, that is, less consumption. Whose consumer habits or incomes were to be cut? One student suggested eliminating welfare payments. Thurow pointed out that such a measure would have a negligible effect and that it would not increase growth appreciably. The students could not suggest any additional income to cut.

Summary and Conclusions

This introduction gave a general overview of economic policy and its relation to economic theory, economic analysis and economic management. Without good theory and good analysis, good policy cannot be devised. Good policy cannot be implemented without good economic management.

Economic policy has to be set in a framework of the ultimate goals of society. These aims or goals are determined by the political process. Most countries, including Canada, aim to achieve full employment, no inflation, a high economic growth rate, an equitable income distribution, and a viable balance of payments. This chapter showed that Canada has not realized these goals; nor have most other industrialized countries, although some have done better than others. Clearly, Canada's performance can be much improved. The aim of this book is to offer suggestions as to how this can be done.

Part I surveys the allocation of resources in the Canadian economy. If the allocation of resources could be made more efficient—if our resources of land, labour and capital could be better utilized—the GNP and employment would increase, bringing the economy closer towards the goals of full employment and economic growth. A more efficient allocation of resources could also have a beneficial effect on price stability and the Balance of Payments. Greater price stability would be achieved if critical bottlenecks and capacity constraints were removed.

The Balance of Payments would be favourably affected if an efficient allocation of resources meant greater efficiency (productivity) in the export sector.

Part II of the book deals directly with the goal of an equitable income distribution, and Part III with full employment, price stability and the Balance of Payments from a macroeconomic viewpoint.

NOTES

1. For a study of economic management in Canada, see Phidd and Doern 1978.
2. Economic Council 1964. The Economic Council was established in 1962 to study medium- and long-term problems of the economy in contrast to the short-term orientation of the department of Finance.
3. See, for example, Beckerman 1978. Other studies tried to incorporate pollution, but found that this factor had a small effect on the estimates.
4. For a philosophical discussion, see Rawls (1971) who argues that an unequal distribution of income is only acceptable if it benefits everyone.
5. This statement does not take into account the foreign investment that takes place through the retained earnings of foreign corporations. For a discussion, see Chapter 13.
6. See, for examples, Frey 1978, Nordhaus 1975 and Lindbeck 1976.

BIBLIOGRAPHY

Beckerman, Wilfred. *Measures of Leisure, Equality and Welfare.* Paris: Organization of Economic Cooperation and Development (OECD), 1978.

Economic Council of Canada. *First Annual Review* 1964, *Fourth Annual Review* 1967; *Ninth Annual Review* 1972; *Fifteenth Annual Review* 1978. Ottawa: Queen's Printer or Supply and Services.

Frey, Bruno S. "Keynesian Thinking in Politico-Economic Models." *Journal of Post-Keynesian Economics* (1), 1978, pp. 71-81.

Hirsch, Fred. *The Social Limits to Growth.* Cambridge, Mass.: Harvard University Press, 1976.

Lindbeck, A. "Stabilization Policy in Open Economies with Endogenous Politicians." *American Economic Review* (66), 1976, pp. 1-19.

Lipsey, R. G. "Economists, Policy-Makers and Economic Policy." In

D. C. Smith (ed.), *Economic Policy Advising in Canada, Essays in Honour of John Deutsch.* Montreal: C. D. Howe Research Institute, 1981.

Meadows, D. *et al. The Limits to Growth.* New York: Universe Books, 1972.

Nordhaus, W. D. "The Political Business Cycle." *The Review of Economic Studies* (42), 1975, pp. 169-90.

Officer, L. and L. B. Smith (eds.). *Issues in Canadian Economics.* Toronto: McGraw-Hill Ryerson, 1974.

Phidd, R. W. and G. Bruce Doern. *The Politics and Management of Canadian Economic Policy.* Toronto: Macmillan, 1978.

Rawls, John. *A Theory of Justice.* Cambridge, Mass: Harvard University Press, 1971.

Rosenbluth, Gideon. "Economists and the Growth Controversy." *Canadian Public Policy* (II) 1976, pp. 225-39.

Thurow, L. *The Zero-Sum Society: Distribution and the Possibilities for Economic Change.* New York: Basic Books, 1980.

PART I

The Allocation of Resources

Resources such as land, labour and capital are used to produce the goods and services consumed in an economy. What goods and services are produced is largely determined by the price mechanism—by the market.[1] A sector expands if the public wants it to expand. The public signals its wants by its demand. If the demand for a good increases because people have changed their tastes or lifestyle, the price of the good will increase, profits in the production of the good will increase and production will expand. The expansion in production will attract more resources into the sector. Some sectors of the economy expand because of technological improvements in production which lower the costs and increase profits, others because the demand for the goods they are producing is income elastic. Some sectors contract because (1) cost and developments in productivity have made production unprofitable, or (2) the demand for the product has become income inelastic, or (3) tastes have changed.

The allocation of output between various sectors in the Canadian economy is given in Table 2. As can be seen, there have been some changes over the years. Resources have shifted out of agriculture and manufacturing into services, particularly community, business and personal services. These shifts are not unusual for a developed economy. Services are considered to have a high income elasticity of demand, and therefore the demand expands at a faster rate than the economy expands. It is interesting to note that manufacturing's share of output and the share of output of personal and community services have not changed as much as their share of employment. This can be explained by productivity. Manufacturing, which has always had a high productivity of output, has been able to expand output and therefore (almost) maintain its share of output by economizing on labour, whereas community and personal services, being highly labour intensive and having low productivity, can only expand output by attracting substantial amounts of additional labour.

15

No discussion of the allocation of resources is complete without a discussion of the many ways governments affect the allocation of resources. Production of services by government is an obvious example, but governments can also interfere with the market by making regulations, by giving subsidies, or by implementing discriminatory taxation policies that affect the prices or profits of private industry. Reasons for government interference are political and economic. There are three economic arguments for government interference in the allocation of resources. One is the need for government to produce public goods, a second is the need to correct for externalities, and a third is the need to correct monopoly elements in the economy. Since these reasons are frequently alluded to in the book, they deserve some explanation.

A public good is a good which everybody can consume at the same time, without reducing the total amount available. Nobody can be excluded from consuming it. An example is national defence. Every citizen receives protection from an army, regardless of whether he/she has paid his/her taxes. In practice, a public good must be produced by the government because not enough would be produced if the good were produced privately. In theory, a private firm could raise money for an army by subscription, and patriotic citizens would probably give a voluntary contribution towards it. However, some people, even if they wanted an army, would be reluctant to contribute towards its upkeep, knowing that as long as other people were contributing, they could enjoy the benefits of an army without giving a penny. They can act as free riders on other people's contributions.

The second reason for government interference in the allocation of resources is to correct for externalities. A firm or an individual takes only private benefits and costs into consideration—not social benefits and costs. A firm that operates a factory which belches out smoke, which in turn becomes acid rain, which in turn pollutes lakes imposes a considerable cost on society, a cost which is not entered in its calculations of marginal costs. By equating marginal revenue with its own private marginal costs, the firm selects an output which is not optimal—it is too high. One way to correct this is for the government to levy a tax on output equal to the cost (damage) imposed by the firm's actions on the environment. The firm should then voluntarily cut back production to a level in which marginal revenue is equal to marginal social cost. The government could use the tax revenue to compensate the people who are adversely affected by the firm's actions.

In the case where a firm's production yields a beneficial spillover on another activity, the government could give the firm a subsidy, so that production could be expanded to a point where marginal social benefits are equal to marginal social costs. An example of a service with considerable external benefits is the production of primary education. The individual benefits but so does society. Presumably a society in which every-body is literate functions better than one in which everybody is not.

The third reason for government intervention is to curb monopoli-zation. In a monopoly, output is underproduced at too high a price, and too few resources are channelled into this particular sector of the econ-omy. Through legislation, government can interfere to remove barriers to entry and anticompetitive practices. In those cases where monopoly is unavoidable (natural monopoly), the government can regulate the industry in such a way that prices and output would be the same as if the firm operated in a competitive environment.

For these reasons and others, the role of government in the econ-omy has expanded. However, to measure the growth of government is not easy. In Table 2 the role of government as a producer of goods and services (and as a regulator of the private sector) is hidden in the data; the government is not shown as a separate sector. The service sector, in particular, carries a large proportion of government services (examples are education, health services, utilities, public transit, some rail and air

TABLE 2
Percentage Distribution of Output and Employment
by Sectors in the Economy

	Output				Employment	
	1950	1960	1970	1980	1970	1980
Agriculture	10.1	4.9	3.3	2.6	6.4	4.5
Non-agricultural primary industries	6.6	5.5	5.0	4.1	2.7	2.8
Manufacturing	29.1	26.4	23.3	21.4	22.3	19.7
Construction	5.8	6.0	6.3	6.3	5.9	5.8
Total goods	51.6	42.8	37.9	34.4	37.3	32.8
Transportation, storage, communications, utilities	11.5	12.4	11.9	13.7	8.8	8.5
Trade	12.3	12.8	12.4	11.8	16.8	17.2
Finance, insurance, real estate	9.2	11.6	11.3	13.6	4.8	5.7
Community, business, personal services	10.3	13.5	19.2	19.6	25.8	28.9
Public Administration	5.1	6.9	7.3	6.9	6.4	6.9
Total services*	48.4	57.2	62.1	65.6	62.6	67.2

Sources: Statistics Canada, *National Income and Expenditure Accounts* (Cat. 13−201, 13−531)
* The total for goods and services may not add up to 100 because of rounding.
and *Historical Labour Force Statistics* (Cat. 71−201).

services), but how much is not apparent. In practice the most commonly quoted measure of the role of government in the economy is total government expenditures as a proportion of GNE (Gross National Expenditures). Using this measure, it can be shown (Table 3) that in twenty years the share of government (federal, provincial and municipal) has increased from approximately 30 percent to 40 percent of GNE. However, a large part of government expenditures takes the form of transfer payments to individuals, through which it is the individual who decides what goods and services to buy, not the government. Therefore government expenditures should be adjusted for transfer payments. Table 3

TABLE 3

The Role of Government in the Economy, 1960–80

(% of GNE at current prices)

Year	Total government expenditures	Transfer payments*	Government expenditures adjusted for transfers
1960	29.7	12.0	17.7
1961	30.8	10.9	19.9
1962	30.7	10.9	19.8
1963	30.3	10.8	19.5
1964	29.6	10.6	19.0
1965	29.9	10.4	19.5
1966	30.9	10.5	20.4
1967	32.9	11.6	21.3
1968	33.7	12.1	21.6
1969	34.1	12.4	21.7
1970	36.4	13.3	23.1
1971	37.3	13.9	23.4
1972	37.8	14.7	23.1
1973	36.4	14.3	22.1
1974	37.9	15.4	22.6
1975	41.3	17.3	24.0
1976	40.3	16.8	23.5
1977	41.4	17.3	24.1
1978	42.0	17.9	24.1
1979	40.3	17.3	23.0
1980	41.7	18.8	22.7

* Transfers are calculated by subtracting government expenditures on goods and services and gross capital formation from total government expenditures.
Source: Statistics Canada, *National Income and Expenditure Accounts* (Cat. 13–001, 13–531).

shows that after this adjustment has been made, government expenditures as a share of GNE increase from 18 to 23 percent.

Table 3 is based on figures quoted in current dollars. If the goods and services on which the government spends its money have increased more in price than other goods and services, the government's share of money GNE must increase without its share of real GNE increasing. This has actually occurred. In real terms, the share of government expenditure on goods and services has remained approximately constant over the last twenty years, and has even shown a small decline in the 1970s (Bird 1979:20). However, because productivity increases in the public sector (which is mainly engaged in the production of services) have been slower than in the private sector, it could be expected that an almost constant output share for the public sector implies an increased share of resources. Table 4 shows that the proportion of the labour force in the public sector has not increased appreciably.

There has been considerable alarm over what is considered government intrusion in private business through crown corporations. The recent acquisition of Petrofina by Petro-Canada has fuelled this concern. In December 1977 the Treasury Board, after an incomplete count, was reputed to have found 373 federal-government-owned enterprises.

TABLE 4
Public-Sector Employment
as a Percentage of Total Employment, 1961–75

Year	Percentage
1961	22.7
1962	22.7
1963	22.9
1964	22.8
1965	22.7
1966	22.5
1967	23.2
1968	23.4
1969	23.5
1970	23.7
1971	23.7
1972	23.6
1973	23.5
1974	23.5
1975	24.0

Source: Bird, *Financing Canadian Government: A Quantitative Overview*, Tables A1 and A4.

Because of the lack of sufficient data, it is difficult to estimate the importance of public enterprise in the economy. Bird (p. 4) related sales revenue of government enterprise to GNE but found no real trend. In 1961 it was 8.7 percent of GNE, and in 1975, 8.3 percent.

The chapters making up Part I provide a detailed analysis of problems in some of the major sectors of the Canadian economy, of how government has reacted to these problems, and of more efficient alternatives to current policies. Agriculture, resources and manufacturing are included among the goods-producing sectors; health, education and transportation among the service-producing sectors. The emphasis in the analysis is on how to achieve efficiency. Distribution issues are only touched upon, as they are discussed in Part II.

NOTE

1. There is considerable controversy over the role of the market in contemporary society. Some economists believe that the consumer is still sovereign, whereas others like Galbraith believe that large corporations are powerful enough to dictate to the consumer what he or she should buy.

BIBLIOGRAPHY

Bird, Richard M. *Financing Canadian Government: A Quantitative Overview*. Toronto: Canadian Tax Foundation, 1979.

CHAPTER 1

Agriculture

As in all other industrialized countries, the relative importance of agriculture as an industry in Canada has declined substantially over the last eighty years. In 1900 approximately 75 percent of the population was engaged in farming compared to 4.5 percent in 1980. Farming was easy to enter because of the homesteading policy of the federal government, whereby a farmer could claim 160 acres of land provided he had lived on it and worked it for five years. The farms were usually self-sufficient, yielding a variety of crops and livestock.

After World War II, the exodus from agriculture escalated, and agriculture's share of GNP dropped from 11.8 percent in 1951 to 2.6 percent in 1980.[1] Agriculture's share of exports in the same time period declined from 26 percent to 10.8 percent. The number of farms decreased by over 20 percent. Yet total agricultural output increased because of substantial increases in productivity. The increase was caused by mechanisation, specialization, better technology, and improvement in seed and livestock varieties. Farmers also became increasingly dependent on other industries for supplies, food processing and distribution (known collectively as *agribusiness*). The traditional mixed farm all but disappeared. Between 1971 and 1976, the number of farms reporting milk cows decreased by 30 percent, and the number reporting hogs by 45 percent. Poultry and livestock production became separate enterprises. Farms became bigger and the value of land increased. The real value of land and buildings per farm nearly doubled between 1971 and 1976, the average capital value of a farm being $200,000 by the end of 1976. The increased value created substantial barriers to entry into farming and led to the fear that the family farm would disappear. However, so far the majority of farms are family-owned.[2]

Many Canadians see the agricultural sector as one in which Canada has a considerable comparative advantage from a world-wide perspective. We do indeed have a trade surplus in food products, but this surplus is mainly due to wheat production. We have only moderate trade surpluses in oil seed, and oil seed products, in animal feeds and in animals, meat and meat products. We have a growing deficit in fruit, vegetables, nuts, and in other products such as seeds for sowing, honey, sugar, tobacco, and vegetable fibre (Wilkinson 1980:98). Many analysts predict that Canada will be a net food importer within the foreseeable future.

In this chapter the problems in agriculture will be surveyed, as well as government policies and a critique of them. A particular section will be devoted to Canada's role as a major food supplier.

Problems in Canadian Agriculture

The traditional problems of agriculture as seen by farmers, the agribusiness sector and government are low income and instability. In no other industry are worker incomes as closely tied to the supply and demand for the product. The gross income of a farm family is, after all, equal to the total revenue it receives from sales.

The long-term decline in the importance of agriculture in the economy and the tendency towards low farm prices and incomes can be attributed to Engel's Law and to improvements in productivity. Engel observed that as real incomes increase, the proportion of income spent on food tends to decline (the income elasticity is less than one, as there is clearly a limit as to how much food a person is capable of consuming), whereas the proportion spent on manufactured products tends to increase (the income elasticity is greater than one). This means that over time, the demand for manufactured products will expand at a faster rate than the demand for food, leading to a relative decline in the price of food, assuming constant supply.

Technological change has been very rapid in agriculture, probably moreso than in most other industries. This fact, combined with substitution of capital for labour, led to great increases in productivity, shifting the agricultural supply curve to the right, thus exacerbating the effects of the demand-induced changes on prices. However, technological change has probably declined considerably over the last decades. Shute (1975) estimates *yearly* increases in total-factor productivity at only 0.07 percent between 1962 and 1974.

The tendency of farm incomes to lag behind incomes in other sectors of the economy came to a halt in the mid-1970s, partly because of crop-induced shortages of grain and other cereals which pushed up prices, and partly because of the increased influence of marketing boards. The real income of farmers increased substantially, almost doubling between 1971 and 1976. Recent research by the Economic Council of Canada (1981) indicates that the average farmer, at least in Ontario, receives a real rate of return on his or her effort (and capital) close to that achieved in other industries. Yet, it is true to say that there is a large poverty-ridden sector in Canadian agriculture (Veeman and Veeman 1978). The majority of farms are too small to provide adequate family incomes.

Another problem closely associated with the problem of low income is that of price and income instability. Agricultural prices tend to be unstable, mainly because of weather-induced changes in supplies of grains, vegetables and fruit. Since the demand and supply of many agricultural products are inelastic, the supply changes are translated into relatively substantial price changes. Changes in grain prices will in turn affect livestock prices through the cost of feed. The effects on livestock prices tend to lag behind grain prices, as farmers will adjust by either slaughtering or building up their herds, which can take some time. Cattle prices and hog prices in particular tend to follow a cobweb-type cycle. In Ontario, the annual variations in farm cash receipts are greatest for grain growers and smallest for dairy, poultry and egg producers.

Price instability is usually considered harmful and discouraging to investment in farming. It is also claimed that neither producers nor consumers like the uncertainty associated with vast price fluctuations, and that fluctuations in food prices affect the consumer price index which in turn can give false signals as to the proper conduct of monetary and fiscal policy. The first claim rests on the assumption that farmers are "risk averse": the greater the price fluctuations, the greater the uncertainty about the future and therefore the less will be invested. However, the opposite view that instability increases the propensity to invest may also be true.[3] A substantial amount of investments in agriculture takes place in periods of high prices, since high farm incomes imply a large cash flow and a potential source for investment. Reinvesting this cash back into the farm usually leads to considerable tax savings.

The second claim implies that instability adversely affects consumer and producer welfare. Recent theoretical research has demonstrated that instability is more beneficial to consumers than if prices were stabilized at their arithmetic average.[4] When the effects on producers are introduced in addition to the effects on consumers, the problem becomes complex and it is not clear if the net effects on welfare are positive or negative.[5]

It is obviously true that unstable farm prices will affect the consumer price index,[6] particularly if the price cycles of different agricultural products happen to coincide. Whether or not this is a problem depends on how well informed the public and politicians are about the way in which the price mechanism operates and about the components of the consumer price index. To increase information on these matters may well be a better option than to stabilize prices. Most economists would tend to opt for instability, provided society took some measures to alleviate the plight of those whose survival is threatened by instability. It is possible that extremely high food prices in a particular year may lead to mass starvation in some countries.

Current Policies
Used to Alleviate the Income and Instability Problems

There are two ways to raise farm incomes: by increasing the price of agricultural products (assuming inelastic demand), or by giving the farmers more money through direct income transfers and/or subsidies to food production. The government has tried both approaches. Policies to raise incomes through transfers have included assistance to farmers in low crop-yield areas (the Prairie Farm Assistance Act of 1939), grants for agricultural improvements (FRED, the Fund for Rural Economic Development, 1967), funds designated specifically for small farmers (The Small Farm Development Program, 1971), and various credit programs. The other means of raising incomes through price increases is mainly accomplished through a policy of supply restrictions by marketing boards (discussed below).

The government's approach to instability has included attempts to stabilize prices through subsidies and supply management programs, and to stabilize incomes through income subsidies or deficiency payments. The 1975 amendments to the Agricultural Stabilization Act gives the Agricultural Stabilization Board the power to stabilize the price of agricultural products by buying products at minimum prices set by the board and by making deficiency payments (subsidies), or other payments to farmers (*Canada Yearbook* 1978–79:464). The commodities include slaughter cattle, hogs, sheep, industrial milk, industrial cream, corn, soybeans, and oats and barley produced outside the jurisdiction of the Canadian Wheat Board (eastern Canada and southern British Columbia). The Western Grain Stabilization Act guarantees that the net cash flow of grain growers in the current year will not fall below the average of the previous five years.

Supply management programs are undertaken through marketing boards. Stability is usually attempted by allocating production quotas to farmers and/or establishing buffer stocks when the commodity can be stored. The buffer stocks would be added to in periods of overproduction and depleted in periods of shortages.

Marketing Boards have objectives other than stability, including standardizing the terms of sale of the product. Such an objective can be interpreted as an attempt to equalize returns between different producers (Hiscock and Bennet 1977). Another objective is to raise incomes for producers. Indeed, the most frequently heard justification for marketing boards is the bad bargaining position of the farmers *vis-à-vis* agribusiness. Farming is competitive, whereas agribusiness (for example, food processing) is not because it is dominated by relatively few firms.[7] These large firms can collude and extract low prices from farmers who, not organized, have no bargaining power. Therefore one way for farmers to receive a fair price is to organize into marketing boards that can then bargain collectively with agribusiness.

Farm incomes can certainly be raised through marketing boards. If supply management aims not only to even out fluctuations in price, but also to restrict supplies at all times, a marketing board can push up prices to monopoly levels. If demand is inelastic—which it is for many food products—this will lead to higher gross incomes for producers.

The growth in marketing boards has been spectacular. During 1975–76, there were 108 provincially authorized marketing boards (*Canada Yearbook* 1978–79:482). All provinces have egg-marketing boards, nine have milk-marketing boards and eight have broiler boards. In addition, there are provincial grain, sheep, cattle, hog, turkey, fruit, vegetable, tobacco, and honey-marketing boards. These boards vary substantially in their powers and their exercise of powers. Many impose quotas and minimum prices, and almost all require of its members a licence to produce. The most restrictive boards are the fluid milk boards, followed by the egg and poultry boards (Hiscock and Bennet 1977). At the other extreme, there are boards such as the Alberta Cattle Commission, which functions merely as a promotion organization.

Before 1972 there were only two federal marketing boards: the Canadian Wheat Board and the Canadian Dairy Commission. There was a definite need, however, for some coordination of provincial boards, as the actions of one provincial board could nullify those of a board in another province. The enabling legislation for federal boards was passed in 1972 in the Farm Products Marketing Agencies Act (Canada Yearbook 1978–79:481-82). Since then the Canadian Egg Marketing Agency (CEMA), the Canadian Turkey Marketing Agency and the Canadian Chicken Marketing Agency have been established. Plans have also been made to establish a national potato agency. Each national marketing agency has the authority to set production levels and to allocate provincial market shares.

The Canadian Dairy Commission is a crown corporation which has jurisdiction over industrial milk used for butter, skim milk powder, cheese, yoghurt, and other products. The commission administers a price support system for these products. The marketing of fresh milk is handled by the provincial marketing boards.

The Canadian Wheat Board is also a crown corporation, controlling the marketing of wheat, barley and oats. It has jurisdiction only in the three Prairie provinces and the Peace River region in British Columbia. Its only function is to regulate international and interprovincial movements of grain. The Wheat Board's mandate includes marketing as much grain as possible, providing producers with price stability, and ensuring that each producer gets his share of the available market.

The Board uses a pooled-pricing mechanism and a delivery quota system. The quotas are set each year and are determined by demand. The pooled-pricing mechanism operates in such a way that the farmers are first paid by the Wheat Board at a price set by the government. The final payment to the farmers is based on what the Wheat Board receives in the international market for its grain, less the initial payment and the cost to the Wheat Board. In general, the Wheat Board is not a very restrictive agency and has not engaged in price and income support measures, as indicated by the fact that the guaranteed price has usually been set below the market price (McCalla and Schmitz 1979).

The Wheat Board has recently set a target for the expansion of Canadian grain supplies by 50 percent by the year 1990. In order to achieve this target and to induce the farmers to grow more wheat, the Board proposed a new market assurance plan. According to this plan farmers would be paid for all grain they committed to the Board even if it could not be sold. The unsold grain would be stored by farmers, a service for which they would receive compensation. This proposal had to be shelved because of opposition from Alberta and Manitoba (The Financial Post, 2 May 1981).

The operations of the Wheat Board have come under increasing attack, particularly by Alberta. Some farmers feel that they could do better if they were allowed the option to sell their own wheat through the commodities exchanges. It is believed that the Wheat Board, by being too sluggish, missed out on some of the price increases in 1973–74. However, whether the farmers could do better by themselves is open to debate. The world grain trade is not a competitive market, but is dominated by a handful of multinational corporations (Continental, Cargill, Dreyfus, Bunge, and Andre), the power and influence of which have been documented in The Merchants of Grain (Morgan 1980). Therefore, world grain marketing resembles a monopsony—or rather an oligopsony (few buyers)—where the sellers in a sense are at the mercy of the buyers. The Wheat Board can circumvent these private companies; apparently 75 percent of Canada's wheat deals and 50 percent of barley deals are made between the Wheat Board and other governments (The Globe and Mail, 20 Oct. 1980). However, in periods of oversupply, even the Wheat Board has had to resort to the private grain traders.

Other marketing boards, particularly those involved with the marketing of milk and poultry products have also received adverse publicity during the last few years—in many cases entirely justified. The most infamous incident was in 1974, when nine million eggs had to be destroyed because of overproduction. The newly formed Canadian Egg Marketing Agency had not been successful in coordinating the quotas between the provinces, which failure resulted in too high production at the prevailing prices.[8] The massive egg surplus had to be stored in areas normally reserved for apples. Too high temperatures resulted in rotten eggs and a public outcry.

Recently, there has been an increased public concern over high egg prices. Limited entry, strict quota and import controls have led to very high prices with considerable profits for producers. When higher than normal profits are earned, a quota or a licence to produce becomes a desirable property and therefore receives a value in its own right. The initial recipient of the quota did not have to pay, but many recipients later sold their quota allocations for substantial sums of money. In those provinces where quota rights could not be sold, the value of the quota became capitalized in the value of the farm. According to the ECC (1981:54), the aggregate value of quotas was close to three billion dollars in 1980. Egg quotas alone were worth $280 million. Using a discount rate of 12 percent, this figure converts into an annual income stream for the average egg farmer of $15,000.

Some milk marketing boards also appear to have been plagued by mismanagement and inefficiency, and have pushed up consumer prices towards monopoly levels. The B.C. milk marketing board seems to be particularly restrictive. In Vancouver consumers paid 76 cents per litre of milk compared to 60.7 cents per litre in Toronto and 58.5 cents per litre in Montreal (*The Globe and Mail*, 24 Jan. 1981). An earlier study by Grubel and Schwindt (1977) found that the B.C. board had succeeded in raising prices by 7 cents per quart, a yearly cost to the average consumer of $48. The benefit to the average milk farmer was estimated at $12,000 and the cost to the economy at twelve million dollars. A recent study by the ECC (1981) estimated that as much as 200 million dollars may be lost to the Canadian economy every year as a result of the inefficiencies introduced by the milk marketing boards.

Clearly, then, the egg and the milk boards impose a considerable cost on the economy. It is interesting to note in this context that Canada's labour productivity in farming lags behind that of the United States. Indeed, one study by Auer (1970) estimates productivity in Canadian agriculture to be 80 percent of that in the United States. How much of this differential is caused by our restrictive marketing boards is, of course, open to debate in view of the fact that the majority of the boards are not restrictive, and that a number of boards have provided real improvements in products and in marketing. However, it can be concluded that substantial efficiency gains and real benefits to consumers can probably be achieved if quota sizes were expanded. This would lower prices and lower quota values to reasonable levels.

Canada and World Food Supplies

So far only the supply side of agriculture has been discussed. In the early years of agriculture, supply-induced changes were probably the prime cause of instability in grain markets, whereas in the last decade, shifts in export demand have probably been more important. Earlier, Canada had reasonably secure markets in western Europe and therefore export demand did not show great variation. Two factors changed this: the development of the European Common Market (EEC), and the erratic behaviour of the Soviet Union and China as purchasers of grain.

The Common Agricultural Policy (CAP) of the Common Market administers the restriction of imports from non-member countries (e.g., Canada), free trade among member countries, price support, and export subsidies. The CAP has led to increased production, large surpluses for many products and a declining market for Canadian grains and other agricultural products. To keep prices from falling, storage facilities held 240,000 tons of skim milk powder, 190,000 tons of butter, 290,000 tons of beef, 40,000 tons of pork, and 7 million tons of grain at the end of 1980 (*The Economist*, 8 Nov. 1980).

Ever since John Diefenbaker negotiated the first wheat sale to the Soviet Union, the welfare of the western farmer has been closely tied to the crop situation in that country. Even though Canada's production of food grains is modest compared with global needs, because of her small domestic consumption, Canada is a major exporter of wheat. Since 1950, Canadian wheat exports have, on the average, provided 20 percent of the world's trade in grain (Cohn 1977). Canada has also consistently been one of the largest holders of wheat reserves.

During the '50s and '60s, the Canadian Wheat Board was unsuccessful in selling the whole wheat crop, partly because of above-average yields, increased acreage and aggressive selling by the United States, and partly because of increased production in importing countries. This led to mounting surpluses and low prices. As a result, Canadian food aid to the Third World increased, since, apart from humanitarian reasons, it was a good way of disposing of the surplus. Attempts were also made to achieve stability through International Wheat Agreements, which are administered by the International Wheat Council. However, the agreements have no economic provisions and their main purpose is to facilitate trade in wheat and wheat flour.

Another attempt to solve the problem of surplus was made in 1970, when the Canadian government introduced an acreage restriction program called LIFT (Lower Inventory for Tomorrow). LIFT was designed to reduce wheat acreage and to discourage farmers from using this land for production of other crops. Farmers were paid $6 per acre for converting wheat acreage into summer fallow, and $10 for converting it into perennial forage (Cohn 1977).

In 1972–73 the agricultural situation changed radically. There were poor crops in the Soviet Union in 1972 and unfavourable harvest conditions in the United States. Another factor was the temporary disappearance of anchovies from the coast of Peru in 1972–73—a source of protein for animal feed far more important in the world food supplies than people had imagined. World food stocks fell to the lowest level in twenty years. All of these factors combined into an unexpected escalation of grain and food prices, the aftermath of which is still with us.

This food crisis precipitated the World Food Conference in 1974, which was concerned with the effects of higher food prices on the Third World. The conference suggested the establishment of a World Food Emergency Fund, to which Canada pledged substantial contributions, despite a buoyant market.

There has recently been increasing concern about the desirability of food aid.[9] The long-run solution to food shortages in Third World countries is an increase in their own agricultural output. It has been argued that food aid has depressed farm prices in Third World countries and therefore discouraged local farmers from expanding supplies. It is also contended that food aid has discouraged Third World governments from placing sufficient emphasis on agricultural support. This may very well be so in some countries. However, it could also be argued that food aid provides food for the hungry, frequently to nutritionally bereft groups such as children,[10] and may keep prices down to levels that these groups can afford to buy. Food aid can be used to build up buffer stocks to reduce fluctuations and remove a major constraint on growth. Two-thirds of workers' incomes are spent on food. Therefore employment can only be expanded if food production is expanded (Iseman and Singer 1977).

The future market for grain is difficult to predict, but world population growth will remain high in the foreseeable future. One factor that might influence the grain market is that some Third World countries are rapidly becoming wealthy (the oil-producing countries and some of the Southeast Asian countries). The income elasticity of grain for bread is low, while the income elasticity of grain for cattle feed is high. (The income elasticity of meat is high. Many animals are grain-fed, which means that when meat production expands, so does the demand for grain.) Another factor is that more and more cultures are adopting the western habit of eating bread, apparently aided and abetted by the international grain traders (Morgan 1980).

On the supply side, grain production is not likely to expand substantially. Many areas which were thought to hold potential as bread baskets, for example, Sudan, no longer seem to offer much hope because of the high cost of energy; irrigation and fertilizer are both energy-intensive. In addition, because of inadequate land use practices and population pressures, many areas formerly used for food production are today unproductive; soil erosion is rampant in the Third World.

For these reasons some analysts foresee excellent future prospects for Canadian grain growers. Other analysts, including the U.S. Department of Agriculture, believe that it is possible that cereal surpluses will reemerge by 1985, despite growing food deficits in the Third World (Veeman and Veeman 1976). The Canadian Wheat Board obviously concurs with the opinion that prospects look good, since the Board wants an expansion of wheat production of 50 percent by 1990.

Even if the Wheat Board is correct in its projections for the demand for Canadian wheat, it is probably unrealistic to assume that grain production can be increased by 50 percent, the main limiting factor being soil moisture. The spring season in 1981, after a winter with little snowfall, brought high winds with dust storms reminiscent of those in the dirty thirties, when much of the top soil on the Prairies blew away. Another factor is the short growing season. A marginal change in temperature would make the climate unsuitable for wheat growing. Daryl Kraft, an agricultural economist at the University of Manitoba, does not think that increased fertilizer or new crop varieties would lead to major increases in production (*The Financial Post*, 22 March 1980).

A major limitation on Canada's potential as a major food supplier is the grain transport system. Antiquated, it has remained basically unchanged since the early part of the century. The farmer uses his own vehicle to deliver grain to the local elevator, located on a rail branch line, usually close to his farm. At each elevator, the grain is loaded on individual railcars, which are then assembled into trains for the long haul to Vancouver or Thunder Bay. Given the economies of scale in elevator operations and the cost advantages of trucks over railways on hauls under 100 miles, an efficient system would restrict grain collection to a few large terminals. However, such a system would lead to massive abandonment of branch lines and an increase in cost for farmers because they would have to truck their grain a longer distance. Any attempt at rationing or restricting grain collection would therefore meet with substantial resistance from farmers.

The problems in grain transport are also a result of Crow Rates. Crow Rates stem from the Crow's Nest Pass Agreements of 1897 between the Canadian Pacific Railway and the federal government, whereby the CPR agreed to lower the rate of moving grain to the Lakehead by 3 cents per hundredweight in return for a 3 million dollar federal subsidy to extend the rail line from Lethbridge to the Kooteney Valley in British Columbia. According to the findings of the Snavely Commission, the Crow Rates, which vary from 14 to 26 cents per hundredweight do not even cover variable costs (Canada 1976). A realistic rate would probably range from 70 to 80 cents per hundredweight. Moving grain at these low rates accounts for 30 percent of the railways' ton/mile output and only 12 percent of rail revenue. The projected losses for the railways for 1981 were expected at $538 million. (*The Globe and Mail*, 26 January 1981).

The effects of the Crow Rates may have been many. In the first place, the railways had no incentive to maintain track on uneconomic branch lines, nor to invest in box-cars for grain. Secondly, as the westbound route over the Rockies was more expensive to run than the eastbound route to Thunder Bay, it was in the interest of the railways to encourage eastward movements, given that the revenues were the same under the Crow Rates.[11] This apparently led to their underinvestment of the port of Vancouver compared to the port of Thunder Bay, which in turn led to underinvestment by West Coast port operators in cleaning facilities for grain. All of these factors led to a crisis in grain transportation in the mid-1970s, which meant that several export sale commitments could not be honoured.

Indications are, however, that the problems in grain transport are being sorted out. Following the recommendations of the Hall Commission, the rail network is being rationalized. Uneconomic branch lines are being abandoned and others improved. The Wheat Board and the federal and provincial governments have added 7,400 new grain-hopper cars to the rail fleet in 1980–81. The federal government is also building a new grain terminal at Prince Rupert, British Columbia (*The Financial Post*, 9 Dec. 1979).

Canadian Agricultural Policies: An Overview

The problem of lagging farm incomes appears to have temporarily (?) disappeared, but the problems of income distribution have not. One of the reasons is that the policy solutions to low farm incomes have been general, not selective, benefitting rich farmers more than poor farmers. An example is the federal dairy program. Payments to dairy producers are distributed on the basis of sales and therefore large farmers get more than small farmers. These types of non-selective programs, of which marketing boards are another example, tend to worsen the income distribution problem in agriculture (Veeman and Veeman 1977). It could therefore be argued that if federal or provincial governments really wanted to come to grips with the poverty problem in farming, they should do one of two things: either small, inefficient farmers should be encouraged to leave farming (an unlikely solution, as a positive small farm policy has been one of the cornerstones of Canadian agricultural policies), or selective programs to help needy farmers should be instituted, such as guaranteed income programs or graduated subsidy payments. These solutions are unlikely for political reasons: farmers like the present arrangements better. Governments like them as well, since marketing boards do not drain the federal treasury, and since consumers bear the brunt of the responsibility through higher food prices, which cannot be blamed on the government but on the greedy farmers and marketing boards.

The growth of marketing boards and of the power of farmers in a period when the absolute number of farmers is declining is puzzling. The explanations may be found in the general growth and pressure of interest groups in society, and the rosy markets for agriculture in the mid-70s which made boards easier to establish and keep together. It is well known from industrial organization theory that anti-competitive producer associations, such as cartels, are more successful in periods of buoyant markets than in periods of recession, as chiselling is more likely to take place in periods of excess capacity. Another important aspect of Canadian agricultural policy is trade. At the international level, the Canadian Wheat Board and other organizations have been looking for new markets and have been pushing for less restricted trade in (some) agricultural products, as well as for expanding agricultural assistance to Third World countries. At the same time, Canada offers relatively high protection for its own food-processing industry, and has displayed highly erratic behaviour in its import policies. An example is the live-stock industry.[12]

In February 1973, Canada removed tariffs on beef and live cattle as an anti-inflation measure. In March, the United States, also fighting inflation, imposed temporary price ceilings on beef and other meat, the beef ceiling to be removed in September. U.S. beef producers withheld beef supplies from the market in order to benefit from higher prices in September. Canadian beef flooded the U.S. market, resulting in an increase in Canadian beef prices due to the increase in demand. This ran against the federal government's inflation policy and export controls were imposed, which were subsequently removed in September. How-ever, with the removal of price ceilings in the United States, the U.S. mar-ket became flooded with U.S. beef and prices dropped. Canada imposed import surcharges on beef and cattle to protect Canadian producers from cheap U.S. beef. These surcharges were removed in 1974. In 1974 escalating grain prices threatened feedlot operations. The government instituted a subsidy to producers, as well as import quotas. The United States retaliated by imposing temporary quotas on hogs, beef and pork. The quotas were removed, but imports were controlled again in 1976 because of distortions in world beef markets.

Clearly, much instability in agricultural markets is caused by gov-ernment actions of this type. A consistent bilateral trade policy is defi-nitely needed.

It can be concluded that Canada does not have a coherent agricul-tural policy.[13] There are several possible reasons for this. First, agricul-ture has a regional dimension which makes the development of coherent policies difficult, as there are always pressures on the government for special treatment from different regions. Second, the farmers do not speak with one voice. There are two national farm organizations (the Canadian Federation of Agriculture and the National Farmer's Union), as well as all the different producer organizations (marketing boards). All of these represent different farm interests, making it difficult for the policy-makers to know what the farmers really want. Third, policy is made at two levels: provincial and federal. The BNA (British North America) Act gave the federal government and the provinces joint responsibility for agriculture. This presents additional difficulties of coordination. A fourth factor is pressure from consumers. Policies which benefit farmers do not necessarily benefit consumers.

Consumers in the mid-'70s launched a drive for a national food policy to supplement the traditional agricultural (farm) policies. A food policy would be attuned to the needs of consumers and customers of all sectors of the food industry. The prime aim was to get consumer representation on marketing boards. The government responded by proclaiming *A Food Strategy for Canada* (1977). The food strategy recognizes that farmers need a stable income; consumers need safe, nutritious food at reasonable prices that will be responsive to competitive conditions over time; and that in any future government involvement, interests of both consumers and producers should be considered. In 1978 a national food strategy conference was held. Following the conference the government asked the Economic Council of Canada to examine the objectives, activities and power of marketing boards as part of the council's ongoing study on regulation. In its report (*Reforming Regulation*) the ECC recommended that the power of the more restrictive boards should be curtailed and quotas expanded, but so far the government has taken no action.

Summary and Conclusions

In this chapter the problems of the agriculture industry were surveyed and government agricultural policies discussed. Agriculture has traditionally suffered from low and unstable incomes. The problem of low incomes seemed to disappear during the latter part of the 1970s, and the problem of unstable incomes has been alleviated through various income support schemes and through marketing boards. Marketing boards have helped farmers but have come under attack from various consumer groups and recently from the Economic Council of Canada for restricting output for the purposes of raising prices and increasing profits for producers. The milk, egg and poultry boards are particularly restrictive. The efficiency gains which could be achieved by an expansion of agricultural quotas are substantial.

The chapter also examined Canada's role as a major food exporter. World food imports are growing, but Canada's reputation as a major food exporter mainly rests on grains, a reputation which has been tarnished by an inadequate grain transport system. Some of the problems are being solved, but the major anomaly in grain transportation, the Crow Rates, still exists. The Crow Rates have created substantial distortions both in transportation and in the location and marketing of grain and related products. The beneficiaries of the rates (the western grain farmers) have mounted substantial resistance to any suggestions for change.

The chapter concluded with an overview and criticism of Canadian agricultural policies. It was argued that they suffered from a lack of coordination and that many policies have benefitted rich farmers more than poor farmers.

NOTES

1. The following data are based on Veeman and Veeman 1978.
2. Yet the number of corporate farms nearly doubled between 1971 and 1976. Corporate farms and cooperatives made up 4.4% of the farms in 1976 (Veeman and Veeman 1978).
3. See Robinson 1975.
4. Earlier studies showed that if welfare were measured by consumer surplus, both producers and consumers would gain from instability, whereas society would lose, assuming the gainers would compensate the losers. More recent research, using the less controversial indirect utility function, has demonstrated that if only one commodity is stabilized, consumers are likely to gain from instability. They gain more from instability the larger are the income and price elasticities of demand, and the lower is the degree of risk aversion. If the analysis is extended to more than one commodity, the necessary and sufficient conditions for gains are very stringent (Turnovsky, Shalit and Schmitz 1980).
5. Recent research has shown that attempts by producers to insulate themselves from world markets can actually lead to *more* price instability as small shocks in international demand and supply become exaggerated, because domestic supplies and demand are not permitted to respond, at least not in the short run (Zwart and Meilke 1979).
6. For an explanation of the components of the Canadian consumer price index and the weight of food in the index, see Chapter 12.

7. The Canadian food and beverage processing industry shows relatively high levels of concentration. This is also true for the retail sector (Veeman and Veeman 1978).
8. Yorgason (1976) maintains that egg prices were not deliberately raised to increase profits for producers. The surplus was caused partly by the cost-induced high prices and partly by the effects of the U.S. market where egg prices were lower at the time.
9. See Schultz 1960 and Fischer 1963.
10. It is well known that an inadequate diet in children and pregnant mothers can stunt both the intellectual and physical development of children.
11. See Maister 1978.
12. The following is based on Anderson 1978.
13. For a good discussion, see Lee 1978.

BIBLIOGRAPHY

Agriculture Canada and Consumer and Corporate Affairs. *A Food Strategy for Canada*. Ottawa: Supply and Services, 1977.

Anderson, W.J. "North American Food and Agricultural Policies." *American Journal of Agricultural Economics* (60), 1978, pp. 797–9.

Auer, L. "Labour Productivity in Agriculture: A Canada-U.S. Comparison." *Canadian Journal of Agricultural Economics* (18), 1970, pp. 43–55.

Canada. *Report of the Commission on the Cost of Transporting Grain by Rail*, Vol. 1. Ottawa: Information Canada, 1976.

Cohn, Theodore. "Food Surplus and Canadian Food Aid." *Canadian Public Policy*. (III), 1977, pp. 141–55.

Economic Council of Canada. *Reforming Regulation*. Ottawa: Supply and Services, 1981.

Fischer, F.M. "A Theoretical Analysis of the Impact of Food Surplus Disposal on Agricultural Production in Recipient Countries. *Journal of Farm Economics* (45), 1963, pp. 863–75.

Grubel, H.G. and Schwindt, R. *The Real Cost of the B.C. Milk Board*. Vancouver: The Fraser Institute, 1977.

Hiscock, G.A. and T.A. Bennet. "Marketing Boards and Pricing in Canada." In G.C. Ruggeri (ed.), pp. 265–73, *The Canadian Economy: Problems and Policies*. Toronto: Gage Educational Publishing, 1977.

Iseman, Paul J. and H.W. Singer. "Food Aid, Disincentive Effects and Their Policy Implications." *Economic Development and Cultural Change* (25), 1977, pp. 205–37.

Lee, George E. "Regional Policies for Agriculture: The Effects and the

Future." *American Journal of Agricultural Economics* (60), 1978, pp. 1038−43.

Maister, David H. "Technical and Organizational Change in a Regulated Industry: The Case of Canadian Grain Transport." In W.J. Stanbury (ed.), *Studies of Regulation in Canada*. Toronto: Institute for Research on Public Policy and Butterworths, 1978.

McCalla, Alex F. and A. Schmitz. "Grain Marketing Systems: The Case of the United States versus Canada." *American Journal of Agricultural Economics* (61), 1979, pp. 199−213.

Morgan, Dan. *Merchants of Grain*. New York: Penguin Books, 1980.

Robinson, K.L. "Unstable Farm Prices: Economic Consequences and Policy Options." *American Journal of Agricultural Economics* (57), 1975, pp. 769−77.

Schultz, T.W. "Value of U.S. Farm Surplus to Underdeveloped Countries." *Journal of Farm Economics* (42), 1960, pp. 1031−42.

Shute, D.M. "National and Regional Productivity of Canadian Agriculture, 1961 to 1974." *Canadian Farm Economics* (10), 1975, pp. 1−6.

Turnovsky, S.J., Haim Shalit and Andrew Schmitz. "Consumer Surplus Price Instability, and Consumer Welfare." *Econometrica* (48), 1980, 135−52.

Veeman, M.M. and T.S. Veeman. "The Directions of Canadian Agricultural Policy." *Canadian Journal of Agricultural Economics* (24), 1976, pp. 78−90.

Veeman, T.S. and M.M. Veeman. "The Changing Organization, Structure and Control of Canadian Agriculture." *American Journal of Agricultural Economics* (60), 1978, pp. 759−68.

Wilkinson, B.W. *Canada in the Changing World Economy*. Montreal: C.D. Howe Research Institute, 1980.

Yorgason, Vernon W. "But Who Reviews the Reviewers? The Case of Eggs." *Canadian Public Policy* (II), 1976, pp. 511−20.

Zwart, A.C. and K.D. Meilke. "The Influence of Domestic Pricing Policies and Buffer Stocks on Price Stability in the World Wheat Industry." *American Journal of Agricultural Economics* (61), 1979, pp. 434−48.

CHAPTER 2

Renewable and Nonrenewable Resources

The production and exports of renewable and nonrenewable resources (staple products) have played a dominant role in Canadian economic development. Most Canadians are familiar with the importance of the fur trade and the Hudson's Bay Company in the exploration and settlement of Canada. There were, of course, other important staples: lumber, fish, wheat, and minerals. Even today a substantial proportion of employment and income is generated in the production of staples. Sixty percent of exports leave the country in raw or semi-processed form—the highest proportion of any developed country.

The importance of staples in economic growth was developed and formalized into a theory of growth called the Staples Theory by the Canadian economic historian, Harold Innis (1956), and further elaborated by Mel Watkins (1967). When a new territory was settled, the migrants brought with them certain cultural traits and expectations of living standards. Unable to supply all the necessary goods to maintain their culture and living standards, the migrants had to purchase them from the mother country. The goods had to be paid for and hence the settler was in constant search for goods which could be sold to the mother country to earn the necessary revenue. The exports had to be transported over large distances at high freight rates, and therefore they had to fetch high prices in the mother country. The earliest commodities to fit these requirements were cod caught off the Grand Banks of Newfoundland and fur, particularly beaver. With the collapse of the fur trade, lumber became the dominant commodity, followed by gold, wheat and minerals.

The Staples Theory rests on the assumption that the staple export is the leading sector in the economy, and development will take the form of diversification around the export base (see Watkins 1967). The extent of diversification depends on the linkages that the export product has with other sectors of the economy. There are three types of linkages:

backward, forward and final-demand linkages. A backward linkage takes place if there is investment in the domestic production of goods that are inputs in the production of the export good. For example, if the export product is fish, a backward linkage would be the production of nets and boats. A forward linkage, by contrast, is the production of goods that use the export good as an input (e.g., the production of fish meal). A final-demand linkage is the production of consumer goods demanded by people who receive payments from the export industry in the form of wages, salaries, interest, rents, or dividends. The larger these linkages are, the more beneficial is the effect of the export product on the economy as a whole.

According to Watkins, the success of a staple economy depends on its ability to shift resources from one staple product to another according to the dictates of the market. If this ability to shift ceases, the economy could become caught in a staple trap and would then stagnate. Another pitfall is that too much attention may be given to exports to the detriment of development of linkages, particularly forward linkages. Some maintain that Canada suffers from an export mentality out of which a boom-and-bust psychology has developed with regard to staples. During boom conditions, excessive optimism leads to overreaction. An example is the building of two transcontinental railways during the wheat boom of 1896–1913 (The Canadian Northern and the Grand Trunk Pacific) in addition to the already existing CPR which was completed in 1885. Depressions were met by tariff increases.

Canada's current staples are minerals, which account for nearly 30 percent of merchandise exports and which to some extent also determine our comparative advantage in the few manufactured products exported. Fish is still an important staple commodity at the regional level. In Newfoundland, for example, the fisheries account for 15.8 percent of employment. Forestry-related products are also important staples in many areas of Canada.

There are two problems in resource management: the problem of optimum exploitation and the problem of resource pricing and revenues. Optimum exploitation and production is an economic problem, but in the case of nonrenewable resources it is also an ethical problem, for it involves making a decision about how much of the resource should be left for our children to exploit and use. The problem of resource revenues has probably received more attention in Canada than anywhere else, and has centred on the question of who is entitled to the economic rent generated by a resource. (Any excess profits earned in resource exploitation are a scarcity rent.) The debate has concentrated on how much of this rent belongs to the landlord (the federal government or provincial government or the tenant (the corporation or the individual which has acquired the right to exploit the resource). The situation is further complicated by the competing interests of the provincial governments as rent collectors, and the federal government as tax collector on earnings of capital.

This chapter examines the problems of optimum exploitation of renewable and nonrenewable resources, with particular examples from fisheries, timber and non-fuel minerals. The question of who is entitled to resource rents will be left to chapter 11 where the distribution of income between provinces, and between provinces and the federal government will be discussed.

Resource Management Problems in the Oceans

The oceans contain a vast amount of resources, many of which have not been exploited because of the lack of technology. The traditional ocean resources are fish, shellfish, seaweed as fertilizer, salt (30 percent of salt production comes from sea water), sand, and gravel. The energy crisis has led to a search for non-conventional sources of energy, including energy generated from the oceans, such as tidal power and wave power and even making fuel out of seaweed. Much interest has been shown in the development of deep-sea mining of manganese nodules.[1] The nodules are actually composed of a large number of chemical elements including copper, nickel, cobalt, and manganese (Crutchfield 1979). The nodules are scattered over the ocean floor in great profusion at depths of 12,000 to 20,000 feet, and range in size from a grain of rice to a football. A report in *The Financial Post* (4 Oct. 1980) estimated that a six-million-square km area in the Pacific could contain 30 to 50 billion tons of nodules with a nickel content of between 300 and 600 million tons. These nodules are technically a renewable resource as more are formed every year from sea water.

Ocean resources have one factor in common which sets them apart from most land-based resources. So far, they are common property and everyone is free to use them. They therefore suffer from the tragedy of the "commons" so aptly described by Garett Hardin (1968). A single user of a common property resource will take into account only his own costs and benefits in calculations as to how much of the common property he should use; unless forced to do so, he or she will not consider the effects of his or her production or consumption on other people's production and consumption. This situation is not threatening as long as the resource is in abundant supply, but it becomes critical when scarcity ensues. Overgrazing by one farmer's herd on common grassland results in less fodder for other herds. Similarly, overfishing by one fisherman leads to less fish for others today and less for all in the future. However, unless all fishermen agree to cut back, it is not in the interest of a single fisherman to do so, because he knows that what he does not catch will be caught by someone else. Therefore everyone will overfish, even though everyone knows it will lead to long-term disaster.[2] For these reasons free access and common property resources tend to become overexploited.

The economic solution to common-property problems is to assign property rights to someone and enclose the commons. The owner will then be able to exploit his resource in an efficient manner, and the users can be taxed or subsidized depending on whether or not their production or consumption is leading to external economies or diseconomies.

Until recently, the oceans were decreed an open space by international law. Each country had jurisdiction over coastal waters extending 3 miles from the island furthest out. This arrangement had not led to any problems until technology created long-distance fishing fleets, making exploitation of fish resources possible outside the zone of coastal jurisdiction. A dramatic shift occurred from abundance to scarcity. In 1946, world fish production had been 20 million tons, in late 1960, 70 million tons. Between 1970 and 1976 there were no further increases in landings despite tremendous improvements in technology (Crutchfield 1979:269). The output of fish for human consumption has actually been declining. At the present time, most fish species that have been exploited by U.S. and Canadian fishing fleets are on the endangered species list compiled by the U.S. National Marine Fisheries Service (Wilkinson 1979:252). Depletion has been methodical: fishermen have moved from one stock exhibiting falling yields to the next most promising species.

Some attempts were made to come to grips with the situation by the International Commission for the Northwest Atlantic Fisheries (ICNAF) (Copes 1978). Like most international organizations, its effectiveness was limited by national rivalries, unclear objectives and the lack of enforcement authorities, although it had some success in controlling catches. During the early '70s, it became obvious that international commissions were not the solution to the depletion of fisheries. The Third Law of the Sea Conference was convened in 1974 to deal with the fisheries and the exploitation of oceans in general. Agreement was relatively easy in the case of fisheries. The solution advocated was traditional: enclosures— the assignment of property rights. It was recommended that each coastal nation should be given the exclusive right to fish within 200 nautical miles from its coast.[3] (More than 90 percent of the world's fish catch takes place within the 200-mile limit.) This solution has not yet received the status of an international convention; however, many countries, including Canada, have already declared a 200-mile exclusive economic zone.

The reason why the fisheries convention is not yet finalized is that the Law of the Sea conference is not yet over. It bogged down at an early stage in arguments concerning who owns and who has the right to exploit the ocean floor (beyond the exclusive economic zone). In general, everyone pays lip service to the idea that the sea belongs to everyone, but it is not yet clear who should be allowed to exploit and who should get economic rent from the resource. The United States, Germany and Japan have argued that an interim agreement, under which secure title to seabed mining tracts could be obtained, is essential, whereas the developing countries argue that the seabed is the heritage of all mankind, and they see no reason why the industrialized countries should be able to stake claims before others are in a position to partake (Crutchfield 1979:267). An agreement was actually announced in 1980, but the new Reagan administration in the United States decided not to honour it.

The document ICNT[4] allows coastal states a 12-mile territorial sea in which they may exercise complete sovereignty, and beyond that an exclusive 200-mile economic zone in which certain rights may be exercised, including the sovereign rights over fisheries for the purpose of exploiting and managing fish stocks. However, if a country does not have the capacity to harvest the optimum allowable catch, it should give other countries access to the surplus. The ICNT recognizes that fish do not know international borders and encourages states to co-operate in the joint management of trans-boundary stocks, for example the rich George's Bank area which overlaps both Canadian and U.S. coastal waters. There are also special provisions for the management of anadromous species (e.g., salmon) which spawns in rivers and then migrates to the high seas. From a fisheries management viewpoint, these species are best caught and managed in the coastal waters before they ascend the rivers. Further, the coastal states incur costs in the management of these species. (For example bypasses must be built around hydroelectric power stations.) For these reasons it is contended that the coastal states should have exclusive rights to these species. Therefore, according to ICNT, fishing on the high seas for these species should not be allowed—except when the ban would result in an economic dislocation for a state other than the coastal state.

Extended jurisdiction, by giving each coastal state an opportunity to manage its fisheries scientifically, should improve the situation in world fisheries. However, scientific management is very difficult as surprisingly little is known about the behaviour of fish populations. Until recently the objective of management has been to achieve maximum sustainable yield. The concept of maximum sustainable yield is based on a model of biological growth (see Figure 1). At any population level less than K, there is a surplus population which can be harvested without any ill effects on future populations. If this harvest is not taken, the population will expand towards K, where there is no longer a surplus. Open access to fisheries will, in most cases, expand production beyond M. Fishermen will continue to fish until total revenue is equal to total cost

FIGURE 1
Biological Growth of a Fish Population

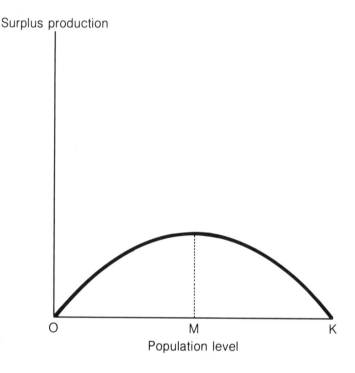

Surplus production

O   M   K

Population level

(including opportunity costs), at which point profits and resources rents will have become completely dissipated.[5] The traditional solution has been to attempt to cut back production towards M by limiting access (or limiting the fishing season, or by issuing quotas, or restricting the design of nets, and so on).

Recently, there has been increased criticism of maximum sustainable yield as the criterion for management of fisheries.[6] In the first place, if two species are interdependent ecologically, maximum sustainable yield for one may lead to less than maximum sustainable yield of the other. Second, many fish populations are subject to unpredictable fluctuations in populations. Therefore, a quota based on a relatively large population will not be appropriate if the population suddenly declines. Third, the concept ignores economic considerations as it looks only at the benefits, not the costs. If costs are taken into account, it is likely that the maximum sustainable yield will not correspond to the optimum level of exploitation.

The appropriate principle for managing the fisheries should be to maximize the standard net present value of the fishery resources (i.e., benefits minus costs discounted at an appropriate rate of interest) (Clark 1976). This principle sounds good in theory, but is extremely difficult to apply because of lack of information. Another factor which makes management difficult is the distributional implication of policies (Huppert 1977). Proper management in most cases would restrict access to the fisheries, and those fishermen denied access would want to be compensated. Furthermore, the fishermen who received access would earn excess profits (or rather positive economic rents) which should rightly belong to the owners of the resources who are the people of the country.

Should rents be confiscated through auctioning of quotas, taxes or licence fees? Should the aim be to maximize world welfare, domestic welfare or fishermen's welfare? These are important questions which have to be answered before any effective policy can be implemented.

The Management of Canadian Fisheries

The waters off Canada's Maritime coastline contain some of the world's best fishing grounds—an asset which has made Canada the world's largest fish exporter. Even though the fisheries generate only 1 percent of GNP and a minute proportion of employment, they can be of substantial local importance (Mitchell 1978). During the seventies, 75 percent of communities along the Atlantic coast had some connection with the fisheries (ECC 1981:68).

The Atlantic fisheries have been a problem area for some time. The problems can be attributed to two factors: overfishing by foreign fleets and little alternative employment for fishermen in any particular region. Fishing has therefore served as a safety valve: when the unemployment rate increases, the fishing effort will increase as well.

The fishing industry is divided into the off-shore and inshore fisheries and processing. The inshore fishery has been traditionally prosecuted with small boats and modest capital equipment, and therefore entry is easy. It is estimated that in the Atlantic fishery there are roughly 35,000 inshore fishermen living in 2,000 inshore communities, a number far in excess of the available resources (MacDonald 1979). The offshore industry, by contrast, is modern, capital-intensive and is controlled by company-owned trawler fleets, which are vertically integrated with the processing industry and therefore has monopsony power in its relations with the inshore fishermen.

According to the BNA act, the federal government has full legislative jurisdiction over the coastal and inland fisheries, but the management is sometimes shared with provincial governments. The federal fisheries department controls all fisheries in Newfoundland, Prince Edward Island, Nova Scotia, New Brunswick, the Yukon, and the Northwest

Territories, whereas in Ontario, Manitoba, Saskatchewan, Alberta, and Quebec, all fisheries are managed by the province. In British Columbia, saltwater and migrating fish are managed by the federal government, whereas the provincial government manages freshwater fisheries (*Canada Yearbook* 1978–79).

Federal fishery policy in the immediate postwar era was characterized by a lack of understanding of fisheries as an open-access, common property resource (See Copes 1978). For example, even though the inshore fisheries were over-exploited, it seemed that a fisherman with better equipment could increase his catch. The policy response was to subsidize all fishermen to enable them to acquire better boats and gear. The predictable outcome was a total catch of the same size as before, but obtained at higher cost.

In the mid-1960s the problems of low catches and low incomes became acute. The federal government appears to have realized that the root of the problem was the excess number of fishermen in the inshore fisheries, and in 1965 announced a Newfoundland Fisheries Household Resettlement Program. The alleged purpose of the program was to relocate the population to larger centres which would offer a more comprehensive set of services to the local population (education and medical services). At the same time, the offshore fishery and fish processing were promoted in these centres. A similar program was initiated in Prince Edward Island in 1969. Resettlement was encouraged through substantial relocation subsidies (given if more than 80 percent of a community wanted to move) combined with regional economic development grants and incentives to industry. In its first five years 14,116 people were evacuated from 119 communities (Matthews 1975:206).[7]

Meanwhile, the provincial governments of Newfoundland and Prince Edward Island were still under the illusion that it was the inshore fisheries which offered the greatest development potential, and were therefore pressing for continued assistance to the overexploited inshore (Copes 1978). During the early '70s the resettlement programs fell into bad repute as more people had been induced to move than could possibly be accommodated in the larger centres. Overfishing by foreign fleets and the subsequent quotas imposed by ICNAF led to a crisis in the offshore fisheries which could not absorb any more people. Increased unemployment levels in the national economy and overexploitation of the off-shore sector saw the inshore sector reverting to its traditional role of being an employer-of-last-resort. These developments led to the so-called ground fish (cod) crisis of 1974. The crisis led to a federal emergency subsidy program for ground fish and a major review of fisheries policies which resulted in the policy document: *Policies for Canada's Commercial Fisheries* (Canada, 1976).

The immediate objective of the policy was to reduce the foreign fishing effort in order to expand fish stocks beyond their depleted level, and then to expand the Canadian fishing effort. Part of this strategy was the declaration of a 200-mile exclusive economic zone. The approach to management advocated in the policy document is a broad one of net benefits to society, not the narrow biological one of maximum sustainable yield. The federal government is now faced with two immediate problems: regulating the size of the catch and distributing the catch between off-shore and inshore. The size of the catch is most efficiently regulated by a decrease in the number of licences and shifting of activity from inshore to off-shore. There are still too many people in the inshore industry, resulting in low incomes and the need for subsidies. The ECC (1981:73) argues that the current fisheries policy has led to a substantial misallocation of resources with losses to the economy of between 750 million and 1 billion dollars.

A good fisheries policy would limit the catch to maximize the present value of the fishery resource and decrease the amount of labour and capital in the industry in order to increase the income of fishermen. The ECC maintains that this is most efficiently achieved through a system of stinting rights. A stinting right is a licence which gives a fisherman the right to catch a certain amount of one or more species. This right should be transferrable, and the total number of rights should add up to the optimum sustainable yield. In order to reduce the amount of labour and capital in the industry, the ECC recommends the use of landing taxes or licence fees. Taxes or fees would make the fishermen more efficient and induce them to economize on labour and capital. The council also recommends the phasing out of any subsidies to the commercial fisheries as these encourage increased fishing effort and therefore contribute towards excessive use of labour and capital.

Whether or not this type of policy could be implemented is open to doubt. Any policy of landing or licence fees, or decreased subsidies would be vigorously opposed by fishermen (Copes 1978).

Forestry Resources

The management of forestry resources is similar to the management of fisheries: both are renewable resources. Forestry-related industries still play an important role in the economy, with the pulp and paper industry being the largest single employer in the manufacturing sector (See Table 13, Chapter 7). Exports of wood products constitute 18 percent of the value of all commodity exports. Most provinces generate some income from forestry-related activities, with British Columbia being the largest producer, followed by Ontario and Quebec. However, it is in New Brunswick that forestry is most important to the local economy.

The federal government is responsible for the protection and administration of forestry resources in the Yukon and Northwest Territories, and in national parks, Indian reserves, military areas, and forestry experimental stations. The provinces have jurisdiction over all other crown land. According to the *Canada Yearbook* (1978–79:416), 92 percent of forest land in Canada is owned by the crown (either the provincial or federal government). Cutting rights on crown land is usually sold to corporations or individuals through leases or licences. Economic rent is collected by a form of royalty: stumpage fees, assessed per thousand board feet of cut timber. Several provinces have restrictions on exports of timber, a policy designed to encourage further processing.

Canada is at present the world's largest newsprint exporter, and is second to the United States in the production and export of wood pulp. Even though the future world market for forestry products is likely to be good, there are some clouds on the horizon. First, many pulp mills are obsolete, with relatively low productivity which could obliterate our comparative advantage. This situation is exacerbated by mandatory anti-pollution adjustments which are necessary to reduce emissions, following the public uproar surrounding the mercury contamination of the English Wabagon River system in the Kenora region of northwestern Ontario. The industry is also a high user of energy and so far has not adjusted to the new wave of higher energy costs compared to, for example, the Swedish pulp and paper industry. The Swedish industry reduced fuel consumption by 17 percent between 1973 and 1979 despite increases in capacity; almost 60 percent of total heat demand is being met by internally generated fuels (*Globe and Mail*, 12 May 1981). The second discouraging factor is that there is increased competition from regions with more favourable climates (e.g., southern United States), where a tree grows in 20 years compared to 60 to 80 years in Canada. The third is that even though 37 percent of the Canadian land area is classified as forest land, only half is productive. The remainder is muskeg, barren or unstocked because of the ravages of forest fires and spruce budworms. Twenty-five percent of the area classified as productive is not accessible because of present lumber prices and transportation costs (Statistics Canada, 1978 Tables 1–3). Many sawmills and pulpmills are in difficulties at the moment, as they no longer can secure an adequate supply of wood at realistic costs. Forestry has been subjected to the same psychology as the fisheries in the sense that people have regarded forestry as an infinite self-renewable resource. Cut areas were generally left to regenerate themselves with the frequent result that tall-standing conifers have been replaced by a wilderness of bush and inferior hardwood species of little commercial value.

Recently, however, provinces have made a serious effort at reforestation. There is even some indication that too much reforestation is being done in terms of what is economically efficient. An example is

Ontario's recent reforestation policies. An annual average of 100,000 acres were reforested in the 1960s, after which 175,000 acres were reforested annually. The present plan is to increase the annual average to 275,000 acres, which together with the 125,000 acres expected to regenerate naturally would maintain stock, giving a yield of 400,000 acres per year. A provincial cost-benefit study confirmed that such a yield would give net benefits to the province. But another study, using a different methodology, estimates that the costs actually exceed the benefits by $18 to $20 million per year, and concludes that reforestation should probably be done on a more selective basis (Anderson 1979). Neither study takes into account the social costs and benefits, but only the direct costs and benefits to the province. For example, the importance of forestry in ensuring the survival of many northern communities was not included in the analysis.

British Columbia, in contrast, has had a policy of sustained yield management since 1948. Crown land was made available to large operators free of charge provided they were willing to take on the duties of forest management. The remainder of crown land was divided into Public Sustained Yield units whose forests are managed by the provincial forest service, and whose annual cutting quotas are sold to the forest companies through traditional timber sale licences.

The policy (in British Columbia) of allocating free timber rights to the large forest-product companies has probably led to considerable distortions in the economy, as it has allowed the companies to collect a large amount of rent (Copithorne 1979). The companies pay the B.C. government a stumpage fee equal to the average price of logs divided by an expression of one plus a profit allowance minus average operating costs. Given this type of formula, it is obviously in the interests of logging companies either to inflate the costs or to depress prices. Because of vertical integration in the forest companies and their size, the easiest solution was apparently to depress prices. Pearse (1976) has shown that U.S. log prices have been double those in Vancouver—and these low prices show up as large profits in sawmill operations. Given the large number of workers employed in forestry-related operations, the union involved in sawmill operations and logging has probably influenced the wages of workers in other sectors of the B.C. economy. This powerful union can extract very high wages (twice those in Nova Scotia) from the logging companies. The wages can be financed by the large profits in sawmill operations and are also deductible in the calculation of stumpage fees. If high wages spread into other sectors that have no resource rents, then these sectors will be adversely affected. This situation may explain the regionally high unemployment rate in British Columbia (Copithorne 1979). The problem could be rectified by introducing competitive bidding for licences which would tax away some of the resource rents and force the unions to accept lower wages. Another solution would be to force log prices up by easing export prohibitions on cut logs.

The Management of Nonrenewable Resources

In contrast to fishery and forestry resources, mineral resources are not reproducible. They can be recycled, but their total stock can never be increased. Nor can mineral resources be completely recycled because of the laws of thermodynamics, and therefore the stock is always decreasing if the mineral is being used. The problem here is how quickly the resource should be used, in contrast to fisheries and forestry where the problem is the determination of the optimum size of stock.

A mineral deposit can be compared to any type of asset.[8] The value of a deposit stems from the discounted future income-flows the owner expects to earn from its extraction and sale. The profit is then equal to the discounted income-stream minus the discounted cost of extraction. The owner wants to get the maximum return on his portfolio of assets. The only way a mineral deposit can increase in value is if the price increases or the extraction cost decreases. In equilibrium, the value of a deposit must be growing at a rate equal to the rate of interest.[9] If the value increases at a rate less than the rate of interest, it does not pay the owner to hold on to the ore. If the owner expects the marginal profits—to be gained from holding on to his ore deposit—to increase by 5 percent per year, and prevailing interest rates are 7 percent, the owner would be better off exploiting his resource quickly and investing his profit somewhere else at 7 percent. Leaving the ore in the ground to appreciate is not the best policy. The higher the interest rates, the faster the ore will be exploited. However, if values were increasing quickly, it would pay the owners to delay production and thereby enjoy substantial capital gains. It can be demonstrated theoretically that scarcity will finally have forced the market price to such a high level that demand will fall to zero, and if markets have operated smoothly this will also be the time when the last ton produced will be the last ton left in the ground.

According to this analysis a sequence of mines would be brought into operation. A high-cost mine and a low-cost mine cannot operate concurrently, because net profits cannot increase at the same rate for both, given that the market price would be the same, but costs would not. As time goes on, production will exhaust the 'good' deposits, and the higher-cost deposits will be put into production. For many resources it is possible that there is a technology capable of producing at high cost but at an almost inexhaustible resource base: a 'backstop' technology. Fusion energy or solar energy may be examples of backstop technologies. As there is no scarcity rent, the technology would come into production as soon as present energy prices had risen to a sufficiently high level, providing a ceiling for the market price of energy. The main point here is that for most natural resources, substitutes or perhaps backstop technologies may be available, and would come into production at a sufficiently high price.

Another factor is how to estimate the amount of resources in the ground. The doomsday people have tended to base their estimates of resources on the ratio of reserves to current yearly consumption. This is rather pessimistic, as proven reserves are comparable to working capital or inventory: when reserves are running low the mining company will go out and look for more (Nordhaus 1974). At the other extreme, some optimists have calculated the crustal abundance of different materials, showing that for most important minerals there is more than a million years' supply. This approach is also unrealistic as it assumes that everything can be recovered. Obviously, the market price of the resource, as well as the extraction costs have to be taken into consideration.

Unfortunately, the market price of a resource, for various reasons such as government interference in pricing, or monopoly, or uncertainty, may not always reflect 'true' prices and therefore there is no guarantee that the market mechanism will ensure that resources will be efficiently allocated over time.

As mentioned above, the rate of interest plays a crucial role in deciding whether to produce now or later. The higher the interest rate chosen, the more will be produced now, at the expense of future generations. A mine operator would select the interest rate or rate of return that he would earn on his capital in its best alternative use. The question is, however, whether or not this interest rate is optimal from society's viewpoint. There are several reasons why this rate may be too high. First, the rate of interest is a reward for waiting, because for most people, a dollar earned today is worth more than a dollar earned ten years from now. People tend to be myopic (or realistic: "you may be dead in ten years time"). But this myopia (or realism) also means that we value the welfare of our own generation more than the welfare of the next generation (our children's generation). Therefore, if we are truly concerned for our children—or in fancy terminology, about intergenerational equity—we should use a zero rate of interest in evaluating a mine deposit. It is only if we expect our children to be richer than we that we would be justified in using a positive interest rate.

The second reason why the rate may be too high is that a mine operator will choose his rate of interest so that it compensates him for taking risks—the rate of return earned in business contains a risk premium. The operator is, for example, risking his being driven out of business by a lower-cost supplier of whom he was previously unaware. From society's viewpoint, this type of risk premium is not necessary because this risk involves income transfers between people, not a loss in output. From society's viewpoint the discount rate should not contain this type of risk premium.

Third, a private operator will equate the growth of his after-tax marginal profit rate with the rate of interest, whereas society would equate the before-tax profit rate, as taxes are merely transfers of income from people to government and do not affect total output (ideally). Therefore from society's viewpoint, the mine owner's required profit will be too high.

All these factors, the first stemming from concern for the welfare of our children, the last two from concern for allocative efficiency over time, indicate that resources can be exploited too quickly and therefore exploitation should be slowed down. This could be accomplished either by a conservation subsidy or a system of severance taxes.

Mineral Resources and Mineral Policy in Canada

Mineral production and mineral-related production play an important part in our economy, making up approximately 30 percent of exports. Mineral production can be divided into four sectors: metallics, non-metallics (asbestos, potash and sulphur), mineral fuels (coal, uranium, oil, and gas), and structural materials (cement, sand and gravel). The largest output comes from fuels (over 50 percent of the value of mineral production), followed by metallic minerals (over 30 percent) (*Canada Yearbook* 1978−79:507). Mineral fuels will be discussed in the next chapter.

Canada is the third leading producer and the largest exporter of minerals in the world. Our most important non-fuel minerals are iron ore, copper, nickel, and zinc. We are the largest exporter of nickel, zinc, sulphur, and asbestos and one of the leading producers of copper, silver, platinum, molybdenum, and potash (see Table 5). Perhaps surprisingly Canada also imports minerals: oil and bauxite. Aluminum production, which uses bauxite as a raw material, tends to be located near hydroelectric resources, as refining is extremely energy-intensive. Canada is the world's fifth largest producer of aluminum.

Minerals can probably be regarded as our current staple export. Canada certainly has a comparative advantage in this area. Yearly productivity increases have been high in the mining sector—between 1948 and 1970 it was 5 percent compared to 2.6 percent for the economy as a whole (ECC 1974:178−79). The productivity increases can be largely attributed to increased investments in the industry. However, Canada's comparative advantage is declining because our best ore bodies have already been depleted; in addition Canada is faced with increasingly aggressive competition from Third World countries, many of which are actively encouraging rapid exploitation of their ore bodies to earn foreign exchange.[10]

Given the importance of minerals in our trade, mineral production as a generator of growth is not very impressive. The importance of a staple in generating growth is determined by the three linkages referred to above. Both backward and forward linkages for minerals are lower than for other industries (Stahl and McCuila 1975).

Forward linkages—the processing of ores—have not been well developed in Canada. Indeed, today more than ever, the country seems to be exporting raw rather than processed minerals; for example, a larger proportion of minerals are currently shipped abroad in unprocessed form than in 1928–29 (Wilkinson 1980:82). Raw mineral exports

TABLE 5
Canadian Non-Fuel Mineral Production
in a World Context, 1974–75

Metals	Average share of world production (%)	Average rank among world producers	Rank as source of economically recoverable world reserves
Iron ore	5	6	2
Nickel	35	1	2
Cobalt	6	4	5
Columbium	13	2	2
Molybdenum	16	2	3
Tantalum	14	3	3
Tungsten	3	6	2
Copper	11	3	4
Lead	10	4	4
Zinc	20	1	1
Germanium	6	5	?
Gold	4	3	4
Mercury	4	7	7
Platinum group	7	3	3
Selenium	20	3	3
Silver	14	2	4
Strontium	40	1	?
Uranium	19 (1973–74)	2	3
Other minerals			
Asbestos	40	1	1
Feldspars	3	11	12
Potash	21	2	?

Source: Wilkinson, *Canada in the Changing World Economy*, Table 14.

account for a two to three times larger share of the GNP than they did then. The traditional explanation for the lack of processing is the large degree of foreign ownership in the mining sector. Fifty-eight percent of metal mining assets are controlled by foreign corporations and 60 percent of exports go to parents or affiliates of these companies for processing. A high degree of foreign ownership also means that unless taxes are designed to capture resource rents, these rents will leave the country immediately in the form of interests and dividends; or they will be reinvested in the company, in which case interests and dividends arising from the profits will leave the country at a later date.

The production of base metals is extremely sensitive to the state of the world economy because of low, short-run elasticities of supply and demand. Supply elasticities are low because of the time lags involved in opening up or closing down mines. Low demand elasticities can be explained by the lack of substitutes in the short run. Any event, such as a big strike, or a shift in industrial demand because of recession or a boom period will send the price up and down like a yo-yo. Between October 1973 and April 1974 base metal prices (copper, zink, tin and lead) rose by 53 percent. World recession sent the prices down by 52 percent in the next six months (*The Economist*, 13 Oct. 1979). In 1976 and early 1979, prices started to rise again, followed by an immediate plunge at the prospect of an impending U.S. recession. In late 1979 and early 1980, world unrest and currency speculation hit the gold and silver markets; base metals were also affected and prices reached record-high levels.

These severe fluctuations, which incidentally have not been as great as for commodities such as sugar, cocoa and rubber, can create substantial hardships for towns or regions whose economy depends on mining. Most Canadians are aware of the fate of Dawson City, the rise and fall of which was connected to the fortunes of gold. Many northern communities have suffered similar fates. For this reason a major aim of government policy has been to encourage further processing in order to maintain some stability in local economies.

Both the federal and provincial governments are involved in formulating policies for the mineral sector. The main roles of the federal government in the resource field are as manager of resources in the North and as collector of income taxes. In the North, it administers the allocation of mineral rights and collects royalties (discussed in the next chapter). In the taxation field, the federal government formulates a policy for the mining sector, which has traditionally been very generous—in the opinion of some, because of our staple export mentality (Kierans 1973). Also, the private-resource operators were able to convince both governments and people that because natural resources are of no value to anyone until discovered and exploited, the ancient principle of 'finders keepers' should apply.

Until 1955, most of the tax concessions were renewed on a three-year basis, but subsequently became a permanent part of the tax laws. They included a three-year tax holiday for new mines, a depletion allowance of 33 percent set against taxable income, and an immediate write-off of exploration and development expenses. This situation led to many cases in which large multinational corporations did not pay any tax at all. The federal government also gave substantial subsidies under the Emergency Gold Mining Assistance Act and the Coal Production Assistance Act. After 1973, with the energy crisis and sky-rocketing prices for base metals, mining companies were labelled "corporate welfare bums," and taxation was tightened up by both federal and provincial governments. The three-year tax holiday for new mines was abolished and depletion was substituted for earned depletion which could be claimed only if exploration and development were carried out. Provincial royalties were also made nondeductible in computing federal taxable income.

One of the aims of provincial mining policies has been to collect any rent arising from the sale of mineral resources. Economic rent is payment for a resource that is in scarce supply, and should accrue to the owner of the resource (the province), not the mining company or the purchaser of the resource. If the purchaser of the resource pays less than the market price, the purchaser collects some of the rent. If the government could identify the actual rent, then it would be able to take over the rent from the mining companies without any effect on the demand and supply of the resource. In practice, the chief rent collection instruments have been royalties and to a lesser extent mineral leases. A royalty, which is a tax per unit of output produced, is an inefficient means of appropriating rent. The effect of a royalty is similar to that of a production tax. It can be shown that if the stock of natural resources is fixed, but the supply is not (more will be produced at higher prices), then a royalty is likely to lower future investments in the industry (Grubel and Smith 1975). It can also be demonstrated that a royalty will result in a higher initial price of mineral rights and a longer period of extraction (Campbell, Gainer and Scott 1976). For these reasons, a royalty is not a neutral tax and does not collect pure economic rent. It has been suggested that royalties should be abolished and mining profit taxes put in their place (Leith 1978).[11]

Apart from this problem of isolating economic rent, there is the problem of foreign ownership. In the resource sector close to 50 percent of total assets are owned by foreigners. It is well known that multinationals can minimize their taxes by manipulating the prices at which the subsidiary in one country sells to the subsidiary in another country. This could mean that foreign-owned corporations do not pay their due rent either in the form of provincial mining taxes or corporate income taxes, and therefore that the rent is appropriated by foreign shareholders through an outflow of dividends at present or will be in the future.

Summary and Conclusions

In this chapter some of the problems in the resource sector were surveyed. The fisheries sector is particularly plagued by inefficiencies in the sense that it has attracted an excessive amount of labour and capital. A more efficient allocation of resources would be achieved by policies designed to reduce the amount of resources in this sector. The forestry sector suffers from some of the resource management problems found in the fisheries, but not as severely. However, forestry policies in British Columbia appear to have been badly designed, resulting in substantial distortions in the local economy.

Minerals are Canada's current staple products. The economic benefits derived from this sector are modest compared to the potential the sector had for generating growth. The main reason is the poor forward linkages with the rest of the economy. The aim of government policies to develop more processing has not been achieved, with subsequent loss of potential income and employment for Canadians. A related factor is the high degree of foreign ownership which makes it difficult for governments, both federal and provincial, to appropriate rents. Failure to collect all the rents implies a loss of income for Canadians. It is also possible that a more orderly conservation-oriented development of mines would have given Canadians greater benefit in the long run. Many of our best ore bodies have been depleted, and will not survive competition from newly opened mines in other countries.

NOTES

1. At present there are four leading North American-based conglomerates involved in deep-sea mining: the Kennecott consortium, Ocean Mining Associates, Ocean Management Incorporated, and Ocean Minerals Co. INCO is a member of Ocean Management Incorporated. This consortium conducted full-scale at-sea tests of a prototype mining system in the Pacific during the spring of 1978. The test has stopped, but before it did, 750 tons of nodules were recovered at a depth of 17,000 feet (*Seatrade*, July 1979).
2. It is estimated that the value of the total yield lost by mismanagement of North American fisheries is nearly 300 million dollars per year (Huppert 1977).
3. United Nations 1977. *Informal Composite Negotiating Tract*. Third Conference on the Law of the Sea.
4. See note 3.
5. The path-breaking analysis was supplied by R.L. Gordon 1954.

6. For a good analysis, see Clark 1976:1–23.
7. The program was actually a continuation of a more limited program operated by the Newfoundland government.
8. The following section is based on Solow 1974.
9. This is the so-called Hotelling Rule, after Hotelling 1931.
10. For an interesting discussion of the effects of increased competition on the Canadian nickel industry, see Cairns 1981.
11. Note, however, the argument above that mineral resources tend to be exploited at too fast a rate and therefore should be taxed to encourage slower extraction (or subsidized for conservation). Therefore, if royalties prove to lead to a longer period of extraction, they are not necessarily a bad tax. Yet there may be more efficient tax regimes available that encourage conservation and tax rents at the same time.

BIBLIOGRAPHY

Anderson, F.J. "Ontario's Reforestation Policy: Benefits and Costs." *Canadian Public Policy* (V), 1979 pp. 348–66.

Cairns, R.D. "A Reconsideration of Ontario Nickel Policy." *Canadian Public Policy* (VII), 1981, pp. 526–34.

Campbell, Harry, W.D. Gainer and A. Scott. "Resource Rents, How Much and for Whom?" In A. Scott (ed.), pp. 118–37, *Natural Resource Revenue: A Test of Federalism*. Vancouver: UBC Press, 1976.

Clark, Colin W. *Mathematical Bioeconomics: The Optimal Management of Renewable Resources*. New York: John Wiley & Sons, 1976.

Copes, P. "Canada's Atlantic Coast Fisheries: Policy Development and the Impact of Extended Jurisdiction." *Canadian Public Policy* (IV), 1978, pp. 155–72.

Copithorne, L. "Resources and Regional Disparities." *Canadian Public Policy* (V), 1979, pp. 181–95.

Crutchfield, James A. "Marine Resources: The Economics of U.S. Ocean Policy." *The American Economic Review, Papers and Proceedings* (69), 1979, pp. 266–71.

Department of the Environment. *Policy for Canada's Commercial Fisheries*. Ottawa, 1976.

Economic Council of Canada. *Eleventh Annual Review*. Ottawa: Information Canada, 1974.

Economic Council of Canada. *Reforming Regulation*. Ottawa: Supply and Services, 1981.

Gordon, H.S. "A Reinterpretation of the Pure Theory of Exhaustion." *Journal of Political Economy* (75), 1967, pp. 274–86.

Gordon, R.L. "The Economic Theory of a Common Property Resource." *Journal of Political Economy* (62), 1954, pp. 124-42.

Grubel, H.G. and S. Sydney Smith. "The Taxation of Windfall Gains on Stocks of Natural Resources." *Canadian Public Policy* (I), 1975, pp. 13–30.

Hardin, S. "The Tragedy of the Commons." *Science.* (162), 1968, pp. 1243-47.

Hotelling, H. "The Economics of Exhaustible Resources." *Journal of Political Economy* (39), 1931, pp. 137–73.

Huppert, Daniel D. "Constraints to Welfare Gains under Extended Jurisdiction Fisheries Management." *American Journal of Agricultural Economics* (59), 1977, pp. 877–83.

Innis, H.A. *The Fur Trade in Canada: An Introduction to Canadian Economic History.* Rev. Ed. Toronto: University of Toronto Press, 1956.

Kierans, E. *Report on Natural Resource Policy in Manitoba.* (Prepared for the Secretariat for the Planning and Priorities Committee of Cabinet, Government of Manitoba), 1973.

Leith, J.C. "What is Ontario's Mineral Resource Policy?" *Canadian Public Policy* (IV), 1978, pp. 352–64.

MacDonald, R.D.S. "Inshore Fishing Interests on the Atlantic Coast." *Marine Policy* (3), 1979, pp. 171–89.

Matthews, R. "Ethical Issues in Policy Research: The Investigation of Community Resettlement in Newfoundland." *Canadian Public Policy* (I), 1975, pp. 204–19.

Meadows, D.H. *et al. The Limits to Growth.* New York: Universe Books, 1972.

Mitchell, C.L. "The 200-Mile Limit: New Issues, Old Problems for Canada's East Coast Fisheries." *Canadian Public Policy* (IV), 1978, pp. 172–84.

Nordhaus, William D. "Resources as a Constraint on Growth." *American Economic Review,* Papers and Proceedings (CXIV), 1974, pp. 22–6.

Pearse, Peter H. *Timber Rights and Forest Policy in British Columbia.* Report of the Royal Commission on Forestry Resources, Victoria, B.C., 1976.

Solow, Robert. "The Economics of Resources and the Resources of Economics." *American Economic Review* (64), 1974, pp. 1–14.

Stahl, J.E. and D.J. McCulla. *The Canadian Mineral Industry and Economic Development.* Ottawa: Energy, Mines and Resources, 1975.

Statistics Canada. *Canadian Forestry Statistics, 1978.* Ottawa: Supply and Services, 1979.

United Nations. *Informal Composite Negotiating Tract.* Third Conference on the Law of the Sea. A/CONF.62/WP.10, New York, 1977.

Watkins, M.H. "A Staple Theory of Economic Growth." In W.T. Easterbrooke and M.H. Watkins (eds.), pp. 49-74, *Approaches to Canadian Economic History*. Toronto: McClelland & Stewart, 1967.

Wilkinson, B.W. *Canada in the Changing World Economy*. Montreal: C.D. Howe Research Institute, 1980.

Wilkinson, Maurice. "The Economics of the Ocean: Environment, Issues and Economic Analysis." *American Economic Review,* Papers and Proceedings (69), 1979, pp. 251−55.

CHAPTER 3

Energy Resources

The 1970s can probably be described as the first decade of the energy age. At no other time were people so obsessed with energy resources and energy demands. In 1973, at the height of the energy crisis, many people were convinced that Doomsday had arrived, and that the world economy would start its long downward slide as predicted by the Club of Rome—admittedly a few decades too early. At the start of 1980, energy was still at the forefront in people's minds, but the world had changed rather dramatically since 1970. On the positive side, the world had not run out of energy, and the world economy did not collapse. What did happen, however, was that energy made some people fabulously wealthy, while its high costs made considerable dents in the pocketbooks of others. We saw a massive redistribution of money, mainly from the industrialized countries to some Arab countries (the Third World countries did not have much to be redistributed), and inflation rates unheard of in the postwar period. The search for alternative energy resources continues, as well as a sometimes hysterical debate on the pros and cons of nuclear energy.

In this chapter, the events of the 1970s will be surveyed, and world supply of and demand for energy discussed. This survey will set the background for an assessment of the Canadian energy scene and a critical examination of Canadian energy policy in Chapter 4.

OPEC and the Energy Crises of 1973 and 1979

The dependence on oil in the industrialized countries goes back to the Second World War. Before then, coal was the dominant energy source, and oil was used mainly as fuel for road and air transport, and as an input into a growing petrochemical industry. The oil industry has always tried to match supply and demand by keeping the level of proven reserves well ahead of immediate demand. However, oil discoveries typically do not happen in small increments; on the contrary new wells tend to be discovered in large lumps. This means that occasional surpluses and shortages appear. From the 1920s to the late '60s, there were mainly surpluses, leading to cutthroat competition and falling prices and therefore increased oil consumption. The surplus led to attempts at cartelization already in the 1920s, and government imposed production quotas in the form of prorationing (in Texas and Alberta). In 1960, following a couple of years of falling prices, the Organization for Petroleum Exporting Countries (OPEC) was formed, consisting of Venezuela, Iran, Iraq, Indonesia, Nigeria, Algeria, Abu Dhabi, Kuwait, Saudi Arabia, the United Arab Emirates, Libya, Qatar, and Oman. OPEC's immediate aim was to stabilize prices. In its first decade of existence, OPEC did not operate as an effective cartel, as it was unable to agree on production quotas and therefore could not push up the price toward the monopoly level. In fact, all through the '60s the real price of oil fell, stimulating further increases in demand by industrialized countries and therefore increasing their dependence on oil.

A cartel can be successful in increasing profits for its members only when three conditions are present. First, demand for the product must be inelastic. A cartel may control 100 percent of the output, but if demand is elastic because of the existence of good substitutes, the prospects of increasing profits by raising prices are slim. Second, a cartel can raise prices only by reducing output. Output restrictions usually mean that the cartel has to agree on the allocation of quotas. Third, the cartel must have an effective policing mechanism because an individual producer can increase his profit by selling his product at a slightly lower price than the cartel price and increasing his output beyond the quota. Unless a producer is effectively prevented from doing so, the cartel will fail.

In the case of OPEC, the first condition for successive cartelization was certainly present: demand is highly inelastic, at least in the short- and medium-term. Estimated short-run elasticities for crude oil are in the range of -0.3 to -0.5 (Berndt 1977:62). The second precondition of agreeing on quotas was not present during the 1960s—the reason why high prices were not achieved. The reason for the failure to agree on quotas was the diverging interests of the producing countries. They had different resource endowments, a different need for revenues and a different outlook on development. Some countries (e.g., Libya, Algeria and Venezuela) were more favourably located in relation to the markets than others and demanded compensation for this in the form of a premium (location rent); this demand led to dissension. Some countries had higher production costs. An optimum allocation of quotas would have required higher reserve-to-production ratios in some countries than in others. There was no political mechanism for solving these problems, little common tradition and no habit of cooperation (McKie 1974).

The third condition—an effective policing mechanism—was present. Adelman (1972) maintained that it was the western oil companies that served this function, being the sellers and distributors of oil. The reason was their position as tax collectors for the oil-producing countries. In the early '60s OPEC set the posted price of a barrel of oil at $1.80. The royalty that had to be paid at the time was $0.225 per barrel, but in addition the companies had to pay a profits tax of 50 percent (Adelman 1972:207). Assume the cost of production was $0.10 per barrel. Profits were $1.80 − $0.225 − $0.10 = $1.47. The tax was then $0.737. Total payments due were $0.225 + $0.737 = $0.972 and the total cost to the oil company $0.972 + $0.10 = $1.072. This cost served as an effective floor on the price, as under no circumstances would an oil company accept a price lower than $1.072. The oil companies therefore guaranteed that prices would never fall to their competitive level which was then at a marginal cost of $0.10 to $0.20. Under these circumstances the cartel would be more likely to disintegrate if the OPEC countries had to do their own producing and selling, that is, if they nationalized the oil companies. Cheating would then be far more difficult to detect, and there would be no floor (except marginal cost) to the price, assuming the national oil company would not have to pay production taxes and income taxes.

In September 1969, Colonel Gadaffi came to power in Libya.[1] He forcibly argued for an increase in posted prices and for cutbacks in production. In 1970 Libya reduced production by 800,000 barrels per day. At the time there was also a break in the vital pipeline from the Middle East through Syria, resulting in a further cutback of 500,000 barrels per day. Because of this induced scarcity, the market could allow an increase in prices. The Teheran and Tripoli agreements of 1971 between the oil companies and OPEC increased the posted price by 35 cents per barrel and made provisions for annual upward adjustments in prices by 2½ percent. This was followed by further cutbacks in Libya and Kuwait.

On 6 October 1973, Egypt attacked Israel, and when an Arab victory—despite early successes—did not seem assured, it was decided that oil should be used as a bargaining lever. The Arab members of OPEC vowed to decrease output by 5 percent each month until Israel had withdrawn from occupied Arab land. Saudi Arabia reduced production immediately and set up an embargo on exports to the United States and Holland. These cutbacks could not have come at a worse time. Buoyant world markets had increased the demand for oil substantially, so the normal surplus capacity had already all but disappeared. The United States, partly because of its oil-pricing program, had seen its proven reserves dwindle and had come to rely increasingly on OPEC oil for its domestic consumption.

Confronted with cutbacks, the industrialized countries did not put up a unified front, which made the cutbacks a great political and financial success. The Europeans and the Japanese stood clear of the Americans and were falling over themselves in attempts to collaborate with the Arabs. Existing inventories were not spread over time by rationing, nor were there any attempts to pool resources.[2] Instead, reserves were being run down as a means of putting off unpopular decisions of curbing demand. Oil companies scrambled to the Rotterdam spot markets to build up reserves. The spot market normally handles a minute fraction of oil, as most companies obtain their oil from long-term contracts with the oil-producing countries.[3] With more and more companies turning to the spot market, spot prices soared. This upswing in turn convinced OPEC that they had been too modest in their price demands and revised posted prices upwards. Table 6 gives an account of the price movements.

Following the price increases, the world experienced double-digit inflation and a recession, the worst since the Great Depression of the 1920s. This led to a decrease in energy demand. Further, illustrating the fact that demand for oil is not perfectly inelastic, consumers cut back on their consumption when they were confronted with higher prices. Higher prices also made other sources of oil economical (North Sea oil and Alaskan oil). These factors contributed to a potential surplus during the remainder of the '70s, and again the price of oil fell in real terms. (Compare the price in 1974 in Table 6 with the January price in 1979, and consider the rate of inflation in the intervening period and the fall in the value of the U.S. dollar). It is possible that had it not been for Saudi Arabia's willingness to cut production to control the surplus, oil prices would have fallen in nominal terms as well. The management of the cartel during this period was firmly in the hands of Saudi Arabia which was by far the largest producer.[4]

By 1978, demand was creeping up again as the world economy began to improve, and as the lower real prices made their way to consumers. The consumers were cushioned from the price rises to a considerable degree in most countries. For example, the increase in oil prices between 1973 and 1974 of 400 percent was translated into an average real increase in prices to consumers of 22 percent. In seven of the fourteen industrialized countries, gasoline prices at the pump were actually lower in real terms in 1978 than *in 1972* (before the 400% increase in the price of oil) (*The Economist*, 22 Dec. 1979). Furthermore, Saudi Arabia's hold over OPEC seemed to decline in the late '70s. Keeping OPEC in line used to be a matter of having sufficient spare capacity to undermine prices if the other OPEC countries pushed up prices to a higher level than Saudi Arabia wanted, and cutting back if prices threatened to drop. However, in 1977 there were signs that some fields in Saudi Arabia had been overexploited, harming their ultimate recoverable potential (*The Economist*, 22 May 1979). Recoverable reserves therefore had to be

TABLE 6
Posted Prices for Oil, 1973–1981
($ per barrel)

Type of Oil	1973 Oct. 1	1973 Oct. 16	1974 Jan.	1978 Dec.	1979 Jan.	1980 Jan.	1980 July	1980 Dec.	1981 Jan.
Arabian Light	3.011	5.119	11.651	12.70	13.34	26.00	28.00	30.00	32.00
Iranian Light	2.995	5.091	11.875	12.81	13.45	30.00	35.87	35.37	37.00
Iraq Basrah	2.977	5.061	11.671	12.88	13.52	26.18	33.29	31.96	35.96
Kuwait	2.884	4.903	11.545	12.22	12.83	27.50	31.50	31.50	35.50
Qatar	3.143	5.343	12.298	13.09	14.03	27.42	33.42	33.42	37.23
Libya	4.604	8.925	15.768	13.85	14.69	34.67	37.00	37.00	40.78

Sources: *The Petroleum Economist* (various issues); Hill and Vielvoge, *Energy in Crisis*, p. 66.

downgraded and the Saudis no longer had the spare capacity necessary to exercise their control over OPEC. With the Saudis converted to a policy of slow (or no) growth in oil production, and with world demand soaring, the stage was set for another circus. This time the circus was started by a strike by oil workers in Iran in the winter of 1978−79 which depleted most of the oil reserves that had accumulated in the West over the last few years. The strike was followed by the fall of the Shah of Iran and the rise of a new regime. The oil fields were opened again but they were operating at a low capacity.

When the OPEC countries met in Abu Dhabi in December 1978 they reached a compromise agreement for oil prices during 1979. The marker (light Arabian crude) would rise in four quarterly installments from $12.70 to $14.54. By the summer, supply shortages were such that a new conference in Geneva was called, at which the Saudis agreed to raise the price immediately to $18, while others were charging more. There was an agreement, however, that the limit was to be $23.50. (*The Petroleum Economist*, Jan. 1980).

Despite a modest *increase* in world oil production during 1979, buyers continued to stockpile, again turning to the Rotterdam spot market. Oil supplies were diverted from the oil companies to government-to-government deals, which sent even the major oil companies to the spot market, bidding for oil. By October 1979, the spot price had soared to $45 a barrel, again sending signals back to OPEC that they had been too bashful in determining prices. Once again, posted prices leap-frogged in disarray. In an attempt to stabilize them, the Saudis announced in mid-December that they would raise prices to $24 and backdate the raise to November. All the other OPEC countries were near that price at the time. Yet, at the beginning of the conference in Caracas at the end of December, Libya announced an increase in price to $29.40 and Iran to $28.50 (*The Petroleum Economist*, Jan. 1980). No agreement on prices was achieved. (Table 6 shows the spread of prices quoted in January 1980.) Following the outbreak of war between Iran and Iraq and subsequent fears of disruptions of oil supplies from the Persian Gulf area, further price increases were announced in 1980 (see Table 6). These disruptions never materialized and another glut emerged at the end of 1980. Higher prices led to a considerable reduction in consumption. Indeed, by the middle of 1980 consumption of oil in the non-communist world averaged 46.1 million barrels a day compared to 49.4 million a year earlier (*Globe and Mail*, 21 May 1981). In the summer of 1981 some of the higher-priced OPEC countries had to reduce their prices.

World Energy Demand and Supply

It is extremely difficult to forecast world energy demand-and-supply for reasons indicated by the above events. Energy demand depends not only on price but also on income, population and climatic conditions. The demand for a particular type of energy depends on its relative price compared with the price of other forms of energy. Supply of energy also depends on price—the higher the price, the more will be supplied and the greater the effort to find new supplies of the same resource and to develop alternate resources. However, supply also depends on technology, as well as on politics. After all, oil supplies were being withheld by the OPEC countries partly for political reasons. Energy prices are also controlled by governments to placate voters; the development of nuclear power, in particular, has been hindered for political reasons.

All these factors make it impossible to forecast with any accuracy the future path of prices, when the world is going to run out of fossil fuels, and so on. The question is whether there are hitherto unfound sources of oil and gas, or a backstop technology which would set a limit on the maximum price of oil.

Conventional Oil and Gas

The immediate future for hydrocarbons is not impressive. A report by the Central Intelligence Agency in the United States shows that oil production in OECD will decline by 1982 (*The Petroleum Economist*, Nov. 1979). The production of oil in Alaska has already reached a plateau. Oil production is rising in some Third World countries such as Mexico, India, Egypt, and Malaysia, but it is expected that these increases will only keep up with the increase in consumption in these countries. Output in eastern European countries is expected to peak in the early 1980s, at which time they will try to enter the world market as buyers. OPEC production is also expected to fall, since capital expenditures on exploration have been declining. There are some, however, who believe that vast areas of South America, Antarctica, Southeast Asia, and Africa have been underexplored in view of the fact that they contain 50 percent of the world's oil-bearing geological structures (*The Petroleum Economist*, Jan. 1980). Many of the countries in these areas lack the technological expertise to find and develop oil, whereas the multinational oil companies tend to regard these areas as too risky politically. The major oil companies are not renowned for their diplomatic acumen.[5]

Shale Oil and Tar Sands

The United States is by far the largest buyer of oil in the world. If the United States could be made self-sufficient in energy, the pressure would be taken off world energy demands. Indeed, this country has large energy reserves in coal and shale oil. Much has been written but little done about the vast deposits of shale oil which are located in

Colorado, Wyoming and Utah, covering an area of approximately 17,000 square miles. The American government estimates that 80 billion barrels are recoverable, given the present technology (compared to 27.8 billion barrels of proven conventional oil reserves in the United States and 169.5 billion barrels in Saudi Arabia). A ton of high-grade shale will yield 25 or more U.S. gallons of raw shale oil (*The Petroleum Economist*, Jan. 1980).

The best-developed method for extracting shale oil involves the heating of crushed shale to 900°F, at which temperature the hydrocarbons are released as vapour. When the vapour condenses, it forms what is known as raw shale oil. Atlantic Richfield is involved in a pilot plant to perfect this technology. In another pilot project, on-site recovery is being attempted. This entails fracturing the shale in place, followed by combustion. The condensed vapour is then pumped to the surface as raw shale oil. It is not yet certain whether the latter technology is economically feasible, but at present prices the former technology is.

Legal and environmental obstacles are delaying implementation of shale oil production. Legal wranglings over leases are such that production in Utah, for example, does not seem likely in the foreseeable future. Colorado seems a more probable site for large-scale production, but even here, the would-be shale producer would have to get past a hurdle of 44 necessary permits; failure to obtain one could block the project. These factors, as well as the recent oil glut and the free-market orientation of the Reagan administration, make it unlikely that large-scale shale oil production will commence (*The Economist*, 4 July 1981).

Tar sands production has progressed further, but is also unlikely to make a dent in world energy supply prospects despite vast reserves. The deposits in Alberta and Saskatchewan are estimated to hold up to 1,000 billion barrels of oil, with perhaps 10 to 20 percent being ultimately recoverable (Gander and Belair 1979:38). Together, they constitute the largest-known single deposit of oil, and after the price increase in 1979, tar sands production seemed a profitable enterprise. The costs are substantial, however, with the capital cost of a new plant estimated at 6 billion dollars. This figure was translated into a per barrel cost (as measured by capital investment related to productive capacity) of approximately $30,000 compared to $8,000 for North Sea oil and $2,000 for low-cost Persian crude (*The Petroleum Economist*, Feb. 1980). In 1981 the cost estimate of a new plant had increased to 12 or 13 billion dollars. The prohibitive cost, together with falling oil prices, make even oil sands production a dubious investment.

The deposits have been known to exist since the early part of the century. Tar sands were used in the 1920s to provide material for roof and paving roads; the first Jasper-Banff highway was paved with tar sands material. The Alberta Research Council has been engaged in research on ways to extract the crude from the sand since the '20s. At one stage there was serious talk about using underground nuclear explosions, the heat from which would separate the oil from the sands, which would then be collected in big underground caverns.[6] One of the researchers, Mr. Clark, designed a flotation process which involved dumping the sands in big flotation tanks filled with warm water. When the slurry was heated, the oil rose to the surface and could be skimmed off to form the basis for synthetic crude. A similar process is used by the current producers of synthetic oil.

The first commercial plant for producing synthetic oil commenced operations in 1967. It was operated by Sun Oil first under the name of GCOS (Great Canadian Oil Sands plant) and more recently under the name SUNCOR. This plant has a production capacity of 45,000 barrels per day. It operated at a loss until 1973 but was expected to have cleared its cumulative deficit by 1980. Another plant, the Syncrude plant (which is sponsored by Esso Resources, Canada Cities Service, Gulf Canada Resources, Petro-Canada Exploration, Alberta Energy Company, the Province of Alberta, Hudson's Bay Oil and Gas, Petrofina, and Pan Canadian Petroleum), with a capacity of 100,000 barrels per day, started production in 1978. Both plants have at times had severe production problems; each has had a major fire, and have frequently operated below capacity. A third plant, the Alsands plant (sponsored by Shell Canada Resources, Shell Explorer, Amoco, Pacific Petroleum (Petro-Canada), Gulf Oil, Chevron, Petrofina, Dome, and Hudson's Bay Oil and Gas), is planned and construction was expected to start early 1980; however, disagreement over energy pricing between the Alberta and federal governments postponed construction. There are also several pilot plants in operation, experimenting with on-site steam extraction of heavy oil in the Cold Lake region of Alberta.

It is possible that by the 1990s, additional plants will have increased total capacity to between 1 and 2 million barrels per day, which would improve Canada's energy situation but not the world's as a whole.

Coal

Coal is expected to play an increasing role in future world energy supplies. Most of the known recoverable coal reserves are located in the United States (37%). The remainder can be found in the USSR and eastern Europe (26%), China (15%), western Europe (10%), Australia (4%), South Africa (2%), and Canada (1%) (Gander and Belair 1978:38). The coal reserves are huge: in the United States they are estimated at 300 to 500 times current annual consumption, given present technology and prices. However, there are some important drawbacks to a massive changeover to coal. First, the large reserves are concentrated in Montana, Wyoming and Utah, in deposits where only stripmining is feasible.

Land reclamation in these areas poses substantial problems, given the scarcity of water. Grass cover can be achieved only with intensive use of water and fertilizer; therefore reclamation on a large scale would take water away from agricultural use, making the process very costly. The second problem is air pollution. The coal would be used in eastern industrial areas where air pollution problems are bad already because of frequent inversions and periods of air stagnation. Apart from the health-induced effects of smog, there are the environmental effects of increased acidity; sulphur oxides, nitrogen oxides and chlorine are emitted from coal-generated electricity plants. These gases react with water vapors to form sulphuric, nitric and hydrochloric acids which pose severe threats to aquatic and plant life. Many lakes in Ontario are contaminated beyond repair already because of excess acidity. The water looks beautifully clear and clean, but the lakes are dead. Some of the sulphur dioxide can be removed by using "scrubbers" and some of the newer stations have these. It is estimated that the cost of cutting the emission of sulphurdioxide in half would be $350 million in Canada and 5 to 7 billion dollars in the United States (*The Financial Post*, 28 July 1979).

The answers to the environmental problems of using coal may be (1) coal gasification or liquefaction at the site; (2) conversion of coal into electricity at the site; or (3) learning to use coal more efficiently. Coal liquefaction is not an unknown technology, but has so far only been used for political and strategic reasons. Nazi Germany ran several plants and SASOL, the state-owned energy company in South Africa, has operated a plant since 1960. Another plant was scheduled to start operating in 1981. The two plants will produce 40,000 barrels per day of gasoline, as well as some chemical feedstocks. However, a SASOL spokesman admitted that the second plant will be only marginally profitable at 1978 oil prices (*The Petroleum Economist*, Feb. 1979); however this situation will likely have changed, given recent oil price increases.

The Americans are presently involved in improving the technology of coal liquefaction. Three separate hydrogen processes have been developed that are technologically feasible. These operate with conversion factors of 2.5 to 3 barrels of liquid per ton of coal. The Electricity Producers Joint Research Institute reckons that the three processes can be made commercially viable, with a yield of 450,000 barrels per day by 1990 and 950,000 per day by 1995 (*The Petroleum Economist*, Feb. 1979).

There is some speculation coal-fired ships will come into limited use again. Indeed, the Australian National Line and a Japanese shipping firm have bulk carriers on order which would run on coal (*Seatrade*, Jan. 1980). The estimated cost-saving over diesel-powered ships is between 15 and 22 percent. A large-scale return to coal in the shipping industry would, however, require substantial modifications in the design of ports, as storage facilities for coal would have to be provided.

Nuclear Energy

Cheap nuclear energy was touted as the solution to the world's energy problems, immediately following the energy crisis of 1973. It was widely believed that a massive buildup of nuclear energy could supply electricity at a generating cost half that of an oil-fired station.[7] Since then the nuclear option has been put in doubt—even though it still has proponents—partly because of cost and partly because of environmental considerations. It no longer seems particularly cheap. The early cost estimates were based on private, not social costs, with most of the research and development costs assumed to be undertaken by the government at no cost to the utility. When all costs are taken into account (research into safety measures, environmental impact studies, cost of storage, and long-term guarding of the station after the reactor core is spent), it is clear that nuclear energy is not cheap.[8]

The costs are also high because many stations have difficulty maintaining full operating capacity. The reliability of operations at present power stations has been erratic—with no customary improvement in reliability. The average period of time when a nuclear station is inoperative is in the region of 40 to 45 percent, which is worse than for most fossil-using stations.[9] Another factor is the limited supply of high-grade uranium, which in turn will escalate the cost of uranium as it becomes scarce. It is expected that the solution to this is to economize on uranium by the use of so-called fast-breeder reactors. The breeder reactor can extract almost all the energy contained in uranium and it produces more energy than it consumes. A breeder reactor is being constructed in France which, more than any other country, has chosen to take the nuclear option. France hopes to generate 70 percent of electricity by nuclear power by 1985 (*The Financial Post*, 28 Jan. 1978).

The environmental hazards of nuclear energy are well known. They can be divided into three problem areas: the safety of the reactors themselves, the problem of safe storage and dismantling of stations with spent reactor cores, and the terrorist problem. As far as the safety of individual reactors are concerned, the record is good. The nuclear industry has pointed out that there has not yet been a lethal accident at a nuclear power plant, and even better safety could probably be obtained—at a price. The Harrisburg incident in 1979 showed that things can go wrong, however. The risk of a reactor melt-down ("the China Syndrome") is acceptably low, even though a melt-down almost occurred at the Three-Mile Island plant (*The Economist*, 2 Feb. 1980). It is still possible to argue that in terms of injuries and fatalities, nuclear power is considerably safer than coal.

The problems of the storage of wastes and what to do with the power stations after the core has become spent are perhaps the most serious. At present the amount of waste is insignificant and therefore the problem may seem insignificant too. However, the energy economy envisaged by the end of the century would be generating substantial amounts of wastes. The wastes do not become harmless in a few years' time—the time involved for the least noxious waste is one thousand years. A major research effort is underway into methods to solidify the wastes and to enclose them in ceramic-like solid forms which can be stored deep down in geologically stable structures. However, according to geologists there is no such thing as a perfectly stable structure, and if the container breaks the radioactive material could contaminate the ground-water.

Another factor of nuclear energy is the terrorist threat and the proliferation of nuclear weapons. If terrorists got hold of waste in surface storage, or occupied an outdated plant, or seized hold of spent fuel on its way to reprocessing plants, the possibilities of large-scale blackmail are terrifying: the waste could be spread over a large area using conventional explosives. Some people argue that the security measures necessary in a fully nuclear society would seriously affect our civil liberties.

The proliferation of nuclear weapons and the accessibility of the technical know-how were made clear a few years ago when a physics undergraduate at Princeton wrote a term paper on how to make a workable nuclear bomb. Plutonium is the main raw material and can be made from reprocessed wastes from conventional nuclear power stations. It is produced as a waste product from the Canadian-developed Candu reactor, and from the newly designed breeder reactors. One conventional reactor can produce enough raw material to make 330 lbs. of plutonium—enough to make fifteen bombs of Hiroshima strength (*The Economist*, 6 Dec. 1975). It was from plutonium waste from the Candu reactor that India made and exploded its first nuclear bomb. One Candu reactor is in use in Pakistan, two are ready for Argentina and two are on order for South Korea. When Iran and Brazil negotiated contracts for their nuclear power plants, they insisted their plants should also have enrichment-fuel fabrication and plutonium-separation facilities. The United States refused to sell a reactor under these conditions, but Germany complied with the request. With the advent of breeder reactors, plutonium production will increase substantially.

All these factors, combined with a perhaps irrational fear of radioactivity, have led to a considerable slowdown in the construction of nuclear power plants in OECD countries, the major exception being France where public resistance to nuclear power has been minimal and not well organized.

Renewable Energy: Biomass

Much interest has been generated in the possibilities of biomass as a source of energy. Biomass includes all types of organic materials, ranging from fast-growing trees (eucalyptus and poplar), energy-rich crops (sugar cane, cassava and maize), water weeds and algae, and petroleum-bearing plants (euphorbia), to waste products from the agriculture and forestry industries, garbage and sewage.

The use of biomass for energy is not new. Wood had been the dominant heating fuel in most of the world until the production and transportation of coal were made economically feasible. Today, wood and dung are used as fuels for cooking by most people in Third World countries, where excessive use by too many people has led to deforestation of large areas with resulting wind and soil erosion problems.[10] The lack of firewood is frequently referred to as "the other energy problem" and has received little attention in the West. Only two countries appear to have made serious efforts to halt this dangerous trend: China and South Korea. In China, it is claimed that the proportion of forested land has increased by 5 to 13 percent over the past twenty years, and in South Korea, one-half the land is said to be restocked with trees less than ten years old.

In the industrialized countries, interest in biomass has gone beyond wood to the manufacture of methanol, ethanol, hydrogen, and ammonia. Ethanol (alcohol) can be produced from wood residue, sugar cane and other plants. Present-day technology allows the use of ethanol mixed with gasoline as a fuel for cars ("gasohol"). Brazil has used gasohol for some time with apparent success (*The Financial Post*, 16 Feb. 1980), and it has also been marketed in the United States since 1979 with less success. The mixture of 90 percent gasoline and 10 percent alcohol costs consumers a few cents more than conventional gasoline.[11] The alcohol is made from sugarcane in Brazil ("the sweet solution"), and from grain and corn in the United States. Given present fluctuations in the grain markets, it is unlikely that alcohol from grain would be a secure energy source. It could also be argued that a full-scale changeover to gasohol would be immoral as it would raise grain prices even higher and have severe implications on the food situation in the Third World.

Oil and gas can also be produced from plants such as euphorbia and seaweed. Researchers at the Hebrew University in Jerusalem have discovered a way of processing a salt-water seaweed into a high-grade oil (*The Economist*, 27 March 1976). Cultivated in ponds, the seaweed needs only sunlight and carbon dioxide to grow.

On the one hand, it is unlikely that biomass production could fill the gap left by the depletion of oil and gas resources, since plants and trees grown for biomass would in many cases infringe on land used for food production, and therefore the opportunity cost of the land would be high. On the other hand, plants such as euphorbia are known to thrive on arid lands with little alternative use; similarly cultivation of seaweed would not have high opportunity costs. It is also possible that agricultural research could produce new plant varieties with higher energy output-input ratios.

Solar Energy

Solar energy is of course the ultimate source of energy for the whole of planet earth. Without the sun there can be no energy. American scientists estimate that the solar energy falling on the United States each year is 700 times the nation's total consumption (*The Economist*, 26 March 1974). However, when we speak of solar energy, we usually mean the marshalling of the sun's rays for heat transfer or electricity generation.

Heat transfers for space- or hot-water heating has come to be regarded as the most promising short-term application of solar power, both in a "passive system" and "active system." A passive system involves the construction of houses with large window panes situated in a way that maximizes the heat collection from the sun's rays. An "active" system involves the use of solar collectors normally installed on rooftops. These collectors contain circulating water which is heated, stored and pumped into the house. At present in Canada, commercially supplied solar systems involve a high capital outlay of $7,000 to $10,000 or more.[12] The saving in energy costs have to be substantial to make this outlay worthwhile, particularly in Canada where solar heat is not great during the winter months. Solar heating may be the answer in many of the warm countries of the world; in Israel, for example, most of the houses have a collector on the roof for heating water. However, this form of heating is unlikely to have more than a modest impact in colder regions.

The real solar breakthrough may come in "photovoltaics"—the direct transfer of sunlight into electricity. Photovoltaic cells consist of a semi-conducting material and a metal which can transform light into a current. Five companies have decided to massproduce photovoltaic cells, thereby hoping to achieve economies of scale (*The Economist*, 9 Feb. 1980). The present production cost of solar energy is ten to twenty times the cost of conventional energy. It is expected that mass production could bring the cost of solar energy down to two or three times the present cost.

Wind Energy

Wind energy has been used for milling and irrigation since ancient times (and still is in many parts of the world). Wind power can take two forms: direct mechanical conversion, through, for example, wind mills, or conversion first into electricity. Present technology can produce energy at a cost sufficiently low to make wind energy viable for low-grade electricity or heating, particularly in agriculture (*The Economist*, 27 March 1976). It is unlikely, however, that wind could power large-scale electrical generation. The problem with wind energy, as with solar energy, is one of storage. The wind does not blow all the time and occasionally blows too hard for a mill to operate. Energy can be stored in batteries, but this increases the cost of the system.

The United States, Sweden and Denmark are in the forefront in developing wind energy. Most of the experiments involve windmills using giant blades with diameters of several hundred feet. A small company in the United States has experimented with windmill farms and claims that the capital cost does not exceed $1 per peak watt of electricity capacity (*The Globe and Mail*, 11 May 1981).

There are also some attempts to return to the use of sails in bulk shipping, with the help of computers and backup engines. In 1979 the Soviet Union built a 60,000-ton ore carrier with computer-controlled Dacron sails (*Seatrade*, July 1979). The economics of such an adaptation are apparently dubious. A computer-outfitted sailing bulk carrier would probably be able to compete with a small steamship, but not with a big one. Yet, if the price of crude oil increased to $80 per barrel, sailing ships would become economical.

Water

Like wind and biomass, water has been used as a source of energy since ancient times, and since this century to generate hydroelectric power. Current research is concentrating on developing tidal and wave power. In fact, on the Rance estuary in France, a tidal power station has been in use since 1970, and has proven to be a greater success than expected (*The Economist*, 27 March 1979). It is reputed to generate electricity more efficiently than other hydro sites, working at full capacity since 1973. A second French tidal plant, as well as one in Britain on the Severn, are being planned.

Of more immediate interest for Canadians is the proposed project on the Bay of Fundy in Nova Scotia. Because of its 50-foot tidal range, the Bay of Fundy is one of the best sites in the world for a tidal power plant. The current state of planning calls for a 4,000 megawatt station at Cobequid Bay to be built in the 1990s at an estimated cost of $10 billion (*The Financial Post*, 21 Feb. 1981). One site alone could produce 2,000 megawatts, more than enough to meet Maritime needs well into the twenty-first century. However, there is one problem: the silt. A leading sedimentologist argues that silt could turn the area into an expensive wasteland, producing nothing but marsh grass. Silt accumulation at existing causeways appears to be reaching 14 cm (about 6 inches) a month.

Wave power is different. Experiments are being conducted to utilize the energy stored in waves through the use of floating power stations. Wave movements would power floating turbines, from which electricity would be transmitted via cable to land. British scientists estimate that a third of British power needs could be met by a floating power station 1,000 miles long (*The Economist*, 27 March 1976). No cost estimates were given.

Geothermal Energy

Another potential source of energy is obtained from heat generated inside the earth. Iceland has used heat generated from hot springs as a source of home heating for a long time, and the United States, Japan and New Zealand also derive some energy from hot springs.

Most countries do not have hot springs, but most do have hot rock formations far beneath the surface of the earth. In theory, cold water could be transported to this layer of rock via a borehole. The water would then evaporate and be released as steam through an adjacent borehole. The two holes would be connected by fracturing the rocks between them. However, the technology for this type of fracturing has not been developed (*The Economist*, 27 March 1976).

Fusion Energy

The development of fusion energy has been heralded as the ultimate solution to the world's energy problems. Fusion is the method by which energy is produced by the sun, and involves fusing, or joining, the nuclei of two atoms.[13] A new material of less-total-mass is formed and the remainder is converted into energy in the form of extraordinarily intense heat. (This is the process utilized in making the hydrogen bomb.) If the heat explosion could be harnessed, a massive amount of energy would be produced, and the only raw material needed would be heavy water (which can be found in the oceans) and lithium. There would be little radioactive waste.

However, the technological challenge is daunting. A temperature of 100 million degrees Celsius must be achieved and sustained in a special vacuum environment. Scientists at Princeton have achieved 60 million degrees Celsius and have demonstrated that the necessary temperature may be technically feasible within the next ten to twenty years. We do not know, however, if it will be economically feasible.

Summary and Conclusions

It is unlikely that the world will run out of energy in the foreseeable future. The 1979 oil price increases caused a surge in research for alternative energy resources and led to substantial cuts in oil consumption. In particular, coal liquefaction, coal gasification, oil sands development, and biomass production seemed feasible alternatives. Solar and wind energy also seemed possible in many areas. Table 7 gives some comparable cost estimates for these sources of energy—given 1979 prices. A forecast by the World Energy Conference predicts that a five-fold increase in the supply of energy can be achieved over the next fifty years, making use of energy resources whose existence is reasonably well known. Table 8 projects a possible breakdown of energy use by the year 2020.

TABLE 7
Production Cost of Alternative Energy
(1979 dollars per barrel equivalent of crude oil)

Energy Source	Cost
Conventional crude oil (1980 dollars)	26–35
Synthetic natural gas from coal (U.S.)	23–35
Oil from coal (U.S.)	30–37
Oil from coal (Europe)	30–44
Oil from tar sands	15–25
Oil from shale oil	15–35
Biomass energy	30–60
Solar hot water (35° latitude)	50–130

Source: *The Petroleum Economist* Feb. 1980.

TABLE 8
Percentage Breakdown of World Energy Use, 1972–2020

Sources of Energy	1972	1985	2000	2020
Hydrocarbons				
Oil	42.8	44.2	28.3	10.6
Gas	17.1	15.8	20.7	12.5
Unconventional	0	0	.6	4.0
Total hydrocarbons	59.9	60.0	49.6	27.1
Coal	24.5	23.6	24.6	25.9
Nuclear	.7	4.7	12.8	31.4
Renewable energy:				
Hydraulic	5.2	4.9	4.9	5.6
Other	9.7	6.8	8.1	10.0
Total	14.9	11.7	13.0	15.6

Source: *The Petroleum Economist* Feb. 1979.

The recent oil glut and falling crude prices, however, may temporarily stall the changeover from oil to other energy resources. This would be regrettable. The lower oil prices could once again increase the world's dependence on OPEC oil and therefore set the stage for a repetition of the events of 1973 and 1978–79. Industrialized countries would do well to prevent lower crude prices from reaching consumers by increasing excise taxes on oil.

NOTES

1. The following account is based on Hill and Vielvoge (1974), pp. 51–100.
2. See Adelman 1974.
3. The spot market covers two trading activities: barge trading and oil cargo trading. The latter is not restricted to Rotterdam. The oil cargo trading acts as a buffer for the oil companies when they fail to match supply and demand. Normally, the spot market handles 3 to 4% of the world's traded petroleum, but in the panic of 1979, the share of the spot market increased to 20 percent as the major oil companies scrambled to divert their sales to the spot market where prices were sometimes double the posted prices (*Seatrade*, July 1979).
4. OPEC in this period resembled more an oligolopoly under price leadership (the price leader being Saudi Arabia) than a properly functioning cartel (Erickson and Winokur 1977).
5. For a devastating account of the activities of the major oil companies, see Sampson 1976.
6. Gray (1970:299–305) describes some of the early attempts.
7. *The Economist*, 6 Dec. 1975. Yet in 1975 it was estimated that the cost of a nuclear power station was 50 to 70 percent higher than a fossil fuel station.
8. Conventional cost-benefit analysis is of course unfair to future generations as it discounts future costs and benefits. For example, assume that the cost of a nuclear accident to a future generation is $1 billion. Assume that the probability of this occurring is 0.1, and assume that the discount rate is 10 percent. The expected value (costs) to the future generation of this occurrence is 0.1 times $1 billion which is equal to $100 million. If this accident were to happen in fifty years time, the discounted cost entered in the cost/benefit analysis would only be $100 million times .009 (.009 is the discount factor assuming 50 years and a discount rate of 10 percent) which is only $900,000 (Pearce 1979).
9. Figure quoted in Crutchfield 1978, p. 393. The Candu reactor is

reported to have the best record of the present generation of reactors.
10. The severe implications of these problems on world agriculture and the food problem are described in Eckholm 1976.
11. The cost would have been even higher, had there not been substantial subsidies to distilling.
12. Gander and Belaire 1978:143. *Quest* magazine (May 1981) has an interesting account of the expense and maintenance problems of solar heating in Canada.
13. Fission is the process wherein a heavy atom is split into lighter atoms, with the remaining mass converted into energy.

BIBLIOGRAPHY

Adelman, F.A. *The World Petroleum Market*. Baltimore: Johns Hopkins University Press, 1972.
―――――. "Politics, Economics and World Oil." *American Economic Review*, Papers and Proceedings (LXIV), 1974, pp. 58−68.
Berndt, E.R., "Canadian Energy Demand and Economic Growth." In Berndt *et al.* (eds.), pp. 44−86, *Oil in the Seventies*. Vancouver: The Fraser Institute, 1977.
Crutchfield, James. "Nuclear Power in Long-Run Energy Supply." In B.R. Dowling and J. Durkan (eds.), *Irish Economic Policy*. Dublin: The Economic and Social Research Institute, 1978.
Eckholm, Erik. *Losing Ground*. New York: W.W. Norbon, 1976.
Erickson, Edward W. and Herbert S. Winokur. "Nations, Companies and Markets: International Oil and Multinational Corporations." In Berndt *et al.* (eds.), pp. 170−212, *Oil in the Seventies*. Vancouver: The Fraser Institute, 1977.
Gander, James E. and Fred W. Belaire. *Energy Futures for Canadians* (A Summary): *Long-Term Energy Assessment Program (LEAP)*. A study prepared for Dept. of Energy, Mines and Resources. Hull: Minister of Supply and Services, 1978.
Gray, Earle. *The Great Canadian Oil Patch*. Toronto: Maclean Hunter, 1970.
Hill, Peter and Roger Vielvoge. *Energy in Crisis*. London: Robert Yeatman, 1974.
McKie, James. "The Political Economy of World Petroleum." *American Economic Review*, Papers and Proceedings (LXIV), 1974, pp. 51−7.
Pearce, D.W., "Social Cost-Benefit Analysis and Nuclear Futures." *Energy Economics*, April 1979, pp. 66−71.
Sampson, Anthony. *The Seven Sisters: The Great Oil Companies and the World They Shaped*. New York: The Viking Press, 1975.

CHAPTER 4

The Canadian Energy Scene

Canadians are great energy guzzlers by international standards, being outdone by no country on a per capita basis, not even the United States.[1] We are well ahead of the Scandinavian countries, whose climate, living standards and population densities are similar to those of Canada. Compared with other countries we are also well endowed with energy and have a considerable surplus on hand. However, like most other countries Canada will, within a relatively near future, experience a shortage of oil, and with the current situation in the world market, the possibility of compensating for this shortage by increasing imports cannot be counted on. Therefore substitutes for conventional oil have to be developed rapidly, which will require some fundamental adjustments in people's energy use.

In this chapter Canadian energy demand and supply are surveyed, and the criteria for a rational energy policy explained. Canada's energy policy is then assessed in the light of these criteria.

Energy Demand in Canada

Canada's energy demand grew at an average yearly rate of 5.3 percent between 1960 and 1977; more recently the growth rate has been between 3 and 4 percent. Even if the demand were scaled down to 3 percent, energy use would double its present level by 2000. Most energy is used for industrial needs (40%), for heating purposes (30%) and for transportation (25%). Industrial and transport use account for 70 percent of all the oil consumed.[2] Table 9 gives the percentage breakdown in energy use since 1950. As shown, it was in the period 1950–60 that the changeover from coal to oil occurred, mainly because of the decline in the real price of oil. Since the increase in the price of oil in 1973, however, there has been a gradual substitution from oil to coal, nuclear power and natural gas, a substitution which is still going on. The prob-

TABLE 9
Sources of Canada's Primary Energy Consumption, 1950–77
(percentage distribution)

Sources	1950	1960	1970	1975	1977
Petroleum	29.8	48.6	48.1	46.8	44.7
Natural gas	2.5	9.0	16.5	18.8	18.8
Coal and coke	47.6	14.7	10.7	8.0	8.9
Hydro electricity	20.1	27.7	24.6	24.9	24.6
Nuclear electricity	—	—	0.1	1.5	3.0

Source: Gander and Belair, *Energy Futures for Canadians*, p. 303.

lem is if the market can do the substitution quickly enough, particularly in view of the fact that oil prices in Canada are kept below world market levels. Changing from oil for heating and industrial purposes is relatively simple, but it is more difficult in the field of transportation.

Energy demand can be scaled down. If Canada were to decrease its growth rate to 2 percent in energy use, instead of 3 percent, we would save in terms of energy the equivalent of ten large oil sands plants or 40 Pickering-sized nuclear reactors by 1990 (Gander and Belaire 1978:70). Energy demand can be decreased by imposing higher taxes on energy, by raising prices, subsidizing conservation, spreading propaganda, by making people poorer (an option not usually tried overtly), and by making institutional changes (e.g., in town planning or building designs). The most effective is probably increasing the price of energy. Demand elasticities appear to be in the region of −.5 in the short run and may be as high as −1.3 in the long run (Thirsk and Wright 1977). The relative merits of these measures will be discussed below.

Canada's Energy Supply

Canada is currently a net importer of oil and is likely to remain so in the foreseeable future. It is expected that production of conventional oil, even with enhanced recovery methods, will decline by the year 2000. If there are no major discoveries and if there is continued growth in energy demand, there will be a need for increasing oil imports. According to the National Energy Board, imported oil will soon be needed to supply Ontario's needs and by 1995, 50 to 85 percent of Canada's total requirements if present trends continue.[3] Canadian oil production is at present 1.8 million barrels per day, supplemented by approximately 600,000 barrels per day of imports.[4] Even the huge recent find by Chevron off the coast of Newfoundland would not appreciably decrease our dependence on imports. This find may contain 1 billion barrels and produce 330,000 barrels per day within the next five years (*The Financial Post*, 9 Feb. 1980). This find is the most significant since Leduc, and a few more finds of this size would undoubtedly alter our energy situation considerably.

On an international scale, Canada's reserves of conventional oil and gas are modest—unlike Saudi-Arabia's. The hydrocarbon deposits are concentrated in the Western Canada Sedimentary Basin, stretching from the Beaufort Sea, the Mackenzie Delta and along The Rockies through Alberta and southern Saskatchewan; in the Sverdrup basin in the High Arctic; in the Hudson Bay region; and the Scotia shelf-Grand Banks area off the east coast of Nova Scotia and Newfoundland. Until the Newfoundland discovery, no major oil find had been made outside the Albertan section of the Western Sedimentary basin.

Estimates for potential reserves (undiscovered but probable reserves) of oil and gas were continually revised downward through the seventies. However, the oil industry still believes there are significant resources of oil and gas in Alberta. These may occur in the deeper part of the basin, in low-productivity gas sands and in heavy oils in the shallow part of the basin. An example is in the Elmworth area of northwestern Alberta, where unconventional techniques involving fracturing of surrounding rocks are used to release the oil from the rock. This is very costly, with exploration and development costs running up to $800,000 per well (*The Globe and Mail*, 14 May 1979). It is also likely that the Arctic will yield more oil, but again at great cost because of adverse drilling conditions and the distance involved in getting the oil to the market.

Canadians used to think that development of the Arctic would provide a solution to all their problems. However, except for a small well at Norman Wells on the Mackenzie River which has been producing since the 1920s, exploration in the Arctic did not begin until 1960. At that time, the federal government issued a set of regulations mainly aimed at getting exploration moving; for example, no rental had to be paid on federal land, and the only obligation on the part of the companies was that they had to do a stated amount of exploration to retain their permits. The first (dry) well was drilled at Winter Harbour on Melville Island in 1962 by Dome Petroleum.[5] Two more dry wells materialized in 1963 and 1964, at which point many companies wanted to give up on the Arctic because of the hostile conditions and lack of success. It was only because of the persistent effort of Calgary geologist J.C. Sproule, to get a joint venture started, that exploration continued. He argued that the companies should pool their land and money, and thereby coordinate exploration of the region. None of the major oil companies showed interest in joining, however, and the lack of funds did not brighten the prospect of Sproule's plan. Finally, Sproule persuaded the federal government to contribute 45 percent of the money, and Panarctic was formed.

Panarctic was later successful in finding a substantial amount of gas on the arctic islands. Indeed, Panarctic, together with its partners in the Arctic Islands Exploration Group—Petro-Canada, Esso Resources Canada and Gulf Canada Resources—have recently made a major gas discovery from an ice platform west of Lougheed Island, which could bring the Arctic within the reach of commercial exploitation. Before this find, 15 trillion cu. ft. were shown to exist, and another 5 to 10 trillion were thought to be necessary to justify the massive cost of getting the gas to the market (*The Petroleum Economist*, Feb. 1980). In 1968, Atlantic Richfield found a vast oilfield off the North Slope of Alaska, not far from where Canadian exploration teams were operating in the Mackenzie Delta. In the following twelve months the amount of federal land under exploration almost doubled.

Imperial Oil was the first to announce the discovery of oil at Atkinson Point in 1970 (Maxwell 1973:31). By 1973, the company had announced three major gas finds and two oil discoveries. Gulf, Shell and Mobile also made significant gas discoveries in 1972 and 1973. Attention was then shifted to the Beaufort Sea just off the Delta. Drilling conditions in the Beaufort Sea are extremely hazardous because of shallow waters and the resulting potential for very high waves. Nevertheless, Dome Petroleum discovered oil in the Beaufort Sea from a well 50 miles offshore in 180 feet of water. (*The Petroleum Economist*, Nov. 1979). It is not yet known how much oil this well contains.

In general, the oil discovery rate in the Arctic has been disappointing. It is instructive to note that in 1970 Federal Energy Minister Greene told the country: "Don't worry about U.S. gas and oil exports from the Province of Alberta, for we have approximately nine hundred and twenty three years supply of oil and three hundred and ninety years supply of natural gas left to play around with."[6] Three years later the National Energy Board wrote that Canada had only a decade's supply left of conventional oil, and that the frontier potential appeared disappointing in size and in cost.

Canada has of course vast reserves of oil locked up in the tar sands of northern Alberta. However, as mentioned above, the possibility of tar sands supplying a large proportion of our oil consumption is limited. It is estimated that even if a new oil sands plant were brought into production every eighteen months (compared with the present rate of one plant every five or six years), Canadian oil would supply less than one third of Canada's total energy requirement in the 1990s compared with the current 40 percent (Gander and Belaire 1978:114). Additions of plants on such a scale do not seem feasible at present.

Canadian Gas Reserves and the Pipeline Question

The Canadian gas situation is more hopeful, with a considerable surplus on hand. In 1979 2,676 billion cu. ft. were produced, 38 percent of which was exported (*Department of Finance, 1980*:39). Present reserves are likely to last another 15 to 20 years with the potential of new discoveries in the Arctic and on the East Coast. The recent find at Sable Island off Nova Scotia by a consortium (Mobile, Texaco, Petro-Canada and Kaiser Petroleum) is encouraging.[7] Gas might replace oil as a major heating source; however, at present, the marketing of gas is hampered because heating oil is produced relatively cheaply as a by-product of oil refining. It is also claimed that marketing of gas is hampered by the monopoly position of Trans Canada Pipelines which is the sole seller and distributor of gas.

In addition, there is also the problem of getting the gas to the market. Additional pipelines would have to be built. To reach eastern regions, a gas pipeline would have to be extended from Montreal to the Maritimes. This pipeline would ideally have a reversible flow capacity: the gas would first flow from Alberta to the Maritimes, then from the Mackenzie Delta and the Beaufort Sea via a new pipeline, and finally it would be pumped the other way from the Labrador-East Coast region to central Canada.

Pipelines have been a controversial issue in Canadian politics ever since the great pipeline debate in Parliament during the Diefenbaker era. The Canadian pipeline scene is intimately connected with the situation in the United States. After the Prudhoe Bay find in Alaska, an oil pipeline was built across Alaska to the icefree port of Valdez, where the oil was loaded onto tankers. The Prudhoe Bay reserves, like most oil reserves, contain a substantial amount of natural gas. Normally gas associated with oil is "flared off," but in this case, the state of Alaska prohibited such wastage of energy and planned to transport the gas to markets in the United States. It appeared that the vicinity of the Prudhoe Bay gas and the Mackenzie Delta gas would make a joint pipeline possible. In 1974, the Canadian Arctic Gas Pipeline Company (a consortium of 27 companies, including the major oil companies) submitted an application to the National Energy Board to construct a 2,600-mile 48-inch diameter pipeline from Prudhoe Bay through the Mackenzie Delta to southern Canada. The line would run parallel to existing lines in Alberta and then split into two branches, one moving towards California, and the other to eastern Canadian and U.S. markets. The estimated cost was 5 billion dollars. It was expected that construction would start in the winter of 1976/77, and the pipeline would start carrying gas in 1978.

The Mackenzie pipeline proposal generated a vast amount of discussion centering around the likely impact of a pipeline on the delicate Arctic environment and on the native population. There was also the question of whether the pipeline should be built then or in the future, since there was no need for arctic gas at the time.[8] The federal government launched a large-scale enquiry in 1974, headed by Mr. Justice Thomas Berger, into the social, environmental and economic impact of the pipeline. This became an out-of-the-ordinary undertaking in the history of Canadian commissions of enquiry. Mr. Justice Berger travelled around the arctic communities which would be affected, inviting anyone who had an opinion to speak up—and they did.[9] Berger presented his report in April 1977 (Berger, 1977). By then he had become a populist hero, and Canadian public opinion had swung firmly against a pipeline along the Mackenzie. Berger recommended that no pipeline be built across northern Yukon between the North Slope and the Mackenzie Delta because of its environmental implications. He gave a qualified approval to a pipeline along the Mackenzie River, but only after a ten-year moratorium on construction, which would provide the necessary time to settle land claims and do more research into critical environmental questions.

Meanwhile, another proposal was gaining ground: the so-called Alcan proposal (now known as the Alaska Highway Proposal). In 1976, a joint proposal by Alberta Gas Trunkline, Westcoast Transmission and Foothills Pipelines was filed with the National Energy Board (*The Petroleum Economist*, Aug. 1977). It called for a 48-inch line with an initial capacity of 2.4 billion cu. ft. per day to be built parallel to the existing Alyeska oil pipeline as far as Fairbanks. From Fairbanks the line would follow the Alaska Highway through the Yukon (with a detour through Dawson City) into British Columbia and Alberta. A smaller pipeline would be constructed along the Dempster Highway between Dawson City and Inuvik, joining the main line at Dawson. Some of the gas transported would be routed to eastern markets.

After the Berger report was published, the federal government hurriedly appointed another commission (the Lysyk Enquiry) to investigate the environmental implications of the new route. The environmental damage was thought to be less severe as the pipeline would follow an already existing transportation corridor. In July 1977, the National Energy Board rejected the Mackenzie Valley line proposal in favour of the Alaska Highway proposal (before the results of the Lysyk enquiry had been published). Federal control over the project was to be assured by a corporate restructuring to give Foothills a major share in the regional companies building the line. The Alaska Highway sponsors would also be required to conduct feasibility studies for the Dempster Highway extension, and make a formal application by 1 July 1979. They would also be expected to provide spare capacity for 1.2 billion cu. ft. in the mainline by 1 January 1984, and to apply $200 million to cover the socioeconomic effects on the regions involved. The estimated cost was

$10 billion with an additional cost for the spurline along the Dempster Highway of $2 billion (*The Petroleum Economist*, Aug. 1977).

The Alaska Highway project ran into difficulties regarding financing, particularly since the United States was slow to decide a number of crucial pricing questions, including who would pay for the plant facilities to process gas. The Canadian government made it clear that it would not provide financial guarantees. By 1981, the estimated total cost of the project had reached $35 billion (*The Globe and Mail*, 21 Sept. 1981). At one stage it was hoped that the National Energy Board would grant large export permits for existing Albertan surplus gas, the sale of which could finance the preliminary building of the southern section of the pipeline. The National Energy Board granted increased export sales in 1980, but not in volumes considered necessary. However, the construction of the southern portion of the line will be started in 1982.

The Polar Gas Project was set up in 1972 (managed by Trans Canada Gas Pipelines) with the purpose of investigating the feasibility of getting gas from the Arctic islands to the market. The project concluded that if modest amounts of gas were found, the gas could probably be brought down by ice-strengthened LNG tankers—an expensive option but without the high capital costs of a pipeline.[10] However, in 1977, Polar Gas filed an application with the National Energy Board to build a pipeline starting 800 miles above the Arctic Circle, reaching west towards the Mackenzie River and then turning south to Longlac Ontario (*The Financial Post*, 17 March 1979). The estimated cost was then $7 billion (*The Petroleum Economist*, Feb. 1980). This pipeline has not yet been approved. In 1982, the National Energy Board started hearings on the Arctic Pilot Project, a joint venture between Dome Petroleum, Petro-Canada and the Nova Corporation, to transport gas form the High Arctic in LNG tankers.

In 1979, two competing applications were filed with the National Energy Board for a pipeline to the Maritimes: one by Alberta Gas Trunk Line Company's subsidiary, Trans Quebec, and Maritimes Pipelines Incorporated to build a 2.15 billion-dollar 1,900-mile gas pipeline from west of Montreal to Halifax; the other by Trans Canada Pipelines to extend the existing pipeline to Quebec City with a proposal to develop Maritime markets for propane first, before going ahead with a full pipeline (*The Financial Post*, 28 April 1979). The National Energy Board approved the construction of the Trans Quebec and Maritimes pipeline, the first stage of which will be completed in 1982. But there is controversy over the pricing of gas in the Maritimes. The federal government insists that the gas should be sold at the same price as that in Ontario and Quebec. This would mean that the Alberta gas producers would have to absorb the additional transport costs to the Maritimes, for which they want compensation (*Globe and Mail*, 26 March 1981).

In May 1981 the National Energy Board gave its approval for a new oil pipeline going from Norman Wells on the Mackenzie River to Alberta. Imperial Oil wants to expand production from its existing wells in this area. Approval for this pipeline was given without any settlement of existing land claims, contrary to the recommendations in the Berger report. Maps 1 and 2 show the extension of this and other pipelines.

Coal

Canada has substantial reserves of coal. Current reserves of recoverable coal are estimated at 717 million tons of coking coal and 5.2 billion tons of thermal coal (1973 prices). Current production is 25.5 million tons of coal (*Canada Yearbook*, 1979:568). Most of the reserves are found in Alberta and British Columbia, with smaller deposits in Saskatchewan and Nova Scotia.

Because of the long distances to the principal markets in eastern Canada, much coal is still imported. There would have to be substantial improvements in transportation networks to make western coal competitive in eastern markets. Environmental considerations associated with strip mining and with burning may also restrict the expansion of coal production unless underground gasification and liquefaction at the site can be carried out.

Peat

Peat is a well-established energy resource in the Soviet Union, as well as in Ireland where it supplies 25 percent of electricity and some home heating. It is estimated that Canada has 89 billion tons of peat, the energy equivalent of 500 trillion cubic feet of natural gas (*The Financial Post*, February 1980). However, harvesting peat is expensive. The peat has to be dried and cut before it can be used, and transportation costs may be too high. Quebec and the Maritime provinces are doing research into how to utilize peat most effectively.

Hydroelectric Power

Hydro power has long been the principal source of electricity generation in Canada. In 1976, over 58 percent of electrical energy came from hydro. Further hydroelectric developments are possible in the James Bay area, at Gull Island in Labrador, at the Nelson and Churchill rivers in Manitoba, and at a number of rivers in British Columbia (Gander and Belair, 1978:133).

Nuclear Energy

Canada has large deposits of uranium, 60 percent of which are in Ontario. Electrical generation from nuclear power dates to 1962, when the first small station was put into use at Rolphton, Ontario (*Canada*

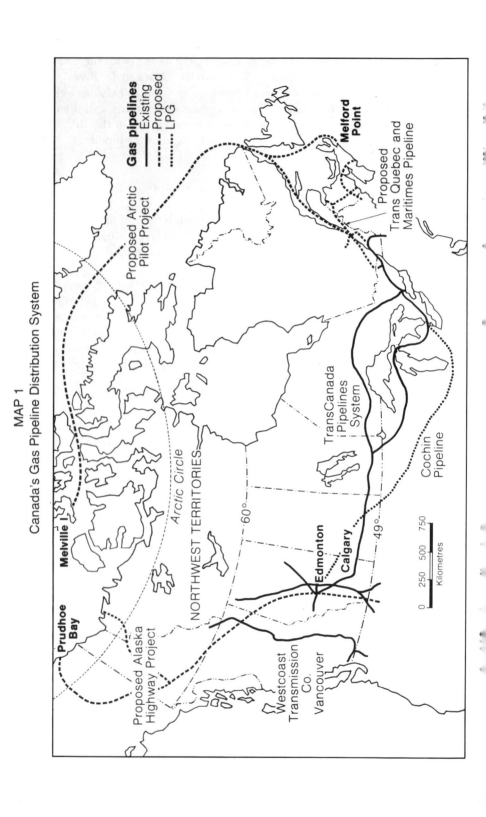

MAP 1
Canada's Gas Pipeline Distribution System

Gas pipelines
Existing
Proposed
LPG

Proposed Arctic
Pilot Project

Melford
Point

Proposed
Trans Quebec and
Maritimes Pipeline

TransCanada
Pipelines
System

Cochin
Pipeline

Arctic Circle

NORTHWEST TERRITORIES

60°

49°

Edmonton

Calgary

0   250   500   750
Kilometres

Melville I.

Prudhoe
Bay

Proposed Alaska
Highway Project

Westcoast
Transmission
Co.
Vancouver

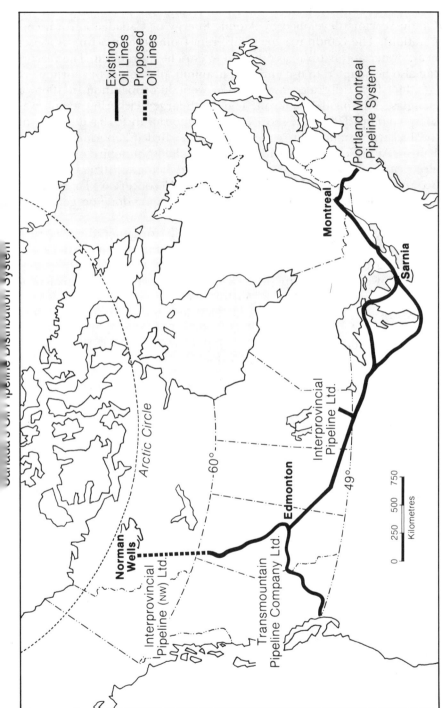

Existing
Oil Lines

Proposed
Oil Lines

Portland Montreal
Pipeline System

Montreal

Sarnia

Interprovincial
Pipeline Ltd.

Arctic Circle

60°

Edmonton

49°

0   250   500   750

Kilometres

Norman
Wells

Interprovincial
Pipeline (NW) Ltd.

Transmountain
Pipeline Company Ltd.

Source: *Report of the Special Committee on Alternative Energy and Oil Substitutions to the Parliament of Canada.* House of Commons, Ottawa, 1981, pp. 42-43.

Yearbook, 1979:575). Canada's nuclear technology is embodied in the Candu reactor (developed by Atomic Energy of Canada, a crown corporation). The Candu reactor is different from other reactors as it uses heavy water and natural, as opposed to enriched, uranium. The reactor can also be adapted to use enriched uranium, plutonium or thorium.

The first full-scale power station went into operation in 1966 at Douglas Point on Lake Huron. The much larger Pickering station was completed in 1973 on the shores of Lake Ontario. In 1979 a duplicate of the Pickering station was completed on the Bruce Peninsula on Lake Huron. At present nuclear energy supplies almost one-third of Ontario's electricity. Two additional Candu stations are being constructed in Quebec and New Brunswick. At present there is no concerted plan for dealing with nuclear wastes, but some research is being done on geological disposal.

At present, Canada has a surplus capacity for generating electrical energy, which has made exporting possible. Ontario Hydro had a spare generating capacity of 17 percent in 1979 (*The Financial Post*, 4 Aug. 1979). However, to take up the slack left over from the decline in oil production, it is estimated that a fourfold increase in generating capacity will be needed between now and 2000 and an additional threefold increase by 2025 (Gander and Belaire 1978:128). The Ontario government has made it clear that it intends to proceed with its proposed expansion of nuclear generating facilities.

Canada's Energy Policy

Both the federal and provincial governments are involved in energy matters, the provincial governments as landlords of the natural resources in their respective provinces and the federal government as landlord of those found in the Yukon and the Northwest Territories. The federal government also has responsibility for interprovincial and external trade, as well as the fiscal control, of the energy industries. The National Energy Board regulates the export of gas, hydroelectricity and oil. It also approves the construction of pipelines and their tolls.

All these areas of involvement with energy of course means that Canada has always had energy policies. However, like most other industrialized countries, we have until recently lacked a coherent policy, that is, a policy designed to achieve specific long-term objectives. Given the present energy scene, the objectives of a rational energy policy should be:

(a) to ease the adaptation from conventional oil to alternative energy resources;

(b) to encourage conservation. Conservation makes adaptation less severe and should be pursued out of concern for posterity (see Chapter 3 for a discussion);

(c) to encourage the exploration and development of new and efficient energy resources suited to Canadian needs and resource availability;

(d) to encourage efficient use of energy resources over time and to enable Canadians to earn an adequate return on their resources.

The first two objectives can be achieved through a variety of policies, some more efficient than others. They include pricing policies, rationing, regulations, "save energy" campaigns, and subsidies to conservation. Policies aimed at encouraging exploration and the development of new energy sources include pricing policies and also taxation and investment policies. To achieve the last objective, adequate taxation and export policies are needed. Each of these policies will be discussed in turn.

Policies Aimed at Adjusting the Changing Energy Scene

Theoretically, the most efficient means of encouraging conservation and substitution is to decontrol the price of oil and let it rise towards world levels. A price rise would decrease consumption because the demand for oil is not perfectly inelastic. People will attempt to conserve oil by insulating their homes, by buying smaller cars and by changing to substitutes (gas, coal, wood, or electricity). Concerning the supply of oil a price increase would in turn increase the profit potential of oil companies, which would then be expected to increase the supply of oil from existing reserves (by pumping faster, by investing in better recovery techniques and by decapping wells), and to reinvest profits into exploration.

In practice, however, there are some problems in implementing such a policy. First, higher oil prices would impose hardships on some people. Waverman (1975) has shown that lower-income groups spend a larger proportion of their income on energy than higher-income groups. It follows that some low-income people would not be able to afford adequate heating at higher prices. Second, an increase in the price of oil would affect the consumer price index by increasing the price of transportation and heating, and also the prices of manufactured products. This could set off further increases in the consumer price index through the concomitant effects on wages. Third, some manufacturing industries would be adversely affected (in Canada, the auto industry in particular), causing unemployment. Yet, several studies have shown that capital and energy are complements, whereas energy and labour are substitutes (Denny *et al.* 1978). This means that an increase in the price of energy would decrease the demand for capital and increase the demand for labour, all of which would have little effect on manufacturing costs in the long run. Fourth, if oil company profits were increased, it is possible, given the preponderance of foreign ownership in Canada, that the profits would be siphoned off into foreign exploration, into more takeovers of Canadian firms and into dividends to foreign shareholders.[11]

The first two drawbacks have led to suggestions that other methods should be used to curtail the demand for oil, such as rationing, imposing regulations and offering conservation subsidies. Rationing is probably more effective than raising oil prices in the short run if the demand has to be cut back rapidly. If there were an immediate shortage, rationing would also be fairer than making people line up for their supply of oil. However, queueing would be necessary if the increase in price did not immediately clear the excess demand. Whether rationing is fairer than the price mechanism in the long run involves quite a difficult argument. The price mechanism is a sophisticated system for matching a scarce commodity to those who need it most, simply by giving consumers an opportunity to express their preference in the market place: those who want the commodity most will be the ones who are prepared to pay the most for it. Rationing, in contrast, cannot effectively take account of individual differences. A rationing scheme would overdeliver goods to some people who do not really want them and not give enough to people in great need or want—unless the scheme allowed trading of coupons and rations.

The counterargument is that rationing is fairer in ensuring that real needs are met. The price mechanism may drive up prices to such a level that only those who could afford to pay would end up with most of the commodity. Therefore a fair way of making certain that everyone will have an equal chance to satisfy his needs would be to give the same share to each consumer.

Which argument is correct? On the one hand, it can be proven that the price system is more effective in getting the commodities to those who need them most when need is widely dispersed, or when income distribution is relatively even (Weitzman 1977). On the other hand, rationing is more effective in looking after people's needs if these are more uniform, or if there is greater income inequality. Even if the last conditions are met, the case for long-term rationing is not necessarily made, as rationing imposes a cost on society in the form of administration.

A decrease in energy use can also be achieved by "save-energy" campaigns conducted through the media. However, these campaigns are quite costly in relation to the modest and frequently short-term effects which are achieved.

Directives, regulations and conservation subsidies can also be effective in achieving lower energy use if they are properly enforced. Regulations may include insulation standards, temperature control in public buildings, standards for energy efficiency in appliances, maximum speed limits, and so on. Again, though, recent research into the effectiveness of regulations has demonstrated that many regulations have very high cost in relation to the modest benefits achieved.[12] Subsidies to conservation (for example, insulation grants) are also likely to be inefficient as the people who received them would probably be willing to conserve energy anyway.

The fourth and final point is controversial. Available data show that oil companies do indeed reinvest most of their funds, but not necessarily into exploration (but into takeovers and diversification), and not necessarily in Canada. Data provided by the federal government (Canada 1980:17) show that in addition to paying interest and dividends to shareholders outside Canada, the oil and gas industries invested a net amount of $2.1 billion abroad in the period 1975−79. If interest and dividends are added to this figure, the total outflow of payments abroad reaches $3.7 billion.

Clearly, investment in exploration in Canada would only be undertaken by the oil companies if the expected rate of return from this activity were higher than the rate of return in other areas. According to one study by Quirin and Kalymon (1977), a significant risk premium has to be earned before exploration can take place; normal profit is insufficient. They showed that profits in 1975 were insufficient to generate this risk premium. The rate of return was 14 percent (nominal value) as opposed to a required rate of return of 19 percent on debt capital. According to figures for 1979, only one firm (Western Superior Oil) achieved a rate of return of 19 percent (*Financial Post*, 8 Dec. 1979). Therefore an argument could be made that if prices were allowed to rise to world levels, the oil companies should be allowed to pocket the windfall. However, rates of return are determined not only by prices, but also by the probability of finding oil and the cost of exploration and exploitation. It is then conceivable that even if energy prices were high, profits would not be reinvested in Canada, in which case Canadians would get small benefit from their resources.

It follows from the preceding discussion that a good energy policy should include an increase in the price of oil towards world level. Low-income people should get some additional compensation either through a reduction in taxes or an increase in transfers. If sudden shortages appear, short-term rationing may be necessary, but the rationing coupons should be freely transferable so that a person not using them can sell them to people who do. Some of the necessary price increase should be achieved by the imposition of an excise tax on crude oil consumption.

Canadian Pricing Policies

The discussion above was based on suggested policies and their possible effects. Now we turn to actual, existing policies. Canadian oil policy and oil pricing policy can be divided into three periods. The first covers the time from the discovery of oil at Leduc in 1947—which made Alberta into an oil province—to the implementation of the National Oil Policy in 1961.

After completion of the interprovincial pipeline from Edmonton to Sarnia in 1950, Canadian crude oil prices (at the wellhead) were determined at the Canadian dollar equivalent of U.S. prices at Sarnia and adjusted for the pipeline transport cost from Edmonton to Sarnia (Anderson 1976). In 1959, U.S. oil prices were reduced in line with declining international prices. To protect U.S. producers from cheaper imports, an oil import quota was established by the U.S. government. Canada obtained an exemption after its oil exports had been affected by this quota. The Royal Commission on Energy in 1959 addressed the problem of declining markets and prices, and recommended a division of the Canadian market for crude oil at the Ottawa Valley. This recommendation became implemented in the National Oil Policy in 1961, when the markets west of the Ottawa Valley were to be supplied by Canadian crude, and the markets to the east by imported crude. This policy gave full protection to Canadian producers against imported oil.

The second period, between 1961 and 1973, saw Canadian oil enjoying stable and high prices, but the difference in price between Canadian and imported oil resulted in Ontario's paying Alberta a subsidy. For the cost of Canadian crude at Sarnia averaged $3.12 to $3.14 a barrel, whereas the cost of imported crude declined to $2.45. If imported crude had been delivered to the Sarnia refineries, the transport cost would probably have added an additional $.25 to the price. This means that the National Oil Policy cost the Ontario consumer $3.12 − ($2.45 + $0.25) = $0.42 per barrel as a premium (Anderson 1976 and 1977:110-11).

After 1971, the OPEC countries began to increase the price of oil. The United States started to encounter domestic oil shortages, which helped to increase the price of Canadian oil, as the demand for imports from Canada increased.

The third period starts in 1973, when the federal government moved to control the volume of oil exports and imposed a freeze on Canadian wellhead prices at the same time. An export tax was levied on oil exported to the United States to equalize the price of Canadian oil with American oil at Chicago. The revenue from the export tax was earmarked to subsidize consumers of imported oil in Quebec and the Maritimes. The export tax started at $0.40 per barrel in September 1973, rose to $1.90 per barrel by December, to $2.20 in January of 1974, and to $6.40 per barrel in February 1974 (Anderson 1976:10). Not surprisingly, this confiscation by the federal government of resource rents which belonged to the owner-province, Alberta, led to a confrontation with Alberta as to the constitutional legality of such a move. In 1975, Alberta gained some ground when wellhead prices were raised to $8.00 per barrel (see Table 10), and the export tax was reduced by a corresponding amount. A further adjustment was made in July 1976 when the export tax was set at $3.65 per barrel and Alberta wellhead prices at $9.175 per barrel. The landed price of OPEC oil was $13.29 per barrel (Watkins 1977:99). On 1 July 1979 the domestic price was $13.75 compared with the world price of $17 U.S. The Conservative government, in its first budget, planned to increase domestic prices by $4.00 in 1980, but the budget was defeated along with the government.

The situation with natural gas was similar, moving from a surplus to buoyant demand and resulting in a two-price system. After the Leduc discovery, Alberta saw its reserves of natural gas build up partly from independent gas wells, and partly from gas associated with oil wells. In 1947 gas reserves were about 5.1 trillion cu. ft., with an annual rate of production of 33 billion cu. ft. (Watkins 1977:100). After the completion of three major gas trunkline systems (the Trans Canada Pipeline system, serving eastern Canada but not the Maritimes; the Alberta and Southern system, serving northern California; and the West Coast system serving the U.S. Pacific Northwest), Albertan gas was exported under long-term permits granted by the National Energy Board. Prices were fixed in the permits, but with some allowance for minor escalations and adjustments. In 1970, 17 percent of gas was consumed within the province, 39 percent in other parts of Canada and 44 percent was exported (Watkins 1977).

Gas prices were stable. The average Alberta field price was 10.2 c/mcf (cents per thousand cubic feet) in 1957, 12.7 cents in 1962 and 15.7 cents in 1967 (Watkins 1977:101). These prices were low compared with oil prices (in terms of energy content). The equivalent price of oil would have been 45 c/mcf. The low prices can be explained by the yet undeveloped markets and by the price control imposed by the federal Power Commission in the United States.

By the late '60s, the price ceiling in the United States had led to shortages, and some natural gas distributors started a campaign to buy more Albertan gas. The National Energy Board refused to issue more long-term export contracts, arguing that Alberta no longer had an exportable surplus.[13] This curtailment of exports left only one potential buyer of future Albertan Gas: Trans Canada Pipelines, the sole buyer for the big Ontario distributors.

Given this monopoly situation, the Alberta government started a campaign to increase natural gas prices by renegotiating the price in existing contracts, and by putting pressure on Trans Canada Pipelines to accept a higher price. In 1975, the Alberta government proved successful. The natural gas reference price (the Toronto city-gate price) was set at $1.25 mcf (including transport costs), and prices at the Canadian border were set at $1.60 mcf (Watkins 1977:103). The price differential amounts to an export tax. In 1979, Toronto city-gate prices were $2.15, and in February 1980, export prices were set at $4.47 (Table 10). The proceeds from the export price do not accrue to the federal government, but are shared among producers. The higher wellhead prices have led to a considerable increase in exploratory effort. The average yearly net finding rate has jumped from 2.9 tcf (trillion cu. ft.) to 4.2 tcf (*The Financial Post*, 4 Aug. 1979).

In 1980, the industry again found itself in a surplus position. In the early part of the year the National Energy Board approved exports of 3.75 tcf of gas to the United States, an amount considered to be insufficient by industry officials (*The Financial Post*, 28 Feb. 1980). The National Energy Board has been reluctant to approve a larger amount, for even though as much as 10 tcf was considered to be surplus, only a third of this amount could be delivered to markets. Therefore, a "Catch-22" situation has developed: on the one hand, the industry will not get permission to export more unless the extra gas can be delivered to the market; on the other, the industry is reluctant to invest in pipelines (or drilling) to prove that gas can be delivered from existing wells unless it is assured of markets.

In October 1980, the federal government announced a new energy policy with far-reaching implications for the producing provinces: the National Energy Program. The policy touched almost every aspect of the energy scene, and attempted to accomplish three things: to promote security of supply and self-sufficiency in energy; to make it possible for

TABLE 10

Prices of Canadian Crude Oil and Natural Gas, 1973–80 (year-end)

Year	Crude oil well-head prices ($/barrel)	Natural gas Toronto city-gate price ($/1000 cu. ft.)	Natural gas export price ($/1000 cu. ft.)
1973	3.80	—	—
1974	6.50	0.82	—
1975	8.00	1.25	1.60
1976	9.05	1.405	1.80
1977	10.75	1.68	2.16 (U.S.)
1978	12.75	2.00	2.16 (U.S.)
1979	13.75	2.15	3.45 (U.S.)
1980	16.75	2.60	4.47 (U.S.)

Source: Helliwell, "Energy," p. 26 and Canada, *The National Energy Program 1980*.

Canadians to participate and share in the benefits of energy-related industries, particularly the petroleum industry; to establish a pricing and revenue-sharing scheme that would be fair to all Canadians. To achieve these goals the program contained a new pricing scheme for oil and gas, as well as for oil sands; a new tax on revenue derived from oil and gas production; various incentives for exploration and development; subsidies for conservation and development of renewable energy; and a Canadianization program with the ultimate aim of reducing foreign ownership of oil and gas production to 50 percent by 1990.

The new oil pricing scheme stipulated a gradual increase in the wellhead price of oil as well as an excise tax called the Petroleum Compensation Charge. This tax was intended to raise revenue for the federal government to cover the subsidies on imported oil, and replaced the so-called Syncrude Levy which had been imposed by the federal government to finance subsidies to refineries buying the more expensive synthetic oil from tar sands. Table 11 gives the proposed price increases. The wellhead price of oil was to increase by one dollar every six months until the end of 1983, by $2.25 every six months until 1985 and after 1986 by $3.50 every six months. The Petroleum Compensation Charge would increase by $2.50 a barrel until it reached $10.05. According to this blended price system, the federal government claimed that the price to Canadian consumers would never exceed 85 percent of the OPEC price or the average price of oil in the United States, whichever was lower.

The program also included a gradual increase in the price of natural gas and a new excise tax on gas. The price increases to consumers were not as high as those for oil, reflecting a deliberate policy on the part of the federal governnment to encourage consumers to shift from oil to natural gas.

The National Energy Program, however, was met with hostility from the producing provinces, particularly from Alberta. The main sources of discontent were the wellhead prices, the division of revenue between the provinces and the federal government, and the right of the federal government to impose a tax on natural gas (see Chapter 10). The Alberta government in protest initiated a program of cutbacks in oil production designed to last until the National Energy Policy was changed. Prolonged negotiations resulted in a new energy pricing deal, which was announced in September 1981. According to the new agreement, the controversial excise tax on natural gas was removed, oil and gas prices increase at a faster rate than previously planned (see Table 11), with oil prices increasing until they reach 75 percent of the world price. World price is to be paid on newly discovered oil and on synthetic oil until 1982. There is also a new incremental profit tax of 50 percent to be paid after royalty payments have been deducted.

It is obvious from the National Energy Program and the new pric-

TABLE 11
Price Increases for Oil:
The National Energy Program and the Energy Accord, 1980–86
(year-end)
($/barrel)

Year	Crude oil wellhead prices		Petroleum compensation charge	Total (blended) price	
	NEP	Energy Acc.		NEP	Energy Acc.
1980	16.75		2.55	19.30	
1981	18.75	21.25	5.05	23.80	26.30
1982	20.75	25.75	7.55	28.30	33.30
1983	22.75	33.75	10.05	32.80	43.80
1984	27.25	41.75	10.05	37.30	51.05
1985	31.75	49.75	10.05	41.80	59.80
1986	38.75	57.75	10.05	48.80	67.80

Source: Canada, *The National Energy Program 1980*, and Energy, Mines and Resources Canada, "Communique," 1 Sept. 1981.

ing agreement that the federal government has no intention of increasing the price of oil to world levels. Low-priced oil has become a permanent feature of the energy scene, because of public resistance to higher energy prices. The prices are substantially out of joint with the rest of the world. This discrepancy has several ramifications: (1) The discrepancy results in a net loss to the Canadian economy (see Appendix); (2) Canadian prices may divert exploration to other countries where the return is better; (3) The low-price policy also gives false signals to the economy by implying that Canada has a substantial comparative advantage in energy-intensive production; (4) Apart from encouraging American motorists to fill up in Canada, it encourages multinational corporations to shift their energy-intensive production to Canada and encourage energy-intensive exports.

Compared with many other countries, we may indeed have a comparative advantage in energy-intensive production, but the signals given by present price differentials must be excessive.

Investment, Research and Exploration Policies
There are two arguments for governments to be involved in direct investment or in exploration. The first is based on national security. Energy is too important in the national economy to be left entirely in the hands of the private sector. The private sector, for business reasons, may

not furnish the government with sufficient information on reserves, thus preventing the government from making informed judgments on future planning. The second argument is that a government is in a better position to provide risky undertakings than private business, for the risk can be spread among a larger number of people—the whole taxpaying population (Arrow and Lind 1970).[14] If a $10 million government venture in the Arctic fails to find anything, the cost could be recovered by a levy on 10 million taxpayers of one dollar, whereas if a small company failed in the same venture, the loss to the company might be disastrous.

In practice, indirect subsidies to private industry had been given through the tax structure by the government's allowing an immediate write-off of 125 percent of exploration and development expenditures (25 percent in the form of earned depletion). The National Energy Program, however, changed these incentives. The depletion allowance has been phased out and in its place there are new incentives for exploration and development which are particularly generous if a company is more than 60 percent Canadian-owned (the company receives from the government 35 percent of eligible exploration costs).

The federal government has also been directly involved in exploration through its part ownership of Panarctic. Since 1976, Canada has also had a national oil company: Petro-Canada (or Petrocan).

Petro-Canada has been marred by controversy, but it has also had some successes. The role envisaged for Petro-Canada was largely determined by a realization that most of the energy needs in the near future would come from petroleum and natural gas, with an insignificant amount from other non-renewable and renewable resources. Ottawa was probably concerned that 90 percent of the oil industry is controlled from abroad, and in many cases the government had to rely on the major oil companies for information on resource potential, particularly in the Arctic. Some regulatory control was exercised by the National Energy Board, the Department of Energy, Mines and Resources and by the provinces in their territories, but no adequate instrument was on hand for ensuring orderly development of frontier areas and of unconventional oil and gas—resources considered to be necessary for the government to achieve its objectives of self-sufficiency. Therefore the first priority of Petro-Canada was to ensure that the frontier areas off the East Coast and in the Arctic were sufficiently explored to delineate reserves.

Petro-Canada inherited Ottawa's 45-percent holdings in Panarctic and 15-percent holdings in Syncrude. In August 1976, it acquired the assets of Atlantic Richfield of Canada for $342.4 million, which made Petrocan the sixteenth-largest producer of gas and the seventeenth-largest of oil in Canada (*The Petroleum Economist*, April 1978). The name of Atlantic Richfield was changed to Petro-Canada Exploration. Petro-Canada has been involved in joint exploration ventures in offshore areas of Nova Scotia and Newfoundland, where the results were a major gas find at Sable Island and a major oil find off the east coast of Newfoundland. Petro-Canada has also been involved in successful exploration on the Arctic Islands. The company is not directly involved in the pipeline game, but supports feasibility studies on alternative transportation routes. It is also involved in researching development of tar sands and heavy oil, as well as having a share in Syncrude and the proposed Alsands plant. New federal regulations allow Petro-Canada a 25 percent initial preference option on new federal land being opened for exploration and a 25 percent share of any new oil and gas finds in the Arctic or offshore.

In late 1978, Petro-Canada first staked an unsuccessful bid for Husky Oil and then a successful $1.4 billion bid for Pacific Petroleum, which put Petro-Canada in the country's big-oil league (fourth in oil and third in gas production) (*The Financial Post*, 18 Nov. 1978). The takeover was probably designed to give the company more muscle in negotiations with the major oil companies, as well as a larger cash flow. The government allotted the company $200 million each year, which was insufficient for the projects envisaged. The acquisition of Petrofina gave Petro-Canada a network of gas stations across western Canada and therefore a presence in distribution.

During the 1979 election campaign, the Conservatives vowed to dismantle Petro-Canada, partly because of the hostile reaction of business to its expansion. This was probably unwise politically, for even though Canadians are no lovers of big government, they love multinational oil companies even less. The renewed energy crisis of 1979 also made it clear that a national oil company was of strategic importance in negotiations with some OPEC countries. The Conservative government had to water down the proposal to make Petro-Canada private, and in the election of 1980 Prime Minister Trudeau promised to make the company even more powerful. In 1981, Petro-Canada successfully bid for Petrofina (at a cost of $1.46 billion), a Belgian-owned firm that has oil wells in western Canada, a refinery in Montreal and a network of gas stations in eastern Canada (*The Financial Post*, 14 Feb. 1981). The government, in its National Energy Program, proposed a Canadian ownership account to finance this and other takeovers. The account would get its funds from special charges on all oil and gas consumption.

The same argument for exploration holds for research into *alternative* energy resources. Again, because of the inherent risk and the possibility of long lead times for resource development, an argument could be made for government involvement. The federal government is indeed funding research in the exploration of solar energy, the harnessing of biomass and utilization of wastes, but no funding has so far gone into fusion. Research is in most cases not done directly by the government, but by grants given to industry for energy research and development. Research funds were increased from $4.4 million in the fiscal year 1976–77 and $7.4 million in 1977–78 to $13.5 million in 1978–79, half of which was earmarked for solar research (*Canada Yearbook* 1979).[15] The National Research Council is conducting a solar energy program and was directly involved in the design of the electricity-generating windmill on the Magdalen Islands.

Although federal spending on research into *renewable* resources has increased, it is, nevertheless, very small. However, in view of our relatively large reserves of conventional energy resources, it is probably wiser to spend money developing these, and letting other countries develop the technology for renewable energy resources. Canadian research should perhaps be aimed at adapting foreign technology to suit Canadian needs. After all, our climate is more severe than that in all other countries with the exception of the Soviet Union.

The federal government recently allocated $1.4 billion to grants for home insulation. The cost effectiveness of energy conservation programs can be questioned. From society's viewpoint it would probably be better to let the price of oil rise to world levels, and let people adjust their oil consumption accordingly. Generally, people are rational: if home insulation saves X dollars per year, people will insulate if the savings outweigh the costs. However, some federal money should be allocated to disseminate information on ways to conserve energy.

Export Policy

The decision as to whether to export Canada's surplus gas to the energy-hungry United States is a difficult one. In theory, the answer is simple: Canada should keep the surplus in the ground for future use if it is expected that scarcity will be such that real prices (assuming constant extraction costs) will increase at a rate greater than, or equal to, the real rate of interest (the real rate of return on the best alternative investment). Or we should get the gas to the market now and export it, if we expect prices to escalate more slowly than the rate of interest. We could then invest the revenue in ventures yielding a better rate of return. As was discussed in Chapter 3, a relatively low interest rate should be used in making these decisions in fairness to future generations, as the market probably acts imperfectly with regard to future generations.

In practice, the question is very difficult, as governments do not have perfect foresight, nor does industry. It is conceivable that during the years that surplus gas is being stored for future use (should such a decision be made) and pipeline development is postponed, a massive breakthrough in solar energy or fusion technology might occur. In such an event, energy prices would come tumbling down and Canada's high-cost arctic gas and oil sands plants would turn into white elephants.

Given that such a scenario is unlikely, but not impossible, the appropriate policy is to proceed with caution, particularly in granting long-term export permits. In the case of renewable energy resources (e.g., hydroelectricity), obviously any surplus should be exported, as it cannot be stored.

The question of what constitutes an adequate division of resource revenues between governments and the private sector will be discussed in Chapter 11.

Summary and Conclusions

Canada, compared with all other industrialized countries, has ample supplies of energy resources, but has a shortfall of conventional oil. The main thrusts of policy-making should therefore be encouragement of substitution and development of other energy resources, as well as the conservation of oil. The implementation of the National Energy Program and the recent oil-pricing agreement with Alberta are steps in the right direction, but cannot be considered efficient until Canadian oil prices approach world levels. Indeed, it can be demonstrated that the current pricing policy imposes a net loss on the economy. Policies relating to exploration, research and export may be regarded as reasonably efficient.

NOTES

1. *The OECD Observer* (March 1978) gives comparative statistics on energy consumption.
2. For these and other statistics, see Gander and Belair 1978:81–5. However, many of these estimates of energy demand have turned out to be wrong. Data for the first 10 months of 1981 show that petroleum product consumption fell by 10.3 percent. The decline for motor gasoline was 2.7 percent and for fuel oil 12.3 percent (*The Financial Post*, 12 December 1981).
3. See Gander and Belair 1978:109.
4. Table 5.1, p. 36 in Department of Finance 1980.
5. For an account of oil and gas exploration in the Arctic, see Maxwell 1973:17–28.
6. Quoted in McDougall 1975:50.
7. It may contain 1 trillion cu. ft. (*Globe and Mail*, 9 May 1979).
8. Helliwell (1977) has demonstrated convincingly that arctic gas, be it

from the Delta or the islands, is not needed until 1990 (unless new export permits are granted).

9. For a vivid and sympathetic account, read O'Malley 1976.

10. The environmental hazards of LNG tankers in ice-infested arctic waters are great. An LNG tanker contains supercool ($-164°$) inflammable gas, compressed to 1/600th of its volume. The tankers are believed to have great catastrophic potential. Leaks make steel as brittle as nutty toffee. In the event of a collision, the LNG can freeze the sea for a 20-mile radius or act like a nuclear missile if the gas were ignited (*Seatrade*, July 1979). In June 1979 an LNG tanker ran aground at a speed of 16 knots in the narrowest section of the Straits of Gibraltar. Fortunately salvage ships were able to pump the gas from the disabled tanker without incident. Industry officials did not believe that this could be done (*Seatrade*, Oct. 1979).

11. For a discussion, see Wilkinson and Scarfe 1980. They estimate that for each dollar increase in the price of oil, 21 cents leaves the country in the form of payment to foreign shareholders.

12. See, for example, Posner 1975.

13. The criterion used in determining what is an exportable surplus is simple. A surplus is the difference between proven reserves and estimated consumption in Alberta for 30 years and in the rest of Canada for 25 years.

14. For an application to Canada, see Cohen and Krashinsky 1976.

15. For an account of the solar energy program, see Berkowitz 1979.

BIBLIOGRAPHY

Anderson, F.J. "Price Formation in the Canadian Crude Oil Sector." *Canadian Public Policy* (II), 1976, pp. 1–17.

——— "Canadian Petroleum Prices and Policies." In G.C. Ruggeri (ed.), pp. 110–13, *The Canadian Economy: Problems and Policies*. Toronto: Gage, 1977.

Arrow, K.J. and R.C. Lind. "Uncertainty and Evaluation of Public Investment Decisions." *American Economic Review* (LX), 1970, pp. 364–78.

Berger, T. *Northern Frontier, Northern Homeland: The Report of the Mackenzie Valley Pipeline Enquiry*, Vol. 1, Ottawa: Supply and Services, 1978.

Berndt, Ernst R. "Canadian Energy Demand and Economic Growth." In E. Berndt *et al.* (eds.), pp. 46–84, *Oil in the Seventies*, Vancouver: The Fraser Institute, 1978.

Berkowitz, M.K. "A Review of Canadian and U.S. Solar Energy Policies." *Canadian Public Policy* (V), 1979, pp. 257–63.

Canada. *The Canada Yearbook 1978–79.* Ottawa: Supply and Services, 1979.

Canada, Dept. of Finance. *Economic Review.* Ottawa: Supply and Services, 1980.

Canada, Dept. of Energy, Mines and Resources. *The National Energy Program 1980.* Ottawa: Supply and Services, 1980.

Canada. House of Commons. *Energy Alternatives.* Report of Special Committee on Alternative Energy to Parliament. Ottawa: Supply and Services, 1981.

Cohen, J. and M. Krashinsky. "Capturing the Rents on Resource Land for the Public Landowner: The Case for a Crown Corporation." *Canadian Public Policy* (II), 1976, pp. 411–23.

Denny, M., J.D. May and C. Pinto. "The Demand for Energy in Canadian Manufacturing, Prologue to an Energy Policy." *Canadian Journal of Economics* (XI), 1978, pp. 300–14.

Gander, J.E. and F.W. Belaire. *Energy Futures for Canadians.* Ottawa: Supply and Services, 1978.

Helliwell, J. "Arctic Pipelines in the Context of Canadian Energy Requirements." *Canadian Public Policy* (III), 1977, pp. 344–54.

——————. "Energy." In R. Bellan and W.H. Pope (eds.), pp. 19–41, *The Canadian Economy: Problems and Options.* Toronto: McGraw-Hill Ryerson, 1981.

McDougall, I. "Canada's Oil and Gas: An Eleventh Hour Option that Must Not Be Ignored." *Canadian Public Policy* (I), 1975, pp. 47–58.

Maxwell, Judith. *Energy from the Arctic: Facts and Issues.* Montreal: C.D. Howe Research Institute, 1973.

O'Malley, Martin. *The Past and Future Land: An Account of the Berger Inquiry into the Mackenzie Valley Pipeline.* Toronto: McClelland & Stewart, 1976.

Posner, Richard. *An Economic Analysis of Law.* Chicago: University of Chicago Press, 1975.

Quirin, G.D. and B.A. Kalymon. "The Financial Position of the Petroleum Industry." In E. Berndt *et al.* (eds.), pp. 213–46, *Oil in the Seventies* Vancouver: The Fraser Institute, 1977.

Scarfe, B.L. "The Federal Budget and Energy Program, Oct. 28th, 1980: A Review." *Canadian Public Policy* (VII), 1981, pp. 1–15.

Thirsk, W.R. and R.A. Wright. "The Impact of the Crude Oil Subsidy on Economic Efficiency in Canada." *Canadian Public Policy* (III), 1977, pp. 355–65.

Watkins, G.C. "Canadian Oil and Gas Pricing." In E. Berndt *et al.* (eds.), pp. 86–126, *Oil in the Seventies.* Vancouver: The Fraser Institute, 1977.

Waverman, L. "The Two Price System in Energy: Subsidies Forgotten." *Canadian Public Policy* (I), 1975, pp. 76–89.

Weitzman, Martin L. "Is the Price System or Rationing More Effective in Getting a Commodity to Those Who Need It Most?." *Bell Journal of Economics* (8), 1977, pp. 517–24.

Wilkinson, B.W. and B.L. Scarfe. "The Recycling Problem." In *Energy Policy for the 1980's: An Economic Analysis.* Toronto: Ontario Economic Council, 1980:145–73.

Appendix 4.1:
Welfare Implications of Low Oil Prices

Figure 2 shows schematically the quantities of Canadian oil demanded and supplied, and the amount of foreign oil that would have to be imported if the Canadian price equalled the world price and if the Canadian price were kept below the world price. If the Canadian price is

FIGURE 2
Welfare Implications of Low Oil Prices

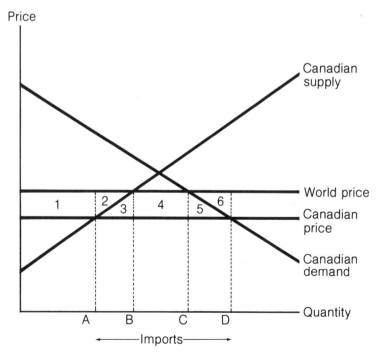

equal to the world price, Canada has to import BC units of oil. If the Canadian price is lower (for example, at the level indicated in the diagram) oil imports will increase to AD.

The diagram also illustrates the benefits and costs of artificially low Canadian oil prices using the concepts of consumer and producer surpluses. The consumer's surplus is the benefit received from being able to buy a commodity at the market price instead of the maximum the consumer would be prepared to pay for the product according to his or her demand curve. At a price of oil equal to the Canadian price, the consumer's surplus is the triangle bounded by the demand curve, the Canadian price line and the price axis. At a price of oil equal to the world price, the surplus is the triangle bounded by the Canadian demand curve, the world price line and the price axis. An artificially low Canadian price therefore increases consumer's surplus by the areas 1, 2, 3, 4 and 5.

The equivalent concept for producers is the producer's surplus— the amount the producer gains from being able to sell a product at the market price instead of at the minimum price he or she demands according to the supply curve. At a price of oil equal to the Canadian price, the producer's surplus is the triangle bounded by the Canadian price line, the supply curve and the price axis. At a price of oil equal to the world price, the producer's surplus is equal to the triangle bounded by the world price line, the supply curve and the price axis. An artificially low Canadian price of oil leads to a loss in producer's surplus of areas 1 and 2.

The preceding analysis neglects the cost to the federal government of subsidizing oil imports. According to current policy, oil is imported at the world price, but is sold to consumers at the lower Canadian price. The cost of this subsidy is equal to areas 2, 3, 4, 5 and 6 (the difference between the Canadian price and the world price times the quantity imported). The net effect on the Canadian economy of low oil prices is therefore equal to the gain in consumer's surplus (areas 1, 2, 3, 4 and 5) minus the loss of producer's surplus (areas 1 and 2) minus the cost of the oil import subsidy (areas 2, 3, 4, 5 and 6). This equals a net loss to the economy of areas 2 and 3, a loss which increases with the size of the price differential.

CHAPTER 5

Canadian Manufacturing: Problems

The Canadian economy has traditionally been a staple economy, dependent to a large degree on revenue from sales of a succession of staple products: fish, fur, wheat, timber, and minerals. Other countries have done most of the processing; indeed, despite a longstanding policy to encourage manufacturing, 60 percent of our products still leave the country in a semi-finished state.

This arrangement may be optimal, given Canada's wealth of natural resources relative to labour and capital. However, it is and always has been unpopular, particularly among Canadian nationalists whose objections against remaining "hewers of wood and drawers of water" are well known. Similar sentiments are not unusual in new countries. There is a common belief that economic development can be achieved only by means of industrialization. Embedded in this belief is a tendency to regard certain industries as strategic in the development process: for example, a steel industry in the first stage; and an auto manufacturing industry, together with some service industries such as a national airline or a national fleet, in the second stage. More recently it has been argued that more advanced countries, such as Canada, must have a high technology industry—presumably in a third stage—in order to survive in today's competitive world.

Harry Johnson argued that these and similar convictions are suspect as they are often advanced by economic nationalists, usually belonging to the upper middle classes, who would stand to gain from such economic development (Johnson 1968:1–16, 124–41). This may very well be true, but as was shown in the last chapter, there are problems of relying on resource exports to generate income in the sense that Canada appears to be losing its comparative advantage in several areas and in the sense that most resource products have a low income elasticity of demand.

Canada's industrial policy dates to Confederation. Prior to Confederation, British North America had become dependent on the economic structure and protectionism of the British Empire. In the 1840s some of this protection was dismantled (the Corn Laws, Navigation Acts and the preferential timber duties), after which the British colonies then for a period considered joining the United States. The Reciprocity Treaty of 1854 offered the colonies partial economic annexation to the United States by free trade. However, following victory by the protectionist north in the American Civil War and abandonment of reciprocity in 1866, the prospect of union with the United States disappeared. Canadians found themselves in a situation where the only direction to turn was towards themselves. The British North America Act of 1867 united politically Upper and Lower Canada with Nova Scotia and New Brunswick; Manitoba entered Confederation in 1870, British Columbia in 1871 and Prince Edward Island in 1873. The political unity was to be reinforced by measures to achieve economic unity. These measures became known as the National Policy.

The National Policy had several goals, the most important being the construction of the transcontinental railway. The railway was set as a precondition for British Columbia's entering Confederation. The railway would keep the country together by fostering east-west trade which would counter the prevailing north-south pull. The railway would make agricultural expansion in the Prairies possible and also transport agricultural produce to the central Canadian markets. Central Canada in turn could get a captive market for its manufactured products. A protective tariff would keep American manufacturers out, and the western provinces would therefore be forced to buy the more expensive Canadian goods. The protective tariff was implemented in 1878, although the Canadian Pacific Railway was not completed until 1885.

Since that time, the policy of high tariffs has remained. Canada has one of the highest levels of tariff protection in the industrial world (the non-tariff barriers, however, appear to be lower). The tariff policy has been successful insofar as there is today a sizable manufacturing sector. Whether this growth would have occurred without high tariffs is open to question. As it is, the tariff policy is blamed for all the evils which have befallen the industry, such as low productivity and the high degree of foreign ownership. In this chapter some of the issues involved will be examined, including the problem of productivity, the need for high technology and the pros and cons of foreign ownership. Government policies designed to deal with these problems will be discussed in the next chapter.

An Overview of Canadian Manufacturing

Manufacturing makes up approximately one-fifth of total output and accounts for approximately the same share of employment (see Table 2). (As in most other industrialized countries, the service sector is the main employer.) Moreover, the share of manufacturing jobs in total employment has decreased over the sixties and seventies. In terms of sales (value of shipments), the largest industry is petroleum refining, followed by motor vehicle manufacturing, pulp and paper, slaughtering and meat processing, and iron and steel (Table 12). In terms of employment, if the auto parts industry is included with vehicle manufacturing, the auto industry is the largest employer, but pulp and paper is the largest single employer (petroleum refining is one of the smallest). Most manufacturing activity is concentrated in Ontario and Quebec.

Canadian manufacturing is highly concentrated, with a four-firm concentration ratio varying from 94 percent for cane and beet sugar processors, 96 percent for breweries to 7.5 percent for women's clothing manufacturers.[1] Of the 40 top industries, fifteen had concentration ratios in excess of 50 percent. According to the *Report of the Royal Commission on Corporate Concentration* (Canada, 1978:11−42), Canadian industry is more concentrated than that in the United States, and also more con-

TABLE 12
Canada's Leading Industries, 1979*

Industry	Number of production workers	Value of shipments of goods of own manufacture (000')
Petroleum refining	7,373	12,143,763
Motor vehicle manufacturers	39,008	10,724,399
Pulp and paper mills	66,878	9,282,403
Slaughtering and meat processors	25,462	6.587,418
Iron and steel mills	46,977	5.859,261
Saw mills and planing mills	57,441	5,676,033
Motor vehicle parts and accessories manufacturers	45,340	4.472,779
Misc. machinery and equipment manufacturers	48,053	4,280,346
Dairy products industry	14,076	3,789,563
Metal stamping and pressing	21,759	2,913,926

Source: Statistics Canada *Manufacturing Industries of Canada 1979, National and Provincial Areas* (Cat. 31-203).
* Ranked according to value of shipment of own manufacture.
Note: Not included in the table are men's clothing factories ranked in 24th place, with a total number of 29,553 workers and women's clothing in 26th place with a total number of 26,968 workers.

centrated than in countries of similar population size (for example, West Germany, France, Japan, and Sweden). In a sample of nine industries, only one (pulp and paper) was more concentrated in West Germany and Sweden than in Canada. Concentration increased substantially between 1948 and 1954, but has changed very little since 1965.

It is claimed that Canada has the highest level of foreign ownership of any industrialized country. Seventy percent of the total assets in manufacturing are foreign-owned. Rates of foreign ownership in particular industries are 100 percent in tobacco products, 96 percent in auto manufacturing, 99 percent in rubber manufacturing, 92 percent in petroleum refining, and 85 percent in the chemical industry. Of the top 200 industrial corporations, 68 were completely owned by foreign corporations (Wilkinson 1980:73).

High concentration levels and a large degree of foreign ownership are problems for Canadian industry only insofar as they affect industry performance. The main problems facing Canadian manufacturing are high labour costs and low productivity. The extent to which these problems can be attributed to foreign ownership and high concentration levels will be discussed below. If productivity increases at a faster rate than costs, then high costs are not a serious problem. If an industry is faced with both high costs and low productivity, it will encounter increasing difficulty in competing both in home and world markets.

Another problem facing the manufacturing sector is that it is dominated by slow-growing industries producing semi-processed agricultural, forestry and mineral products. These are products with low income elasticities. As income levels increase in other countries, the purchase of these products by other countries will increase less than proportionately, with the result that output and employment in these industries will expand slowly, as well.

Canada's comparative disadvantage in so-called high-technology production appears to be well documented. The Science Council of Canada has recently devoted three publications to this.[2] However, what is meant by high technology is a matter for debate. Most people include only secondary manufacturing, such as production of instruments or computers, in high-technology industries, where Canada is lagging behind. Agriculture is usually not included, and yet many sectors (wine growing, development of new crops) are technology-oriented.[3] Other examples of unconventional high-technology industries are chartered banks, which have gained a substantial lead in the international market partly through computer applications; and the oil industry, which has made substantial advances in production technology.

Productivity in Canadian Manufacturing

Productivity is a measure of how efficiently inputs are converted into outputs. The more output that can be squeezed from a unit of input, the more a firm will prosper. As long as productivity increases outstrip cost increases, a firm does not have to raise prices. Productivity estimates at the national level are usually taken as a measure of how well a country is using its scarce resources. Productivity increases are a major component of economic growth, and without economic growth there cannot be any improvements in our standard of living.

There are three measures of productivity: productivity of labour, productivity of capital and total factor productivity. The ideal concept is perhaps total factor productivity, which measures how efficiently input is being utilized.[4] In practice this concept is difficult to arrive at empirically because of the problems involved in measuring capital. The most commonly used productivity measure is labour productivity: the value of output per worker or per manhour (average product of labour times price).

In interpreting measures of labour productivity, one has to be very careful about the effect of the business cycle on the measures. When the economy enters a recession, productivity tends to drop. The reason is that output falls as sales slacken, but employers usually wait until they get a feeling of how serious the situation is before they lay off workers. At the bottom of the recession, both output and employment will be low. When the upturn begins, output will grow rapidly, the slack in capacity will be exploited and for a while employers will have to make do with the existing supply of labour. Productivity will then increase. For these reasons short-run fluctuations in productivity may reflect merely the stage of the business cycle.

Several studies have been done on labour productivity, some comparing Canada's level of productivity with that of other countries, and others comparing the rates of productivity growth. The results demonstrate that the level of productivity in Canada is low compared with that in most other industrialized countries. The United States also exhibit a poor performance, but Canada's is even worse on the average. One study (West 1971), using 1963 data, shows Canadian labour productivity varying from 67 percent below U.S. productivity for sectors of the textile industry to 92 percent above for sawmills. The average was 25 percent below U.S. standards. A more recent study done for the Conference Board of Canada demonstrated, using 1974 data, that the average productivity level of the durable goods industry (which includes wood, metal and motor vehicle production) was 94 percent of the U.S. level, but for the non-durable goods sector (food processing, textiles, paper and petroleum refining) it was only 68 percent (Frank 1977). In general, Canadian productivity was not poor in the large-scale export-oriented industries such as wood products, iron and steel, and motor vehicles and parts. It was poor in food-processing and petroleum-refining.

The Conference Board study also showed that the productivity gap narrowed between 1967 and 1974, which indicates that Canadian productivity must have grown at a faster rate than U.S. productivity. This is correct for most of the postwar period and could be taken to mean that Canada has become more competitive, at least compared with the United States. Unfortunately, this does not seem to be the case as any gains in productivity growth have been nullified by increases in labour costs. Our unit labour costs rose at a faster rate than those in the United States.

The reasons for low productivity could be many. In theory, we learn that the average product of labour depends on the amount of capital per worker, the technology used, the skill levels of workers, and the quality of management. Each of these will be examined in turn.

Capital and Economies of Scale

Simple production theory postulates that the larger the amount of capital per worker, the more productive the worker becomes (up to a point). The Conference Board study showed that in 1967 machinery and equipment per employee (the capital-labour ratio) was 1.4 times that in the United States. By 1974, this figure had risen to 1.6. These figures indicate that the expected link between productivity and the amount of capital per worker appears to be missing. We have more capital per worker, but our labour productivity is lower. Capital is not efficiently utilized. The reasons for this are complex, and need to be examined in more detail.

According to Scherer (1973), there are three types of economies in production: product-specific, plant-specific and multiplant specific. Product-specific economies are achieved by lengthening the production run. Only then is full-scale specialization possible with one worker being assigned to a specific task. If full volume is not achieved, a worker may have to shift from task to task to keep himself or herself occupied. Similarly, a general-purpose machine may have to change from one task to another, with subsequent time loss for retooling. Plant-specific economies are created by fixed costs of plant management, maintenance and repair. If product-specific economies are exhausted before plant-specific economies are, it may be worthwhile to have several product lines. Multiplant economies become viable when transport costs are so high that it is cheaper to produce a product in short runs at many plants rather than in one large plant and then sell over long distances.

There may also be firm-specific economies of scale. A firm can consist of several plants producing many product lines. A firm, in contrast to a plant, is involved not only in production but also in distribution, finance and exporting. If there are large fixed costs associated with these functions, large firms may have considerable cost advantages.

Two important issues emerge: one is how significant the economies of scale are for manufacturing in general, and the other is whether Canadian manufacturing operations are sufficiently large to take advantage of these economies, where the economies exist.

Several studies have been conducted on plant-specific economies but the evidence from these is not conclusive.[5] However, there is some support to the claim that Canadian plants are too small to be efficient, but the actual cost disadvantage this incurs is not clear. Scherer (1973) showed that suboptimal plant size led to large cost increases for only three out of twelve industries. For six of the industries covered, costs were only 5 to 6 percent higher when the plant was one-third the optimal size. However, most studies do not take into account the scattered markets and large distances in Canada, factors whose effects could mean that Canadian plants are efficient at a smaller size and in larger number. One study done for Consumer and Corporate Affairs (Skoulas 1981) shows that transport costs are an important cost element for many Canadian industries. Indeed, total transport costs exceeded 10 percent of the producers' value of goods for 28 of 137 industries and 10 percent of the purchasing price for 123 of 521 commodities. This finding indicates that transport costs may impose considerable cost disadvantages on Canadian producers.

There is little evidence on the effects of firm size on per unit cost. Canadian firms on the average are smaller than U.S. firms. Large firms appear to have some cost advantages in marketing, but whether or not this advantage extends to other areas as well is open to question.

Findings on product-specific economies are more conclusive. Researchers and representatives of industries alike agree that each Canadian plant produces too many products to be efficient. Most economists argue that this is so because of the small Canadian market for the goods produced, in combination with high domestic and foreign tariff barriers. Because the Canadian market is small and because foreign tariffs prevent access to large markets, world-scale plants and corporations cannot be built. However, it is also true in many cases that where one plant would have been sufficient to serve the Canadian market, Canada has many, each operating at high costs. For example, Eastman and Stykolt (1967) found, using 1960 data, that the Canadian market was not large enough to absorb the output of even one plant manufacturing optimum-size refrigerators or electric ranges. Yet, in 1960 there were ten plants producing refrigerators and twenty-three producing ranges. The size of the domestic market and lack of access to foreign markets obviously do not constitute the whole story. It is more justifiable to blame the Canadian tariff and, possibly, transport costs that have protected inefficient producers. The tariff allows firms to price their product at a higher than normal price. The Canadian manufacturer regards a combination of the American domestic price plus tariff plus transport costs as the upper limit to the price that can be charged. Indeed, one study has shown that manufacturers mark up their prices by 0.5 percent for every percent of tariff protection (ECC 1978:67). High-cost inefficient producers can therefore afford to remain in business. Gorecki (1976) has provided some evidence to show that Canadian plants come closer to being of efficient size in low-tariff industries than in high-tariff industries.

If the tariff protects a collection of highly inefficient industries, the question is why does an aggressive firm not cut prices to increase volume and thereby achieve cost reductions and higher profit? The answer usually given is that the existing firms are assumed to be too frightened to rock the boat. A cut in prices may lead to an all-out price war, which may result in a status quo in market shares but with lower profits for all of the firms in the industry. Such a situation implies that the stronger the monopoly element in an industry (i.e., the higher the concentration ratio), the less the competition and the closer the price will be to the world price plus tariff level. Indeed, the Economic Council's fifteenth annual review (1978:67) quotes a study showing that the price markup is positively related to the concentration ratio.

Another factor of increasing concern is the existence of barriers to trade within Canada. Not only are local producers protected from foreign competition, but often from competition from other parts of Canada as well. All provinces exercise government procurement policies favouring goods produced in the home province (Safarian 1979). Often, more efficient out-of-province producers cannot compete for contracts. The interprovincial barriers to trade in agricultural products are well known, and are reinforced by the federal government through the national marketing boards.

Worker and Management Skills

The more highly trained workers are, the more productive they should be, provided they are trained in something relevant to their tasks. Training for industrial work can be acquired at schools or on the job. The Canadian labour force is highly educated, but perhaps not well trained. Compared with the United States, Canada turns out proportionately fewer skilled people from the school system. For example, the proportion of the technical and professional categories in manufacturing was 5.3 percent in Canada in 1971, compared to 9.1 percent in the United States in 1970 (Britton and Gilmore 1978:75). If present trends continue it is unlikely that the situation will improve. For years, Canada imported a large proportion of skilled trades people. With tighter immigration rules, however, this is no longer the case, and little attempt has been made to train skilled workers in Canada to fill the gap. Such a situation could lead to a severe shortage of skilled labour in the future.

This lack of skilled workers apparently holds true for management as well. The average Canadian manager is not as well trained as the average U.S. manager. In 1961, 16 percent of Canadian male managers had university degrees compared to 35 percent in the United States in 1960 (Daly and Globerman 1976:36). Canadian managers have probably become better trained since then, but this trend began later in Canada and has not kept up with the United States. Furthermore, at least in the late '60s, U.S. universities were graduating proportionately four times the number of commerce students than Canadian universities. It is possible that formal training in management skills has facilitated a more rapid adoption of advanced methods of production and organization in U.S. business compared to Canadian business (*ibid.*).[6]

Technology

New or better technology, by definition, leads to more output, the output of better-quality products or new products. When the issue of low productivity in Canadian manufacturing is under discussion, the emphasis is on output. When the debate centres around the lack of comparative advantage in high technology production, the emphasis is on the other effects.

In assessing the effects of technology on productivity in Canadian manufacturing, the first question to be answered is whether our technology is inferior to that of other countries. The difficulty here is separating technology from capital equipment, as in most cases new technology is embodied in new machinery. There is some indication that the rate of technological change is slower in Canadian manufacturing than in other countries. Hufbauer (1966) found that the production of a new synthetic was undertaken in Canada fourteen years after it had been introduced by the innovating country. Globerman studied the tool-and-die industry and found that the adoption of numerical-control machine tools was faster in the United States than in Canada (Daly and Globerman 1976). This innovation was introduced around 1960; by 1968, 20 percent of the surveyed firms used it in the United States compared with 10 percent in Canada. Globerman also showed that Canada lagged behind the United States by three years in the adoption of tufting equipment for carpet-making. Globerman blames tariff protection and inadequate management for slow technological change. Tariffs work in two ways: they reduce competitive pressure and therefore weaken incentives to improve efficiency; and insofar as the tariff has induced excessively short production runs, economies are not large enough for innovations to be adopted, given that innovations are capital-intensive.

Another aspect that needs examining in assessing the effects of technology on production in Canada is the extent of technological innovation taking place in Canada. Our record in this area is also poor. In a recent OECD (1977) study, Canada was ranked last (tenth) in technological innovation. Given the fact that Canada was ranked sixth in terms of total expenditures on research and development, this indicates that Canadians are not getting good value for their dollars; in other words, research and development are not efficient.

There has been substantial debate recently on the relationship between productivity and basic research. Some argue that the adoption and adaptation of the best available technology could be just as fruitful as the development of new technology through basic research. A key feature of American industrialization, for example, was the application of similar production techniques to an ever-widening circle of final products. A study by Terleckyj (1974) shows that productivity returns of research and development concerning purchases of capital or intermediate goods from other industries was twice the return obtained from private research and development. However, a more recent study (Mansfield 1980) demonstrates that expenditure on basic research in manufacturing results in improvements in total factor productivity. Yet this finding does not prove that more research and development of an industry results in higher productivity. Obviously there has to be a link at the plant level between basic and applied research. Nelson's survey (1981) of studies on productivity also points out that not all industries benefit from research and development, for to derive any benefits, the technology in the industry must have a strong scientific and engineering base. Research and development must also be integrated with the other functions of the firm to ensure continuous feedback between production and research. Learning-by-doing and research and development appear to be closely connected.

Other Factors Affecting Canadian Manufacturing

Traditional economics has treated productivity within very narrow bounds, with the quantity produced strictly related to the amount of labour, capital and technology employed. The production function was seen as an engineering formula, wherein the same amount of output is always generated by the same amount of input. This is, of course, not an accurate description of reality, as people are involved as well as machines. Actions must be coordinated and information must flow between all levels of a business for the operation to flow smoothly. There are times when this information flow is severed and also when the objectives of employees do not coincide with those of management. Under such circumstances, production may well be suboptimal, despite optimal plant size, skilled management and workers, and the best technology.

Organizational theory has become an important area of study, but has so far not yielded many firm conclusions. For example, according to Nelson (1981), some researchers report that greater worker participation in management decisions increases productivity. Similarly, job enrichment has been found to make some workers more content and productive, others more content but not more productive, and still others less content but not less productive. At any rate, labour-management relations seem to be important, as many studies on the low productivity in British industry point out. British industry tends to be overmanned, the reasons for which are restrictive union practices, general union pressure and lack of effective response from management. In addition, it appears to be difficult to persuade British labour to accept changes in general.

It is possible that problems in labour-management relations contribute to Canada's low productivity, also. If we take the number of mandays lost due to strikes to be a good measure of labour relations, Canada and Italy can pride themselves in having the worst labour relations among OECD countries. Bad labour relations in turn could be caused by inadequate management training.

Foreign Investment

The issue of foreign control over Canadian industry is hotly debated and involves the alleged effects of foreign investment not only on the performance of manufacturing industries, but also on the economy as a whole. In this section the effects of foreign firms on efficiency will be discussed.

Foreign investment is of two types: direct investment and portfolio investment. Portfolio investment involves cross-border purchases of securities—bonds or shares—with no change in control of the companies in which assets were bought. Direct investment involves the purchase of securities for the purpose of acquiring control. Portfolio investment is very volatile and tends to follow interest rates, shifting from country to country in search of the highest return. The most serious concern about portfolio investment is their effect on the Balance of Payments and on a country's indebtedness—issues which will be discussed later. The motives behind, and the effects of, direct investment are more complex.

Direct investment can take place horizontally or vertically, or take the form of conglomerate diversification. Horizontal investment consists of more or less duplicating one's facilities in other countries: the branch-plant phenomenon. Vertical investment usually involves investing in the extraction of raw materials and assuming control over raw material supplies located in other countries. Conglomerate diversification is far more unusual and involves branching out into completely new lines of production abroad.

Economic theory states that direct investment, like portfolio investment, is also in search of the highest possible return. Pattison (1978) has shown that direct investment is largely determined by macroeconomic conditions; that is, the state of the economy, in general, (including interest rates) and of the stock market, in particular. The question then is why direct investment takes the form of ownership. In other words, why does direct investment exist at all—what is the particular advantage of having ownership and control as opposed to having a licence to sell or having direct selling rights to a patent or trademark in foreign markets? Horizontal and vertical investment tend to occur only in industries dominated by oligopoly. Direct investment is unusual in textiles and agriculture, but common in mining, petroleum and car assembly. The branch-plant phenomenon is particularly prevalent in differentiated oligopolies; the question is why?

The most commonly suggested reason for foreign control in Canadian industry is the Canadian tariff. The tariff stops corporations from exporting directly to a country. Therefore in order to get access to Canadian markets the corporation will set up a branch plant inside the borders. However, the tariff cannot be the only explanation, since a corporation could earn access to the market by a licensing agreement or the selling of a patent right or trademark. In addition, there does not seem to be a positive association between the tariff level in an industry and the extent of foreign investment. It is well known that an increase in tariffs will stimulate domestic production, but no statistical analysis has been able to show conclusively that foreign firms will expand production more than domestically owned firms (McManus 1972). If tariffs are the cause of foreign investment, any lowering of tariffs would cause foreign firms to leave Canada, the result of which would be a loss of jobs.

A more promising avenue of research arises out of Steven Hymer's work (see Hymer and Rowthorn 1970). He emphasized the importance of the investing firm's having a unique asset, one which could be exploited only through foreign production, as opposed to exports or licensing. Hymer stressed that this asset must be fairly substantial, since a foreign producer would be at some disadvantage, compared with a domestic producer, because of the foreign producer's lack of familiarity with the market. An example of such an asset is the advantage created through product differentiation. In industries characterized by product differentiation, producers try to create real differences (for example, in varieties of beer) or imagined differences (for example, in varieties of aspirin) in their products to gain a marketing advantage. The product is usually protected from imitations by trademarks, or by the high cost of advertising.

The successful firm has a unique knowledge (core skill) in production and/or marketing. The firm can capitalize on this advantage (capture the economic rent associated with it) by exporting the product, by selling a licence to produce the product, or by the expansion of production through branch plants. Hymer argues that the presence of multinational corporations in some industries indicates that expansion through branch plants is the most profitable manner of exploiting the particular core skill the corporation enjoys.

There appears to be some evidence that there is a connection between product differentiation and foreign investment (Caves 1971). A test of this hypothesis is to argue that what is true across the border is true within countries as well. Firms that find foreign investment profitable also find it profitable to establish a large number of domestic plants. Therefore industries with high concentration levels inside a country will also be those with many foreign investments. Indeed, McManus (1972) reports a positive correlation between investment and concentration, as does Caves (1978) in a study for the Royal Commission on Corporate Concentration.

In general, foreign investment is not spread evenly across all industries. It is low and declining in industries dominated by public enterprise (public utilities and transportation), or in industries characterized by small business (wholesale, retail or construction). In such industries, the possibility of transferring core skills is limited.

Vertical foreign investment is less general and usually involves the expansion of a firm's activities into raw material production. The main motives for vertical foreign investment are probably avoidance of uncertainty and erection of barriers to the entry of new rivals. However, McManus (1972) argues that vertical foreign investment is not different from horizontal foreign investment in that the prime motive is organizational: foreign investment is the most efficient means of transferring a core skill.

Turning now to the effects of foreign investment, there are two separate issues to be considered: the performance of foreign-owned firms compared with that of Canadian firms and the effects of foreign firms on the performance of Canadian firms. It is sometimes claimed that foreign-owned firms export less than Canadian firms; that exporting is done from headquarters in the home country; that foreign-owned firms import more than other firms; and that they do all of their research and development at headquarters. It is also claimed that they build miniature replicas of their operations in the home country, which is usually the United States, but on such a small scale that they are extremely inefficient. Most of these allegations are not confirmed by empirical evidence.

Safarian (1969) did an extremely thorough study to see if any of these charges were true. He found that foreign-owned firms were more diversified than Canadian-owned firms, but otherwise there were few differences. No statistically significant difference was found in behaviour between Canadian-owned and foreign-owned firms with regard to export performance, expenditures on research and development. Foreign-owned firms tended to do more importing than Canadian-owned firms. Safarian found that differences in behaviour between firms could be explained more often by size than foreign ownership in itself.

Safarian's results have been confirmed by other studies.[7] Other researchers have found that foreign-owned firms appear to be more productive. For example, Caves *et al.* (1978) found that labour productivity was 19 percent lower in domestically owned firms than in foreign-owned firms. Raynauld (1972), in an earlier study, found that the value-added per worker in a foreign-controlled plant was 1.5 times higher than the value-added in an English-Canadian-owned plant and 1.8 times higher than in a French-Canadian-owned plant. Another study by McFetridge and Weatherly (1978) revealed that subsidiaries of foreign firms export more than domestically owned firms.

A study for the Science Council of Canada, *The Weakest Link,* (Britton and Gilmore, 1978) concluded that Canada's poor performance in the export of manufactured products can be attributed to foreign ownership. Foreign ownership has led to the "truncation" of firms—firms which do not carry out innovative functions. The results are low-level technology, failure to export and dependence on imports. However, this study is more polemic than scientific, and there is little statistical analysis to substantiate these claims. On the basis of all these studies, therefore, it can be concluded that foreign-owned firms are no worse than Canadian firms with respect to export performance, expenditures on research and development, and productivity. Indeed, they appear to be more productive than Canadian-owned firms. However, foreign-owned firms appear to import more than Canadian-owned firms and may therefore establish fewer linkages with the local economy (Britton and Gilmore 1978:94).

As for the effects of the operations of foreign-owned firms on Canadian firms, a few observations can be made. It is possible that foreign direct investment increases product differentiation and promotional behaviour and therefore strengthens barriers against entry into the market for domestic firms. Foreign firms entering raw material production may act as a barrier to entry by domestic firms as the domestic firms may not get access to the raw materials. Barriers to entry decrease competition and increase concentration to the detriment of productivity and efficiency of the Canadian economy. It is also contended that the presence of foreign firms makes Canadian firms reluctant to engage in price competition as the former operate with all of the resources of the multinational corporation behind it. The outcome of any price war would be stacked against a Canadian firm.

All of these factors decrease efficiency in Canadian industry. However, it can also be argued that the presence of foreign-owned firms can have a beneficial effect on the operations of Canadian-owned firms by decreasing market imperfections in the movement of capital and core skills, and therefore making an industry more competitive. A study by Rosenbluth (1970) could not detect any statistically significant relationship between the concentration ratios in an industry and the level of foreign ownership in the industry. In other words, we cannot tell if foreign ownership leads to more or less concentration in industry. However, Globerman's recent study (1979) demonstrated that the presence of foreign ownership in an industry tended to increase labour productivity in the industry, indicating that the presence of foreign-owned firms had a salutory effect on competition. The evidence is not particularly strong in either direction.

Summary and Conclusions

Canadian manufacturing is dominated by slow-growing industries which in some areas suffer substantial competition from the newer industrialized countries. Many industries are plagued by low productivity and high labour costs. Low productivity is usually attributed to too many and excessively short product runs at the plant level. Production remains inefficient because of the lack of competition in the Canadian market and the sheltering of Canadian producers from foreign competition by the high tariff policy.

Another factor that contributes to low productivity is insufficient research and development expenditures (basic or applied), which in turn means that industries will be slow to adopt new technologies. The reason for this situation could also be the lack of competition, in the sense that the market position of established firms may be too secure. A secure market means that it could take considerable time before management realizes that the market has changed and that economic success requires adjustments. Technological advancement goes hand in hand with a technically trained labour force and some technical sophistication on the part of management, both of which Canadian industry appears to be lacking.

Critics attribute many of the problems in manufacturing to the high level of foreign ownership in Canadian industry. Although it is possible that foreign ownership has inhibited the development of technology and large-scale efficiency of corporations in Canada, there is no conclusive evidence to prove that this is the case.

NOTES

1. Concentration ratios usually show the value-added or the sales of the largest four firms in the, industry as a proportion of total value-added or sales. The higher the concentration ratio, the less competitive the industry.
2. Britton and Gilmore (1978), Science Council of Canada (1977, 1979).
3. See the very negative review of *The Weakest Link* by Palda (1979:22–26).
4. May and Denny (1979) did a study on total factor productivity in Canada. Their results suggest that the growth in total factor productivity declined in the 1970s.
5. For a review of the evidence, see Canada 1978:43–67.
6. See Daly and Globerman 1976:36. Several studies on British productivity have pointed to the lack of technical expertise in management as a contributive factor to low productivity (Nelson 1981).
7. See Lithwick 1969 and Wilkinson 1968.

BIBLIOGRAPHY

Britton, John N.H., Gilmore James M. *The Weakest Link, A Technological Perspective on Canadian Industrial Underdevelopment.* Background Study No. 43, Science Council of Canada. Ottawa: Supply and Services, 1978.

Canada. *Report of the Royal Commission on Corporate Concentration* Ottawa: Supply and Services, 1978.

Caves, R.E. "International Corporations and the Industrial Economics of Foreign Investment." *Economica* (38), 1971, pp. 1–27.

——————. *et al. Studies in Canadian Industrial Organization.* Royal Commission on Corporate Concentration, Study No. 26, 1978.

D.J. Daly and S. Globerman. *Tariff and Science Policies: Applications of a Model of Nationalism.* Toronto: Ontario Economic Council, 1976.

Eastman, H.C. and S. Stykolt. *The Tariff and Competition in Canada.* Toronto: Macmillan, 1967.

Economic Council of Canada. *Fifteenth Annual Review: A Time for Reason.* Ottawa: Supply and Services, 1978.

Frank, James G. *Assessing Trends in Canada's Competitive Position: The Case of Canada and the U.S.* Ottawa: The Conference Board, 1977.

Globerman, S. "Foreign Direct Investment and 'Spill Over' Efficiency Benefits in Canadian Manufacturing Industries." *Canadian Journal of Economics* (XII), 1979, pp. 42–57.

Gorecki, P.K. *Economies of Scale and Efficient Plant Size in Canadian Manufacturing Industries.* Ottawa: Consumer and Corporate Affairs, 1976.

Hufbauer, G.C. *Synthetic Materials and the Theory of International Trade.* Cambridge: Harvard University Press, 1966.

Hymer, Stephen and Robert Rowthorn. "Multinational Corporations and International Oligopoly: the Non-American Challenge." In C.P. Kindleberger (ed.), *The International Corporation.* Cambridge: MIT Press, 1970.

Johnson, H.G. *Economic Nationalism in Old and New States.* London: Allen & Unwin, 1968.

Lithwick, N.H. (ed.) *Canada's Science Policy and the Economy.* Toronto: Methuen, 1969.

Mansfield, E. "Basic Research and Productivity Increase in Manufacturing." *American Economic Review* (70), 1980, pp. 863−74.

May, J.D. and M. Denny. "Post-War Productivity in Canadian Manufacturing." *Canadian Journal of Economics* (XII), 1979, pp. 29−42.

McFetridge, D.G. and L.J. Weatherley. *Notes on the Economies of Large Firm Size.* Royal Commission on Corporate Concentration, Study No. 20, 1978.

McManus, John. "The Theory of the International Firm." In G. Paquet (ed.), *The Multinational Firm and the Nation State.* Don Mills: Collier Macmillan, 1972.

Nelson, R.R., "Research on Productivity Growth and Differences." *Journal of Economic Literature* (XIX), 1981, pp. 1029-65.

OECD. *Science Resources Newsletter*, Spring, 1977.

Palda, Kristian S. *The Science Council's Weakest Link.* Vancouver: The Fraser Institute, 1979.

Pattison, J.C. *Financial Markets and Foreign Ownership.* Occasional Paper No. 8. Toronto: Ontario Economic Council, 1978.

Paquet, Gilles (ed.) *The Multinational Firm and the Nation State.* Don Mills: Collier Macmillan, 1972.

Raynauld, André. "The Ownership and Performance of Firms." In G. Paquet (ed.), *The Multinational Firm and the Nation State.* Don Mills: Collier Macmillan, 1972.

Rosenbluth, G. "The Relation Between Foreign Control and Concentration in Canadian Industry." *Canadian Journal of Economics* (3), 1970, pp. 14−38.

Safarian, A.E. *The Performance of Foreign-Owned Firms in Canada.* Montreal: The Private Planning Association, 1969.

_____. "Ten Markets or One? Regional Barriers to Economic Activity in Canada." Lecture delivered in the Ryerson Lecture Series in Economics, 18 Oct. 1979.

Scherer, F.M. *et al*. *The Economics of Multi-Plant Operation*. Cambridge: MIT Press, 1975.

_____. "The Determinants of Industrial Plant Sizes in Six Nations." *Review of Economics and Statistics* (54), 1973, pp. 135–45.

Science Council of Canada. *"Forging the Links: A Technology Policy for Canada."* 1979.

Science Council Committee on Industrial Policies. "Uncertain Prospects: Canadian Manufacturing Industries, 1971–77." 1977.

Skoulas, N. 1981. *Transport Costs and Their Implications for Price Competiveness in Canadian Goods Producing Industries*. Research Monograph No. 9. Consumer and Corporate Affairs. Ottawa: Supply and Services.

Terleckyj, Nestor. *Effects of R and D on the Productivity Growth of Industries*. Washington: U.S. Government Printing Office, 1974.

West, E.C. *Canada–U.S. Price and Productivity Differences in Manufacturing Industries, 1963*. ECC Staff Study 32. Ottawa: Information Canada, 1971.

Wilkinson, B.W. *Canada's International Trade*. Montreal: Canadian Trade Committee, 1968.

_____. *Canada in the Changing World Economy*. Montreal: C.D. Howe Research Institute and the National Planning Association, 1980.

CHAPTER 6

Government Policies
and Canadian Manufacturing

Policies and solutions to the problems of Canadian manufacturing obviously have to be designed around what are identified to be the causes of the problems. If low productivity and lagging performance in high growth industries are caused by high Canadian tariffs, the obvious solution is a free-trade policy. If the problem is seen to be a lack of competition, with high concentration levels, a policy of active competition should be implemented. If foreign investment is seen as the problem, control of foreign investment should be strengthened, and so on. This chapter will concentrate on four types of policies: trade policies, competition policies, foreign investment policies, and research and development policies.

Canadian Trade Policy

After the implementation of the National Policy which established a protected market in Canada, there were proposals at various times to open up trade with the United States. Indeed, reciprocity, that is, reciprocal free trade, was a major issue in the elections of 1891 and 1911. With the end of World War II there was a world movement towards multilateral reductions in tariff barriers, a movement focussed on GATT (the General Agreement on Tariffs and Trade). GATT was established in 1947, and Canada, being one of the founding nations, agreed to apply the most-favoured-nation tariff rates to phase out Commonwealth preference. Canada also agreed to the principle that national commercial policy measures should be used to promote the growth of world trade, and not primarily to achieve and maintain employment in high-growth industries.

Canada in the postwar period came to be increasingly dependent on trade with the United States because of the erosion of traditional European markets due to the creation of the Common Market in Europe. In particular, the entry of Britain to the Common Market in 1973 was a serious blow to Canada's trade prospects. The interdependence of Canadian and American economies was reinforced by the Defence Production Sharing Agreement of 1959 and the Canada-United States Automotive Agreement of 1965 that established free trade in autos and parts.

During the last decade, interdependence between the two countries has become a major political concern. In 1972, Secretary of State for External Affairs Mitchell Sharp outlined three possibilities for Canadian trade policy (see ECC 1976:6-7). The first option would maintain the current relationship with the United States, with minimum policy adjustments; the second option would move towards closer integration with the United States; and the third would pursue a long-term strategy to develop and strengthen the Canadian economy and other aspects of national life, in the process reducing Canada's vulnerability. Mr. Sharp chose the third option as being the most likely to ensure Canadian sovereignty, independence and distinctness.

There is, however, a powerful lobby in Canada that is advocating free trade with the United States, led by the Economic Council of Canada, the Standing Senate Committee on Foreign Affairs and the C.D. Howe Research Institute. Free trade is seen to be a panacea for Canada's troubled manufacturing sector. Free trade would remove U.S. tariffs and thereby increase the size of the markets for Canadian products; producers should then be able to achieve longer production runs and lower the costs of production. Indeed, European experience has shown that free trade increases specialization to such a degree that trade within an industry increases; for example, both steel exports and imports increase at the same time, but involve slightly different categories of steel (Grubel and Lloyd 1976). Free trade would also remove the protective barriers from many Canadian industries and force them to rationalize and become more efficient. Free trade could also stimulate more research and development in Canadian industry as it would increase competitive pressures.

The *Royal Commission on Canada's Economic Prospects* (Canada, 1957) estimated that the benefits from free trade with the United States would increase the real income of Canadians by approximately 4 percent. The benefit would come from the reduction in consumer prices. Ten years later Wonnacott and Wonnacott (1967) estimated the benefits to be approximately 10 percent of GNP, including the production effects. A more recent study (ECC 1976) estimated the benefits to be at least 5 percent of GNP. However, Britton (1978) argues that these figures are far too high as the studies have not allowed for the locational pull of southwestern United States. Removal of Canadian tariffs would decrease the profits of firms in Canada, many of which would then migrate to southwestern United States—much to the detriment of Canadian employment.

The autopact is an example of relatively free trade. The autopact was concluded in 1965 and called for the removal of the 15 percent tariff on imported automobiles and parts from the United States for producers (not consumers), and U.S. removal of its corresponding tariff. The agreement included special protection for Canadian automobile assembly. The ratio of vehicle production to sales in Canada for each class of vehicle had to be at least 75 percent or the percentage attained in the 1964 model year, whichever was the highest (Emerson 1975:4). Further, value-added in vehicles produced in Canada had to be no less than the dollar amount achieved in 1964.

The effect of the agreement was to make the Canadian auto industry far more specialized. This led to increases in efficiency—about 90 percent in auto assembly and 20 percent in parts (ECC 1976:124-27), which in turn resulted in lower prices for Canadian consumers, at least initially. The gap between Canadian and U.S. list prices narrowed until 1969, but has widened again since then. The reason for the gap could be that the Canadian tariff on imported cars from countries other than the United States remained at 15 percent. Whereas the corresponding U.S. tariff remained at 3 percent. As mentioned above, Canadian producers tend to "price up" to the tariff.

The autopact has received much attention lately, partly because of pressure from the industry to change the safeguards, and partly because there is a huge deficit in the parts trade. The safeguards are indeed restrictive, particularly in periods of falling sales in the United States. It is claimed that because of the safeguards, Canadian vehicle producers have to continue to produce for export to the United States just to meet the safeguards, even though the market there has collapsed (*The Financial Post*, 23 Aug. 1980). This has obviously helped maintain employment in Canada but has made it difficult for producers.

The autopact contained no safeguards to parts production, and although assembly has flourished, the parts industry has increased its sales but not in pace with the demand. The deficiency between domestic production and demand must therefore be filled by imports. The need for parts imports becomes particularly great when car sales are booming in Canada but slumping in the States. In these periods, the traditional surplus in the trade in assembled vehicles decreases, whereas the deficit in parts increases. For these reasons, the parts manufacturers are pressing for safeguards to parts production.

Although the autopact can be described as a success—Wilton (1976) estimates that Canadian disposable income in 1969 would have been 4.7 percent lower without the autopact—conditions in other sectors of the manufacturing industry may not be as favourable to trade liberalization. An example of an industry which has not gained from the removal of the Canadian tariff is the farm machinery industry. Canada has maintained tariff-free imports in this industry since 1944. If the rationalization argument is correct, one would expect Canadian productivity levels to approximate U.S. productivity levels and the inefficient firms to have been weeded out. However, this is not the case. Productivity levels are still well below U.S. levels. In 1973–74 the average product of labour in the farm machinery industry ranged from 78 to 86 percent of U.S. levels (Wilkinson 1980:160).

There are additional factors which should be considered. Free trade with the United States could lead to a considerable loss of freedom for Canada in economic and perhaps political matters. For example, a free-trade agreement may preclude Canadian action in controlling exports of oil, gas and water. Full economic integration would probably lead to the adoption of a common currency with subsequent loss of control over monetary policy. It is even possible, given the similarities between the two cultures, that full political union would ensue (Wilkinson 1980:168–70).

To overcome the possible loss of economic and political independence, various proposals have been made for Canada to join, or be instrumental in forming, other free trade alliances. One possibility would be a Pacific Free Trade Area (PAFTA) involving free trade with Japan, Australia and New Zealand. Another possibility would be to seek closer association with the Common Market. These alternative arrangements, however, may not be as beneficial as trade with the United States since they would involve a far lower volume of trade.

Others argue that free trade should be our ultimate goal, but it should not be undertaken until Canadian industry has become prepared, that is, become rationalized.[1] This could be achieved by an appropriate merger policy which would encourage the establishment of world-scale corporations. Mergers would probably be necessary, since one firm would be reluctant to specialize in one product, given the increased risks this would entail. Therefore big firms should be formed, each in control of a number of plants, each plant specializing in a product. This policy would obviously lead to an even higher concentration in Canadian industry, but the proponents say that it should be made clear to the merging firms that free trade would be the ultimate aim—that they would not be protected behind a tariff wall to capture economic rents. The firms would therefore have an incentive to become efficient and to lower prices. The proponents of the policy also call for active government partnership in some industries and increased support for research and development.

In 1976, Canada signed an agreement with the European Common

Market (EEC) for increased economic cooperation. It was seen at the time as a concrete example of the third option. However, there were no preferential tariffs involved, nor were there tax concessions. Not surprisingly, an agreement for mere cooperation did not lead to any concrete results (*The Financial Post*, 28 July 1979). On the contrary, since then, Canadian trade with the EEC has either stagnated or declined because of cyclical conditions.

More recently, Canada has been one of the driving forces behind multilateral tariff negotiations conducted under the auspices of GATT. The first round of tariff negotiations was the so-called Kennedy round. Congress, in 1963, gave President Kennedy an initiative to partake in a round of negotiations on multilateral tariff reductions. Concluded in 1967, it led to quite substantial tariff concessions. The latest round of tariff negotiations was launched in Tokyo in 1973 and was to have been concluded by 1975. However, the energy crisis of 1973 halted negotiations, so that by 1975, they had barely started. These talks centred on non-tariff barriers to trade but also involved bargaining over tariffs. The talks concluded in 1979.

According to the agreement, tariff reductions will be phased in over a period of eight years, starting 1 June 1980. Tariff reductions on Canadian exports to the United States, the Common Market and Japan average about 40 percent. After the reductions, Canadian tariffs on industrial products average 9 percent compared to the previous 14 percent (*Globe and Mail*, 14 April 1979). This still leaves Canada as one of the higher-tariff countries in the West. The average tariff for most of the goods entering Canada is 5 to 7 percent, compared to the average U.S. tariff of 4 percent. Canadian tariffs and quotas on textiles, clothing, footwear, and ships are largely unaffected. It will obviously take time before the full impact of these reductions will be seen.

Competition Policy

Another avenue for promoting efficiency in Canadian industry is to promote more active competition; free trade would, of course, do this by making firms more open to competition. Therefore a competition policy can be seen as an alternative to free trade. However, a competition policy could not achieve simultaneously both the promotion of efficiency through mergers and the promotion of efficiency through competition.

In Canada, anticombines policy dates to an act in 1889 when it became a criminal offence (1) to limit unduly facilities for transporting or manufacturing, (2) to restrain or injure trade or commerce, (3) to prevent unduly or limit the production of an article in order to increase its price, and (4) to prevent unduly or lessen competition in the production or sale of any commodity.[2] This act also covered insurance, but not other services. Because the act fell under the jurisdiction of criminal law, all investigation took place in a criminal court which did not have adequate staff to assemble evidence. For this reason the Combines Investigation Act was passed in 1910 and a special investigative body was created. Later, resale price maintenance and price discrimination were added to the list of prohibited practices.

Compared with that in the United States, Canadian anticombines law has been very lenient, partly because combines investigation falls under criminal law, meaning that it has to be proven beyond reasonable doubt that an anticompetitive activity is against the public interest. The government (the prosecution) has won only four cases since 1945. No firm has been convicted for merger (monopolization) in Canada (Green 1981:185−89), and three celebrated acquittals have more or less confirmed that Canadian anticombines law is ineffective in proving that a merger is detrimental to the public interest. In the Canadian Breweries case, a merger was allowed because the defence maintained that a merger would not threaten competition in the market. In the B.C. sugar refining case, the Crown lost because, even though the merger monopolized the industry in western Canada, there was still competition from refiners in eastern Canada; nor could the prosecution demonstrate that prices and profits had increased because of the merger. The most spectacular defeat for the government occurred in 1976, when the Supreme Court of Canada upheld an acquittal on merger and monopoly charges against the K.C. Irving Co. which had bought up all five English-language daily newspapers in New Brunswick. In the court's judgment, the Crown had not been able to establish that the decrease in competition was detrimental to the public.

Another monopolization and merger case is currently under investigation by the courts. Thomson Newspapers Ltd. and Southam Inc. have been charged with illegally conspiring to unduly lessen competition and monopolize the production and sale of major English-language newspapers in four Canadian cities (*Globe and Mail*, 2 May 1981). The charges followed the closing, in 1980, of the Thomson-owned *Ottawa Journal* and the Southam-owned *Winnipeg Tribune*.

In 1966, the Economic Council of Canada was given a mandate to study and advise on competition policy, with special emphasis on combines, mergers, monopolies, and the restraint of trade. The council published an *Interim Report on Competition Policy* in July 1969, proposing (1) that services should be included among the industries in the Combines Investigation Act (for example, doctors, lawyers and sports activities); (2) that five practices should remain under criminal law: price-fixing between producers, market-allocation schemes, collusion to prevent entry, resale price maintenance, and misleading advertising; (3) that provisions relating to mergers and monopolies should be removed from the criminal code; and (4) that a new competitive practices tribunal would decide if mergers and certain other business practices were in the public interest.

In 1971, Bill C−256, the *Competition Act*, was introduced in Parliament, adopting the proposals made by the Economic Council. Public reaction was fierce, particularly with respect to the merger policy provisions. In the end, the bill was divided into an amendment to the Combines Act that included the less controversial regulations, and a proposal for the merger provisions to receive more study. The amendment was passed in 1976. In 1977, Bill C−42 was introduced, concerning the merger proposals. It contained changes in legislation with regard to mergers, monopoly, monopolization export and import agreements, and price discrimination. It also contained new elements regarding class actions, price differentiation and systematic delivered pricing. However, Bill C−42 was not passed; nor was its successor, Bill C−13. In Bill C−13 a competition board was given authority to deal with any mergers involving market shares in excess of 20 percent of the market. Any merger would be judged on the basis of twenty criteria. If the merger were considered detrimental, it could be dissolved, or approved subject to tariff reductions or other changes.

As the debate continued about merger policy, public opinion was directed towards the issue of corporate concentration. In March 1975, two corporate giants were involved in a takeover bid: the Power Corporation bid for control of Argus corporations. The bid was unsuccessful, but it led to considerable debate on the issue of corporate concentration and its effects on the Canadian economy. The government appointed Robert Bryce to chair a commission to report on (1) the nature and role of major concentrations of corporate power in Canada, and (2) the economic and social implications for the public interest of such concentrations, and whether safeguards were needed to protect the public interest. After receiving 200 written briefs and after holding public hearings in all major Canadian cities involving 127 witnesses, the commission released its report (Canada, 1978) complete with 33 separate research studies.

The concensus of opinion seems to be that the report was unexpectedly uncritical of big business.[3] The commission concluded that the level of concentration in Canadian industry was not too high, given the size of the market. The commission agreed in principle with the competition policy in Bill C−13, but had some reservations about merger policy, arguing that the effects of a merger should be judged after it has been undertaken and not before.

Public Policy Concerning Foreign Investment

Since Confederation, Canada has looked abroad for foreign investment to supply the necessary savings. About 30 percent of capital has been received from abroad; in the early years most had come from Britain, and later from the United States. Most capital was in the form of portfolio investment (60 percent). After World War II, two fundamental changes took place; a shift from portfolio to direct investment, and a vast increase in the size of the investment from $8.7 billion in 1950 to $68.9 billion in 1975 (Statistics Canada 1976:Table 1). The major sources of foreign investment were corporations as opposed to governments or individuals.

These developments did not go unnoticed by Canadians—indeed, they created widespread concern. The peak of public opinion probably came in the late '60s and early '70s with the publication of books such as Kari Levitt's *Silent Surrender* (1970) and Harry Pope's *The Elephant and the Mouse* (1972). Government responded to public opinion with studies. The Gordon Commission—the *Royal Commission on Canada's Economic Prospects*—included a discussion of the issue of foreign ownership. It was particularly concerned with the conflict of interests of foreign subsidiaries, and recommended that financial intermediates (banks, trust companies and insurance companies) should be in Canadian hands. It also recommended that foreign subsidiaries should be required to offer equity to Canadians.

The first major investigation into foreign ownership was a task force headed by Mel Watkins. This task force was an outcome of a directive from the U.S. government outlining the desirable behaviour of American-owned subsidiaries operating abroad. At the time, the United States was concerned about problems in the Balance of Payments. The directive involved guidelines to encourage repatriation of earnings. There had also been several attempts by the U.S. government to apply American laws to their subsidiaries operating in Canada, particularly the Trading with the Enemy Act that forbade U.S. citizens and corporations to trade with countries such as Cuba, North Vietnam and China. There was one incident in the late '50s in which it was claimed that Ford of Canada had to refuse an export order for vehicles to mainland China.

The Canadian government responded to U.S. government action by issuing its own Guiding Principles of Good Corporate Citizenship for foreign subsidiaries in 1966. The Watkins Report, released in 1968 (Canada, 1968), recommended the formation of an agency to survey the activities of multinational corporations in Canada. It also recommended the establishment of a federal agency to promote investments in Canadian corporations, tax incentives to foreign-owned companies to offer shares to Canadians, subsidization of research and development and management education. Following the recommendations, the Canada Development Corporation was formed in 1971 to develop strong Canadian-controlled corporations in the private sector and to increase investment opportunities for Canadians.

The government then set up an inquiry to assess the costs and benefits of foreign investment under the chairmanship of Minister of Consumer and Corporate Affairs Herb Gray. The Gray Report (Canada, 1972) came out in 1972, and its major emphasis was on technology. Access to foreign technology was seen to be the major benefit of foreign investment. However, it was pointed out that much of this benefit never accrued to Canada as most of the technology used by U.S.-owned subsidiaries had been developed in the United States. Subsidiaries, therefore, did not perform the full range of enterprise they were expected to perform—they were truncated, to the detriment of Canadian research and development capabilities. The report also recommended the establishment of a foreign investment review agency to maximize net benefits to Canada from direct foreign investment.

Both federal and provincial governments have since then passed legislation reserving certain key sectors of the economy to Canadian firms: banking, transport, finance, and communications.[4] Nonrenewable resources have also been treated as a key sector with the creation of several crown corporations, both federal and provincial (the Saskatchewan Potash Corporation, the Quebec Asbestos Corporation and Petro-Canada).

The Foreign Investment Review Act of 1973 established the Foreign Investment Review Agency (FIRA) to screen all new foreign investment, be it a takeover of a Canadian firm or a completely new enterprise. FIRA is directed to take five factors into consideration in determining whether a foreign acquisition or establishment (an investment) is of net benefit to Canadians. These are (1) the effect of the investment on the level and nature of economic activity; for example, on employment, processing of resources, on imports and exports and the purchases of Canadian parts, components and services; (2) participation by Canadians as managers, shareholders and directors in the business enterprise; (3) effects of the investment on efficiency, technology, product innovation and variety; (4) the effect of the investment on competition; and (5) the compatibility of the new investment with government industrial and economic policies.

FIRA has been attacked for being a welcome wagon for foreign investment in view of the small number of applications which have been turned down (approximately 10 percent) (*Maclean's*, 1 Nov. 1976). However, this is not a measure of FIRA's effectiveness as some firms will not bother to apply if they are reasonably certain their application will be turned down. It is claimed that no other country has as stringent regulations as Canada (Safarian 1978). FIRA bargains actively with applicants to reduce costs and increase benefits to Canadians of any proposed establishment or takeover—another reason why the rejection rate may not indicate FIRA's influence. FIRA has also been accused of being arbitrary, but it is not known if this accusation is well founded as most decisions are surrounded by secrecy. The present minister of Industry, Trade and Commerce, Herb Gray, has promised to make the operations of FIRA more open. A third charge against FIRA is that it adversely affects investments by Canadian firms: if the actions of FIRA significantly influenced the demand for Canadian shares, then share prices would be lower than normal. This in turn would decrease the asset value of Canadian firms, making it more difficult to raise capital for expansion. There is no empirical evidence to support this contention.

In the election campaign of 1980, the Liberals promised to work towards Canadianization of the oil industry and to increase the role of FIRA and the Canada Development Corporation. They proceeded on all three counts. The National Energy Policy of 1980 attempts to achieve a larger degree of Canadian ownership by granting substantial cash incentives to exploration and development if a firm is Canadian-owned, and by expansion of the role of Petro-Canada. The policy has three aims: (1) at least 50 percent Canadian ownership of oil and gas production by 1990; (2) Canadian control of a significant number of the larger oil and gas firms; and (3) an increase in the size of the share of the oil and gas sector owned by the federal government.

Initial reactions by the oil industry indicate that the incentives are sufficiently generous for the industry to want to play the government's game. Several companies have already 'Canadianized' and others such as Chevron, Mobil Oil and Suncor are seeking ways to increase equity holdings by Canadians (*The Financial Times*, 23 Feb. 1981). Some analysts predict that Canadian ownership will have reached 50 percent well before 1990.

The government has also announced its intention of expanding the role of FIRA (*Globe and Mail*, 31 March 1981). Three changes are being considered: (1) a performance review of major foreign-owned firms to see if they meet the criterion of bringing substantial benefits to Canada; (2) publication of major proposed takeovers by foreign firms before they are accepted or rejected by FIRA so that Canadian-owned firms can make counter-offers; and (3) government assistance for Canadian companies to make bids on proposed takeovers.

The government is apparently not pleased with the development of the Canada Development Corporation. The CDC has turned into a reasonably profitable venture, with assets of $3.4 billion in mining, oil and gas, fish processing, and venture capital (*Globe and Mail*, 12 May, 1981). It owns Polysar Ltd. (a manufacturer of synthetic rubber), and has significant interests in companies such as Texagulf, Petrosar of Sarnia and Connlab. AES Data Ltd., a new company, and Wordplex Corporation were developed by venture capital affiliates of the CDC (*Globe and Mail*, 14 April, 1979). The government has a 49 percent ownership in the CDC but until recently showed little interest in running the company. However, the government would at present like the CDC to play the same role in manufacturing as Petro-Canada does in the oil and gas industry (*Globe and Mail*, 12 May, 1981). Federal officials feel that the CDC has not fulfilled its mandate to encourage more entrepreneurial activity in Canada but has instead concentrated on safe, profitable investments. The government apparently approached the CDC in the fall of 1980 to acquire shares in the troubled Massey Ferguson, but the CDC refused. One may perhaps question whether partial interest in Massey-Ferguson would have encouraged more entrepreneurial activity in Canada.

Research and Development Policies

The final section of this chapter deals with government policies concerning technology. Advanced technology, or rather, the lack of it in Canadian industry has become a very live issue, particularly after the publication of a report by the Science Council. *The Weakest Link* (Britton and Gilmore 1978) argues that the reasons for our lacklustre trade performance is the behaviour of foreign-owned firms. It is suggested that foreign-owned firms are truncated, technologically dependent and lacking in innovative ability, and the smaller Canadian-owned firms are too unprogressive and imitative. Therefore Canadian industry needs to revitalize technological development. This could be achieved by various means: (1) increasing demand for Canadian technology, partly through government purchasing; (2) increasing the capacity for technological development through the creation of large-scale high technology companies in areas where we 'should' have technological sovereignty (communications and arctic resources); (3) subsidizing small-scale enterprise; and (4) regulating technology imports through an expanded role for FIRA. The whole approach calls for an active role of government in promoting and selecting industries worthy of support.

Two important issues are involved here. One is the effectiveness of subsidies to research and development and the other the effectiveness of actively encouraging large companies and world-scale corporations in key areas. Are subsidies to research and development the most efficient way of increasing productivity growth and developing new growth industries? Mansfield (1980) established a link between basic research and productivity. However, Daly and Globerman (1977) and others have shown the importance of a competitive environment; a firm that has to compete to survive is more likely to develop new technology and products. Therefore, a more efficient policy may be to remove barriers to competition.

Subsidies to research and development date as far back as 1967, when the federal government gave cash grants or equivalent tax credits to corporations that carried out research and development of benefit to Canada. This program ceased in 1978 because of budgetary restraints. However, in the same year, the federal government announced a new program of support aimed at increasing research and development expenditures as a proportion of GNP from a meagre .92 percent in 1977 to 1.5 percent by 1983, with an emphasis on applied research.[5] At present most of the research conducted in Canada is done by the government in contrast to other countries where most is done in the private sector.

The second issue is whether increases in corporate size through mergers and government involvement would increase Canada's innovative capabilities. Again the available evidence casts doubt on this policy. Anything that decreases competition appears to work to the detriment of innovations and product capabilities. Further, government involvement in industry does not guarantee success. France is sometimes given as an example of a country whose government is successfully involved in high technology. However, one must ask, success at what price? The development of the supersonic aircraft, Concorde, a collaboration between two governments, was indeed an impressive achievement—at a cost of $6 billion (Palda 1978:41-3). Canada's involvement could also be deemed successful in its development of Candu. However, according to the annual report of the Atomic Energy of Canada, in 1977 Candu's long-term debt to the government of Canada reached $1.7 billion and the prospects of developing a large market for the reactor are dim.

Another question of concern is what is a key area? Presumably it should be an area in which Canada has a potential comparative advantage which, for various reasons, has not been realized. A case could then be made for the provision of an initial subsidy to get the industry off the ground. The Science Council study has identified communications and the development of arctic resources as being potentially promising areas. However, it is extremely difficult for governments to single out industries worthy of support, to pick "winners." The record of provincial governments in this area is abysmal and aptly described by Philip Mathias in his book *Forced Growth* (1971). It is possible (but hardly likely) that the federal government will be more successful.

At present most industrialized countries are worried about import competition from some of the rapidly industrializing third-world countries and are therefore looking for new products to develop. High-technology products are seen as being the answer to all problems. Japan's industrial policy is held up as an example; however, Japanese society is not Canadian society, and what works in Japan may not necessarily work here. The Japanese have a long history of government involvement.

The experience of Sweden, whose economy is much like ours, may be more relevant. Sweden's economy is centred on the exploitation of natural resources, that is, on industries that will face increasing difficulties in competing with low-wage producers (e.g., forest products, ship-building and steel). Sweden does not have an explicit industrial policy involving subsidies to technology and spends little on research and development. Indeed, Sweden's total expenditure on research and development in manufacturing is not bigger than the research budget of General Electric (*The Economist,* 24 Nov. 1979). This has forced Swedish industrialists to borrow foreign technology and focus on specific markets, producing specialized products such as pulp digesters—which are scarcely glamorous but profitable. Sweden has a market share in this industry of 90 percent. Restricted research and development also results in concentration on one or two technologies which are then applied in all possible directions; for example, Atlas Copco developed the technology involving compressed air and currently makes one thousand products based on it. An additional factor is that concentration is on process equipment rather than on end products, that is, on less expensive ways of making old products instead of inventing new ones.

It can be concluded that subsidization to research and development does not guarantee the development of a high-growth, high-technology manufacturing industry, nor does active government involvement. The whole subject of industrial strategy is highly controversial with no clear-cut answers.

Summary and Conclusions

This chapter surveyed government policies related to Canadian manufacturing. Good policies should encourage efficiency in manufacturing; however, Canadian trade policy has led to an inefficient, highly protected, slow-growing manufacturing sector. Various proposals for change were examined, including free trade with the United States. Some studies predict substantial gains from free trade, others are more skeptical. The autopact, which has been of some benefit to Canada, was examined as an example of limited free trade.

Another avenue of promoting efficiency is through an active competition policy. Canadian competition policy has been particularly ineffective in preventing mergers. The courts have been unable to prove that any merger has been against the public interest, and all attempts at reform have failed so far.

Canadian foreign investment policy is an area which has attracted much attention and controversy with the establishment of the Foreign Investment Review Agency, and more recently with the substantial incentives offered for Canadianization of the oil and gas industry. The operations of the Foreign Investment Review Agency were examined in some detail, but there is no empirical evidence to show whether the agency has been beneficial to Canada or Canadian manufacturing.

The chapter ended with a discussion of research and development policies—another controversial topic. It was concluded that subsidies to research and development would not necessarily make the manufacturing industry strong and competitive. The survey presented in Chapter 5 showed that technology is only one of the problems affecting Canadian manufacturing, and that a comprehensive industrial policy should include manpower training policies and perhaps, above all, measures to encourage competition in the Canadian economy.

NOTES

1. The example is taken from Wilkinson 1980.
2. See Legislative History of the Combines Investigation Act in Rea and McLeod 1976.
3. For a critical assessment, see Gorecki and Stanbury 1979.
4. The new Bank Act allows foreign banks to operate in Canada on a limited basis.
5. The policy appears to be working. Research and development expenditures climbed to 1.1 percent of GNP in 1981. A survey of 94 firms, which together accounted for 70 percent of Canada's research and development expenditures, showed that these firms were planning substantial new outlays on research and development (*The Financial Post,* 28 November 1981).

BIBLIOGRAPHY

Britton, J. "Locational Perspectives on Free Trade for Canada." *Canadian Public Policy* (IV), 1978, pp. 4–20.
Britton, J. and J. Gilmore. *The Weakest Link.* Background Study No. 43, Science Council of Canada. Ottawa: Supply and Services, 1978.
Canada. *Royal Commission on Canada's Economic Prospects, Canadian Commercial Policies.* Ottawa: Queen's Printer, 1957.
_____. *Foreign Ownership and the Structure of Canadian Industry.* Ottawa: Queen's Printers, 1968.
_____. *Foreign Direct Investment in Canada.* Ottawa: Information Canada, 1972.
_____. *Report of the Royal Commission on Corporate Concentration.* Ottawa: Supply and Services, 1978.
Daly, D.J. and S. Globerman. *Tariff and Science Policies: Applications of a Model of Nationalism.* Toronto: Ontario Economic Council, 1976.

Economic Council of Canada. *Interim Report on Competition Policy.* Ottawa: Queen's Printer, 1969.

_____. *Looking Outward: A New Trade Strategy for Canada.* Ottawa: Supply and Services, 1976.

Emerson, D.L. *Production, Location and the Automotive Agreement.* A report for the Economic Council of Canada. Ottawa: Information Canada, 1975.

Gorecki, P.K. and W.T. Stanbury (eds.) *Perspectives on the Royal Commission on Corporate Concentration.* Montreal: Institute for Research on Public Policy, 1979.

Green, Christopher. *Canadian Industrial Organization and Policy.* Toronto: McGraw Hill-Ryerson, 1980.

Grubel, H.J. and P.J. Lloyd. *Intra-Industry Trade: The Theory and Measurement of International Trade in Differentiated Products.* New York: John Wiley, 1975.

Levitt, Kari. *Silent Surrender.* Toronto: Macmillan, 1970.

Mansfield, E. "Basic Research and Productivity Increase in Manufacturing." *American Economic Review* (70), 1980, pp. 863–74.

Mathias, P.M. *Forced Growth.* Toronto: James Lewis & Samuel, 1971.

Palda, Kristian. *The Science Council's Weakest Link.* Vancouver: The Fraser Institute, 1979.

Pope, W.H. *The Elephant and the Mouse: A Handbook on Regaining Control of Canada's Economy.* Toronto: McClelland and Stewart, 1971.

Rea, K.J. and J.T. McLeod (eds). *Business and Government in Canada.* Toronto: Methuen Publications, 1976.

Safarian, R.E. "Presidential Address: Policy on Multinational Enterprises in Developed Countries." *Canadian Journal of Economics* (XI), 1978, pp. 641–55.

Statistics Canada. *Canada's Balance of International Indebtedness, 1976.* Ottawa: Supply and Services, 1977.

Wilkinson, B.W. *Canada in the Changing World Economy.* Montreal: C.D. Howe Research Institute, 1980.

Wilton, David A. *An Econometric Analysis of the Canada-U.S. Automotive Agreement: The First Seven Years.* A report for the Economic Council. Ottawa: Information Canada, 1976.

Wonnacott R.J. and P. Wonnacott. *Free Trade Between the United States and Canada: The Potential Economic Effects.* Cambridge: Harvard University Press, 1967.

CHAPTER 7

Health and Education

Some of the problems in the service sector of Canadian industry are similar to the problems in manufacturing, particularly in the search for greater efficiency. Other problems are fundamentally different and stem from the fact that many services are financed and produced by government. In this chapter the problems encountered in the provision of health and education services will be analysed, and in the next those in transportation.

Health and education services are supplied mainly by provincial governments and financed by taxes. At the time of Confederation the federal government was given power over what were considered the most important activities for a government, and health and education were left to the provinces. This was probably a good division of power at the time, since the tremendous increase in the demand for health and education services that was to occur in the present century could not have been forseen. However, this division left the provinces with inadequate taxing power to finance these expensive services. Perceiving a strong national interest in these two areas, the federal government began to offer financial assistance after World War II. Today the federal government finances, either directly through specific transfers, or indirectly through general purpose (equalization) grants, a large share of total provincial expenditures on health and education programs.

Equalization payments were designed to even out the different standards of government services across the country. Relatively rich provinces, such as Ontario, have a good taxation base with which to raise money, whereas poor provinces, such as Nova Scotia and P.E.I. have not. Equalization grants are designed to equalize provincial tax revenue on a per capita basis. These will be discussed in greater detail in Chapter 10.

The special financial arrangements for health and education initially took the form of conditional grants. The grants provided approximately half the cost of a program, provided the province agreed to abide by certain standards. Examples of programs financed in this fashion are Medicare, postsecondary education, the Canada Assistance Plan and hospitalization. Such conditional grants became unpopular with both the federal and provincial governments. The provincial governments saw the grants as an intrusion into provincial areas of jurisdiction, whereas the federal government, because of its open-ended cost commitment, saw the grants as an expenditure commitment over which they had no control. The Quebec government never took part in this shared-cost program, but instead received a tax abatement of 24 percent of the federal tax. In the 1975 budget, the federal government put a limit on its contributions to the grant program. In 1977, three large conditional grants were abolished (the exception was the Canada Assistance Plan) and in their place the Quebec arrangements were extended to the other provinces in a more complex fashion, through what became known as "Established Program Financing."

The remainder of the chapter will focus attention on the reasons behind escalating health costs, how these can be controlled in theory and how governments have chosen to approach the problems. The problems in education will also be addressed, with particular emphasis on equity in education.

Health Care

Health expenditures have increased at a faster rate than other expenditures. In 1962, they amounted to 5.2 percent of GDP and in 1974 this figure had risen to 6.8 percent (Bird 1979:73). Health expenditures as a share of GDP are today as important as agriculture and mining together (Department of Finance 1980:25). *Public* health expenditures have risen at an even faster rate, from 2.5 percent to 5.1 percent of GDP, the reason being the introduction of medicare in 1967, which transferred the responsibility of health insurance from the private to the public sector.

Canada is not alone in experiencing an escalation in health costs. In 1974 health expenditures accounted for 7.4 percent of GDP in the United States, 7.3 percent in Sweden and 5.2 percent in the United Kingdom (Bird 1979:73). The proportion financed by public expenditures was 41 percent in the United States, 92 percent in Sweden, 88 percent in the United Kingdom, and 75 percent in Canada. It is interesting to note that the largest increase in health expenditures between 1962 and 1974 took place in Sweden (2.6 percent) and the United States (2.4 percent), and the lowest in the United Kingdom (1.3 percent), indicating that there is not necessarily a direct link between the explosion of health costs and public provision of health care.

The federal government's formal entry into the health field dates to 1948, when it sponsored a program of national health grants to cover hospital construction, and contributed towards health surveys and public health research (Blomqvist 1979:93). The hospital program, which had added 130,000 hospital beds, was phased out in 1970. Hospital insurance was introduced in 1957, by which all Canadians could receive hospital care. The provinces were responsible for their insurance programs, with the federal government picking up 50 percent of the cost. Each province received approximately 50 percent of the national per capita cost times its population (Broadway 1980:20). Comprehensive health insurance was introduced in 1966 with the Medical Care Act, again with the federal government contributing approximately 50 percent of the cost of eligible programs.

In order to be eligible, a provincial program had to offer the following features: (1) it had to be comprehensive, covering all types of hospital and physician's services which were considered necessary from a medical viewpoint; (2) services had to be available to all eligible residents on equal terms; programs were not allowed to discriminate in their premiums between high-risk and low-risk people; user charges (fees for services) were permitted but only if they did not impede reasonable access to medical care for low-income groups; (3) the program had to be portable; that is, if one were insured in Alberta and fell ill in Ontario, the Alberta program would pay for medical care in Ontario; (4) the final condition was that the plans had to be run on a non-profit basis and be managed on a public basis accountable to the provincial government. This program is still in effect today, and the provinces are free to finance their share of the health cost as they choose: by premiums, by general tax revenue, or by a combination of both. Saskatchewan, Manitoba and the Maritime provinces finance their programs through general tax revenue, the others through a combination of tax revenue and premiums (Broadway 1980:20).

Under the 1977 Fiscal Arrangements Act, three of the major conditional grants (for hospital insurance, medicare and postsecondary education) were consolidated into one unconditional "Established Program Financing" (EPF). No longer was the federal program open-ended, but instead each province received an amount based on the average per capita federal contribution in 1975−76 times its population. The per capita contribution was tied to increases in GNP (a three-year compound average). Some of the payments were to be made in cash, and some in the form of a transfer of tax points. Ottawa has stated that even if grants are no longer conditional, the four conditions on medicare (outlined above) are still to be in force.

Recently, however, the universal aspect of health insurance has been eroded. In Ontario and Alberta, it is claimed that 20 to 50 percent of the doctors overcharged, frequently adding 30 percent to the standard fee (Brown 1980:522). Extra-billing presumably occurs because doctors feel that they are not getting adequate compensation from the present level of fees. The provinces maintain that they cannot afford to raise the fee level. In this context it is interesting to note that with the exception of B.C. and Manitoba, expenditures on health care have dropped as a proportion of gross provincial expenditures in all provinces (Brown 1980:529). For example, in Alberta the share of health expenditures was 26.19 percent in 1973 and 19.69 percent in 1979. Corresponding figures for Ontario were 30.33 percent in 1973 and 25.71 percent in 1979.

Reasons for Escalating Health Costs

For most people the main problem in the area of health care is cost: for governments, the substantial cost increases over time and for private individuals, the threat of deterrent fees and doctors opting out of the publicly provided programs. The cost increases have indeed been substantial. As shown above, the share of health expenditures of GDP increased, at least until the late seventies, which means that health expenditures increased at a faster rate than other goods. The question is why?

Several explanations are possible. One is that the demand for health services has increased at a faster rate than other goods because we are richer (i.e., the demand is highly income-elastic), another that the population has become less healthy. A third explanation is that in contrast to the goods-producing industries, it is difficult to achieve productivity increases in a service industry. In many cases it is impossible (and also undesirable) to achieve automation. This means that increased salary costs are directly translated into increased health costs. A fourth explanation is that since doctors supply the health care, and since doctors advise patients as to how much care is necessary, doctors have been able to create their own demand. A fifth explanation often heard is that the government is at fault, in that publicly provided health care is more expensive than privately financed care. A sixth explanation is that certain changes in society have contributed to the increase in demand. For example, an increasing share of health cost today goes to old-age nursing homes and nursing care; care that was previously provided by the family. Another change is the decline in religion. Previously, when an individual was under severe emotional stress, he or she went to his parish priest or minister who provided consultation free of charge. Today the individual goes to his doctor or psychiatrist.

With the exception of the second explanation—that the population has become less healthy—each explanation has some merit and some deserve more discussion. The first argument certainly has an element of truth in it. There appears to be a relationship between per capita GNP and expenditure on health (the United States and Sweden top the list in both GNP per capita and expenditures on health), which probably means that people are more likely to seek medical help for minor ailments if they can afford it. Similarly, a rich community is more likely to spend a vast amount of money on a flashy new hospital than a poor community. Expensive medical operations such as transplants are also more likely to be undertaken by the well-to-do. The fifth explanation that puts the blame on government-financed health care may also be true. Insurance in general does not make a person cost-conscious. In order to claim car insurance, the claimant has to get three estimates from different body repair shops before the car can be repaired. In health insurance no estimates are necessary. However, there is little relationship between government-provided health services and total health costs. If one compares the public share of health expenditure in Canada, the United States and the United Kingdom, the share is largest in the United Kingdom where the costs as a proportion of GDP are also the lowest. Therefore, the blame should be put on insurance, not government-supplied insurance.

R.G. Evans, a B.C. health economist, has argued persistently that the main reason for escalating health costs is that there are too many doctors (Evans 1976). Given the present structure of medicare, if the number of patients per physician declined, the doctors would not try to cut fees to increase the number of visits and thereby try to maintain income—patients are often not aware of the doctor's fee—but rather increase the service given to each patient; the doctors could increase the number of tests and/or nonemergency operations, for example. When these possibilities are exhausted, they may start to compaign for higher fees. The medical market is therefore an example of a market that works in reverse. Normally an increase in supply would depress prices and increase or decrease incomes, depending on the elasticity of demand. In the case of medical services, demand and supply are interdependent in the sense that the supplier (the physician) can create the demand for his or her services by telling the patient what he or she needs to have done.

For Evans to be correct, it has to be demonstrated (a) that there is a surplus, and (b) that the physician behaves in the manner hypothesized. Whether there are too many doctors is difficult to ascertain, but the economic criterion would be: the optimum amount of medical services is provided when the marginal benefit of an additional service is equal to the marginal resource cost. According to Evans the consensus among health economists is that the marginal benefit in the aggregate is close to zero. There is certainly little correlation between mortality rates in a community and expenditure on health, and a greater number of doctors in a community does not in general lead to better health (in rich countries). An improvement in the present mortality rate could be achieved only if people changed their lifestyle (no alcohol, no smoking, plenty of exercise, moderate eating, and a lowering of traffic speeds), not by increasing the quality of health care.

The second question is whether physicians behave in the prescribed manner; in particular, is there any correlation between the stock of physicians and elective surgery, and between the stock of physicians and the level of fees? It is well known that some surgery is unnecessary. One survey conducted in Saskatchewan showed that the number of hysterectomies decreased significantly when the doctors became aware that they were being studied. Blomqvist (1979:101−03) has shown that there is a significant correlation between the number of physicians per capita and the number of hernia, gall bladder and hemorrhoid operations performed. There is also some evidence for the correlation between the number of physicians and fees. An example is the much publicized surplus of surgeons in the United States. This surplus of close to 50 percent has led to high prices, low surgical workloads and incomes similar to those of other physicians (Evans 1976:151).

Policies Aimed at Promoting Efficiency in Health Care

The first question to be discussed is whether a health care system should guarantee the best for everybody. Clearly not. This would be tantamount to a housing policy's guaranting everybody a five-bedroom house with three bathrooms, air conditioning and swimming pool.[1] Therefore it should not be expected that a comprehensive health insurance will guarantee everybody a private bed in hospital or cosmetic surgery; rather, each patient should be guaranteed the necessary minimum, and any frills should be covered by additional insurance if the patient chooses to have them. In general, the medical insurance system in Canada aims to achieve this goal of a necessary minimum, in which case government policy can control costs either by attempting to control demand, or by controlling supply and promoting efficiency. The latter would be the obvious policy if Evans were right, the former if one believed that the system were abused by patients.

Policies aimed at controlling demand do so by shifting some of the burden of health costs to the individual. Such a policy could take the form of "deterrent fees" which would mean that a nominal charge would be imposed on the patient per visit. It could also take the form of a deductible clause in the health insurance policy, such that the individual would be responsible for the first $100 of medical costs incurred each year. The rationale behind this policy is that if we were more aware of what medical services cost, we would demand less. Another possible avenue, suggested by the Ontario Economic Council, is making the consumption of health services a taxable benefit with an upper limit, subject to various exemptions and qualifications (Reuber 1979:103−10). Sweden has had deterrent fees for some time of 20 kr ($4.50) per visit to out-patients departments at hospitals and 35 kr ($9.00) per visit to a local doctor; however hospital care is free. In May 1979, New Brunswick introduced hospital charges of $10 per day for inpatients and $6 per visit for outpatients, except for senior citizens (Brown 1980:522).

It is not clear whether deterrent fees and similar measures would curb the demand for medical services. For example, Sweden, which has deterrent fees, spends a larger proportion of GDP on health than Canada and the United Kingdom which do not have deterrent fees. One reason why deterrent fees may have little effect on demand is that visits to doctors and hospitals are not completely "free" goods, for most people would rather do something else with their time than wait for hours in a doctor's office to get treatment for minor ailments. Nor are prolonged stays in hospitals a desirable use of time for the majority. It should also be remembered that demand for medical services is to some extent determined by the doctor and not the patient; if the doctor tells a patient to come back for three more tests or check-ups, a deterrent fee is unlikely to curb this demand. Therefore it is possible that deterrent fees may only shift the burden of medical costs to the poor and sickly who cannot afford to pay.

It is possible to devise schemes to promote more efficiency in health care.[2] One way is to make a proportion of health insurance deductible. If, for example, the patient had to pay the first $200 of medical costs out of his or her own pocket, he or she would be more careful in shopping around for a good doctor or clinic to ensure his or her money's worth. However, the deductible feature would deter the poor and the sickly from seeking medical help.

Another option is to introduce a voucher system. Every person would receive an annual voucher from the government, the size of which would be determined by the average amount of medical care required by a person of a certain age. A 40-year-old would, for example, receive a voucher worth $600 and an 80-year-old worth $5,000. The total value of vouchers would add up to the current value of medical care. The patient could then take his voucher to specially designed centres which would provide a comprehensive package of health services. The patient could sign a contract with the centre for a year's service with the voucher as payment. If the patient were not satisfied with the service, he or she could try another centre the following year. The service centre would be cost-conscious, as the total value of the vouchers would set a limit to the amount of money received from the government. The more expensive the individual treatments, the less the profit for the centre. If the centre went too far in cutting costs and did not provide adequate care, it would be assumed that the patient would switch to another centre.

There is some evidence in the United States that prepayment plans are more efficient than other forms of medical care (Blomqvist 1979:82–3). In a prepayment plan the patient buys his or her health insurance directly from a medical centre which provides all the health care. Unfortunately, the full benefits of this type of system can be realized only in areas where the population is sufficiently large to make competition possible.

A third and less radical option would be to put all doctors on salaries. It would then not be in the interest of a doctor to order unnecessary surgery or medicine or tests. Finally, in a somewhat different vein, it could be argued that the whole health care system is inefficient in the sense that most resources are devoted to treating people who are already sick and too little to preventing people from becoming so. The fundamental causes of ill health are, after all, not inadequate hospital facilities and bad medical care, but the lifestyle of Canadians and their environment. Therefore, in the long run it would be more efficient if more emphasis were placed on prevention through community health care centres rather than on physicians and hospitals. These centres could carry on preventative and teaching activities as well as curative care.

Recent Government Policies Affecting the Health Sector

Government response to escalating health costs has been of the "cut, freeze and squeeze type,"[3] the responses to which were a public outcry at hospital closings, and doctors complaining about inadequate fees. The doctors have also responded by extra-billing and by "opting out" of the medicare program. The unpopularity of these developments led to an enquiry under Chief Justice Hall. The mandate of the Hall Commission included advising the government on an appropriate response to the problem of extra-billing. The Hall report was issued in 1980 and recommended that all issues in dispute between doctors and provincial governments should be sent to binding arbitration boards whose decisions would be final. The commission recommended that extra-billing be outlawed, as it denies access to medical service for some and as it violates the principle of portability. Another recent study (Barer, Evans and Stoddart 1979) notes that in addition to shifting the burden of paying for health care to the sick, extra-billing is unlikely to curb demand as it is usually instituted as a form of price discrimination; that is, it increases the price for those who are willing to pay (Manga 1980). Extra-billing will therefore neither curb the demand for health care nor promote efficiency.

The Hall report received qualified support for its ruling on binding arbitration, but outright hostility from doctors for its recommendation to outlaw extra-billing. Clearly, binding arbitration would not help if the right to extra-bill remained. However, even if extra-billing were out-lawed, thereby solving the problems of portability and accessibility, health costs would not be controlled, since the problem of doctors generating their own demand would remain unsolved (Manga, 1980).

Perhaps the commission should have looked into the possibilities of making doctors salaried.

Expenditures on Education

Like health expenditures, most education expenditures are in government hands. Only 3.5 percent of primary and secondary school pupils attend private schools (Husby 1981:181). As is the case with health, government expenditures on education as a percentage of GDP has increased over time. From 4.6 percent in 1965, they peaked at 7 percent in 1970 and dropped to 6.6 percent in 1976. The share of government expenditures on education is larger than that on health.

Despite the fact that the constitution is unambiguous as to which level of government has jurisdiction over education, the federal government has always had a say by providing education to Indian and Inuit children (and the children of military personnel stationed abroad). The federal government has also been involved in post-secondary education since 1910.[4] The justification for the federal presence is a provision in the BNA Act which enables the government to make grants to individuals or institutions to promote the national interest. Since 1967 the federal government has been heavily involved in the financing of post-secondary education, initially through the conditional grants system. In 1961, the federal share of financing post-secondary education was 20 percent; by 1971 it had increased to 48 percent (Bird 1976:215).

The cost-sharing program in education, in contrast to health, had no strings attached and therefore the tremendous increase in expenditures on education was not accompanied by any attempt to achieve minimum standards or national objectives. The Established Program Financing scheme which replaced the conditional grants in 1977 has, in effect, meant that post-secondary education has been handed back to the provinces.

Post-secondary education is perceived to be a problem area because of its high costs, its inequitable financing and the apparent lack of access for students from low-income families. These issues will be discussed in detail.

Post-Secondary Education Costs

Expenditures on post-secondary education skyrocketed in the late '60s and in the first few years of the '70s; indeed, the '60s saw a sevenfold increase. Twenty-one universities were added to the already existing 27. The number of full-time students increased from 191,000 to 501,000 (Bird 1976:216). This increase can be explained partly by demographic factors and partly by an increased participation rate. The increase in birth rate in the late '40s and '50s caused a population explosion of children of university age in the '60s and the '70s. At the same time the participation rate in the 18-to-24-year age group (the proportion of young adults attending post-secondary education) increased from 11 percent in 1961 to 19 percent in 1971.

The interesting feature here is the increased participation rate. Why did so many more young people want a post-secondary education? One possible reason is that the direct cost of an education decreased. In 1961, direct government payments accounted for 69 percent of operating revenues of post-secondary institutions; by 1971 it had increased to 81 percent. This shift of expenses from students to government was made possible by the generous assistance of the federal government in the cost-sharing program.

Another probable reason for the increased demand for education was the attitude of the '60s towards education—investment in education (the popular phrase was "human capital") was seen as a key factor in economic growth. It was widely held that education was a means of improving social mobility for children from low-income families. It was seen as a social leveller that would help build a just society.

Unfortunately, investment in education had very little success in achieving these goals, particularly equality. By the early 1970s, participation rates started to level off as students realized that post-secondary education did not guarantee access to a high-paying job. In addition, the growth in the number of young people in the 18 to 24 age group declined. These two factors combined led to a situation of declining enrollments in the late '70s and early '80s, a situation which is likely to persist unless participation rates again increase. For the present demographic structure will not help: the number of children of primary school age peaked in 1970, the number of secondary school age in 1977 and the number of post-secondary age in 1981 (Reuber, 1979: p. 110). The enrollment in primary schools is expected to decline until 1982, in secondary schools until 1990 and in post-secondary institutions until 1995.

A decrease in enrollment does not mean that education costs decrease in proportion, as such a large proportion of the costs in the system are fixed. Eighty percent of operating costs are in the form of wages and salaries. Governments, to a large extent backed by the public, have started to cut back their support, in most cases indiscriminately (across-the-board). The reason why public support is high compared to public support for cutbacks in health is probably because most people feel that they benefit from expenditures on health, whereas only a privileged few are seen to benefit from post-secondary education. The financial stringency had little impact initially as most universities probably had some excess capacity—or "fat" as it is referred to in the newspapers. However, the cutbacks are now affecting libraries, maintenance support staff and replacement of equipment and supplies. So far there has been little effect on staff because of the tenure system and unionization; the main brunt has been borne by recently qualified university teachers who have not been able to find more than short-term appointments, if any at all. However, layoffs of permanent staff are now expected. Perhaps the most frequently suggested solution to the financial problems of the universities is that students should be made to pay more for their education.

The Problem of Equity in Education

One of the guiding principles of a capitalist economic system is that the consumer pays for what he or she buys. When a good is purchased, the seller receives the money and the buyer receives the good. The benefit or value the buyer derives from the good must be at least as great as what the buyer paid, or the purchase would never have been made. The buyer does not expect the government to pay for part or all of the good. To compare any good with education is perhaps farfetched as education is an investment good (i.e., it enhances earning power). Let us assume instead that an individual plans to go into business, doing some form of consulting, which would require the use of a desk-top computer costing $3,000. Would the government be expected to give the computer to the individual at little or no cost? Post-secondary education is not very different in nature, and yet many people regard it as a right that should be provided almost free of charge.

Most economists agree that there are three reasons for abandoning the basic principle that you should pay for what you receive: (1) if paying the full cost has severe distributional implications; (2) if there are distortions in the money markets that prevent the buyer of the good from raising adequate finances; (3) if the total benefits to society are greater than the benefits to the individual—in the absence of intervention, not enough of this good would be produced.

The distributional argument as applied to education is as follows: if each student had to pay the full cost of his education by paying fees which would reflect the true cost to society of educating him at the university level, it would mean that students from lower-income groups would be denied an education. The educational system would therefore reinforce the present inequities in income distribution.

There is no question that poor students should be given special attention and be subsidized throughout the school system. Countless studies have shown that students from high-income families do better in school than students from low-income families. However, it is unlikely that this anomaly can be corrected at the post-secondary level. Richard Bird puts the issue rather well: "higher education is simply the tail at the end of a very large dog of parental influence, environment, and elementary and secondary education, and tails do not generally wag dogs" (Bird 1976:219). Indeed, much recent evidence on the intellectual development of children shows that the crucial ages of 0 to 3 comprise the period of a child's intellectual and emotional development. This is the time, therefore, when special attention in education should be given to children of disadvantaged or low-income families.

Subsidized post-secondary education has had little, if any, effect on income distribution. Most university students still come from middle- to upper-income brackets. This means that subsidizing universities is the same as giving money to students who would have attended anyway; students from low-income brackets do not benefit as they have dropped out of the educational system at a lower level. There is also the effect of post-secondary education on the income-earning potential of the students themselves. As well as receiving a service far below cost, the students acquire the opportunity to earn a larger income than one they may have earned without a higher education. Therefore tax-financed post-secondary education forces tax payers with relatively low incomes to share the costs of an activity which benefits those who have the highest income potential. Several studies have confirmed that the burden of subsidized post-secondary education is regressive (falls disproportionately on lower-income groups) (Mehmet 1978).

Distortions in the money markets may prevent a student from borrowing money from a bank. Borrowing to buy a house or a car is relatively easy as both can be used as collateral for the debt. Borrowing to finance education is not as easy, for the benefits of education (skills) cannot be used as collateral. Therefore access to money is thwarted for educational purposes, and society ends up with less post-secondary education than is socially optimal. This can be corrected by the government's providing access to capital in the form of loans or guarantees to commercial loans.

The federal government has done more than this. The Canada Student Loans Plan has been in operation since 1966, financed by the federal government but operated by the provincial governments. The federal government allocates money to the provinces on a per capita basis so the provinces can pay the interest on a student loan for six months after the student completes his studies. The federal government also guarantees the loans in case of default. In addition, both the federal and provincial governments provide various types of grants. In the mid-'70s, half the students received some form of subsidy, two-thirds of which was on a nonrepayable basis (Bird 1976). Assistance in most cases is given on basis of need, not ability. Inasmuch as students from low-income groups are the main recipients, this system is clearly desirable. Yet if the main justification for this program is concern for lower-income groups (after all, distortions in the capital market can be overcome by loan guarantees), then loan repayments should be graduated according to ability to pay. Interest and principal payments on a loan of $10,000 is more of a burden on someone who, after graduation, earns $14,000 per year than someone who earns $25,000 per year.

The final argument for government subsidies to education is that education has beneficial spillover effects onto the society in general. For example, post-secondary education may lead to (desirable ?) changes in the values and attitudes of society; it may make people capable of making more informed choices in elections and therefore lead to better government; it may help provide children with a better upbringing in the home; and it may make labour more adaptable to changing labour market conditions. However, it is far from clear how much society benefits from post-secondary education as few studies have been done to substantiate these effects.

In summary, then, the principles of equity dictate that the student should be required to pay a larger share of the cost of his or her education; that the government provide loans at full interest rates but with repayment geared to income (high-income earners would be required to repay at a faster rate than low-income earners); and that special grants be given to students from low-income families.[5] It should be added that this type of scheme would not be without problems. Students who were only marginally interested in getting a post-secondary education would no longer attend, which would further increase the present problem of declining enrollment. Another consideration is that unless all provinces increased fee levels at the same time, many students would move to provinces where the fees were lower (provided the fee differential were large enough to overcome any cost advantages of attending a local institution); however, this situation would probably not persist for long as taxpayers in the low-fee provinces would object to subsidizing students from out of the province.

Recent Government Policies
Affecting Post-Secondary Education

So far there have been four provincial commissions dealing with post-secondary education: in Alberta, Manitoba, Ontario, and Nova Scotia. The Task Force on Post-Secondary Education in Manitoba (1973) recommended no substantial increase in fees; grants to poor students; and increased student loans (Stager 1975). The Alberta Commission on Educational Planning (1972) recommended that students should bear one-quarter of costs in the form of tuition fees, that grants should vary inversely with family income and that student loans should be increased.

The Commission on Post-Secondary Education in Ontario (1972) recommended that students should bear from one-third to two-thirds of costs; the commission also recommended grants for poor students and graduated repayment loans for other students. The Nova Scotia Royal Commission on Education, Public Services and Provincial-Municipal Relations recommended that students should bear *the full cost* of instruction and that grants should be given to freshmen and students from low-income families. Most of these provincial recommendations have not been implemented. For example, in Ontario there has been a very small increase in tuition fees since 1972. In 1978-79, student fees accounted for 9 to 20 percent of university revenue (Leslie 1980:140). Even though the universities technically have the right to set their own fees, it is not in their interest to do so, as their grants from the provincial government would be reduced by the amount the universities would gain.

Summary and Conclusions

Both the health and education fields have recently attracted attention from all levels of government because of the large cost increases and the increased reluctance of taxpayers to carry the financial burden of the increases. In both areas user fees have been suggested, but for different reasons: in health as a means of curbing demand, in education as a means of shifting the cost burden over to the beneficiaries—the students. Implementation of user fees would have more severe distributional implications in health than in education. Both rich and poor get sick, but proportionately fewer people in lower-income groups take advantage of post-secondary education.

Ways of controlling costs in health care include means to infuse competition into the system, the reallocation of expenditures from "curative care" to preventative care, and better utilization of less expensive services (e.g., nurses instead of doctors and home care instead of hospital care). Suggestions for controlling costs in post-secondary education by promoting efficiency are less commonly heard; the only measure of cost control appears to be across-the-board cuts.

NOTES

1. This is a point strongly emphasized by Blomqvist 1979.
2. See Blomqvist 1979:149-176.
3. The description is Reuber's 1979.
4. For a description, see Carter 1980.
5. These, in essence, are Bird's recommendations (Bird 1976).

BIBLIOGRAPHY

Barer, M.C., R.G. Evans and G.L. Stoddart. *Controlling Health Care Costs by Direct Charges to Patients: Snare or Delusion.* Toronto: Ontario Economic Council, 1979.

Bird, R.M. *Charging for Public Services: A New Look at an Old Idea.* Toronto: Canadian Tax Foundation, 1976.

_____. *Financing Canadian Government: A Quantitative Overview.* Toronto: Canadian Tax Foundation, 1979.

Blomqvist, Ake. *The Health Care Business.* Vancouver: The Fraser Institute, 1979.

Boadway, Robin. *Intergovernmental Transfers in Canada.* Toronto: Canadian Tax Foundation, 1980.

Brown, M.C. "The Implications of Established Program Finance for National Health Insurance." *Canadian Public Policy* (VI), 1980, pp. 521–32.

Carter, G.C. "Federal and Provincial Fiscal Arrangements: Some Implications for Financing Education." Paper presented to a conference of the Canadian Teachers Federation, 1980.

Department of Finance. *Economic Review: A Perspective on the Decade.* Ottawa: Supply and Services, 1980.

Evans, R.G. "Does Canada have too many doctors?—Why nobody loves an immigrant physician." *Canadian Public Policy* (II), 1976, pp. 147–60.

Health and Welfare Canada. *Canada's National-Provincial Health Program for the 1980's: A Commitment for Renewal.*

Husby, P.J. "Education." In R. Bellan and W.H. Pope (eds.), pp. 181–97, *The Canadian Economy: Problems and Options.* Toronto: McGraw-Hill Ryerson, 1981.

Leslie, P.M. *Canadian Universities, 1980 and Beyond.* Ottawa: Association of Universities and Colleges of Canada, 1980.

Manga, P. "Arbitration and the Medical Profession: A Comment on the Hall Report." *Canadian Public Policy* (VI), 1980, pp. 670–78.

Mehmet, O. *Who Benefits from the Ontario University System: A Benefit-Cost Analysis by Income Groups.* Toronto: Ontario Economic Council, 1978.

Reuber, Grant C. *Canada's Political Economy.* Toronto: McGraw Hill-Ryerson, 1979.

Stager, D. "The Universities." *Canadian Public Policy* (I), 1975, pp. 393–402.

CHAPTER 8

The Transportation Industry

Transportation is an industry which has played a crucial role in the development of Canada, probably moreso than in other countries, because of the large distances and low population density. The railways in particular were creations and instruments of national policy, built with much financial assistance and concessions from all levels of government, and subsequently regulated to serve various national and regional goals. The idea of transportation being an important instrument of national unity is still with us today, albeit in a modified form.

Transportation of people and goods takes many forms, the most important of which are exhibited in Table 13. In this chapter walking and cycling are not discussed, even though walking constitutes a significant part of urban transportation (probably 10 percent of trips to work), nor is pipeline transportation of oil and gas. The field of transportation is so vast and the policy issues so diverse that it is impossible to do justice to all modes in a short chapter such as this. Instead, this chapter will concentrate on selected policy issues relating to urban passenger transportation, inter-urban passenger and freight transportation, and ocean transportation of freight.

Transportation Policies and Their Justification

Transportation policies are of two types: regulatory and investment. Regulatory policies are usually motivated by the need to achieve economic efficiency and/or a redistribution of income between regions, whereas investment policies are often motivated by such factors as job creation, national unity or even political expediency.

Regulatory Policies

The efficiency rationale of regulatory policies is based on the assump-

TABLE 13
Modes of Transport

Modes		Passenger				Goods			
		Urban	Inter-urban	Extranational U.S.	Extranational Non-U.S.	Urban	Inter-urban	Extranational U.S.	Extranational Non-U.S.
Road	Bus	X	X	X					
	Private car	X	X	X					
	Taxi	X	(X)						
	Truck					X	X	X	
Water	Barge						X	X	
	Bulk carrier						X	X	X
	Tanker						X	X	X
	Liner				X		X	X	X
Rail		X	X	X		?	X	X	
Air		X	X	X	X	?	X	X	X
Pipeline						?	X	X	

tion that without government interference, market forces would not allocate resources efficiently. If an industry, such as railway transportation, has decreasing costs (natural monopoly), only one firm can operate efficiently. The railway would set prices so that marginal revenue equalled marginal costs, resulting in excessively high freight rates for transportation users. The traditional solution to this situation has been to legalize the railway monopoly and to control freight rates. Ideally, rates should be equated to marginal costs to approximate a competitive solution. However, this would be difficult to accomplish, since, under decreasing costs, marginal costs would be lower than average costs, and therefore marginal cost pricing would result in losses to the railway. Instead, average cost pricing is usually attempted, whereby the regulatory agency allows the railway to cover costs plus an average rate of return on capital.

Another reason for regulating a transportation industry is that competition may result in an unacceptable degree of instability with prices fluctuating wildly as firms leave or enter the industry (a boom-and-bust cycle). This rationale for regulation is usually applied to trucking firms and airlines, but the efficiency rationale for regulation is weak. It is possible that instability would lead to an inefficient allocation of resources, as some irreversible investment decisions may be made on the basis of temporary disequilibrium. However, this adverse effect has to be balanced against the inefficiencies introduced by regulation of entry and prices.

All forms of transportation regulation have come under attack, particularly from economists belonging to the so-called Chicago school who argue that regulation seldom achieves its objectives and is expensive compared with the modest benefits achieved.[1] Experience has shown that regulation tends to raise prices on the part of transportation users instead of lowering them. Regulation is frequently of more benefit to the producer (the transportation firm) than the consumer, as the regulators become identified with the welfare of the regulated firms. It is also contended that regulation protects inefficiencies and distorts the allocation of resources in the sense that the regulation may induce the industry to act in a way it would not otherwise do. Certain types of regulations on the rate of return can lead to overcapitalization (Averch and Johnson 1962, and Baumol and Klevorick 1970). The solution, according to the Chicago school, is not to try to improve regulatory control, but to deregulate the economy. Any excess profits reaped by an unregulated natural monopoly can be confiscated by an excess profits tax.

There are cases where deregulation does indeed appear to offer substantial benefits, perhaps particularly in transportation. An often-quoted example is the airline industry in California, which has not been regulated for some time. Although only few companies operate on the main routes, price competition has resulted in fares which are about two-thirds of fares on comparable routes, subject to regulation by the Civil Aeronautics Board.[2] There is also some evidence that the quality of service, in terms of frequency and regularity, is better than in regulated markets.

Another motive behind regulatory policies in transportation is to redistribute income—to assist some freight-transportation users by offering them artifically low (below cost) freight rates. Unless subsidies are offered to transport firms, they will try to recoup their losses by taxing (raising freight rates for) other users. This practice of cross-subsidization is common in airline regulation: the airlines are allowed to charge excessive prices on popular routes to compensate for the losses incurred on services to remote areas. Railroad regulation has also been dominated by cross-subsidization.

Regulation as a form of taxation is popular with governments because the consumer is not aware he or she is being taxed, and because the taxation is not subject to parliamentary review. Deregulation, together with subsidies paid to the transport firms for offering uneconomic but necessary service, should be a more efficient solution. It would then be possible to review these subsidies regularly to assess the benefits and costs of providing the service. This review is particularly important as it is doubtful that transport subsidies are the most efficient means of assisting a group of consumers or a region.

The two philosophies of regulation, efficiency and redistribution of income, have both played an important part in Canadian transport regulation.[3] Direct regulation of transport probably started with the infamous Crow's Nest Pass Agreement of 1897, by which Canadian Pacific agreed to hold constant the rates on transporting grain and grain products from the Prairie provinces to British Columbia (and on certain settlers' supplies inbound from eastern Canada) in return for federal subsidies for extending the railway into British Columbia. Since that time there has been almost continuous warfare between users of railway transportation and the railway firms. This warfare has had to do more with redistribution issues than efficiency issues and frequently resulted in the railways giving in to certain groups of customers, occasionally in return for federal government subsidies. Examples of this are the Crow's Nest Pass Agreements, which became law in 1925; the Maritimes Freight Rates Act of 1927, which provides a 30 percent reduction to customers on some preferred freight movements in the Maritimes; and the movement of feed grains from east to west, which has been subsidized since 1941.

After the Second World War, trucking provided an alternative to the railways as a means of transporting goods. The competition created endless difficulties for the railways as regulatory barriers, particularly the ingrained structure of cross-subsidization, prevented the railways from meeting the competition head on. The railways tried to recoup some of their losses through general rate increases, which were vigorously opposed by the Prairie provinces and the Maritimes. The McPherson Royal Commission was appointed to deal with some of these problems. Following its recommendations, the National Transportation Act of 1967 was passed. This act constituted a major change in the philosophy of transport regulation in Canada by emphasizing efficiency and by recognizing the benefits of competition. The regulatory control over railways was decreased (rate of return regulation was abolished) and the railways gained considerable freedom in setting rates.[4]

With the late 1960s came a renewed interest in national unity and regional needs. It was felt that "free" transport markets unfairly favoured the central provinces. The western provinces, in particular, opposed the National Transportation Act and during the Western Economic Opportunities Conference in 1973, they called for amendments that would establish regional development as a goal for transport policy. The government responded by creating a task force on national transport policy (Studnicki-Gizbert 1975). In 1975, the Ministry of Transport issued a report on transport policy which was followed by Bill C–33 in 1977 (Canada, 1977). However, the bill was not adopted. It paid lip service to efficiency, and reaffirmed that transport policy should be an effective instrument for the achievement of national and regional, social and economic objectives. Transport policy appears to have gone full circle.

Investment Policies

The rationale for transport investments (or disinvestments such as discontinuance of service) should be net social benefits to society; that is, for each project, total social costs and benefits should be calculated and only if benefits exceed costs should a project be undertaken.

However, government may undertake transportation investments for reasons other than providing net benefits to society; national unity, defence, regional employment, and votes are other motivations. Investments motivated by national unity have a time-honoured tradition in Canada. Some examples are the building of the CPR, which was one of the conditions for British Columbia to enter Confederation; the building of the Trans-Canada highway; and the development of Air Canada. Defence, or national security, is frequently cited as a justification for harbour development, highways (the Alaska highway), airports, and even a merchant marine. Examples of transport investments as instruments of regional policy include container terminals in the Maritimes and in Montreal, and Mirabel International Airport outside Montreal. Transportation investment for the purpose of getting votes may be the motivation in provincial highway construction (Munro 1975), and some of the federal transport investments in Quebec may also have been politically motivated.

Problems in Urban Passenger Transportation

Most people single out congestion on roads as being the major problem in urban transportation. Congestion is obviously caused by too many cars using the available space. Some argue that too few expressways have been built, some that there is insufficient public transit; some that transit facilities are adequate, but people are irrational and will not use them; and some that road transportation has been underpriced for years, allowing people to locate their place of work at a distance from their place of residence. Two issues will be discussed here: (1) the economic definition of congestion and whether urban car transport has been underpriced; and (2) factors determining the choice of travel mode and whether people are irrational in their preference for cars.

Congestion and the Cost of Automobile Transportation

Assume that there is an urban expressway with one entry point and one exit point. To travel on this road, the motorist incurs fuel costs, the cost of wear and tear on the car, and the loss of time involved in travelling. This loss of time can be regarded as a cost to the motorist, for the time spent in commuting could have been spent working or engaging in leisure activity. The cost or value of travel time can be determined by observing how much additional money people are willing to spend in order to travel by the fastest means of transportation. Studies have shown that people value their travel time at 20 to 50 percent of their wage rates;[5] that is, if a person's wage is $8.00/hour, he or she spends $1.60 to $4.00 per hour in commuting (plus the cost of running the car).

The time cost of travel will depend on congestion. At off-peak hours, the motorist entering the expressway will be able to travel at maximum speed, but at peak hours the cost of travel will be a direct function of the number of cars entering the expressway: the more cars, the slower the travel and the higher will be the motorist's costs. If these costs are too high, it can be assumed that some motorists will not enter the expressway, but will choose an alternative route or an alternative mode of transport. This principle is the same with any commodity; if the cost or price of a commodity is too high, some consumers will choose not to buy it. As long as the motorist puts a higher value on a trip on the expressway than the trip costs him, the expressway will be used. The number of vehicles will stabilize at a point when the cost to the last car that enters the expressway is exactly equal to the value the last motorist puts on the trip.

However, there are today too many cars on the road, the reason being that the motorist has underestimated the cost involved in using the expressway, for they do not include the effects of the motorist on other drivers, on the environment, and on the wear and tear of the road. At rush hour, a driver imposes a cost on all the other motorists as his or her presence makes them slow down. For efficient allocation of resources, this cost should enter the motorist's calculations and be added to his own private costs. One study places congestion costs at 38 cents per vehicle mile during morning rush hour and 1.4 cents per mile at midday (Dewees 1978). If the motorist were forced to pay this cost in addition to the private costs incurred, less trips would be undertaken and urban congestion would be eased.

Another factor which does not enter into the calculation of the costs of auto-transportation is air pollution—a cost projected not only onto other car-users, but onto everyone, in the form of respiratory illnesses (bronchitis, lung cancer), damage to buildings and damage to crops and vegetation. This cost has been calculated at 0.2 cents per vehicle mile (Dewees 1974). In addition, each motorist should also be assessed a road maintenance charge for contributing to the wear and tear of the road. Estimates for this (based on 1968 data) ranged from 0.2 to 0.6 cents for Ontario (Haritos 1973).

Important Factors in the Selection of Travel Modes

It has been established that expressways are over-used at rush hour. The question then is why public transit is not used to a larger extent, given that transit fares are often low compared with the costs of operating a car. However, besides transit fares and the cost of running a car, travel time must also be considered. The cost of travel time is sometimes broken down into two components: time spent waiting and time spent travelling. It seems that people find waiting for a bus or a train more uncomfortable than travelling in a bus or a train; therefore they put a higher value on the time cost of waiting than the time cost of travelling (two to three times as much).[6] Even if the comparative advantages of travelling by car or by public transit were equal, many people would still choose to commute by car because they find it more comfortable and private. Studies of modal choice include a value for discomfort of the mode.

Statistical analysis of modal choice has yielded some interesting data. The elasticity of demand for public transit is very low. For example, one study for Montreal shows that the elasticity of demand for fares is $-.22$ for adults and $-.52$ for children. In other words, a 100 percent increase in transit fares would lead to a 22 percent drop in ridership for adults and 52 percent for children (Gaudry 1978). Most other studies show similar figures. The elasticity of demand with respect to changes in travel time is higher. The same study for Montreal estimated this to be

−.65 for adults. Other studies have looked at the cross-elasticity of demand for automobile use with respect to transit fares (i.e., the effect of an increase in transit fares on automobile use). These cross-elasticities are also quite low, between −.5 and −.15 (Frankena 1979:22), and if they are correct, few people will switch to public transit because of lower fares. Lower fares would result in less revenue for the transit authority as the elasticity of demand is less than one.

Regulation of Urban Transport

A case can be made for some regulation of urban automobile transport as it is not efficient. At present, the motorist is not responsible for the costs of congestion, pollution, and wear and tear of the road. Several schemes for collecting congestion charges have been suggested. For example, vehicles could be equipped with meters which would record mileage upon the raising of a flag attached to the outside of the car.[7] The flag would have to be raised at rush hour and on certain roads, and failure to do so would lead to heavy fines. The meter in the car would be read at regular intervals and the motorist charged a mileage tax. It would also be possible to have each car equipped with an electronic identifier combined with road-side scanning devices which would automatically record the mileage of each vehicle and the extent of congestion.

However, there is considerable resistance to the idea of user charges in urban transport, and it would take a courageous (if not suicidal) city council to implement them. Therefore, other ways have been suggested or tried to ease congestion and pollution.

It could be argued that since urban road usage is underpriced, urban transit fares should be subsidized so that the relative price of the modes would reflect relative costs. However, because of the low elasticity of demand for urban transit, such a measure would not have a significant effect on modal choice. It has even been argued that the primary effect of subsidizing public transport would be to increase the total amount of travel (Dewees and Waverman 1977). If cheaper public transit fares took some cars off the roads, the travel time of the remaining motorists would decrease. This would lead to an increase in the quantity demanded of expressway trips (remembering the importance of the cost of time in the demand for urban transportation) and therefore an increase in total travel demand. The policy would be self-defeating.

Another way to ease congestion is to increase parking fees. This has been done in several urban areas and is quite effective as the elasticity of demand of automobile use with respect to parking costs is −.32 (Gillen 1977). However, it is not an optimal policy as it does not penalize people that merely traverse the downtown areas on their way to work.

A third way is to increase the price of gas at the pump by means of an excise tax. However, an excise tax levied with the intention of controlling congestion and pollution would scarcely be a fair tax, because it would mean that all car-users, including those in remote areas of the country, would be asked to help to pay the price of urban congestion and pollution.

In most municipalities, the most common form of transport regulation (apart from traffic by-laws) is regulation of the taxi industry. Its rationale is not to promote efficiency but to protect public transit. Restricting the number of licences to run a cab and fare regulation have resulted in high cab fares and large profits for the owners. An indication that profits are large is the market price of a cab licence; in Toronto, a licence sold for $26,500 in 1978. If profits were negligible, no one would want to enter the industry and therefore the market value of a licence would also be negligible. Yet the high price of cab rides adds to, rather than eases, urban transportation problems, since consumers are denied the use of taxis at reasonable fares. In addition, poor people spend a proportionately larger amount of their income on cabs than rich people, and so the burden of regulation falls on them. Deregulation of the cab industry would probably lead to significant benefits to the public.[8]

Investment Policies

Let us assume that a municipality is to build a new system for transporting people between the suburbs and the central business district with a choice between express bus, rapid rail and an expressway. If we assume that each mode would be priced in such a way that all costs would be covered (e.g., in the case of an expressway, the building and maintenance of the expressway, as well as pollution and congestion costs), then the choice should be determined by the number of people expected to use the system.[9] If the system had to transport less than 20,000 people per hour, bus and automobile would be cheaper than rail, with buses being cheapest except at very low travel volumes. Therefore in most cases, efficient investment policy calls for investment in bus travel. Any additional investment in rail transit would be inefficient as it would be economical only in the densest urban corridors with populations above 2 million people. In most of these areas, rapid-rail transit already exists.

Intercity Passenger Transportation

The problems encountered in intercity passenger transportation are more typically regulation problems, such as the need for subsidies and the control of competition. Three problems will be discussed here: subsidization of rail services, regulation of domestic air carriers and airport investments.

Subsidization of Railway Passenger Services

Passenger trains virtually monopolized intercity transportation until the 1920s. The depression and the Second World War delayed the real impact of automobiles and buses until the late 1940s. By 1951, the rail share had dropped to 15 percent of total traffic and automobiles comprised 72 percent (Schreiner 1972:27). Today automobiles probably comprise close to 85 percent, railroads less than 5 percent and the remaining 10 percent is shared by aircraft and buses. The railroads have made some half-hearted attempts to fight off further erosion of their passenger base. CN aggressively tried to improve its services and lower fares in the mid-60s (the "red, white and blue" plan), which temporarily halted the tide, but did not make passenger trains profitable. In 1977, the Liberal government attempted another rescue by integrating CN and CP passenger services in *Via Rail*, intended to make service more efficient and end costly duplications. At present, costs are greater than revenues for all Canadian passenger services, and the federal subsidy paid to Via Rail in the fiscal year 1980s81 was $454.9 million [10] (Canadian Tax Foundation 1981:196).

The reasons for the decline in the popularity of passenger trains are easy to document. Assume again that people make their modal choice on the basis of minimizing costs, and assume that costs can be broken down into direct costs, time costs and a discomfort index. For trips involving a distance over 500 miles, the aircraft has become the dominant mode because of the saving in time costs.[11] For trips of less than 500 miles, the modal choice is more difficult to predict as it depends on local conditions. If it takes a long time to commute to and from the airport at both ends, and if rail offers frequent and fast downtown-to-downtown services, trains may indeed hold their own. In general, profitable passenger trains operate at high speed, at medium-distance runs and between densely populated areas (for example, Toronto–Montreal). CN entered this market with the introduction of the Turbo on the main Montreal–Toronto run. The Turbo was aerodynamically designed and powered by jet-turbine engines which made the train capable of a speed of 160 m.p.h. The train was, however, riddled with endless problems over the heating and the electrical systems. Further, because of track conditions (too many curves and level crossings), the train averaged only 89 m.p.h. (Schreiner 1972:34).

Given that all non-commuter passenger trains lose money, it is not surprising that the Canadian Transport Commission has been inundated with applications from the railways for discontinuance. From 1967 to the end of 1976, there were 72 applications for discontinuance, only eleven of which were approved (McManus 1978:223). All were cases where passengers were few and substitutes available. One example was the London-Windsor service with a daily average of two passengers, another the service between Dauphin and Winnipegosis which in 1974 had an average of ten passengers. The Manitoba service had cost the taxpayer $754 per passenger mile. (The cost of the first Apollo moon project was only $400 per passenger mile, according to Lukasiewicz (1979:524). In 1981, the minister of Transport announced substantial cutbacks in rail passenger services (bypassing any hearings by the Canadian Transport Commission) with the elimination of one of the two transcontinental services and many other shorter routes.

Continuation and subsidization of passenger train services cannot be economically justified on most routes. Even where most people never use a passenger train, it is thought to be bad for a community if the service ceased. As long as the subsidy to keep the train running comes from general tax revenue, a community will voice strong opposition to any rail closure. However, if a user-pay principle were introduced, one in which a community would bear some of the cost of keeping the railway operating, some of the vehement opposition to rail closings might be silenced. A question that needs to be asked is if subsidies to passenger trains are used as a form of regional policy, is the provision of passenger services the most efficient means of assisting a needy community?

Today, the future of passenger trains looks brighter. Before the substantial increase in energy prices of 1973, airlines spent 10 cents of every revenue dollar on fuel, intercity buses 7 cents and trains 3.8 cents (Dewees and Waverman 1977:181). This means that the high energy prices have had the largest effect on airline costs and the least effect on rail costs.[12] If this is translated into prices, a switch to trains can be expected.

Domestic Air Fares and the Question of Regulation

The airline industry in Canada, as in most other countries, has been subject to stringent regulations of entry and price competition. Regulation has usually been promoted for two reasons. In the first place, it was believed that the industry was a natural monopoly and therefore could not function competitively. Secondly, governments have usually had a direct stake in the welfare of the industry in the form of full or partial ownership of an air carrier (e.g., Air Canada); in such cases, it is unlikely that a government would allow competition that might lower the profits of its own airline.

The 1960s brought changes in the airline industry that led to the questioning of the kind of regulation the industry had come to expect. First, the development of alternative charter services on international routes led to a substantial decrease in the cost of flying for consumers and a demand for the introduction of similar services on domestic routes. Second, Texas and California allowed price competition and relatively easy entry within their borders. It was only a matter of time until it became known that competition decreased fares in these markets to roughly two-thirds the level in comparable markets subject to regulation, without any loss in the quality of service (Jordan 1970:202). In 1977, the Air Transport Committee of the Canadian Transport Commission could no longer resist public pressure for change, and the committee addressed itself to the question of domestic ABCs (Advance Booking Charters). During the hearings, Air Canada and CP Air opposed the idea, arguing that ABCs were unnecessary, since they had already introduced this type of service in their new charter class fares.[13] The fact that the number of charter-class seats offered were minute in relation to demand did not deter Air Canada from arguing that the market was limited, and therefore the introduction of ABCs would only lead to a diversion of passengers from the scheduled airlines.[14] The CTC was apparently impressed by this reasoning and decided to allow ABCs on a very limited scale. Air Canada and CP Air were allowed to mount a maximum of 25 interregional return-flight ABCs between points on their present licences, and the regional carriers (PWA, Transair, Nordair, Quebecair, and Eastern Provincial) were granted additional ABCs, but only within their market areas where there was thought to be little potential demand. This decision led to a furor. The *Globe and Mail* called the decision a "charter of stupidity," and the *Ottawa Journal* argued that more people could win government lotteries than would be able to get a reservation on an ABC domestic flight (Kane 1979:55). In view of all the opposition, the cabinet overruled the CTC, the effect of which was to lift the ceiling on ABCs for Air Canada and CP, and to allow the regional air carriers to fly ABCs anywhere in Canada for a trial period of at least three years. In 1979, CP Air was given permission to compete on a more equal footing with Air Canada. Previously, CP Air was limited to carrying 25 percent of passengers on the main trunk lines. This restriction was lifted, but CP Air is still limited on the number of routes on which it can compete. Chartered carriers such as Wardair have also received better treatment.

The easing of regulations has resulted in cheaper domestic air services. Following the Cabinet decision, Suntours introduced Citylink charters, Air Canada Nighthawk fares and CP courier fares. In the last few years a bewildering array of fares has emerged. It could be argued, however, that lowering fares is not enough; there has been no reform in the basic regulatory structure of the airline industry. The Cabinet decision constituted no major change since it was a political decision made after a considerable public outcry. Even though the Air Transport Committee appears to have taken a pro-competitive stance recently, it does not have full regulatory jurisdiction as it cannot exercise full leverage against crown corporations such as Air Canada (Green 1980:227).

In 1981 the Economic Council of Canada (1981) recommended gradual deregulation of the airline industry in Canada, starting with easing of entry restrictions. Any carrier should be given the right to compete on any route currently served by CP or Air Canada. CP and Air Canada should have the right to compete on an equal basis on these routes or on any new route, but should not at present be given the right to enter existing routes served by regional or local carriers. The reason for these asymmetrical recommendations is to give the previously protected local carriers an opportunity to adjust to a new regulation without having to face competition from the strong national carrier. The council also recommended the removal of any restrictions on service competition, the removal of any favouritism towards Air Canada and CP Air, and a vigorous application of the Combines Investigation Act to prohibit predatory behaviour and to control mergers.

Airport Investments and Congestion

Airport investment has become a controversial issue since the building of the Mirabel airport outside Montreal and the proposed new Pickering airport outside Toronto. The alleged justification of both these projects was the congestion problems at Dorval and Malton. As is well known, the building of the new Pickering airport was stopped by a citizen's protest movement based on an antigrowth, antipollution platform. Given that congestion is the justification for additional airports, the question that needs to be examined is whether the building of new airports is the most efficient means of getting rid of this problem.

The traditional remedy to the problem of facilities that are crowded sometime and empty other times is the introduction of peak-load pricing. Charging higher fees during peak periods helps to spread demand over the day (and night) and therefore reduces the requirements for additional capacity. Peak-load pricing as a solution to airport congestion is not practised in Canada, but has been used at Heathrow and Gatwick since 1972. At these airports landing fees for aircraft vary with the time of day. In Canada, the regulatory agency which administers the construction and running of airports, the Canadian Air Transport Administration, levies two fees, one on passengers (the airport tax) and one on aircraft. The tax on aircraft is in the form of landing fees, which are assessed on the basis of the weight of the aircraft and type of flight, and can vary from $1.30 for a small Cessna, to $600 for a 747 (Borins 1978). This fee schedule certainly does not deter the small Cessna from using the airport at the busiest time of the day, whereas peak-load pricing would impose a prohibitive cost of landing and take-off for small aircraft (well over $100), and would lead to more efficient utilization of facilities by passenger aircraft.

There are also ways to reduce passenger congestion of the terminal facilities. Additional measures, apart from rescheduling of departures and arrivals to off-peak times, could include the construction of off-site terminals and various measures to discourage senders and greeters, such as very high parking fees. There is no evidence that these alternatives were examined in evaluating the need for new airports.[15]

Intercity Cargo Transportation

The major share of freight transportation, measured in terms of operating revenue (1978), is held by trucking (53 percent) followed by rail (38 percent) and water (9 percent). Only twelve years earlier, rail had the major share (55 percent), followed by trucking (30 percent) and water (14 percent) (Canadian Transport Commission 1979:19).

The use of freight revenue as a measure, however, understates the importance of water carriers, as these transport bulk commodities at relatively low freight rates. Indeed, if the measure is ton per mile, one study showed that water carriers surpassed CP rail and carried nearly as much freight as CN.[16] This is surprising in view of the nine-month shipping season, compared with the unlimited season for rail. More than half the tonnage moved by water in the domestic trades consists of wheat and other grains (22 percent), fuel oil (19 percent) and iron ore (17 percent). Other commodities moved by water are logs, gasoline, sand, gravel, limestone, and salt.

The water transport industry can be divided into three sectors: Great Lakes shipping, coastal shipping and arctic shipping. Arctic shipping includes seasonal cargo movements on the Mackenzie river, as well as transportation of arctic resources and coastal shipping between arctic communities. The Great Lakes shipping industry consists of nineteen Canadian-owned companies, many of which are still family-owned, that operate a fleet of bulk carriers.[17] The coastal industry consists of tugboat operators on the West Coast and small operators of various types of boats on the East Coast.

The Water Transport Committee of the Canadian Transport Commission (CTC) must license all water carriers and has jurisdiction over rates on general cargo and passenger traffic. Since 1977 the licence to operate in coastal waters has been restricted to Canadian ships. However, it seems that the regulatory control exercised is negligible.[18] There is no evidence that it is difficult to get a licence nor that the control over rates is important, in view of the fact that most of the cargo is bulk and therefore does not fall under CTC jurisdiction. The inland and coastal shipping industry appears to be competitive and relatively healthy.[19]

The Regulation of Trucking
Interprovincial trucking was technically put under the jurisdiction of the

CTC in the National Transportation Act of 1967. However, the power to restrict entry and regulate rates has never been assumed by the federal government. Before this can be done, the federal government has to take back the power to regulate extraprovincial undertakings, a power given to the provinces in 1953 (Janisch 1978:35).

All provinces except Alberta control entry (through the granting of operating authority and licences) and rates in intraprovincial trucking. Alberta truckers do not like the absence of regulation and have apparently tried to persuade the provincial government to assume its regulatory powers, so far to no avail.

The cost to the users of trucking services appears to be quite high. Various estimates show that rates in regulated provinces are 10 to 20 percent higher than those in Alberta (Sloss 1970; McLachlan 1971). That these higher rates are translated into high profits for the truckers is shown in a report (*The Financial Post,* 7 April 1979) of a recent investigation of the Ontario Highway Transport Board by the Standing Resources Development Transport Committee of the Ontario Legislature. In this hearing it was shown that trucking licences "are traded on a sort of a black market," and "several examples were given of permits which cost $700 to obtain from the government being sold for many thousands of dollars." The fact that people are willing to pay many "thousands of dollars" to gain entry into the industry is an indication that a trucking licence is a licence to make above-average profits. It is likely therefore that deregulation of provincial trucking would provide considerable benefits to users of transport services.

The New Transport Policy and Discriminatory Rates

Railway freight rates are an old grievance of the Canadian West, which has been resurrected again, most prominently at the Western Economic Opportunities Conference in Calgary in 1973. According to the National Transportation Act of 1967, railroads are free to set their rates within two limits: a lower limit of average variable cost and an upper limit of average variable cost plus 150 percent. In order for the upper limit to come into effect, a transport-user has to declare himself a captive shipper (he has no alternative mode of transportation). Competition from other modes is meant to regulate rates between these two limits.

Price discrimination is a common feature in most modes of transportation and is known in transport circles as "charging what the traffic will bear." This can be done if the transport firm has some form of monopoly power. For maximum profit, each commodity should be priced in accordance with the elasticity of demand for transportation; that is, a high elasticity of demand should result in a low freight rate and a low elasticity in a high freight rate. People in western Canada feel that they face relatively inelastic demand for transportation services as there is little competition from either water or trucking over the relatively long distances involved. As a result, the West feels that it has to bear a disproportionate share of the fixed costs of the railways.

There are also complaints relating to specific freight charges. For example, it is argued that the rates for exporting raw materials are lower than the rates for exporting processed products, a situation which encourages production close to the market (in eastern Canada) with subsequent loss in manufacturing jobs for Westerners.[20] The Crow's Nest Pass rates are both damned and lauded: they are lauded, since they have assisted the grain farmer in getting a high payment for his grain (he gets the Chicago price minus transport costs); they are damned, since the higher grain prices are translated into high cost of feedgrains for the livestock producer and are therefore killing this industry (see Chapter 1).

However, the demand for transportation is not necessarily inelastic because there is little competition in transport. If the demand and supply for a product is very elastic, the transport firm cannot assess a high freight rate, or the commodity will be priced out of the market and the transport firm will earn no revenue. Indeed, careful analysis shows that many of the West's complaints are difficult to substantiate (see Chapter 11). Further, even if commodities exported from the West are assessed at high freight rates, the welfare implications of this are not straightforward. It is possible that the burden will fall more on the eastern consumer and/or producer, depending on the relative elasticities of supply and demand. It is almost impossible to prove who suffers the most.[21]

It is probably true to say that freight rates have received too prominent a position among all the factors that are assumed to be important in the development of manufacturing in western Canada—with one exception: the Crow Rates (see Chapter 1).

The Carriage of International Trade

This section will look at the problems in deep-sea cargo transport. However, this does not give a complete picture of the carriage of international trade, as some cargo is carried by air, and in Canada's trade with the United States little is carried by sea; most moves by rail, truck or lake carrier. (Many of the problems encountered in road and rail transport have already been discussed.) It is sufficient to say that the problems encountered in the American part of the journey are similar to those in the Canadian part, but often the interaction of two regulatory agencies exacerbates the problems.

There are three broad sectors in deep-sea shipping: liquid bulk carried by tankers; dry bulk (e.g., ores and grains) carried by bulk carriers and general cargo carried by liners. The services of tankers and bulk carriers are purchased on the open market at competitive prices; the cost of a time or a voyage charter is set on exchanges similar to commodity exchanges. Liner services, in contrast, are usually cartelized and controlled by a shipping conference, which is an association of shipping lines that operates in regular traffic on a given route. Each route usually has two conferences, one inbound and one outbound. Each conference attempts to limit entry, fix prices and bind its customers to its services through loyalty contracts. These have an effect similar to that of agreed charges in railway operations, whereby a transport-user receives a lower rate in return for a promise to give continued business to the railway or the shipping line.

In terms of tonnages loaded from Canadian ports, most is bulk cargo (grains 20 percent, ores 30 percent, other bulk cargo 40 percent), with liner cargo accounting for only 10 percent of tonnage. On the import side, petroleum products make up 40 percent of the tonnage, coal and other bulk cargoes 50 percent, and liners 10 percent. However, the share of liner cargo in the *value* of exports and imports is substantially higher than 10 percent, as liner cargo consists of relatively highly valued manufactured and semimanufactured products.

Recent developments in shipping have resulted in larger and more specialized ships (for example, supertankers, LNG (liquid natural gas) carriers, reefers (refrigerated cargo carriers), container ships, OBO (ore/bulk/oil) carriers, and other types of combination carriers). These changes in ship design have resulted in corresponding changes in port use and port design. The importance of small inland ports and also inner-city ports has declined. Many of the new ships cannot clear the St. Lawrence Seaway, and for others it is more economical to unload at Halifax or Montreal and to rail the cargo to its final destination. Inner-city ports are no longer suitable as they cannot provide storage facilities for containers, nor do they have room to accommodate the large bulk carriers or tankers. These factors have led to the decline of the port at Toronto and other Great Lakes ports and boosted the development of the Maritime ports (Halifax and Saint John).

Canadian Shipping Policy: Investment

In 1878, Canada was fourth among the shipowning nations of the world in terms of tonnage owned and operated. It was not until the development of steel hulls that Canada started to lose her competitive advantage, largely because she had no steel industry. By the early twentieth century tonnage had declined by 50 percent. In 1917, the federal government launched a large shipbuilding program, with the ships to be operated by a crown corporation: the Canadian Government Merchant Marine. In the 1920s heavy losses were incurred because of rising construction costs, falling freight rates and the lack of inbound cargo. By 1936 the total losses from the venture had reached $95 million—a large sum of money at the time.

World War II again altered the situation. Four hundred ships were built, many of which were owned and operated through Park Steamships, a fully owned government subsidiary. By the end of the war Canada again had the fourth largest merchant marine in the world. In 1945, the government announced that it planned to sell as many ships as it could and to "lay up" the surplus. However, the purchasers of the ships were under obligation not to transfer any to foreign registry. To ensure the operation of a Canadian fleet, the Canadian Maritime Commission was established, whose terms of reference included finding methods whereby the fleet could be maintained on a permanent basis.

The death blow fell when the United States put up for sale at very low prices hundreds of merchant ships built during the war. This made it possible for other countries to venture into shipping. Freight rates fell. The Canadian government made it clear it was not prepared to subsidize the fleet, and made it possible for shipowners to transfer their ships to British registry, presumably to take advantage of the low wage rates. Since then, Canada has been without a merchant marine. The government has pursued a *laissez-faire* policy in the belief that it will provide Canadians with shipping services at the lowest possible cost, since scarce public funds have been diverted from shipping to other purposes, and since Canada has been able to benefit from the supposedly low freight rates resulting from heavy subsidization of foreign shipping from parent governments.

It should be added, however, that even though Canada has no deep-sea fleet, many Canadian corporations have an active interest in shipping, usually pursued through subsidiaries. For example, Canadian Pacific has two subsidiaries: CP Bermuda Ltd., involved in charter operations; and CP Steamships Ltd., which owns and operates container ships under the British flag. CN has acquired an interest in the Canadian-owned Cast shipping group, involved in a regular non-conference service on the North Atlantic.

Since the demise of the merchant marine, there has been pressure on the federal government to revive the fleet, by making it possible for ships to operate under the Canadian flag (through tax concessions and/or direct subsidies), or by direct investment. The renewed interest in a fleet can probably be attributed to nationalism, reinforced by strong pressure from the Seafarer's International Union which has even guaranteed a ten-year strike-free period in the event of a fleet—and a powerful shipping lobby. Recent developments in world shipping markets have also cast doubt on the wisdom of a continued *laissez-faire* policy.

During the last two decades, Third World countries have built up merchant fleets, frequently with massive government assistance. There are several reasons for this. In liner shipping, Third World countries have felt that they have been exploited by western-dominated shipping conferences, and therefore the only way out is to have one's own ships. Another reason is that shipping is seen as a good earner of scarce foreign exchange. A third reason may be national pride. Some cynics argue that during the last few years, shipping has appeared on the list of Third World status symbols which include steel mills, national airlines and Sheraton hotels.

Heavy investment in shipping has had success in some countries (Brazil and India) but not in others. If a government has a lot of money and prestige invested in ships, it is going to make certain that the ships do not sail empty. This attitude has led to increased use of various cargo reservation policies (flag discrimination), whereby a country's own fleet is guaranteed a share in the carriage of exports and/or imports. Cargo reservation rules (the so-called 40−40−20 rule) have been embedded in the Code of Conduct for Shipping Conferences adopted by the United Nations' Conference on Trade and Development.[22] This code is not yet ratified, but it is likely that it will be.

For a country with no merchant marine these developments are worrying, particularly as cargo reservation rules are threatening to spread into the chartering markets. Flag discrimination is likely to lead to higher costs for users of shipping services for it prevents the exporter or importer from shopping around for the best deal. It may also lead to higher cost for the lines in that they will often have to sail with empty holds, not being able to pick up backhauls.

The Liberal government's response to pressure that something had to be done about shipping was to commission studies. First there was the Menzies report commissioned by the Canadian Transport Commission and published in 1970. Menzies (and Associates) used cost-benefit analysis to show that bulk vessels with an asset cost in excess of $10 million (1970 prices) were potentially of economic benefit to Canada, assuming that freight rates were higher than or equal to the 1970 rates and that Canadian seamen would not seek wage parity with their U.S. counterparts. Next, the Ministry of Transport commissioned Howard Darling, a former chairman of the Water Transport Committee of the Canadian Transport Commission to review Canadian shipping policy. The Darling report, released in 1974, called for a more active and aggressive shipping policy, outlining five areas of potential concern for Canada: the movement of Canadian resources, the role of Canadian ships in arctic development, the implications for Canada of increased concentration in container-shipping, the consequences of flag discrimination, and the implications of recent trends on Canadian ports. The report also gave a qualified approval to the gradual revival of the fleet. The third report was a massive study by Alcan Shipping Services Limited and the Economist Intelligence Unit (1977) prepared for Transport Canada. This was a commercial study showing that there was a commercial potential for shipping services on certain trade routes, such as the coal trade between Vancouver and Japan, the grain trade between the St. Lawrence and Europe and container trades between eastern Canada and Europe.

Early in 1979, the Liberal Minister of Transport released *A Shipping Policy for Canada* (Canada, 1979), a report outlining all the difficulties Canada is facing in the shipping markets as a user of shipping services because of flag discrimination and the decreased freedom of the seas. It referred to the Alcan study and another study by the Ministry of Transport in which the Alcan results were expanded into a full cost-benefit analysis (including social costs and benefits as well as private costs and benefits). This latter study found that costs exceeded benefits for all of the commercially viable trade routes, *given a relatively free market in international shipping*. This is a strange assumption to make in view of present trends. The conclusion in the study is therefore a reaffirmation of the principle of a free market for shipping services. However, the report does outline some measures to help deal with the problem of flag discrimination: "resistance" to any proposals that would deny Canada access to commercial shipping services, the possible designation of foreign shipping lines as Canadian and giving the government broad powers to obtain information from foreign shipping lines.

In the federal election campaign of 1979, Joe Clark promised to work towards a revival of a fleet, an election promise that apparently was honoured by the Conservative government. At the time of their defeat, they had been expected to present a comprehensive package of tax concessions designed to resurrect a fleet.

Canadian Shipping Policy: Regulation

Economic regulation of shipping is usually restricted to shipping conferences, since the charter markets are competitive and are therefore regulated by the market. Shipping conferences are cartels which are illegal under the anti-trust laws of most countries. However, conferences have invariably been exempted from anti-trust laws on grounds that competition in liner shipping would be ruinous, or would lead to instability in freight rates. The claim that competition would be ruinous cannot be substantiated, whereas the claim that freight rates would fluctuate is probably true. The relevant question, however, is stability at what price? Several studies have shown that conferences push up rates to monopoly levels and frequently act as a deterrent to technological innovation.[23]

Canadian regulation of conferences goes back to the so-called Helga Dan incident in 1959. The Helga Dan was a non-conference ship especially fitted for winter navigation in northern waters. Most other ships did not use the St. Lawrence in winter because of ice conditions, and members of conferences moved their services to the Maritimes during the winter months. The Helga Dan was invited by the Industrial and

Trade Bureau of Greater Quebec to sail between the port of Quebec and the United Kingdom in February. In order to use the services of the ship, some shippers had to obtain permission from the Canada-United Kingdom Freight Conference covering the trade, as they had signed loyalty contracts with this conference. The conference refused to release the shipper and a complaint was launched under the Combines Investigation Act, which led to an enquiry before the Restrictive Trade Practices Commission. In 1965, a report was issued in which the commission not only investigated the specific complaints, but also tried to evaluate the whole conference system (Canada 1965). It found that conferences indeed hindered competition and took advantage of shippers. The main brunt of the criticism fell on the use of loyalty contracts by which the shipper received a lower rate in return for a commitment to ship all of his goods with the conference. However, as in most other countries, the commission did not want to apply the Combines Investigation Act, as it felt competition would result in instability. Nor did the commission recommend rate regulation, the reason possibly being that it felt that because of Canadian dependence on foreign shipping, any rate regulation might result in lines' threatening to withdraw from Canadian trades.[24]

The Shipping Conference Exemption Act of 1970 closely followed the recommendations of the commission. The act allowed conferences to restrict entry and control prices, and legalized loyalty contracts, provided the difference between the contract and the non-contract rate did not exceed 15 percent. It also required all contracts and rates to be filed with the Canadian Transport Commission and to be made accessible to the public. In addition, the government recommended the establishment of a shipper's council, the purpose of which was to strengthen the bargaining position of Canadian shippers through the creation of a bilateral monopoly.

The Exemption Act came up for renewal in March 1979. The Water Transport Committee invited briefs from shippers and the industry concerning the need for changes. Several briefs were submitted by conferences in support of the act—which is scarcely surprising (Canadian Transport Commission 1978). Few briefs were received from shipper interests. The Atlantic Provinces Transportation Commission expressed dissatisfaction with conference port pricing: the same freight rate is applicable in Montreal as it is in Saint John and Halifax, despite the longer sailing distance to Montreal. A brief from a shipper complained bitterly about the lack of alternatives to conference services in the Maritimes. Non-conference service is available from Montreal (but not from the Maritimes), a situation which has held down rates on Montreal and central Canadian cargo. The Canadian Shippers' Council does not negotiate as a body with the conferences on rates, making it an ineffective organization to serve as a countervailing power to the conference; instead, each company represented in the organization does its own negotiating.

Since there was no real public outcry for change (except from the Maritimes), the Exemption Act was renewed with few changes. The present act specifies that if a shipper is unhappy with the rate he receives from a conference, he can invoke Section 23 of the National Transportation Act. Under Section 23, a person may appeal to the Canadian Transport Commission to have a rate changed and the Canadian Transport Commission is instructed to conduct an investigation of the rate if a case has been made to the effect that the rate of a carrier may prejudicially affect the public interest. It should be added that any case brought up under Section 23 appears to take an inordinate amount of time because of difficulties in defining the public interest; of the eight cases that have been brought up since 1967, only one has been given a final decision (McManus 1978:224).

The public interest would have been served better if the act had made a more serious attempt to safeguard competition (Bryan and Kotowitz 1978). Competition in Canadian liner trades on the North Atlantic is decreasing, as non-conference competitors either have disappeared, or seem to be contemplating joining a conference.[25] There is at present no effective safeguard against rates set at monopoly levels, and Canadian shippers appear to be apathetic. Apparently many shippers would rather sell f.o.b. (free on board) than c.i.f. (cost, insurance and freight) because of the documentation involved in arranging shipping; they may therefore not be aware of the freights that have to be paid.

Summary and Conclusions

The performance of the transportation industry is of great importance for a country as large as Canada. Indeed, the transportation sector is large by international standards (5.4 percent of GDP; see Table 2), and a significant proportion of total costs of industrial production is made up of transport costs (see Chapter 6, p. 178). Greater efficiency in transportation would therefore yield substantial gains for Canadian producers and consumers. The survey in this chapter has shown that on the one hand efforts to increase competition through deregulation or more active use of the Combines Investigation Act could be particularly beneficial in airline passenger transport, in trucking and in deep-sea shipping. On the other hand, increased regulatory control or interference may be necessary in urban passenger transportation, an area in which social costs and benefits deviate significantly from private costs and benefits.

Transport investments are another controversial area to which few easy solutions can be found and in which cost-benefit studies are plentiful. Often the cost-benefit studies are less than adequate as they do not consider alternatives to investments; for example, building new airports is not necessarily the best solution to airport congestion problems. Also, cost-benefit studies cannot adequately deal with the non-monetary benefits and costs as in, for example, the case of a merchant marine. The main benefit of a fleet may well be national security, which none of the available studies has considered.

NOTES

1. See Posner 1971, 1975. For a summary see Trebing 1976.
2. See Jordan 1970.
3. For a discussion, see Darling 1974.
4. A person can still appeal to the Canadian Transport Commission to have a rate changed under section 23 of the act, and the Commission can order the rate changed if it finds the rate prejudicial to the public interest.
5. For a survey, see Frankena 1979:17.
6. See Frankena 1979:16.
7. This was first suggested by Walters 1961.
8. However, deregulation would adversely affect present licence-holders, as the value of the licence would drop to zero. They would have to be compensated for this loss.
9. See Frankena 1979:93−7.
10. Lukasiewicz (1979) makes the point that a Canadian taxpayer pays more for the support of railways than a taxpayer in any other country in the West, despite having the poorest quality of service.
11. In a model which does not include a discomfort index, Gronau (1970) estimates the switching point from other modes to air to be 590 miles. But in a market with low air fares, the switching point may be as low as 200 miles (Eads 1975:39).
12. Dewees and Waverman 1977. A recent experiment in Sweden indicates that the fare elasticity of train travel may not be as low as expected. In 1979, rail fares were halved on many routes, which led to a remarkable increase in passenger travel. The national railway is even expected to make a profit for the first time in many years on these routes.
13. For an account of the hearings, see Kane 1979.
14. This argument implies that the total elasticity of demand for air travel is zero, which is hardly realistic.
15. Apparently cost-benefit analysis is not used by the Air Transport Administration, only traffic forecasts.

16. See University of Toronto—York University 1978:63-111.
17. *Ibid.* A small amount of cargo is still transported between Valley-field, Hamilton, Windsor, Sarnia, and Thunder Bay by package freighters owned by Canada Steamship Lines.
18. The tow-boat operators on the West Coast would not agree. They feel that the federally imposed safety regulations are excessive. (University of Toronto—York University 1978:132).
19. However, spokesmen for the Great Lakes shipping industry feel that grain rates are not high enough for the operators to get an adequate rate of return, the reason being the monopsony position of the Canadian Wheat Board (University of Toronto—York University 1978:85). The industry has, however, benefited from federal subsidies to shipbuilding.
20. For a summary of the arguments, see Norrie 1979.
21. For a detailed analysis, see Casas and Kotowitz 1976. A recent empirical study has demonstrated that the Crow Rate is subsidizing not only western rapeseed producers but also Japanese rapeseed consumers (Furtan, Nagy and Storey 1979).
22. United Nations 1974. Forty percent of cargo was reserved for the exporting country's fleet, 40 percent for the importing countries, and 20 for outsiders.
23. For a survey, see Bryan and Kotowitz 1978:13—16.
24. An earlier attempt in 1923 to control grain rates on the Great Lakes resulted in American carriers withdrawing their services in protest (Bryan and Kotowitz 1978:80).
25. Cast Line provided a real threat to the conferences operating on the North Atlantic for several years, and probably kept the rates quite low. Recently, the president of Cast was asked if the company might not become a member of a conference. His answer was, "No it is much too early to talk about our joining the Conference. But I think there is now mutual trust between us and an appreciation of each others' problems" (*Seatrade* Aug. 1979:107).

BIBLIOGRAPHY

Alcan Shipping Services Ltd. and the Economist Intelligence Unit Ltd. *Shipping Options for Canadian International Deep-Sea Trade.* Prepared for Transport Canada. Mimeo 1977.
Averch, J. and L.L. Johnson, "Behaviour of the Firm under Regulatory Constraint." *American Economic Review* (52), 1962, pp. 1053—69.
Baumol, W.J. and A.K. Klevorick. "Input Choices and Rate of Return

Regulation: An Overview of the Discussion." *The Bell Journal of Economics and Management Science* (1), 1970, pp. 162–90.

Borins, Sandford F. "Self-Regulation and the Canadian Air Transport Administration: The Case of Pickering Airport." In W.T. Stanbury (ed.), *Studies on Regulation in Canada*. Toronto: Institute for Public Policy and Butterworths, 1979, pp. 131–53.

Bryan, I.A. *Canadian Deep-Sea Shipping Policy and the Merchant Marine Issue,* Transportation Paper No. 3. York University-University of Toronto Joint Program in Transportation, 1977.

_____ and Y. Kotowitz. *Shipping Conferences in Canada.* Research Monograph No. 2, Research Branch, Bureau of Competition Policy. Ottawa: Supply and Services, 1978.

Canada. *An Act to Amend the National Transportation Act* (and other legislation) (Bill C-33), 1977.

_____. Ministry of Transport. *A Shipping Policy for Canada.* Ottawa: Supply and Services, 1979.

_____. *National Transportation Act.* (R.S.C. 1970, N–17), 1967.

_____. Restrictive Trade Practices Commission. *Shipping Conference Arrangements and Practices.* Ottawa: Queen's Printer, 1965.

Canadian Tax Foundation. *The National Finances 1980–81.* Toronto: Canadian Tax Foundation, 1981.

Canadian Transport Commission. *Transport Review, Trends and Selected Issues.* Ottawa: Supply and Services, 1979.

_____. *The Shipping Conference Exemption Act.* Report of the Water Transport Committee. Ottawa, 1978.

Casas, F.R. and Y. Kotowitz. *Transport Subsidies and Regional Redistribution Policies.* Canadian Transport Commission. Mimeo 1976.

Darling H.J. "Transport Policy in Canada: The Struggle of Ideologies vs. Realities." In K.W. Studnicki-Gizbert (ed.), pp. 3–47, *Issues in Canadian Transport Policy.* Toronto: Macmillan, 1974.

_____. *The Elements of an International Shipping Policy for Canada.* Ministry of Transport. Mimeo, 1974.

Dewees, D.N. *Economics and Public Policy: The Automobile Pollution Case.* Cambridge: MIT Press, 1974.

_____ "Simulations of Traffic Congestion in Toronto." *Transportation Research* (12), 1978, pp. 53–61.

_____ and L. Waverman. "Energy Conservation: Policies for the Transport Sector." *Canadian Public Policy* (III), 1977, pp. 171–86.

Eads, George C. "Competition in the Domestic Trunk Airline Industry: Too Much or Too Little." In A. Phillips (ed.), *Promoting Competition in Regulated Markets.* Washington D.C.: The Brookings Institution, 1975, pp. 13–55.

Economic Council of Canada. *Reforming Regulation* Ottawa: Supply and Services, 1981.

Frankena, Mark. "The Demand for Urban Bus Transit in Canada." *Journal of Transport Economics and Policy* (7), 1978, pp. 215–30.

———— *Urban Transportation Economics.* Toronto: Butterworths, 1979.

Furtan, W.H., J.G. Nagy and G.G. Storey. "The Impact on the Canadian Rapeseed Industry from Changes in Transport and Tariff Rates." *American Journal of Agricultural Economics* (61), 1979, pp. 238–48.

Gaudry, M. *A Study of Aggregate Bi-Modal Urban Travel Supply, Demand and Network Behaviour Using Simultaneous Equations with Autoregressive Residuals,* Centre de Recherche sur les Transports, Université de Montréal, 1978.

Gillen, D.W. "Estimation and Specification of the Effects of Parking Costs on Urban Transportation Mode Choice." *Journal of Urban Economics* (4), 1977, pp. 186–99.

Green, C. *Canadian Industrial Organization and Policy,* Toronto: McGraw-Hill Ryerson, 1980.

Gronau, Reuben. "The Effect of Traveling Time on the Demand for Transportation." *Journal of Political Economy* (78), 1970, pp. 377–94.

Haritos, Zis. *Rational Road Pricing Policies in Canada.* Canadian Transport Commission. Mimeo, 1973.

Janisch, H.N. *The Regulatory Process of the Canadian Transport Commission. A Study Prepared for the Law Reform Commission of Canada.* Ottawa: Supply and Services, 1978.

Jordan, W.A. *Airline Regulations in America: Effects and Imperfections.* Baltimore: John Hopkin's Press, 1970.

Kane, Gregory. "Canadian Consumers Learn Their ABC's." In G.B. Reschenthaler and B. Roberts (eds.), *Perspectives on Canadian Airline Regulation.* Toronto: Institute for Research on Public Policy and Butterworths, 1979, pp. 43–65.

Lukasiewicz, J. "Public Policy and Technology. Passenger Rail in Canada as an Issue in Modernization." *Canadian Public Policy* (V), 1979, pp. 518–33.

Maister, David H. "Technical and Organizational Change in a Regulated Industry: The Case of Canadian Grain Transport." In W.T. Stanbury (ed.), *Studies of Regulation in Canada.* Toronto: Institute for Research on Public Policy and Butterworths, 1978, pp. 153–209.

McLachlan, D.L. "Canadian Trucking Regulation." Paper presented to the Canadian Economics Association, June 1971.

McManus, John "On the New Transportation Policy after Ten Years." In W.T. Stanbury (eds.), *Studies on Regulation in Canada.* Toronto: Institute for Research on Public Policy and Butterworths, 1978, pp. 209–31.

Menzies, Hedlin and Associates. *Canadian Merchant Marine — Analysis of Economic Potential.* Canadian Transport Commission. Mimeo, 1970.

Munro, J.M. "Highways in British Columbia — Economics and Politics." *Canadian Journal of Economics* (VIII), 1978, pp. 192–204.

Norrie, K. "Western Economic Grievances: An Overview with Special Reference to Freight Rates." *In Proceedings of the Workshop on the Political Economy of Confederation Nov. 8-10, 1978.* Ottawa: Supply and Services, 1979, pp. 199–235.

Posner, R.A. "Theories of Economic Regulation." *The Bell Journal of Economics and Management Science* (5), 1974, pp. 335–758.

_____"The Social Costs of Monopoly and Regulation." *Journal of Political Economy* (83), 1975, pp. 807–27.

Reschenthaler, G.B. "Direct Regulation in Canada: Some Policies and Problems." In W.T. Stanbury (ed.), *Studies on Regulation in Canada.* Toronto: Institute for Research on Public Policy and Butterworths, 1978, pp. 37–113.

_____"The Canadian Transport Commission and the ABC Issue: Time for Regulatory Reform." In G.B. Reschenthaler and B. Roberts (eds.), *Perspectives on Canadian Airline Regulation.* Toronto: Institute for Research on Public Policy and Butterworths, 1979, pp. 125–39.

_____and Bruce Roberts (eds.), *Perspectives on Canadian Airline Regulation.* Toronto: Institute for Public Policy and Butterworths, 1979.

Schreiner, John. *Transportation, The Evolution of Canada's Networks.* Toronto: McGraw-Hill Ryerson, 1972.

Sloss, J. "Regulation of Motor Freight Transportation: A Quantitative Evaluation of Policy." The *Bell Journal of Economics and Management Science* (1), 1970, pp. 327–66.

Studnicki-Gizbert, K.W. *Transport Policy — Theory and Practice.* Canadian Transport Commission. Mimeo, 1975.

Trebing, Harry, M. "The Chicago School vs. Public Utility Regulation." *Journal of Economic Issues* (10), 1976, pp. 97–126.

United Nations. *United Nations Conference of Plenipotentiaries on a Code of Conduct for Liner Conferences.* Final Act and Annexes, TD/CODE/11/Rev 1. 1974.

University of Toronto–York University, Joint Program in Transportation. *Marine Transportation Policy Project, Final Report.* Research Report No. 48, 1978.

Walters, A.A. "The Theory and Measurement of Private and Social Costs of Highway Congestion." *Econometrica* (29), 1961, pp. 676–99.

Westmacott, Martin W. "The Canadian Transport Commission, Freight Rates, and the Public Interest." In K. Ruppenthal and W.T. Stanbury (eds.), pp. 49–93, *Transportation Policy: Regulation, Competition and the Public Interest.* Vancouver: Centre for Transport Studies and UBC Press, 1976.

PART II

The Distribution of Income

With the slowing down of economic growth in the industrialized world, income distribution issues have become the focus of both economic and political debate. In economics there has been renewed interest in theories of income distribution and in the effectiveness of policies to redistribute income, be it between people or between regions. In addition, the need for redistribution measures has been attacked by the followers of the "new (neo) conservatism."

The new conservatism has as its ideological basis the Chicago school, centred on Milton Friedman and his writings, but it also goes back to the writings of Hayek.[1] The new conservatives believe strongly in the efficiency of the free market. They suggest that the market is competitive and is therefore the most efficient means of allocating scarce resources in the production of goods and goods among people. A free market is alleged to give maximum amount of freedom to people. The consumer is free to choose between sellers; if one seller asks too high a price for an inferior product, the consumer can choose another seller or product. If employees do not like the way they are treated by an employer, they are free to leave and to find other jobs.[2] Nobody is coerced; everybody is free to choose in a pure capitalist system. Any interference with the market mechanism in the form of regulation would lead to inefficiencies and therefore to a wasteful use of resources.

The new conservatives have also joined forces with the supply-side economists. The basic tenet of supply-side economics is that too much emphasis has been placed on demand management. A more effective way of curing inflation and unemployment would be to increase the supply of goods and services by improving productivity. The best way to increase productivity is to remove all the obstacles to a person's earning an honest dollar. Taxes, in particular, are seen to be the culprit of low productivity and inflation. Taxes also interfere with the freedom to choose, as the government chooses how to spend some of the taxpayer's hard-earned money.[3] It is contended that if income taxes, capital gains taxes and corporate taxes were cut, people would work harder and invest more.

The new conservatives also hold that government expenditures are inflationary and expenditures on social welfare programs wasteful; that too many people cheat and that many government programs and services could be administered more efficiently by the private sector. They contend that regional policy is ineffective as it works against the market, which in the end would automatically cure regional disparities by inducing people to migrate. For these reasons, government expenditures should be cut. The shortfall in aggregate demand would be quickly filled by an expansion of the private sector.

Galbraith (1981) argues that the rise of the new conservatism threatens the economic and political consensus which has existed in most industrialized countries since World War II. The consensus centred on three principles: (1) there should be macroeconomic management of the economy to minimize unemployment and inflation; (2) government should provide services not available from the private sector at prices that most people can afford (health care, urban transportation and low-income housing); and (3) government programs such as unemployment insurance, welfare, pensions, medical insurance, job safety, should be available to individuals who, through circumstances beyond their own control, have become disadvantaged. Galbraith argues that if this consensus should break down completely, we can expect a period of increased social and economic unrest, not a society of increased living standards and freedom for all.

In the following three chapters the distribution of income between people and between provinces are discussed. The second aspect of distribution is as important as the first, since the survival of Canada as a nation depends on the satisfactory solution of regional income distribution.

NOTES

1. See Friedman 1972; Friedman and Friedman 1980; and Hayek 1944.
2. Many people have serious reservations about this view of the capitalist system. Many people see the capitalist system as dominated by big corporations and big unions, in which case the freedom to choose may be illusory. Galbraith is the foremost proponent of this view.
3. By the same token, however, very poor people surely have a limited

freedom of choice: If social programs were slashed the choice may be between buying bread or dying of starvation. Many people would agree that the free-to-choose philosophy implies freedom of choice for the rich, but not for the poor.

BIBLIOGRAPHY

Galbraith, J.K. "The Conservative Onslaught." In David Crane (ed.), *Beyond Monetarists. Post-Keynesian Alternatives to Rampant Inflation, Low Growth and High Unemployment*. Ottawa: Canadian Institute for Economic Policy, 1981.

Hayek, Friedrich A. *The Road to Serfdom*. Chicago: University of Chicago Press, 1944.

Friedman, M. *Capitalism and Freedom*. Chicago: University of Chicago Press, 1962.

_____ and R. Friedman. *Free To Choose*. New York: Harcourt Brace Jovanovich, 1980.

CHAPTER 9

The Rich and the Poor: People

Most governments regard equitable distribution of income as being a desirable national goal, a goal usually supported by the public. Yet nobody is willing to define what constitutes an equitable distribution of income, perhaps because the answer necessarily rests on value judgements. However, most people would agree that the present income distribution in Canada is not equitable and that it should be changed. There are considerable pockets of poverty and many people cannot believe they still exist. For example, conditions on some Indian reservations in northern Alberta and northern Ontario are similar to conditions encountered in parts of the Third World. A radio program on CBC's *Sunday Morning* (19 Dec. 1980) reported that children, as well as local transients, line up at the soup kitchens in Winnipeg. In our society of relative affluence, these facts are indeed a disgrace. Article 25 of the United Nations' Universal Declaration of Human Rights states:

> Everyone has the right to a standard of living adequate for the health and well-being of himself and of his family, including food, clothing, housing, medical care and necessary social services, and the right to security in the event of unemployment, sickness, disability, widowhood, old age, or other lack of livelihood in circumstances beyond his control.

In this chapter, the present distribution of income will be examined, with particular emphasis on the poor, as well as the causes of poverty and possible cures. The chapter concludes with a discussion of government policies.

The Size Distribution of Income

The most commonly used measure of income distribution is the size distribution of income. In contrast to the functional distribution which measures how much income goes to labour and how much goes to capital, the size distribution measures the share of income each income class receives. The size distribution is achieved by ranking all incomes in ascending order and dividing the population into five (or ten) equal groups (quintiles or deciles). The percentage of total income earned by each group is then calculated. In 1979, the lowest quintile calculated for families earned 5.8 percent of total income, the second lowest 12.9 percent, the third lowest 18.6 percent, the second highest 24.5 percent and the highest 38.2 percent. This means that in 1979 the top 20 percent of the population of families took home 38.2 percent of total income (see Table 14). As a standard of reference, if the distribution of income were perfectly equal, each quintile would earn an equal share (20 percent) of the total. Statistics Canada also gives information on the upper limits of income quintiles. Table 15 shows that if your family income was less than $11,155 in 1979, your family belonged to the poorest 20 percent of Canadian families. If your family income exceeded $33,000 you belonged to the top 20 percent.

The size distribution of income is usually illustrated diagrammati-

TABLE 14
Income Distribution by Size, 1979 (preliminary estimates)

	Families	Unattached individuals
Lowest quintile	5.8	3.9
Second quintile	12.9	8.6
Third quintile	18.6	15.9
Fourth quintile	24.5	25.4
Highest quintile	38.2	46.2
Total	100.0	100.0

Source: Statistics Canada. *Income Distribution by Size in Canada* (Cat. 13-206).

TABLE 15
Upper Limits of Income Quintiles, 1979 (preliminary estimates)

	Families	Unattached individuals
Lowest quintile	$11,155	$ 3,432
Second quintile	$18,629	$ 5,669
Third quintile	$24,887	$10,394
Fourth quintile	$32,998	$15,868

Source: *Ibid.*

cally by a Lorenz curve. The Lorenz curve plots the cumulative distribution on a graph, with the quintiles on one axis and income shares on the other (see Figure 3). If income distribution were absolutely equal, the Lorenz curve would fall along the diagonal, since each quintile would receive 20 percent. If the distribution of income were absolutely unequal, all incomes would accrue to the top income class (everybody received 0, except Joe Smith who received the whole GNP) and the Lorenz curve would follow the bottom line to the 100 percent point and then take off vertically; It would have the shape of an inverted L.

Sometimes the information from the size distribution and the corresponding Lorenz curve is collapsed into one number: the Gini coefficient. The Gini coefficient is a measure of the distance of the Lorenz curve from the diagonal. More precisely, it is a measure of the proportion the area A takes up of the total area A + B (see Figure 3). Corresponding to the extreme positions of the Lorenz curve, an absolutely equal income distribution would imply a Gini coefficient of 0 whereas an absolutely unequal distribution would have a coefficient of 1. There-

FIGURE 3
The Lorenz Curve, Families, 1979

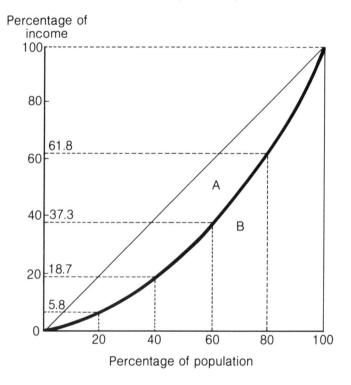

fore, the closer the Gini coefficient is to 0, the more equal is the income distribution.

Most studies show that there has been little change, if any, in income distribution in Canada in the postwar period, at least as measured by the Gini coefficient which fluctuated between 0.37 and 0.40 (see Table 16). Of course it could be argued that because many low-income people are old or young, the fact that the Gini coefficient has not changed could merely reflect that changes in the age distribution have cancelled changes for the better in the income distribution. Attempts have been made to correct this by using Paglin's (1975) adaptation of the Gini coefficient. Paglin replaces the 45q line of absolute equality with an age-adjusted line of absolute equality—where equality would mean that all persons in the same age group have the same income. The justification for this procedure is, given that society wants equality, that equality should not necessarily be extended across age groups: a young person or a very old person does not have the same income needs as a head of household with several children. Armstrong, Friesen and Miller (1977) argue that according to their results based on the Paglin method, the distribution of income in Canada has improved. Subsequently, Needleman (1979) has cast doubts on the statistical accu-

TABLE 16
Gini Coefficients for Families and Unattached Individuals Combined,
Selected Years

Year	Gini coefficient
1951	.390
1954	.377
1957	.381
1959	.371
1961	.368
1965	.370
1967	.379
1969	.386
1971	.400
1972	.395
1973	.392
1974	.389
1975	.392
1976	.402
1977	.388

Source: Ross, D.P. *The Canadian Fact Book on Income Distribution*, Table 8.

racy of the Paglin measure, arguing that it does not properly separate the age distribution. Shedd (1979) has also argued against it on theoretical grounds. The conclusion still holds that any changes in the distribution of income have been minimal. The question is why? After all, the income tax system is progressive and we spend a considerable amount of money to assist low-income people.[1]

The income tax system is indeed progressive: it taxes the affluent at a higher rate than the poor. However, not all taxes are income taxes. Various levels of government earn tax revenues through sales taxes, excise taxes and property taxes. These are not progressive; on the contrary, the poor pay a larger proportion of their income on sales and property taxes than the rich (the rich tend to save more, and therefore avoid paying some of these taxes). Gillespie (1964) showed that in 1961 the highest-income class paid 38.4 percent of its income in taxes, whereas the lowest-income class paid 60 percent. A later study based on 1969 data by Maslove (1972) showed that the total tax system was still regressive.

Given that the tax system does not appear to be an equalizing factor, transfers must be progressive (they must benefit the lower income groups proportionately more); otherwise income distribution would deteriorate. Table 17 gives some interesting information on which income groups receive what proportion of benefits. Some of the changes between 1971 and 1975 can be attributed to the change in age structure in the population. There were proportionately more old people in 1975 than in 1971. Many people in the lowest quintile are old and therefore receive pensions but not family allowances and unemployment insurance. Note that over one-fifth of unemployment insurance benefits and almost one-third of family allowance payments are received by the highest quintile! The benefits system appears to have become less progressive between 1971 and 1975, but it is still true to say that social security benefits are progressive.

The tax system and the benefits system taken together explain why income distribution has not improved. A mildly progressive benefits system cancels a mildly regressive tax structure. To have any effect on income distribution, the social security system has to be revamped and be made more selective.

The above discussion neglects the influence of wealth.[2] The distribution of income among families does not take into account income from capital gains, nor does it take into account the assets a family owns. The distribution of wealth and power in Canada obviously contributes to economic inequality. In 1975 there were eighteen families each with net worth of over $100 million and twenty families with a net worth in excess of $20 million (Newman 1975). The Gini coefficient of the total wealth distribution is 0.746, far more unequal than the distri-

TABLE 17

Distribution of Benefits before Taxes, Selected Programs, 1971 and 1975

Quintile	Family and youth allowances		Unemployment insurance		Canada and Quebec pensions		Old age security		Guaranteed income supplement		Total social security	
	1971	1975	1971	1975	1971	1975	1971	1975	1971	1975	1971	1975
Lowest	6.8	5.7	9.8	8.1	20.2	26.8	34.0	38.0	43.6	47.4	25.1	23.4
Second	15.0	12.6	24.5	22.0	30.2	30.8	32.6	31.3	34.4	33.1	28.9	25.2
Third	23.7	21.9	27.8	25.0	18.8	18.4	12.9	13.6	8.2	7.1	17.5	18.2
Fourth	26.4	27.6	22.0	22.6	11.7	12.7	9.5	8.2	6.6	5.6	14.2	16.2
Highest	28.1	32.2	15.9	22.3	19.1	11.3	11.0	8.9	7.2	6.8	14.3	17.0

Source: Cloutier J.E. *The Distribution of Benefits and Costs of Social Security in Canada*.
Note: The column for total social security includes all five programs as well as other forms of social assistance.

bution of income (Davies 1979). At present the tax structure does little to even out this inequality. Only 50 percent of capital gains are taxed. All provinces have abolished inheritance taxes, which means that the wealth is passed on intact to the next generation.

Who Are the Poor?

In order to identify the poor segment of the population, one has to define poverty. Poverty can be seen as absolute or relative: absolute compared to a minimum standard, or relative compared to other people. A poor person in Canada may be considered rich in some Third World countries, but a poor person in Canada may be worse off than a poor person in Scandinavia.

An ideal concept of poverty would take into account a person's current income, his or her likely future income and his or her assets—information which is usually not available. Instead, poverty is most commonly defined in relation to a cut-off point in monetary income: a poverty line. The cut-off point can be defined in absolute or relative terms. An example of an absolute poverty line is an income which provides an individual's or family's minimal requirements of food, clothing and shelter. A poverty line defined in this fashion would have little relation to the standard of living enjoyed by most Canadians. A relative poverty line, in contrast, is based on a comparison with the average living standard of the population, and is an estimate of the standard required for personal dignity and social survival. The latter approach would always—unless incomes were equalized—define some people as poor.

Several poverty lines have been established in Canada, but none has been accepted officially as *the* poverty line. The first, established in 1961 by Statistics Canada, defined poverty in an absolute fashion.[3] At that time Canadians spent an average of 50 percent of their income on food, clothing and shelter. Statistics Canada defined as poor a person who spent more than 70 percent of his income on basic necessities. In June 1978, the income of a family of four was below the poverty line if it was less than $8,226. Since 1961, the amount an average Canadian family spends on necessities has declined while the living standard has increased. The 1973 revision of the poverty line to a 62-percent cut-off point made the 1978 poverty-line income for a family of four $9,531. Statistics Canada has developed other poverty lines that are adjusted for the size of the area of residence.

The Canadian Council on Social Development and the Special Senate Committee on Poverty have attempted to establish relative poverty lines. The Council uses the Statistics Canada estimate of average family income based on a family of four. The poverty line is then set at 50 percent of average Canadian family income. The Senate Committee's method is slightly more complex and uses 56 percent as a floor. The two poverty lines calculated in this fashion were $10,605 and $11,876.

In 1976 the estimated number of poor people in Canada in 1976 ranged from 2.8 million (Statistics Canada revised poverty line) to 5.4 million (Senate Committee poverty line) (Caskie 1979:26). A poor family is most likely to live in Ontario, in a city of 500,000 or more and to be headed by a male (see Table 18). However, proportionately more poor families are headed by females. The head of the family is likely to be 25 to 34 years old, but proportionately more poor families have heads below 24 years of age and over 70. The largest proportion of both poor and nonpoor families have no children under 16, but the poor are more likely to have three or more children under 16 than the nonpoor. Most of the poor families are headed by persons who had not gone beyond grade 8, whereas most of the better off have had some high school education. Slightly less than 50 percent of poor family heads work, compared with 85 percent of the nonpoor heads. Most of the poor are in service occupations and most of the nonpoor in the professions. Most of the poor families have only one income-earner, whereas most other families have two. The major source of income for poor people is transfer payments.

Statistics for single unattached individuals are different in some respects. For example, two-thirds of the poor are women. The largest single-age group contains people over 70 years of age. Only 25 percent of poor individuals are in the labour force compared to 60 percent of others. According to an article in the *Canadian Homemaker's Magazine* (Sept. 1980), there are more than one million widowed and unmarried women over the age of 55 in Canada, at least two-thirds of whom can be regarded as poor. More than half of all married women between the ages 55 to 64 have no income at all and have been described as being "only one man away from poverty."

Causes and Possible Solutions to Poverty

The poor can be classified into four categories:
(a) Those who are poor because they are unemployed.
(b) Those who are poor because they cannot produce because of disability, old age, or because they have to look after small children.
(c) Those who are poor because they have not acquired sufficient skills or education to qualify for well-paying jobs. "Not only do the wage-earning poor hold low-paying jobs and suffer more and longer spells of unemployment, but they also tend to have hard, dirty, boring and low-prestige jobs with little or no chance for advancement" (Ross 1981:23).
(d) Those who are poor because they are discriminated against; that is,

TABLE 18
Percentage Distribution of Low-Income Families and Unattached Individuals, and of Other Families and Unattached Individuals, Selected Characteristics, 1979

	Families		Unattached Individuals	
	Low-Income	Others	Low-Income	Others
By Size of Family				
One	—	—	100	100
Two	42.5	34.4		
Three	23.3	22.6		
Four	17.8	24.6		
Five or over	16.5	18.4		
By Number of Children Under 16				
None	38.5	48.8	100	100
One	25.6	21.6		
Two	22.3	20.6		
Three	9.3	7.2		
Four or more	4.3	1.8		
By Province of Residence				
Atlantic	11.3	8.5	8.2	6.6
Quebec	30.1	26.4	28.0	21.2
Ontario	32.2	37.3	34.7	36.7
Prairie	17.7	16.6	16.9	20.0
B.C.	8.7	11.2	12.1	15.5
By Size of Area of Residence				
500,000 and over	31.5	30.9	36.6	37.2
100,000−499,990	22.8	24.8	23.6	27.9
30,000− 99,999	8.6	7.8	10.2	8.4
15,000− 29,999	6.6	5.7	6.3	6.0
Small urban areas	10.4	11.7	13.6	9.2
Rural areas	20.1	19.0	9.7	11.2
By Sex of Head				
Male	62.9	93.6	31.1	51.0
Female	37.1	6.4	68.9	49.0
By Age of Head				
24 and under	11.0	5.7	19.6	22.5
25−34	27.0	28.5	8.6	28.1

35–44	17.7	22.4	5.1	11.3
45–54	14.0	17.8	7.9	9.3
55–64	12.7	13.9	15.4	10.7
65–69	6.6	4.9	9.8	5.9
70 and over	11.1	6.8	33.6	12.3
By Employment Status of Head				
Employee	37.0	75.6	22.8	57.0
Employer or own account	13.5	8.7	2.6	3.4
Not in labour force	49.4	15.7	74.6	39.6

Source: Statistics Canada, *Income Distribution by Size in Canada* (13–206), Table 10.
Note: Low-income is defined as income falling below the Statistics Canada revised poverty line.

society does not allow them to participate to their full potential. Examples are Indians, Inuit and women. Lack of education can also be used to discriminate against a person. Even if a job requires only a grade 8 education, job screening is frequently done on the basis of education. The best person does not necessarily get the job, but rather the person with the most formal education.

Poverty of the first type can obviously be eliminated, at least in theory, if the economy is brought to a full employment level. It is interesting to note here that Canada, compared with other industrialized countries, has had a higher unemployment rate and lower inflation rate. Anti-inflation policies have been pursued with more vigour than full-employment policies, frequently with the justification that inflation places a heavy burden on poor people and is one of the major causes of poverty. However, evidence in both the United States and Canada does not support such an attitude.

Inflation is indeed hard on the poor, particularly if their incomes are fixed, but unemployment is worse. Arthur Okun wrote in 1970:[4]

> Welfare recipients and the aged poor may be hurt by inflation even though the predominant effect on the poor is that of improved job opportunities. These facts should once and for all stem the temptation of the political economists to invoke the plight of the poor as one of the reasons for wanting price stability . . . and they should remind us that, when the nation is deliberately pursuing a policy of economic slowdown in order to achieve price stability, it has a special obligation to intensify other efforts to relieve the plight of the poor (p. 297).

The reason why the poor are hit hard is that when a recession strikes, it does not affect all industries equally. The industries most severely affected are investment and durable-goods industries (construction, iron and steel and the light consumer-goods industries), which in turn are forced to lay off their construction workers and other unskilled workers. In 1978 the unemployment rate was 14.8 percent for construction workers and 22.8 percent for workers in forestry and logging—compared with only 2.9 percent for managerial positions.[5]

The people who fall into the nonproducer category can be helped out of their poverty. The plight of the old and the disabled could be alleviated by more generous old-age and disability pensions and subsidized day care could make it possible for many single parents to join the labour force.

The third group comprise the working poor who make up almost 50 percent of the poor. The problems of the working poor are difficult to solve. Minimum-wage laws have been imposed to counter low-paying jobs. They are believed by some to alleviate poverty and still maintain an incentive to work. However, critics argue that minimum wages are not effective as an antipoverty measure for two reasons: they do not allow for different family sizes, and they throw people out of work. The question of whether minimum wages cause unemployment has been the subject of many studies both in Canada and in the United States.[6] Most show that minimum wages have a negligible effect on the total unemployment rate, but have a significant effect on the employment of women and youth.

A better approach would be to attack the reasons for low wages. The economic value of a person (the value of the person's human capital) has two components: the quality of education and skills, and the price at which it is sold. An antipoverty policy should therefore aim to increase the education and training of the poor, as well as the market price of their services. Manpower programs involving education and on-the-job training are obviously important in increasing the number of potential jobs for the poor. Programs aimed at improving labour mobility and job information, as well as the removal of discrimination, would improve the price the poor got for their skills.

Discrimination directed against native groups, women and various ethnic groups probably still occurs.[7] Most Canadians are aware of the low living standards experienced by Canada's native peoples. Indeed, living conditions on some Indian reserves and in some Inuit communities are similar to living conditions of many Third World peoples. Statistics Canada does not publish separate data for Indians, Metis and Inuit, and so it is not clear to what extent low living standards can be explained by discrimination, exploitation, low educational skills, or other factors.

Solutions to the plight of indigenous peoples are exceedingly difficult to achieve. Obviously education and preventive health care should be improved, and concerted efforts to cure the severe alcohol problems made. Measures are also necessary to improve economic conditions on reserves and to increase employment opportunities.

Discrimination against women is well documented in the sense that equal pay for equal work has not been achieved. Women, on the average, earn less than men earn, not only because of outright discrimination but also because of occupational segregation. Gunderson (1979), using 1970 data, found that average earnings of women amounted to 60 percent of average earnings of men. Sixty percent of this difference was attributed to discrimination and 40 percent to other factors. Women tend to hold low-paying jobs partly because many have not been encouraged to acquire the necessary skills through education or on-the-job training. Even if they do acquire them they may not be able to get a good price for it, partly because of outright discrimination, partly because of lack of mobility. It is difficult to move to a better-paying job if the job is not in the same place as the family home, or if the husband is unable to change jobs.

Measures to improve women's earning potential include the opportunity to upgrade education, equal-pay laws, equal-opportunity laws, and affirmative-action programs (Gunderson 1980:353-59). It is widely recognized, however, that equal-pay laws, if enforced, can actually be detrimental to women in the sense that they could decrease employment and on-the-job training opportunities. Equal-opportunity laws, however, are designed to prevent discrimination in recruiting, hiring and promotion; they should, therefore, increase the demand for female labour and increase wages and employment levels. Affirmative-action programs actively promote the employment of women and can be coercive. In the United States court rulings have ordered employers to employ a larger quota of women.

In summary, a good antipoverty program should promote full employment, give adequate income transfers to those unable to join the labour force, give incentives to the working poor to upgrade their skills, and remove any discrimination in the labour force. Current programs are discussed in the next section, with special emphasis on transfers and pensions.

Present Programs in Income Security

At present Canada's programs for income security consist of a Guaranteed Income Supplement; demogrants (old-age security, family allowances and youth allowances); social insurance (the Canada Pension Plan, the Quebec Pension Plan, unemployment insurance, Workmen's Compensation and veteran's pensions); and social assistance. By far the largest share of government expenditures is spent on social assistance. In 1966, Old Age Assistance, Blind Persons Allowance, Disabled Persons

Allowances, Unemployment Assistance, as well as a whole host of programs for child care, needy mothers and nursing homes were consolidated into the Canada Assistance Plan (Boadway 1980:27). The Canada Assistance Plan is a cost-sharing program in which the federal government pays 50 percent of the cost of all provincial programs falling under any of these categories. The conditions to qualify for federal support are not stringent; the provincial programs must only provide the basic requirements for food, clothing and shelter for needy people. The provinces are not allowed to impose residence requirements on applicants for assistance. The federal program does not guarantee uniform standards across the provinces; for example, in 1979–80 maximum annual welfare benefits for a family of four ranged from $6,400 in Nova Scotia to $10,500 in Alberta (see Table 19). Such a discrepancy can occur because the federal government matches each province's expenditures.

The Canada Assistance Plan was not included in the 1977 new financial agreements (Established Program Financing), the main reason being that the welfare system in general was subject to a major review. In 1978, it was agreed that conditional grants would be replaced by block financing—except for grants for welfare which would still be matching grants. The proposed changes have not yet been implemented.

Under the present programs, an elderly couple, even if they had not contributed to the Canada Pension Plan, would get Old Age Security

TABLE 19

Minimum Wage Incomes,
Income Supplements and Social Assistance, by Province, 1979–80

Province	Annual minimum wage income	Net supplementary income	Total net income	Social assistance
Newfoundland	$5,800	$ 700	$6,500	$ 7,200
P.E.I.	5,700	700	6,400	6,900
New Brunswick	5,800	700	6,500	6,700
Nova Scotia	5,700	700	6,400	6,400
Quebec	7,200	1,800	9,000	7,200
Ontario	6,200	1,000	7,200	6,900
Manitoba	6,300	1,200	7,500	8,000
Saskatchewan	7,300	1,500	8,800	6,700
Alberta	6,200	800	7,000	10,500
B.C.	6,200	800	7,000	9,100

Source: Ross D.P. *The Working Poor Wage Earners and the Failure of Security Policies*, Table 5–1.

and a Guaranteed Income Supplement. They would also qualify for provincial assistance. For fatherless or motherless children whose parent(s) cannot work, support is restricted to family allowances, youth allowances and provincial welfare—the generosity or meagreness of which varies considerably between provinces. For the large number of working poor, there is no real program at all.

In general, the income security system is beset by several problems: the various programs are plagued by overlap and duplication, and they vary in generosity across the country. In addition, they provide little incentive to work. When a person on social assistance earns an extra $100, his or her social assistance is usually reduced by a corresponding amount. Table 19 shows that in all provinces except Quebec, Nova Scotia and Saskatchewan, a family of four would be better off on social assistance than if one family member took a full-time job that paid minimum wage. The pension system, in particular, needs overhauling, as it has been estimated that two-thirds of all pensioners live in poverty.

The most commonly suggested solution to the first two problems is a guaranteed income scheme, administered through the tax system (a negative income tax): if a family earns above a certain amount it pays taxes to the government; if it earns below a certain amount, the government pays the family (a negative income tax). There would be a built-in work incentive, compared to existing programs. Let us assume that the guaranteed annual income floor for a family of four is set at $10,000, and that the negative tax rate is 75 percent. If the family's income were zero, it would have an income gap of $10,000. With a negative tax rate of 75 percent, the family would receive $7,500. Similarly, if the family income were $2,000 and the income gap $8,000, with a tax rate of 75 percent it would receive $0.75 \times 8,000 = \$6,000$, which then gives a total income of $6,000 + $2,000. If the family income were $10,000, nothing would be received. Any additional income above $10,000 would be subject to normal tax rates (they would probably have to be increased to recover revenue lost). The system could, of course, be made more or less generous by increasing or decreasing the support level and the negative tax rate.

Negative income taxes were first suggested by Friedman (1962), which is perhaps surprising in view of his conservative philosophy. Friedman proposed the idea because he thought it would be a more efficient way to distribute money than through welfare payments. The system is indeed deceptively simple in theory, but may not be simple in practice (Ross 1981). The government subsidy, in the form of a cheque, would have to be handled through the tax system, and the size of the cheque would be determined by income earned in the previous year. Most people would find it extremely difficult to manage on a once-a-year cheque, particularly if a loss in earned income were sudden and unexpected. If payments are to be made on a monthly basis, the simplicity of the system breaks down as income for the year has to be estimated and allowance made for errors.

The Senate Committee on Poverty recommended a guaranteed income scheme similar to the one described above, and variations have been suggested by the Castonguay–Nepveu Commission and the Canadian Council on Social Development. However, negative income taxes have not been implemented other than on a limited scale, through the Guaranteed Income Supplement, which can be claimed only by old people and therefore does not affect people in the work force. The federal government feels that most of the existing programs cannot be superceded by a guaranteed income scheme, as they are of a contractual nature. Other, perhaps more serious, objections are that the scheme would be too expensive, and that it could not replace all existing programs. Many poor people need more help than a cheque in the mail. The federal government appears instead to have started a policy of refundable tax credits, an example being the new child-tax-credit plan.

The state governments in the United States and the provincial governments in Canada have been more enthusiastic about guaranteed income schemes. Ontario and British Columbia have introduced some limited schemes, and Manitoba ran a pilot project for three years in Dauphin, the results of which are not yet available. It is possible (but perhaps not likely) that each province would end up with a different guaranteed annual income scheme with different residence requirements and income levels. This diversity may serve to fragment the country further by acting as a barrier to labour mobility.

In view of the fact that two-thirds of old-age pensioners are poor, a major antipoverty measure would be to make pensions more generous. At present Old Age Security and Guaranteed Income Supplement are indexed, but not the Canada Pension Plan or pensions in the private sector. Most private pension plans are not transferable between companies. If an employer changes jobs, he or she can usually recover his or her own contributions to a pension plan, but not the employer's contribution. This means that the majority of people do not receive a full pension. Indeed, the Canadian Labour Congress estimates that only 10 percent of workers enrolled in private plans receive a full pension. Other features of current pension schemes are that private pensions do not usually provide any benefits to widows, and until recently it was not possible for women not in the labour force to contribute to the Canada Pension Plan.

The lack of indexation is serious. If the inflation rate is 6 percent and if a person retires at 60 at say $10,000 per year, after fifteen years the real value would have dropped to 45 percent of the initial value: to $4,500. The indexation of civil servants' pensions has raised the ire of the private sector which sees it as another expensive government venture by which the country can ill afford, and a benefit which could not be provided by the private sector.

Two questions are relevant: can the economy afford indexation and can the private sector provide it? The argument that the economy cannot afford it is fallacious (Pesando 1979:81−2). If pensioners' incomes were indexed to the rate of inflation, their claim on the economy's resources would remain constant; it would not increase. Only if real GNP decreased while inflation increased would pensioners increase their share of national income. However, inflation tends to be associated with an increasing GNP, not a decreasing GNP. Recent inflation has indeed been associated with declining output, but this is unusual and was caused by the special circumstances of increasing energy and food prices.

If indexed bonds were available, there would be no problem for the private sector to provide indexed pensions. Indexed bonds, however, do not exist, which in a sense is a puzzle to economists. Firms typically issue bonds to finance the purchase of real assets, the nominal value of which tend to increase with inflation. For this reason, it should not be impossible to issue bonds, the value of which would increase with inflation. Indexed bonds could, however, increase the risk for private insurance companies if the actual inflation rate exceeded the expected rate. Pesando (1979) has suggested a scheme whereby the government could assume some of this risk.

Summary and Conclusions

The distribution of income has not changed radically in the last decades despite substantial efforts by all levels of government. There are several reasons for this. Even though income taxes are progressive, the tax system as a whole is (mildly) regressive. Secondly, many of the major transfers are universal (for example, family allowances) and therefore apply to the rich as well as to the poor. Government support of secondary education can also be regarded as a transfer payment which benefits upper-income groups more than low-income groups. Unemployment insurance is another benefit, little of which goes to low-income groups.

The poor can be divided into two major groups: those who can work and those who cannot, and antipoverty policies have to be designed around these groups. For those who cannot work, there have to be direct transfers; for those who can, a combination of direct transfers, educational upgrading, child-care support services, and affirmative action programs may be necessary.

The current transfer system does not give adequate transfers (particularly pensions) for those unable to work, and provides little incentive to work for those who are able. Guaranteed annual incomes are often suggested as a solution to these problems, but the federal government feels that they would be too expensive to implement. Given current budgetary constraints, it may be more acceptable to cut the universality of schemes such as family allowances and post-secondary education subsidies, and increase direct transfers to those who need them.

There should also be more effort to increase the income of the working poor. Given that almost 40 percent of poor families are headed by women (and that almost 70 percent of low-income individuals are women), special efforts should be made to increase skill levels and on-the-job training of women.

NOTES

1. For a good discussion, see Ross 1980, and on a theoretical level, Sahota 1978.
2. See Osberg 1981.
3. For a survey, see Caskie 1979.
4. Okun as discussant of papers on "Dynamics of Income Distribution." *American Economic Review* Papers and Proceedings. (LX), 1970:297.
5. See Statistics Canada (1978), *Labour Force Annual Averages* (Cat. 71−529).
6. A comprehensive survey is given in West and McKee 1980.
7. There is a gap in salaries between anglophone and francophone Canadians, both inside and outside Quebec. The gap was as large as 52 percent in 1960, but by 1977 it had narrowed to 15 percent. How much of the difference is attributable to discrimination, and how much to different skill levels is not known (Vaillancourt 1978).
8. There has been much interest in pensions recently. Several provincial governments have published reports proposing reforms. The Economic Council of Canada (1979) has also issued a report.

BIBLIOGRAPHY

Adams, Ian, W. Cameron, B. Hill and P. Penz. *The Real Poverty Report.* Edmonton: Hurtig, 1971.
Armstrong, D.E., P.H. Frieson and D. Miller. "The Measurement of Income Distribution in Canada: Some Problems and Some Tentative Data." *Canadian Public Policy* (III), 1977, pp. 479−88.
Boadway, R. *Intergovernmental Transfers in Canada.* Toronto: Canadian Tax Foundation, 1980.

Caskie, D.M. *Canadian Fact Book on Poverty 1979.* Ottawa: Canadian Council for Social Development, 1979.

Cloutier, J.E. *The Distribution of Benefits and Costs of Social Security in Canada.* Discussion Paper No. 108. Ottawa: Economic Council of Canada, 1978.

Davies, J.B. "On the Size Distribution of Wealth in Canada." *Review of Income and Wealth.* 1979, pp. 237–60.

Economic Council of Canada. *One in Three: Pensions for Canadians to 2030.* Hull: The Canadian Government Publishing Centre, 1979.

Friedman, M. *Capitalism and Freedom.* Chicago: University of Chicago Press, 1962.

Gillespie, I. *Incidence of Taxes and Public Expenditures in the Canadian Economy.* Royal Commission on Taxation, Study No. 2, 1964.

Gunderson, M. "Decomposition of the Male/Female Earnings Differential: Canada 1970." *Canadian Journal of Economics* (XII), 1979, pp. 479–84.

_____. *Labour Market Economics: Theory, Evidence and Policy in Canada.* Toronto: McGraw-Hill Ryerson, 1980.

Maslove, A. *The Pattern of Taxation in Canada.* Economic Council of Canada. Ottawa: Information Canada, 1972.

Needleman L. "Income Distribution in Canada and the Disaggregation of the Gini Coefficient of Concentration." *Canadian Public Policy* (V), 1979, pp. 497–506.

Newman, P.C. *The Canadian Establishment.* Toronto: McClelland and Stewart, 1975.

Osberg, Lars. *Economic Inequality in Canada.* Toronto: Butterworths, 1981.

Paglin, M. "The Measurement and Trend of Inequality: A Basic Revision." *American Economic Review* (LXV), 1975, pp. 598–609.

Pesando, James E. "Indexing of Private Pensions." *Canadian Public Policy* (V), 1979, pp. 80–90.

Ross, D.P. *The Canadian Fact Book on Income Distribution.* Ottawa: Canadian Council on Social Development, 1980.

_____ *The Working Poor Wage Earners and the Failure of Income Security Policies.* Ottawa: Canadian Institute for Economic Policy, 1981.

Sahota, C.S. "Theories of Personal Income Distribution: A Survey." *Journal of Economic Literature* (XVI), 1978, pp. 1–55.

Shedd, M.S. "The Measurement of Income Distribution in Canada." *Canadian Public Policy* (V), 1979, pp. 506–10.

Vaillancourt F. "Revenus et langue au Québec: 1961–1971." *Journal of Canadian Studies* (13), 1978, pp. 63–9.

West, E.G. and M. McKee. *Minimum Wages: The New Issues in Theory, Evidence, Policy and Politics.* Ottawa: Economic Council of Canada and the Institute for Research on Public Policy, 1980.

CHAPTER 10

The Rich and the Poor: The Provinces

In few other countries has the regional distribution of income reached such a level of importance as it has in Canada. In Canada the income differential between provinces and regions has always been large, perhaps because of the sheer size of the country and the variations in population, climate and culture. The persistence of the differential has been the source of continual conflict. At times the National Policy has been blamed, as it is alleged to have favoured the industrial heartland of Ontario and Quebec to the detriment of the outlying provinces whose inhabitants were forced into a lower standard of living. The railways have also been a favourite target for criticism. The most recent source of inequality (and envy) is the unequal distribution of energy resources across the country.

In this chapter the regional distribution of income will be analysed, as well as policies to alleviate regional income differentials. The subject of federal-provincial conflict and proposals for a new constitution is so complex that it warrants a separate chapter and will therefore be left until Chapter 11.

Regional Disparities in Income and Employment

A region is defined as a geographic area which is essentially homogeneous in one or more respects. In Canada, regions are usually identified with provinces, even though large provinces such as Ontario and Quebec are too large to be treated as single regions. It is also common to group the provinces into five regions: the Atlantic provinces (the three Maritime provinces and Newfoundland), Ontario, Quebec, the Prairie provinces (Manitoba, Saskatchewan and Alberta), and British Columbia. The whole of northern Canada should also be treated as a separate region.

The most common measure of regional disparity is per capita personal income.[1] According to this measure, in 1979 people in British Columbia were the richest and those in Newfoundland the poorest (see Table 20). This was also the case in 1950. It is interesting to note that whereas in 1960 and 1970, people in Ontario had the highest income per capita, by 1979, Ontario had slipped to third place, having been superceded by both Alberta and British Columbia. Table 20 also suggests that regional disparities have decreased since 1950. In 1950, B.C.'s per capita income was almost 2.5 times higher than that in Newfoundland, whereas in 1979 it was 1.7 times higher.

However, if, instead of per capita incomes, unemployment rates are used as a standard of comparison, the gaps appear to have increased. For example, in 1966 (Table 21) the unemployment rate was 2.4 percent in the Prairie provinces and 5.4 percent in Atlantic Canada. In 1980 the rate was 4.3 percent in the Prairies and 11.2 percent in Atlantic Canada, a difference of over 6 points. This disparity may indicate that had it not been for the generous federal transfer payments in the form of equalization payments and federal financing of health and education, the gap in personal income may well have been larger. Indeed, R. George's data (1981:323) demonstrate that this is so: in 1977 personal income per

TABLE 20
Personal Income per Capita, by Province,* 1950, 1960, 1970 and 1979

Province	1950	1960	1970	1979	1979 $/capita
Newfoundland	50.9	55.5	63.4	65.9	5,862
P.E.I.	55.1	56.9	66.5	68.0	6,057
Nova Scotia	74.4	76.4	77.5	79.6	7,088
New Brunswick	70.2	68.1	72.0	72.7	6,472
Quebec	85.9	87.2	88.7	93.7	8,341
Ontario	121.2	117.8	118.4	107.9	9,608
Manitoba	101.4	99.4	92.9	92.1	8,198
Saskatchewan	83.3	89.2	72.4	93.6	8,335
Alberta	100.6	99.8	99.3	109.2	9,717
B.C.	124.9	115.3	108.8	110.3	9,821
Yukon and NWT	—	105.7	94.6	96.3	8,569
Canada	100	100	100	100	8,902

Source: Department of Finance, *Annual Report* 1981, Reference Table 14.
* As a percentage of personal income per capita at the national level.

TABLE 21
Unemployment Rate by Region, 1966, 1970, 1975, and 1980

Region	1966	1970	1975	1980
Atlantic	5.4	6.2	9.8	11.2
Quebec	4.1	7.0	8.1	9.9
Ontario	2.6	4.4	6.3	6.9
Prairie	2.4	4.9	3.9	4.3
British Columbia	4.6	7.7	8.5	6.8
Canada	3.4	5.7	6.9	7.5

Source: Department of Finance, *Annual Report* 1981, Reference Table 33.

capita for Newfoundland, *excluding* transfer payments, was only 53 percent of the national average—not much of an improvement since the 1950s.

Causes of Regional Disparities

Many explanations have been given for regional disparities. Some of the more common ones are lack of natural resources, market size, transport costs, spatial immobility, and low productivity.[2] Each of these will be discussed in turn.

Natural Resources

It is obvious that natural resources can be an important determinant of a region's prosperity—particularly if the resource is oil—but the lack of a marketable resource does not necessarily lead to low regional income. At the international level, the OPEC countries are rich; however, so are Switzerland and Japan—countries almost entirely lacking in resources. Copithorne (1979) has shown that if the value of primary production per worker is used as a proxy for measuring natural resource endowments, the four poorest provinces and the four western provinces have larger resource endowments than the most industrialized provinces. Newfoundland, which is one of the poorest provinces, is by any measure a resource-rich province; it is the largest producer of iron ore in Canada, and yet in 1978–79, the revenue forecast from mining and royalty taxes was expected to be less than the revenue generated from tobacco taxes.

One reason why mineral resources appear to have so little effect on a region's prosperity is the poor linkages generated from mining. In a study on the impact of minerals on economic development in Canada, McCulla and Stahl (1977) found that compared with other industries both backward and forward linkages in mining were very modest, the reason being that most minerals are exported in raw form. For these reasons, the income and employment multipliers were among the lowest of all industries.

Transportation Costs, Market Size and Aggregate Demand
Transportation costs and the size of the market for a region's products are sometimes given as explanations for regional disparities. Firms that service only a regional market may not be able to achieve economies of scale and therefore low cost, and if transportation costs into the region are less than the cost disadvantage, the firms are forced to pay low wages to survive. Similarly, if a firm sells to outlying regions, it has to absorb the transportation costs in order to compete, which again may mean low wages for the employees. Lower wages are usually associated with lower incomes.

Comparatively little work has been done on the effect of transport costs on regional income. Casas and Kotowitz (1976) demonstrated, using a theoretical model, that transportation subsidies are unlikely to raise regional income in a poor area; that is, the theoretical link between transportation costs and regional income is tenuous. This seems to have been confirmed by empirical work. McRae (1981) found that for most industries, transportation costs are of little consequence as a barrier to competition. If this is correct, it refutes the argument that transportation costs explain low regional incomes.

A related factor is the lack of urban centres in the poorer areas. Urban size appears to have a positive influence on income and productivity because of economies of scale in transportation and distribution and also because of agglomeration economies. Sources of supply may be concentrated and therefore cheaper and quicker to obtain. Industry can get cheaper services because of economies of large-scale production. The supply of electricity is a good example. Hydro rates are far higher in the Atlantic provinces than in Ontario and Quebec, the reason being the high cost of transmission over large, sparsely populated areas.

The importance of aggregate demand in determining regional income was emphasized by the Economic Council of Canada (1977). Unless compensated for by large government expenditures, small markets will lead to low aggregate demand and therefore low income for a region. A related factor is the regional impact of stabilization policies. It was pointed out in Chapter 9 that a recession affects poor people disproportionately in the sense that they are usually the first to be out of work. This is also true for poor provinces. An analysis of unemployment data for 1953–75 demonstrates that a 2 percent increase in the unemployment rate in Canada as a whole implies a 3.7 percent increase in the Atlantic region, 2.6 in Quebec, 1.3 in Ontario, 1.7 on the Prairies, and 1.9 in B.C. (Economic Council 1977:98). This means that stabilization policies should take into consideration the specific needs of the different regions in order to overcome the bias shown to Ontario, for example, which benefits the most during periods of fiscal expansion.

Regionally differentiated stabilization policies are not without problems. Because of the mobility of capital, the Bank of Canada cannot maintain different interest rates in different parts of the country. Government expenditure and taxation policies are already regionally differentiated because of the operations of the automatic stabilizers (a region with high unemployment automatically receives more unemployment insurance payments; a rich region automatically pays more taxes). A regionally discriminatory taxation policy would probably not be politically feasible, unless the provinces themselves shouldered a larger responsibility for fiscal policy-making. Ontario has used sales tax cuts as a stabilization measure, but increased involvement by the provinces in this area would require a surrender by the federal government of some tax room. There is also some doubt as to the efficiency of provincial fiscal policies because of the substantial economic interdependence between the provinces and the concomitant presence of large leakages. Substantial coordination would be required (Maxwell and Pestieau 1980:46−59).

Spatial Immobility

Spatial immobility has often been used as an explanation of persistent regional disparities. According to neo-classical theory, market wages are determined by the intersection of the demand and supply curves for labour. The demand for labour is determined by the productivity of labour (the marginal revenue product of labour). Low regional wages therefore imply low productivity of labour (and high productivity of capital). Assuming there are no obstacles to the movement of labour and capital, labour will move from low-wage to high-wage (high productivity) areas, and capital will move to low-wage areas where the marginal product of capital is high. Because of the law of diminishing returns, this movement of labour and capital will continue until the marginal products of labour and capital are equalized across the country and regional disparities have disappeared.[3] Given that regional disparities still exist, it must mean that there are obstacles to the mobility of labour and capital, either in the form of high transport costs, lack of information, or even federal transfer payments which keep wages and services artificially high in poor regions and therefore retard the migration flows.

Many studies on migration (for example, Courchene 1971; Vanderkamp 1980) confirm that people migrate in response to economic factors. Migration alleviates the problems of a region when there is a sudden decline in an important regional industry. Low wages and unemployment will cause people to move, which in turn may alleviate unemployment and raise wages both for the migrants and the people left behind. However, these results do not necessarily mean that migration always has a beneficial effect on regional income, nor that insufficient migration means persistent regional disparities. According to a study by the Economic Council (1977:179), net outmigration from the Atlantic region has been substantial. Indeed, between 1951 and 1971, 15 percent of the population migrated without any appreciable effect on unemployment or incomes in the Atlantic provinces. There may be several explanations for this. In the first place, it is not necessarily the unemployed or the workers in low-productivity employment who move. Most studies show that it is the young and the educated who migrate (Courchene 1970; Economic Council, 1977:176), leaving behind an older, less-educated population—a mix that will not lessen regional income disparity. Second, as labour moves out, the size of the local market declines, a factor which further depresses local industries. This can lead to a downward spiral: the more people leave, the more the industry will become depressed, so that a region could become depopulated without having achieved income inequality. Third, migration adversely affects the provision of local services; as the tax base becomes eroded, the community can no longer afford good schools and municipal services.

Productivity

Productivity is usually regarded as the main determinant of prosperity. According to recent studies done for the Economic Council, differences in productivity are of major importance in explaining income differentials. Output per worker (labour productivity) varies greatly between the provinces. For example, between 1970 and 1973, labour productivity in Prince Edward Island was only 60 percent of the national average, whereas productivity in Alberta, British Columbia and Ontario was 114 percent, 110 and 104, respectively (see Table 22).

Productivity differences may be explained by differences in industrial mix. If a province has a large proportion of service industries (which traditionally have low productivity) and a low share of manufacturing industries (which traditionally have high productivity), its average productivity will be low. A study by Auer (1978) shows that industrial mix explains only 20 percent of productivity differences among the provinces—with the exception of Prince Edward Island and Saskatchewan where it accounts for more. The remaining productivity differences can be explained by productivity differences within the same industry. For example, a B.C. cow gives 12,000 lbs. of milk per year, an Ontario cow 9,000 per year and a Quebec cow 7,000 per year. A worker bottling soft drinks in Ontario turns out 50,000 bottles per year, whereas a worker in Nova Scotia turns out 30,000 per year. Similar differences exist in some services. Federal offices handling family allowance and old-age pension cheques accomplish more work in one part of the country than in another.

The causes of these and similar productivity differences are difficult to document. Theorists claim that productivity differences can be attributed to differences in the amount of capital per worker, in technology and the amount of human capital per worker, and in management skills (see Chapter 4). However, there seems to be little relationship between regional capital stock and productivity. Alberta and B.C. have high capital stock per capita, but so does Newfoundland, which also has low productivity (Table 22). Differences in the quality of labour exist, with differences in education being the most prominent (Table 22). Alberta has the highest proportion of university graduates and Newfoundland the lowest. British Columbia has the highest proportion of high school graduates. The quality of management varies as well. In a 1970 survey, 32 percent of Canadian managers held university degrees, but the provincial averages varied from 18 percent in Newfoundland to 37 percent in Alberta (ECC 1977:75). There is also some evidence that the adoption of new technology is slower in the Atlantic provinces; for example, they trail behind the others in the use of computers.

Which of these factors (labour quality, management and technol-

TABLE 22

Provincial Differences in Productivity, Labour Quality and Capital*
(1970–73)

Province	Labour productivity	Productivity with adjustment for industrial mix	Labour quality	Capital stock per worker
Newfoundland	91	85	95	124
P.E.I.	60	76	97	80
Nova Scotia	77	78	100	94
New Brunswick	82	81	97	102
Quebec	93	92	97	89
Ontario	104	103	101	88
Manitoba	89	92	99	109
Saskatchewan	99	111	100	144
Alberta	114	118	103	142
B.C.	110	109	105	119
Canada	100	100	100	100

Source: Auer L. *Regional Disparities of Productivity and Growth,* Tables 1–1, 2–4 and 2–8.
* As a proportion of national averages.

ogy) is the most important in explaining productivity differences has not been determined. However, as was pointed out in Chapter 5, the quality of labour, management and technology tend to go hand in hand in promoting a high-productivity, future-oriented industrial structure.

The evidence presented above suggests that a good regional policy should aim to promote efficiency in the movement of goods in the local and national markets; it should aim to upgrade the quality of the labour force and of management in the poor regions; and it should actively promote the dissemination of new technology. The policy should also aim to facilitate the migration of labour in those areas where unemployment reaches crisis proportions. The next section gives an account of Canada's past and present regional policies.

Regional Policy in Canada: An Overview

The 1957 Royal Commission on Canada's Economic Prospects was possibly the first public inquiry to consider the regional dimension of income.[4] Later a Special Senate Committee on land use found that rural poverty was a serious problem, with a large proportion of farmers, particularly in eastern Canada, earning an income barely above subsistence level. The committee recommended the establishment of a national land use policy which would designate certain areas as rural or agricultural, and other areas to be used for other purposes. Subsequently, the federal government introduced the Agricultural Rehabilitation and Development Act in 1961 with the intention of alleviating rural poverty. The main emphasis was on soil and water conservation and land use conversion, with financing split equally between the federal and provincial governments. This program was expanded in 1965 in the Agricultural and Rural Development Act (ARDA), which was followed in 1966 by the Fund for Rural Economic Development (FRED). FRED was to provide additional funds to selected areas in need of assistance. Funds would be forthcoming after the federal and provincial levels of governments had agreed to a basic development program for the region. In 1962, the Atlantic Development Board was set up to inquire into measures and projects for promoting growth and development of the Atlantic provinces. Subsequently the Board received funds to develop growth projects, funds which were mainly used for the development of infrastructure (roads, for example). In 1963, the Area Development Agency (ADA) was formed to provide incentives for firms to locate in specific regions, mainly through tax concessions. In 1965 the program was modified to include capital grants (the Area Development Incentives Act or ADIA).

The provincial governments also entered into a large variety of different development programs with little or no coordination. For this reason the Department of Regional Economic Expansion (DREE) was established in 1969. Its terms of reference are to ensure that growth is widely dispersed across Canada and that employment and income projects in slow-growth regions are brought up to the national average. Most of the existing programs were transferred to DREE. Special areas were demarcated for attention; specifically the development of infrastructure, primarily highways and streets, with secondary importance given to water and sewer systems.

ADIA was replaced by a new Regional Development Incentives Act (RDIA) which was to stimulate industrial expansion in designated areas. The designated areas included all provinces except Alberta and British Columbia and Southern Ontario. Incentives in the form of grants were to be given either for expansion or modernization of existing facilities, or for starting new ventures. The only industries which did not qualify for grants were pulp and newspaper mills and oil refineries. Grants for modernization contributed up to 20 percent of eligible capital costs, and for a new plant and equipment up to 25 percent of eligible capital costs; other grants paid up to 30 percent of the wage bill in the Atlantic provinces (15 percent in other designated regions). Since early 1974 there has been increased provincial participation through General Development Agreements (GDA) signed with each province except PEI.

With all these changes, there is a bewildering array of programs. They can be classified into four major areas: (1) aid to private industry through RDIA and GDA; (2) aid to the public sector in urban areas outside the Atlantic provinces through the Special Area program to the Atlantic provinces, through the Atlantic Development Board; (3) aid to the public sector in rural areas (FRED, ARDA, GDA); (4) various manpower and research programs. Total expenditures in the fiscal year 1980–81 amounted to $543 million, with the largest share going to infrastructure and one third of the total going to the private sector (Canadian Tax Foundation 1981:179). On a per capita basis, Prince Edward Island has been the largest recipient, followed by New Brunswick and Newfoundland.

The DREE program has been subject to substantial criticisms for its terms of reference (Usher 1975) and for its capital bias (Woodward 1974a, 1974b, 1975). According to the RDIA no grant is to be given if it is probable that the facility would have been established without the grant. The grant should not be larger than is necessary to bring forth the investment in the region—an extremely difficult principle to follow. It is also an unusual principle in public finance, for normally a person is subsidized for doing something regardless of whether the person would do it without a subsidy. The principle would operate in the same way as one restricting family allowance to children who were conceived only because of the allowance (Usher 1973).

In assessing the effectiveness of DREE a few words of caution should be added. First, even if the program has added more firms to an area, it may have rendered other investments unprofitable because the new firm(s) could have increased wages and rents in the area; therefore the net effect of the program might be negligible. Secondly, competition from subsidized firms could displace or reduce investments by firms already established. Thirdly, firms that need to be "bribed" to invest in an area may be less likely than other firms to reinvest, and therefore the long-term benefits of subsidized investments may be small.

There have been three studies of the effectiveness of DREE in generating additional investments in the designated areas. Springate (1972) did a survey of 31 firms that had received grants from DREE. In particular, Springate tried to find out the extent to which the availability of a grant affected the location timing and size of a project. Only 30 percent of the larger firms—compared with 45 percent of the smaller firms—indicated that the DREE grant was critical. In 1972–73, the Atlantic Development Council's survey of 51 firms that had received assistance found that 60 percent of the firms thought the DREE grant was instrumental (ECC 1977:161–62). These two surveys may suffer from considerable bias, however. The Springate survey was based on unstructured subjective interviews, and it appears that many of the interviewed executives did not want to convey an impression of relying on government aid. For this reason they could have understated the importance of government aid. The ADC survey was more objective, but unless the questions were carefully phrased, it could also have been subject to bias.

The Economic Council (1977:156–68) tried another approach and looked at the annual births of establishments by industry in the Atlantic region. If the "birth rate" increased significantly after the location grants became available, the grants had worked. It was found that 25 percent of the DREE-supported firms located in the area because of the grant, 41 percent did not, and for the remaining 34 percent, it was impossible to come to any conclusion either way.

Usher (1975) claims that a cursory examination of manufacturing investment trends in the Atlantic provinces before and after the inception of the grants program shows that the large grants could not have had any appreciable effects on the overall level of investments. Similarly, overall employment in the Maritime provinces does not show any appreciable increases after the program was initiated. These observations, of course, do not prove that the program has not worked, since in its absence it is possible (but not likely) that both investments and employment would have declined. It can therefore be concluded that no study has been able to demonstrate how effective DREE has been.

The other criticism of DREE is that despite the fact that the program gives subsidies to labour as well as to capital, the program has a capital bias in the sense that the grant benefits capital-users more than labour-users. The bias can be determined by comparing the wage/rental ration before and after the use of a grant (rental being an estimate of the payments to capital). If a grant leads to an increase in the effective wage-rental ratio, the grant encourages firms to adopt more capital-intensive methods than they would have done otherwise. Woodward (1974a, 1974b, 1975) has demonstrated that the DREE grants do indeed display this bias.

Apart from the policies administered by DREE, the federal government has manpower policies designed to encourage mobility through relocation grants to labour, transport policies which subsidize the transport of some goods in and out of some provinces (see Chapter 12) and fiscal transfer policies (equalization payments, established program financing). The relocation grant program, even though it is quite generous, is not particularly effective. For example, in the 1974–75 period, 50,000 jobs were filled each month, only 1,000 of which fell under the mobility program. (ECC 1977:180). The program accounted for only 2 percent of vacancies filled and less than 5 percent of migrants who moved in Canada. It is possible that many unemployed workers do not know of its existence.

No discussion of federal aid to poorer provinces would be complete without a discussion of equalization payments. The problems which led to equalization payments first surfaced in the 1930s during the depression.[5] The depression led to the collapse of economic activity in many parts of the country. The fall in tax revenues, together with the fiscal stress caused by the high-debt burden and relief payments to the destitute, led to almost insurmountable difficulties for some of the provinces. In response, taxes were raised and the federal government stepped in with grants. A royal commission was appointed to investigate dominion-provincial relations (the Rowell-Sirois Commission). The commission's report in 1940 recommended that the provincial governments retreat from the personal and corporate tax fields (and death duties), which should instead be taken over by the federal government in return for which it would give grants or transfer payments to the provinces. The recommendations were not implemented but the provinces surrendered temporarily (until 1962) their rights to levy income and death taxes in return for cash transfers from the federal government.

The present arrangement dates to the Federal-Provincial Fiscal Arrangements and Established Programs Financing Act of 1977. The purpose of equalization payments is to guarantee citizens in all provinces of Canada equal access to public services. The basis for the payments is the total Canadian tax yield from each revenue source on a per capita basis, against which is calculated the tax yield of each province on a per capita basis. If the provincial per capita tax yield exceeds the federal per

TABLE 23
Equalization Entitlements by Revenue Source and Province, 1977–78

Revenue sources	Nfld.	P.E.I.	N.S.	N.B.	Que.	Ont.	Man.	Sask.	Alta.	B.C.	Receiving provinces
					$ thousands						
1 Personal income taxes	93,142	21,439	100,052	95,638	203,535	-365,968	73,826	71,909	-125,114	-168,459	659,541
2 Business income revenues	32,443	7,194	40,027	21,785	164,598	-1,488	22,163	20,795	-302,217	-5,300	309,005
3 General sales tax	39,731	9,253	49,686	30,885	147,714	-38,251	25,531	5,524	-172,262	-97,811	308,324
4 Tobacco taxes	3,402	263	3,084	-256	-15,168	6,691	2,177	3,800	-3,779	-215	-2,698
5 Gasoline taxes	9,991	71	2,848	-231	24,479	-5,961	3,615	-4,642	-29,981	-189	36,131
6 Diesel fuel taxes	832	941	1,999	689	5,160	1,504	-3	-2,004	-9,464	347	7,614
7 Noncomm. vehicle licences	4,302	223	2,792	1,949	894	-1,294	-250	-1,471	-3,350	-3,796	8,439
8 Commercial vehicle licences	2,268	517	2,966	816	28,063	16,359	-2,395	-8,946	-28,278	-11,371	23,289
9 Revenues from sale of spirits	3,135	-627	-699	6,747	68,455	-19,961	-4,626	-5,064	-22,929	-24,431	67,321
10 Revenues from sale of wine	3,153	456	2,378	3,052	-3,244	2,140	1,585	3,028	-1,276	-11,271	10,408
11 Revenues from sale of beer	143	282	1,503	2,070	-7,769	-121	891	2,666	1,485	-1,150	-214
12 Hospital/medical ins. premiums	3,840	640	1,095	1,564	21,807	-28,921	4,025	5,688	-2,045	-7,692	38,659
13 Succession duties/gift taxes	2,034	402	2,173	2,197	2,087	-8,398	2,080	1,054	-2,720	-910	12,027
14 Race track taxes	2,122	127	1,954	1,811	3,446	-12,611	894	2,535	-1,521	1,242	12,889
15 Forestry revenues	-992	1,160	7,003	-125	20,757	47,153	7,934	5,967	13,546	-102,403	41,704
16 Crown oil revenues	18,952	4,039	28,058	23,080	210,880	280,746	32,995	-56,674	-599,716	57,639	261,330
17 Freehold oil revenues	993	212	1,470	1,210	11,050	14,377	195	-4,777	-29,088	4,359	10,353
18 Crown gas revenues	13,240	2,822	19,602	16,111	147,326	195,186	24,158	12,997	-406,717	-24,725	236,256
19 Freehold gas revenues	499	106	739	608	5,554	7,257	911	513	-18,391	2,203	8,930
20 Sales of crown leases	11,564	2,465	17,120	14,088	128,675	171,060	21,100	13,836	-324,463	-55,445	208,848
21 Other oil and gas revenues	963	205	1,425	1,172	10,711	14,223	1,718	-1,034	-29,797	414	15,160
22 Mineral revenues	-9,348	650	1,436	1,449	7,655	5,655	2,360	-7,568	5,780	-8,069	-3,366
23 Water power rentals	-6,109	197	1,233	604	-4,033	7,383	-242	1,173	2,847	-3,053	-7,177
24 Insurance premium taxes	1,929	271	1,543	837	-4,772	-1,620	1,421	1,295	-1,394	491	2,524
25 Payroll taxes	3,933	923	3,608	3,624	9,993	-20,704	1,808	4,244	-2,074	-5,354	28,133
26 Property school taxes	28,592	5,485	30,201	26,352	93,846	-107,921	3,591	314	-44,362	-36,100	188,381
27 Lottery revenues	1,849	315	1,407	1,518	4,772	-7,933	588	583	-602	-2,495	11,032
28 Miscellaneous provincial taxes	13,560	2,914	14,134	12,353	44,965	-38,072	4,668	341	-40,194	-14,668	92,935
29 Shared federal revenues	211	-74	256	153	640	-660	154	133	-680	-133	1,473
Total entitlements	280,374	62,871	341,093	271,750	1,332,076	109,850	232,872	66,215	-2,178,756	-518,345	2,587,251

Source: Federal-Provincial Relations Office, Department of Finance, Ottawa, 1979.

capita tax yield, no equalization payment is due. If, however, the provincial yield is less than the national yield, the province is paid the difference times the population.

The 1977 arrangements include 29 revenue sources as a basis for calculating tax yields. Table 23 lists these sources. A negative entry means that the provincial per capita tax revenue for this source is above the national average, and a positive entry that it is below. For example, Ontario, Alberta and B.C. appear to receive a lot of revenue from its citizens from lotteries, and Quebec appears not to tax liquor very heavily. For each province, all the positive and negative items are totalled; if the sum is positive, the province will receive the sum from Ottawa in equalization payments. If the sum is negative, no equalization payments are paid, but neither does the province have to pay anything to Ottawa. This is one of the major problems with the equalization scheme. The more oil and gas revenue the Alberta government earns, the more the federal government has to pay in equalization to the other provinces for tax items 16 to 20—without receiving any more revenue from Alberta. Indeed, several sources of oil and gas revenue had to be excluded from the current formula for this reason. Note that because of this problem, in 1977–78 even Ontario was entitled to equalization payments of $109,850,600, a sum it never claimed.

The Fiscal Arrangements Act was recently amended to read that no province can receive equalization payments if its per capita income is above the national average. This excludes Ontario from any claims. (Proposals for reforming equalization payments will be discussed in the next chapter.)

Summary and Conclusions

This chapter gave an overview of regional disparities in Canada, their causes and possible cures. Despite government policies aimed at reducing regional disparities, regional income gaps have not closed appreciably and the differences in unemployment rates have widened.

The causes of regional disparity are elusive. The brief survey presented showed that the presence of natural resources, transportation costs and spatial immobility probably cannot explain the large differentials existing at present. More important factors are the size of the market for a region's products and productivity. It was shown that productivity differences between the provinces are substantial; the Economic Council tentatively attributes these to differences in technology and in the skills of labour and management. If this analysis is correct, regional policies should aim to improve productivity through the upgrading of skills and technology.

The survey of regional policies in Canada showed that little attention has been paid to productivity. Instead, the major emphasis has been on moving labour out of poor regions and/or moving capital (industry) in. An example of the latter approach is the policies administered by DREE. It was shown that these policies have not been effective, on the basis of which it can be argued that regional policies should be more people-oriented in the sense that more money should go to the very poor in a region, and conscious efforts should be made to improve their skill levels. More emphasis should be given to management and technology in determining a region's welfare.

NOTES

1. Just as GNP per capita is not an accurate measure of living standards (see Chapter 1), so too provincial personal income per capita is inaccurate, for it does not take into account the value of products grown and used by farmers and fishermen across the country.

2. Expanding and contracting markets are often used to explain why some regions are advancing and others are contracting. The staple theory of economic growth explains the rise and fall of a region on the basis of the development and decline of a staple product (for a good discussion, see Scott 1978). This is not a particularly interesting explanation, however, for a region that relies on declining industries for its livelihood will obviously see its relative income decline. Similarly, a region that produces a product for which demand is high and growing will obviously expand its income. The theory does not explain, for example, why some regions get caught in a "staple trap" and seem unable to develop relatively fast-growing manufacturing industries.

3. However, trade theory predicts that in a competitive region with more than one industry which trades with the outside world, neither an outflow of labour nor an influx of capital in the form of plant and equipment will raise wages (Copithorne 1979). Instead, the movement of labour and capital will lead to an absolute decrease in the size of labour-intensive industries and an increase in the size of capital-intensive industries. The only factor that could raise wages (apart from taxes or tariffs) would be a change in the production function.

4. I am indebted to Brewis (1978) for the following section.

5. For an account of the development of equalization payments, see Lewis 1978.

BIBLIOGRAPHY

Auer, L. *Regional Disparities of Productivity and Growth.* Ottawa: Supply and Services, 1978.

Bird, R.M. *Charging for Public Services, A New Look at an Old Idea.* Toronto: Canadian Tax Foundation, 1976.

Brewis, T.N. "Regional Development in Canada in Historical Perspective." In N.H. Lithwick (ed.), pp. 215 −30, *Regional Economic Policy: the Canadian Experience.* Toronto: McGraw-Hill Ryerson, 1978.

Canadian Tax Foundation. *The National Finances, 1980−81.* Toronto: Canadian Tax Foundation, 1981.

Casas, F.R. and Y. Kotowitz. *Transport Subsidies and Regional Distribution Policies.* Ottawa: Canadian Transport Commission, 1976.

Courchene, T.J. "Interprovincial Migration and Economic Adjustment." *Canadian Journal of Economics* (III), 1970, pp. 550−76.

Copithorne, L. (1979), "Resources and Regional Disparities." *Canadian Public Policy* (V), 181−95.

Economic Council of Canada. *"Living Together: A Study of Regional Disparities."* Ottawa: Supply and Services, 1977.

George, R. "Regional Assistance." In R. Bellan and W.H. Pope (eds.), pp. 307−27, *Canadian Economic Problems and Policies.* Toronto: McGraw-Hill Ryerson, 1981.

Lewis, Perrin. 1978 "The Tangled Tale of Taxes and Transfers." In Michael Walker (ed.), pp. 39−109, *Canadian Confederation at the Crossroads.* Vancouver: The Fraser Institute, 1978.

Maxwell, J. and C. Prestieau. *Economic Realities of Contemporary Confederation.* Montreal: C.D. Howe Institute, 1980.

McCulla, D.J. and J.E. Stahl. *Quantitative Impact of Minerals on Canadian Economic Development: A Partial Analysis.* Ottawa: Energy, Mines and Resources, 1981.

McRae, J.J. "An Empirical Measure of the Influence of Transportation Costs on Regional Income." *Canadian Journal of Economics* (XIV), 1981, pp. 155−63.

Scott, A.D. "Policy for Declining Regions: A Theoretical Approach." In N.H. Lithwick (ed.), *Regional Economic Policy: The Canadian Experience.* Toronto: McGraw-Hill Ryerson, 1978, pp. 46-68.

Special Senate Committee on Poverty. *Poverty in Canada.* Ottawa: Information Canada, 1971.

Springate, D.J.V. "Regional Development Incentives Grants and Private Investments in Canada." Unpublished PhD thesis, Harvard University, Grad. School of Business Administration.

Usher, Dan. "Some Questions About the Regional Development Incentives Act." *Canadian Public Policy* (I), 1975, pp. 557−76.

Vanderkamp, J. "Interregional Mobility in Canada: A Study of the Time Pattern of Migration." *Canadian Journal of Economics* (I), 1968, pp. 595–608.

Woodward, R.S. "Effective Location Subsidies: An Evaluation of DREE Location Subsidies." *Canadian Journal of Economics* (VII), 1974, pp. 501–10.

——————————. "The Capital Bias of DREE Incentives." *Canadian Journal of Economics* (VII), 1974, pp. 161–73.

——————————. "The Effectiveness of DREE's New Location Subsidies." *Canadian Public Policy* (I), 1975, pp. 217–30.

CHAPTER 11

The Rich and the Poor: Federal-Provincial Conflict and the Constitution

The election of the Parti Quebecois in November 1978 ended the temporary truce in federal-provincial relations which had lasted for some time. There were other occasions when provincial governments had opposed Confederation, but never before had a government been elected whose main aim was to seek secession from Canada. During the remainder of the '70s political debate was dominated by charges and countercharges of the costs versus benefits of Confederation to Quebec and the rest of Canada. Canadians then found to their dismay that the defeat in 1980 of the Quebec referendum proposal for sovereignty-association did not solve the problem of national unity. Instead, western provinces, particularly Alberta, became more vociferous in their demands for change. Indeed, various western separatist organizations appeared to grow in popularity. Recent federal actions to repatriate the constitution have fuelled further political fragmentation of the country.

Canada is not unique in having difficulties containing various separatist movements and in her problems of national unity. The sixties and seventies saw a rise in nationalism which also manifested itself in ethnic nationalism within countries. Well-known examples are the Basque movement in Spain, the Scottish and Welsh nationalist movements in Britain, the Flemish movement in Belgium, and the continuous conflict in northern Ireland. Our national unity problem is similar to that in other countries in one respect: the clash of two cultures and languages. However, the Canadian situation is also quite different because of its regional fragmentation (the West versus Ontario and Quebec, the Maritimes versus the rest of the country). Indeed, many foreign observers maintain that the unique feature of the Canadian situation is that Confederation is evaluated from the particular point of view of how a certain province has fared over the years.[1] Economic considerations appear to have achieved unusual prominence in the debate.

The reasons for the crisis in Confederation are many. Clearly, the clash of two cultures and the language question are important and will always be as long as the French-speaking population makes up a significant proportion of the total. The conflict, as old as Confederation, was addressed in the mid-sixties by the Royal Commission on Bilingualism and Biculturalism which coincided with the Quiet Revolution in Quebec. Some of the recommendations of the commission were included in the Official Languages Acts of 1969, which tried to redress the balance in the federal civil service between English and French. As a result, the participation of French Canadians in the civil service and in federal politics has greatly increased. In Quebec, the legal position on the use of French was expanded first by the Bourassa government (Bill 22), and more recently by the Levesque government (the controversial Bill 101). Both bills intended to improve access of French Canadians to business in Quebec by regulating the language of work and the language of education. These efforts produced a backlash in English-speaking Canada which later culminated in its vehement reaction to the air-traffic controllers' strike (referred to in Quebec as the "Gens de l'air affair"). This perhaps convinced Quebeckers of the lack of understanding in English Canada of their problems.

Another reason for increased friction within Confederation is the development of a backlash against "big government" and the slowdown of economic growth. Big government, which is usually identified with Ottawa, is frequently seen as the source of all evils in modern society (inflation, low productivity in industry, excessive regulation). Ottawa is no longer seen—if it ever was—as a unifying force, but as an unwieldy bureaucracy trying to grab power it should not have. The slowdown in economic growth means that as the cake is no longer growing appreciably, all the cake-eaters are going to make certain that they receive what they regard as their fair share (see Chapter 1). In this context the failure of regional policies to eradicate disparities are important.

In this chapter the economic sources of discontent are analysed, with concentration on tariffs, freight rates, and federal tax and expenditure policies. Then the optimum division of power that is possible in a federal system is examined from a theoretical viewpoint. Finally, some of the proposals for constitutional reform as they pertain to economic issues are discussed.

The Economic Sources of Discontent: The Provinces

Freight Rates

Freight rates have always received a prominent position in the list of grievances, not only on the Prairies, but also in the Maritimes. The most contentious freight rate on the Prairies is the Crow Rate, which nobody in federal politics dares to touch. The Prairie provinces are ambivalent towards the Crow Rate: ambivalent in the sense that the rate assists the grain farmers and hurts the livestock producers. The grain farmer receives the world price minus transport costs for his grain and therefore the lower the transport charges, the higher his revenue, a situation which gives the farmer a vested interest in maintaining the Crow Rate. The livestock farmer, in contrast, suffers from the Crow Rate, since the cost of feed (grain) is higher because of the Crow Rate than it would be otherwise. The position of the grain farmer is the one most often heard.

Other freight rate concerns of the Prairie provinces include the contention that (a) rates on exports of manufactured products are higher than rates on exports of raw materials, thus discouraging exports of processed goods from the West; (b) the West does not receive the same zone or blanket rates on imported goods as the East. This means that smaller communities pay higher rates, thus hampering decentralization of economic activity; (c) the rates on goods shipped to the Prairies are frequently higher than those for the same products shipped to Vancouver at a greater distance. This inhibits the development of wholesaling and distribution centres in the Prairies; (d) westbound rates on manufactured products are frequently lower than eastbound rates, which makes it difficult for western producers to compete both locally and nationally; (e) the across-the-board rate increases in recent years have exacerbated these rate anomalies.[2]

In order to prove whether these charges are true, it has to be demonstrated that the rate anomalies exist and that they have the alleged effects. Norrie (1979) showed that most of the allegations were unfounded and argued that in view of the fact that about 70 percent of the traffic from the Prairies moves at the lowest rate, the overall burden on the Prairie economy cannot be large. However, this argument ignores the possibility that many goods do not move at all because of the high transport costs.

The Maritime provinces have perhaps been more successful in lobbying for freight-rate adjustments than the Prairies. The Maritime Freight Rates Act, after its latest amendments, gives shippers a subsidy of 30 percent of rail or trucking freight rates on preferred movements in select territory. Select territory includes Newfoundland, the Maritime provinces and parts of Quebec. Preferred movements include all movements except to and from the United States, shipments to the Maritimes from abroad or the rest of Canada and passenger traffic. The act therefore subsidizes export movements from the Maritimes but not import movements and is therefore detrimental to other provinces who face the opposite situation. It should be pointed out that the difficulty of assessing who actually bears the economic burden depends on the relative supply and demand elasticities of the commodities involved.

Recently, the Maritimes complained about ocean freight rates on manufactured or semi-manufactured products. The container rates on North Atlantic movements to and from Halifax are the same as those to and from Montreal despite the longer distance to Montreal. Indeed, a Montreal exporter can have his container shipped to Halifax for further export with no extra charge, a privilege not given to Maritime shippers located outside the Halifax area. This anomaly is caused by competitive conditions in the North Atlantic, over which the federal government has little control (Bryan 1980).

Little empirical research has been conducted on how important transport costs are in limiting commodity flows and the location of industry (see Chapter 10). Without more research it is difficult to say whether they are as important as they have been made out to be. If research confirms that they are, one should ask whether the natural locational disadvantage of the West and the Maritimes be tampered with by subsidies to transport users, in many cases paid for by consumers or taxpayers in central Canada. Perhaps it would be more efficient to encourage the development of high-productivity, footloose industries in the outlying regions.

Tariffs

Tariffs have also been of longstanding concern to the West. The National Policy was built around high tariffs to encourage the development of Canadian manufacturing. A manufacturing industry developed, but mainly in Ontario and Quebec. This means that all Canadian consumers have to bear the cost of the tariff, although the benefits accrue only to producers in Ontario and Quebec. If the federal government spent the tariff revenue equally in the provinces, the net burden of the tariff would not be equally distributed.

Several recent studies have been done on the regional impact of the tariff. Pinchin (1979) found that in 1970, 1.7 million Canadians were employed in industries receiving tariff protection; 49 percent of these industries were in Ontario and 31.2 in Quebec. Table 24 indicates that tariff protection may indeed disproportionately favour the central provinces, presumably because most manufacturing industries locate near the markets.

Another complaint from the West is that because raw material producers frequently have to buy tariff protected machinery and because they themselves are not protected by tariffs, their value-added is not as high as it otherwise would be. Producers will therefore make less payments to labour, capital and other natural resources. This argument may also have an element of truth in it, even though there is little empirical evidence of any industry being adversely affected by the tariff structure.[3]

Federal Tax and Expenditure Policies

Federal tax and expenditure policies form perhaps the most contentious issue in the present constitutional debate. The issue has two aspects: (a) some tax policies are alleged to be unconstitutional and discriminatory, and (b) some provinces are alleged to receive more than their fair share of federal expenditures.

The charge that taxation policies are discriminatory comes from the federal treatment of energy. Energy resources, like other resources, are within the provincial domain. According to the western provinces the federal government has no right to levy taxes in this field unless there is a clearly recognized national emergency. The federal government does, however, have unlimited taxing power and jurisdiction over exports and interprovincial trade. Using this prerogative, Ottawa has levied an export tax on oil. In the National Energy Program announced in October 1980, the federal government also imposed a tax on the sales of all natural gas. The western provinces argue that this is unconstitutional because (according to the BNA Act) one level of government cannot tax another level of government, and that taxes on oil and gas are discriminatory. If oil and gas are treated in this fashion, why not hydro, uranium and other resources such as timber and gold?

The introduction of the oil export tax meant that the domestic price of oil was kept artificially low (see Chapter 4). A low domestic oil price imposed a substantial penalty on both the domestic producers and on the Alberta government in terms of revenue foregone. The cost to

TABLE 24
Manufacturing Jobs Protected by Tariffs, 1970
(percentage shares of regions)

Region	Shares of jobs protected by tariffs	Job shares protected by tariffs over 20%	Share of all jobs
Ontario	49	28.8	35.5
Quebec	31.2	61.5	28.2
Atlantic	4.4	1.1	9.5
Prairie	7.4	6.4	16.5
Pacific	8.0	2.2	10
	100	100	100

Source: Pinchin, Hugh M. *The Regional Impact of the Canadian Tariff.*

Alberta in 1974−75 was over $2 billion and must have reached mammoth proportions since then. Even though the Albertans are probably willing to share their wealth, this transfer of money to eastern consumers must seem excessive.

The new energy deal between the federal government and Alberta allows for a more rapid escalation of oil and gas prices and confiscates most of the subsidy, to consumers (but not all as Canadian prices will still be kept below world prices), and gives 25 percent of the revenue from the increased oil and gas prices to the federal government, 30 percent to the Alberta government and 45 percent to industry (*The Financial Post*, 12 Sept. 1981). Both the Alberta and federal governments appeared to be reasonably satisfied over the proposed revenue-sharing, but many producers felt that they received less than their share.

The federal government is alleged to allocate its expenditures in a discriminatory fashion, the argument being that some provinces do not receive their fair share of tax revenue. This is a curious argument as DREE payments and equalization payments are designed to be discriminatory and to favour the poorer provinces. In the debate around the possible separation of Quebec, balance sheets were drawn for Quebec and the rest of Canada to show who benefitted the most from Confederation. Usually, they took account of the taxes the federal government collected in the province (personal and corporate income taxes, sales taxes, tariffs, excise taxes, air transport taxes, gas taxes, unemployment insurance payments), and compared the total with the revenue the province received from the federal government in the form of equalization grants, established program financing, social security payments, civil service payments, the oil price subsidy, family allowances, pensions, and DREE grants. These cost-benefit estimates should be treated with a substantial pinch of salt. Albert Breton of the University of Toronto has been quoted as referring to the issue: "It's a lousy subject. There is nothing you can say with certainty. Any guy who opens his mouth is an ass." (*Maclean's* 7 March 1977) estimated for Quebec that benefits of Confederation exceeded costs by $2,986 million in 1975−76.[4] Other estimates from perhaps more reliable sources (Hazledine 1979) have shown that if one takes into account transfers between provinces, as well as the effects on the economy of the Canadian customs union, the Prairies stand to lose from Confederation as does Ontario, whereas Quebec and the Atlantic provinces gain (the Atlantic provinces gain substantially). The results for British Columbia were not clear-cut.

The Economic Sources of Discontent: The Federal Government

The position of the federal government regarding transportation costs and tariffs is not clearly stated as these issues are largely questions of transfers between the provinces. The position of the federal government with regard to resource taxation is clearly stated, as it involves a transfer from the provinces to the federal government. The stance taken by the federal government is partly determined by its fiscal position. Since 1975 the federal deficit has grown to mammoth proportions (reaching 4.8 percent of GNP in 1978), compared with the period 1963–75 when the federal government consistently ran surpluses on a cyclically adjusted basis (Bird 1979:45). Recently, growth in federal expenditures has been larger than the growth in federal revenue. The popular misconception here is that federal expenditures are out of control and extravagant. Total government expenditures (including transfers) increased from 24 percent of GNP in 1947 to over 40 percent in 1975, but what is usually not realized is that over the entire postwar period, increased provincial and local expenditures accounted for 67 percent of this growth. Whereas the federal government has run deficits, the provincial governments have run surpluses in the past few years. In 1973, their total deficit was $1,756 million and in 1979 their total surplus was $553 million (Department of Finance 1980:122).

The problems of the federal government do not stem from rampant expenditures on goods and services but from a combination of factors. The first factor is that transfer payments have made up 72 to 80 percent of total federal expenditures since 1975 (Table 25). These consist of direct payments to people in the form of unemployment insurance, family allowance, old age pensions, and interests on debt; and payments to provinces in the form of equalization payments, Established Program Financing (EPF), expenditures on social services, and subsidies on imported oil. EPF and social service payments are currently indexed to GNP. Equalization payments also increase in proportion to GNP and work in such a way that when resource revenues to the Alberta Treasury increase, Ottawa must give other provinces more equalization payments without receiving additional revenue from Alberta (see Chapter 10). In recognition of this problem, Ottawa introduced an amendment to the effect that only half of nonrenewable natural resource revenue would be subject to equalization, and the absolute limit for natural resource equalization was one-third of total equalization transfers (1977). Nevertheless, it is estimated that $1 billion of present equalization payments are energy-related.

In addition, Ottawa pays a subsidy to the provinces that have to rely on imported oil in order to equalize the price of oil across the country. The cost of this subsidy has escalated with the increased oil price and increased imports (Table 25), whereas the revenue from the oil export tax has not, as oil exports are being phased out. The cost of the import compensation program was estimated at $3 billion in 1980.[5] In general, the federal government has, until the recent budget, received very little

TABLE 25
Transfer Payments
as a Percentage of Federal Government Expenditures (selected years)

	Transfers to persons	Interest on public debt	Subsidies	Capital assistance	Transfers to non-residents	Transfers to other levels of gov't.	Total transfers
1950	26	18	3	0	1	9	57
1960	29	11	4	0	1	14	59
1970	27	12	4	1	2	22	68
1975	30	10	9	1	2	22	74
1976	30	12	6	1	1	22	72
1977	30	12	5	1	1	23	72
1978	30	13	5	1	2	22	73
1979	30	16	7	1	2	24	80
1980	27	16	9	1	1	21	75

Source: Department of Finance, Annual Review 1981, Reference Table 52.

money from the energy sector because of the liberal corporate tax write-offs for exploration and development expenses. Federal revenue in other areas has not expanded rapidly either, mainly because of actions in the tax field. In successive budgets since 1974, the federal government has cut income taxes, sales taxes and corporate taxes with an implied revenue loss of $14.2 billion in 1979. The indexing of personal income taxes introduced in 1973 is also estimated to have contributed to a cumulative loss of tax revenue of $6 billion (Department of Finance 1980:113).

The increase in the size of the federal deficit and the statutory nature of many of the expenditures mean that Ottawa has very little fiscal leverage with which to stabilize the economy. The National Energy Program and the energy agreement with Alberta should make substantial contributions towards curbing the deficit. However, the basic question still remains: should the federal government be allowed into areas of provincial jurisdiction; indeed, what is an optimum division of power in a federal system? In the next section the theoretical issues will be examined.

Centralization vs. Decentralization: Economic Viewpoint

The recent debate on the need for constitutional change in Canada has sparked interest in the economics of federalism, particularly in issues relating to the most efficient division of power between the various levels of government.[6] If the standard of judging the merits of different constitutional arrangements is to be efficiency, the question is efficiency relating to what? What does the average citizen want from a constitution? It is contended that most citizens want a system of government that (1) protects civil liberties—a government should not be allowed to act in an arbitrary manner towards individuals; (2) responds easily and quickly to changes in citizens' wants—democracy must work; and (3) can perform these two functions at as low a cost to citizens as possible—the tax dollars should be well spent. Recent economic thinking appears to favour a federal system as opposed to a unitary state regarding the second criterion, but is ambivalent about the first and third.

The argument that civil liberties are better protected by a federal system dates to the so-called Federalist Papers.[7] Any government, by definition, restricts individual liberties. A strong, powerful unitary government has the most power to curtail liberty, whereas a fragmented form of government with many competing levels (federal versus provincial, provincial versus municipal) is unable to reduce liberty as much. Overlapping of power and conflict between the levels of governments are in this sense desirable, as they provide checks and balances on the power of a given level of government. The above argument has some flaws, however. West and Winer (1980) point out that a federal system, in itself, does not guarantee civil rights, and that provincial autonomy only results in the local majority depriving the local minority of its civil rights; witness Quebec's Bill 101 depriving some members of the non-French speaking minority of the right to send their children to English-speaking schools. West and Winer argue that in order for a federal system to guarantee maximum protection of civil liberties, a charter of rights should be entrenched in its constitution.

Efficiency in responding to citizens' wants is essentially an economic aim. Small units of government are more likely to promote efficiency than large units (Pennock 1959). Assume that a country has 100 citizens. Assume that 60 citizens favour free education and 40 oppose it. In a unitary democracy free education would be provided, and 40 percent of the citizens would remain dissatisfied. Assume instead that the country contains two provinces with 50 people in each. In one province 40 favour free education and 10 oppose it; in the other province 20 favour free education and 30 are against. Under a federal system free education would be provided in the first province but not in the second, and 30 percent of the total population would remain dissatisfied, which is less than the 40 percent in a unitary state. The smaller the unit of government, the more likely it is to contain like-minded people and therefore the greater the probability that a citizen will be in agreement with government policy. If a minority of people do not agree with a policy pursued in their jurisdiction, it is possible for them to move to a jurisdiction that suits them ("voting with one's feet"). An example of this is the out-migration from Quebec after the controversial language legislation was introduced by the Levesque government.

The question of the most efficient design for providing public service can be discussed and analysed from three different angles: economies of scale, jurisdictional spillovers and leakages. Some public services probably have substantial economies of scale and are therefore produced more cheaply by a central government. National defence is one example. It should be cheaper to run one big central army than for each jurisdiction to run a separate army. It is also claimed that there are economies of scale in tax collection. If many government services are subject to substantial economies of scale, the total cost of production of government services under a loosely federated system would be higher than that under a unitary system. However, little is known about economies of scale in the production of services because it is extremely difficult, if not impossible, to devise a reasonable measure of output of services. The output of a police force, for example, could be measured in terms of the number of arrests or the number of parking tickets, or the number of charges laid. If the amount of police protection were increased, the number of offences would probably decline as people would be afraid of getting caught. As a result, the cost per unit of output would increase greatly, but the quality of service would also improve. There are similar measurement problems in the provision of other services.

McDonald (1979) estimated the cost to Quebec of a decentralized public service to be $182 per family per year. If this figure bears any relation to reality, the benefits of centralization are not small.

Some public services have spillover effects. To take a hypothetical example, if one jurisdiction in a Federal State spent a large amount on defence, and an adjacent jurisdiction did not, the latter jurisdiction would act as a free rider on the protection of the other, a benefit it would not pay for as it could not be taxed by the defence-spending jurisdiction. This would lead to a less than optimum supply of this service under decentralization. For this reason some services should be produced, or at least financed, centrally.

A third argument in favour of centralization is that under a loosely federated system, it would be difficult for each unit to perform stabilization policies because of the large leakages. The larger the leakages, the smaller the multiplier. A Keynesian stimulative policy would not be very effective in dealing with the region's problems as so much of the new demand generated would spill over on imports.

The economic solution to these problems would involve reassigning power to higher and higher jurisdictional levels until all spillovers, leakages and economies of scale will have been captured. Breton and Scott (1980) reject these arguments for centralization of many services and maintain instead that economies of scale, spillovers and leakages can be solved through negotiation between the levels of governments involved. Indeed, Breton and Scott argue that in the Canadian context an extended constitutional assembly should be called whose sole purpose would be to design a constitution. The assembly should consist of government and opposition members from all levels of government, as well as interested citizens. The resulting bargaining should produce an efficient system of government.

It can be concluded that economic theory does not offer solutions as to the 'correct' division of powers in a federal system. A decentralized system of government is more likely to respond quickly to changes in citizens' wants, but some centralization is necessary to handle interjurisdictional spillovers and to capture economies of scale in the provision of services. Which form of government will give the most protection of civil liberties is not clear.

Proposals for Constitutional Change
and/or Adjustments in Federal-Provincial Fiscal Arrangements

Parallelling the economic theory debate, there are two trends in the political debate: province-building or decentralization versus country-building and centralization. The country-builders had their heyday during the immediate postwar period until the mid-sixties. Central control of the fiscal system was thought to be necessary to conduct successful fiscal policy for the promotion of growth and stabilization. More recently, the centralist effort has shifted towards economic regulation. Country-builders see the federal government as the chief instrument of national development. Most problems are defined nationally and solutions are sought nationally (Evenson and Simcon 1979). The Task Force on National Unity (1979) took a definite country-building stance.

The province-building stance was fuelled by the centralist developments. It was caused partly by provincial dissatisfaction over what was perceived as discriminatory federal policies and partly by increased economic importance of the provinces through the transfer of taxing powers. The growth in importance of health and education, areas under provincial jurisdiction, also increased the roles of provincial governments. Also, the wealth that natural resources had brought to some provinces made their governments strong and assertive. An additional factor was the strong economic links with the United States in the form of foreign investment and trade, links which pulled the country in a north-south direction. The province-builders feel that if there is a national interest, it is the sum of provincial interests. This viewpoint was well illustrated in the constitutional conference of premiers held in fall 1980, when Prime Minister Trudeau, after listening to all the diverging viewpoints of the provinces, asked rhetorically, "But who speaks for Canada?" Premier Lougheed of Alberta quickly replied, "We all do."

In the remainder of the chapter recent proposals for equalization payments, resource taxation and the sharing of resource rents are discussed. The federal government has included the principle of equalization in the proposed amending formula for the constitution, but the exact form is not specified. The sharing of resource revenues was not addressed in the Bill of Rights.

Transfers

The public finance literature recognizes three reasons for extending federal grants to provinces: the fiscal gap, interjurisdictional spillovers and fiscal equity (Boadway 1980:41–9). The fiscal gap argument was alluded to in the introduction to Chapter 7. In a federal system each level of government has certain taxing powers and certain expenditures, but the taxing powers may not generate sufficient revenue to cover expenses. Provincial governments in general find that their power in levying taxes is limited, and not just because of the restrictions contained in the BNA Act. The BNA Act does restrict provinces to the levying of direct taxes but in practice the courts have interpreted this point liberally. The major limitation appears to be economic: if a province raises its taxes to a high level, the taxes may deter labour and capital from moving in to this province—to the detriment of economic activity. In many cases the provinces have fallen over themselves in granting tax concessions to attract industry.

Interjurisdictional spillover was discussed above. Spillovers or externalities occur when one province's activity benefits not only the residents in the province itself, but also residents in other provinces. This benefit to other provinces is not taken into consideration by the province providing the activity and so it will not be provided in sufficient amounts. The optimum solution would be for the federal government to provide conditional grants for the province providing the particular activity.

The last argument, fiscal equity, is derived from the basic principles of taxation: vertical and horizontal equity. Horizontal equity means that two persons in the same financial circumstances should pay the same tax, and vertical equity that persons in different circumstances should pay different taxes. One can extend the principle of horizontal equity to the provision of public services: persons in similar circumstances in different parts of the country should have access to the same level of public services. In a unitary state, the government attempts to provide the same services across the country. In a federal system differences obviously arise because of different tax bases. For this reason the federal government should give grants to equalize services across the country. In summary, the fiscal gap argument justifies the demand for getting more money or tax leverage from the federal government, the spillover argument for conditional grants, and the fiscal equity argument for equalization payments. In practice, the federal government is involved in all these forms of payments. The EPF program is a form of conditional grants in that transfers of tax points are given to the provinces to close up any fiscal gaps, and equalization payments are given to equalize public services across the country.

The federal government is not happy about the present system of transfers, since the payments account for the major share of federal expenditures. Equalization payments, in particular, are a problem as they do not involve a direct transfer from a rich province to a poor province, but a transfer from the federal government to a poor province. Indeed, as mentioned in the previous chapter, under the present formula (which equalizes only 50 percent of the oil and gas revenues), Ontario is eligible for equalization. Another objection to the equalization scheme is that it is based only on tax capacity of the provinces, not on revenue need. It is possible that some provinces have higher costs in the provision of services than others because of high transport costs and high dependency ratios. (In the United States equalization payments take account of revenue needs as well as tax capacity.) A third criticism is that the present formula may encourage provinces to pursue policies that maximize their revenue from equalization. For example, before 1977 the corporate tax base excluded provincially-owned crown corporations. This meant that if a province, for example Quebec, nationalized the asbestos industry, the corporate tax yield of the province would decrease and equalization payments to the province would increase. This loophole was closed in 1977. The present formula combines the tax base in both public-enterprise and private sectors. It is possible that there are other loopholes in the system.

There are many suggestions for changing the system of equalization payments, varying from their abolishment to changing their structure. According to the abolishment viewpoint, grants to poor provinces make services better than they would otherwise be; people are therefore better off than they would be if the provinces did not receive grants and are therefore less likely to move to a richer province. Abolitionists conclude that grants retard the economic adjustment process and leave the poor provinces permanently dependent. However, for this argument to hold, it has to be proven that migration is beneficial and that grants retard migration. The effects of outmigration are unclear, as discussed in chapter 10, as some researchers maintain that migration may bleed a region of its best workers and therefore leave the region worse off than before. There is some evidence that grants retard migration (Courchene 1970), but whether this is good or bad obviously depends on whether migration is beneficial.

One of the best-known proposals for reform is Courchene's (1978). Courchene suggests a two-tier system. The first tier would equalize only three sources of tax revenue compared with the present 29. These would be personal, corporate and sales taxes, all of which are levied by the federal government. This means that if one province becomes rich, the others would get equalization, but the rich province would itself contribute most of it. The remaining provincial revenue sources would not be fully equalized, and payments to the poorer provinces would come directly from the coffers of the rich without any interference from the federal government. Under this scheme it would be possible to be both a recipient under the first tier and a donor under the second tier. Courchene's proposal would certainly overcome the first objection to the present scheme.

The Parliamentary Task Force on Federal-Provincial Relations (1981) included in its report a discussion of equalization payments. The Task Force felt that Courchene's proposal of transferring some of the responsibility for equalization to the provinces violated one of the basic principles of federalism. The Task Force recommended that the current structure of equalization payments should be maintained with some minor changes, namely that the equalization formula should include 20 percent of resource revenues rather than the current 50 percent, the argument being that if resource revenue accrued to persons rather than provincial governments, it would be subject to federal and provincial income taxes. Thus, the provincial government would receive only 20 percent of resource revenue (the average provincial income tax rate). The Task Force also recommended that all property taxes be included in the formula. The reason for this recommendation is that under the current scheme, only property taxes related to educational expenditures (not municipal expenditures) are equalized. This means that if a province revamps its property tax structure and collects more for municipal purposes, and less for education, its equalization entitlements and that of other provinces would be changed.

The Task Force also recommended that the formula should not discriminate between provinces and be arbitrarily changed in the light of new circumstances. The example given is the treatment of Ontario under the present scheme. Ontario has qualified for equalization payments for the last five years, but has been prevented from collecting them because of an amendment to the law which stops any province from receiving payment if its per capita income is greater than the Canadian average for the most recent three-year period.

Others argue that the revenue from resource ownership should be spread just as income tax revenue is shared across the country to cover costs of education, health and public services. Why should one form of tax revenue be shared and not another (Moore 1975)?

Alberta maintains that there is a major difference. Revenue from *nonrenewable* natural resources is not the same as revenue from other sources of taxation. Alberta's riches are only temporary and for this reason the province should be allowed to keep most of the money, to be invested in the development of manufacturing and other ventures which could sustain the province when oil and gas has run out. It should also be added that given the rationale for equalization, only resource revenues which are spent by the government on bettering services should be equalized. The revenues put into the Alberta Heritage Savings and Trust Fund should therefore be exempted.

There have also been several proposals for a more equitable treatment of resource revenues for taxation purposes. Gainer and Powrie argued (1975) that since royalties from oil and gas production are income, they would have been subject to income taxes had they accrued to individuals or corporations. It is only because they accrue to the provincial governments that they are not subject to federal taxes. They therefore propose that the federal government should get a 30 percent share of Alberta's royalties—approximately the equivalent of the tax share it would have got if the royalties had gone to individuals.

Courchene[8] argues that the current attempts by the federal government to tax resource revenues are inequitable and essentially arbitrary. He suggests that a solution to the impasse would be to tax crown corporations such as the Alberta Heritage Savings and Trust Fund. Under the BNA Act activities of one level of government—agencies and crown corporations—cannot be taxed by another level of government. This means that if Ottawa nationalized the auto industry, the Ontario government would lose corporate tax revenue. Similarly, if revenue from the trust fund were used to buy a major oil company, the federal government would not receive any tax revenue. Courchene's proposal is therefore to subject public-sector enterprises to the same tax rates as private enterprises. Federal taxes would then be levied on the Alberta trust fund, Ontario Hydro, Quebec Hydro, and all the provincial liquor control boards. It would also work the other way: provincial governments would be able to tax Petro-Canada and the Bank of Canada if they operated within their jurisdictions. Adoption of Courchene's proposal would require constitutional changes.

Summary and Conclusions

In this chapter some of the areas of discontent in current federal-provincial relations were surveyed. Some of the friction stems from the clash of two cultures, but many are caused by economic concerns. In particular freight rates and tariffs are areas of contention, probably as old as Confederation. Economic analysis has shown that the freight rate issue has probably been overblown, but the lack of in-depth studies makes it difficult to draw any firm conclusions.

A more recent area of dispute is the taxation of energy, and it is true to say that the federal government has acted in a discriminatory fashion in this field. Any solution to the conflict must deal with the "correct" allocation of power between the provinces and the federal government. The economic theory of federal systems does not offer much insight, and for this reason no firm policy conclusions can be drawn. Proposals for changes to the equalization formula and to resource taxation abound, but there is no yardstick against which they can be measured. As such, these problems have to be settled politically.

NOTES

1. See the Report of the Task Force on Canadian Unity (1979).
2. For a statement of the West's position, see Blackman 1977 and Norrie 1976 and 1979.
3. Wilkinson and Norrie (1975) measured effective protection given to Canadian industry by the tariff structure. The effective protection

rate measures by how much tariffs allow an industry to increase value added. If an industry has to pay high tariffs on its inputs while its output has no protection, the effective protection rate would be negative. Wilkinson and Norrie demonstrated that this was not common.
4. For a careful analysis of the redistributive impact of major federal transfer programs, see Carter (1980).
5. Courchene, T.J. "The issue is not the price, but how to share the money." *Globe and Mail,* 28 Oct. 1980.
6. This section is based on Breton and Scott 1980.
7. See Breton and Scott 1980.
8. Courchene, *ibid.*

BIBLIOGRAPHY

Bird, R.M. *Financing Canadian Government, A Quantitative Overview* Toronto: Canadian Tax Foundation, 1979.
Blackman, W.J. "A Western Canadian Perspective on the Economics of Confederation." *Canadian Public Policy* (III), 1977, pp. 414–30.
Boadway, R.W. *Intergovernmental Transfers in Canada.* Toronto: Canadian Tax Foundation, 1980.
Breton, A. and A. Scott. *The Design of Federations.* Montreal: Institute for Research on Public Policy, 1980.
Bryan, I.A. *Shipping Conference Pricing Policies and Eastern Canadian Ports.* Discussion Paper No. 24. Department of Geography, York University, Toronto.
Carter, G.E. *New Directions in Financing Canadian Federalism.* Occasional Paper No. 13. Centre for Research on Federal Financial Relations, Canberra, The Australian National University, 1980.
Courchene, T.J. "Interprovincial Migration and Economic Adjustment." *Canadian Journal of Economics* (3), 1970, pp. 550–76.
_____ "Avenues of Adjustment: The Transfer System and Regional Disparities." In Michael Walker (ed.), pp. 145–89, *Canadian Confederation at the Crossroads.* Vancouver: The Fraser Institute, 1978.
Department of Finance. *Economic Review.* Ottawa: Supply and Services, 1980, 1981.
Evenson, J. and R. Simeon. "The Roots of Discontent." In *Proceedings of the Workshop on the Political Economy of Confederation, Nov. 8–10, 1978.* Ottawa: Supply and Services, 1979, pp. 165–99.
Gainer, W.D. and T.L. Powrie. "Public Revenue from Canadian Crude Petroleum Production." *Canadian Public Policy* (I), 1975 pp. 1–13.
Hazledine, T. "The Economic Costs and Benefits of the Canadian Federal Customs Union." In *Proceedings of the Workshop on the Political Economy of Confederation,* Nov. 8–10, 1978. Ottawa: Supply and Services, 1979, pp. 1–25.

MacDonald, B. "Decentralization and Provincial Replication of the Canadian Federal Public Services." In *Proceedings of the Workshop on the Political Economy of Confederation,* Nov. 8–10, 1978. Ottawa: Supply and Services, 1979; pp. 129–65.

Moore, A.M. "The Concept of the Nation and Entitlements to Economic Rents." In A. Scott (ed.), pp. 240–46, *Natural Resource Revenues, A Test of Federalism.* Vancouver: UBC Press, 1975.

Norrie, K.H. "Some Comments on Prairie Economic Alienation." *Canadian Public Policy* (II), 1976, pp. 211–24.

———— "Western Economic Grievances: An Overview with Special Reference to Freight Rates." In *Proceedings of the Workshop on the Political Economy of Confederation,* Nov. 8–10, 1978. Ottawa: Supply and Services, 1979, pp. 199–235.

Parliamentary Task Force on Federal-Provincial Fiscal Arrangements. *Fiscal Federalism in Canada.* Ottawa: Supply and Services, 1981.

Pennock, J.R. "Federal and Unitary Government — Disharmony and Frustration." *Behavioural Science* (4), 1959, pp. 147–57.

Pinchin, Hugh McA. *The Regional Impact of the Canadian Tariff.* Economic Council of Canada. Ottawa: Supply and Services, 1979.

Task Force on Canadian Unity. *A Future Together: Observations and Recommendations.* Ottawa: Supply and Services, 1979.

West, E.G. and S.L. Winer. "The Individual, Political Tension and Canada's Quest for a New Constitution." *Canadian Public Policy* (VI), 1980, pp. 3–16.

Wilkinson, B.W. and K.H. Norrie, *Effective Protection and the Return to Capital.* Economic Council of Canada. Ottawa: Information Canada, 1975.

PART III

Stabilization Issues

In this part of the book the stabilization of the economy will be dealt with—the most controversial area in economics. Economists in general agree on microeconomic issues, such as the effects of tariffs on welfare, the detrimental effects of minimum wages on employment of the young and unskilled, and the effects of rent control. They do not agree on issues such as the fundamental causes of inflation and of unemployment, nor on whether monetary policy should be conducted with interest rates or money supply as a target. In a recent survey in the United States (Kearl *et al.* 1979), 57 percent of economists agreed, with some qualifications, that inflation is primarily a monetary phenomenon (43 percent disagreed). However 61 percent did not think that the federal reserve should be instructed to increase the money supply at a fixed rate. Fifty-seven percent thought that government spending should be reduced from its present levels. As a comparison, a full 98 percent of economists agreed that rent controls decreased the quantity and quality of housing.

The reasons for disagreements on macroeconomic issues are probably within the ideological realm. A person of a conservative bent is more likely to espouse the monetarism of Milton Friedman with its basic philosophy of non-interference. A liberal economist is more likely to be a neo-Keynesian (post-Keynesian). A conservative economist believes that the market should be free and that the market will sort everything out if given time. A liberal economist tends to believe that a market does not function or clear perfectly.. A liberal economist agrees with Galbraith that a substantial sector of the economy is not competitive but is dominated by large monopolistic or oligopolistic firms. There are market failures, sometimes caused by traditions and institutions. For somebody caught in the middle between the "isms" there is no easy way out. Solow puts the dilemma rather well:

237

A hopeless eclectic, like me has a terrible time of it . . . I need only listen to Milton Friedman talk for a minute and my mind floods with thoughts of increasing returns to scale, oligopolistic interdependence, consumer ignorance, environmental pollution, intergenerational equity and on and on. There is almost no cure for it, except to listen for a minute to John Kenneth Galbraith, in which case all I can think of are the discipline of competition, the large number of substitutes for any commodity, the stupidity of regulation . . . and on and on. Sometimes I think it is only my weakness of character that keeps me from making obvious errors (1980:2).

The next three chapters follow Solow and are shamefully eclectic at the risk of being wishy-washy. Chapter 12 explains how unemployment and inflation are measured and briefly reviews current theories; chapter 13 reviews Balance of Payments and exchange rates. Both chapters serve as a background to Chapter 14, a discussion of economic stabilization policies in Canada.

BIBLIOGRAPHY

Kearl, J.R., *et al.* "What Economists Think: A Confusion of Economists." *American Economic Review,* Papers and Proceedings (69), 1979, pp. 28–38.
Solow, R.M. "On Theories of Unemployment." *American Economic Review* (70), 1980, pp. 1–11.

CHAPTER 12

Unemployment and Inflation

The pattern of economic development during the 1970s was markedly different from that of the '50s and the '60s. The economic cycles during the latter two decades were characterized by mildly inflationary periods with little or no unemployment, followed by periods of stable prices with rising unemployment. These swings were thought to be amenable to stabilization policies. Monetary policy was believed to be relatively ineffective because neither consumption nor investment were thought to be responsive to movements in the rate of interest. Fiscal policy was regarded to have the potential of bringing the economy to full employment and no inflation. In periods of excess supply and unemployment, all that was necessary was to give additional stimulus to the economy through increased spending either by governments or by consumers. In periods of excess demand, demand could be decreased by curbing government expenditure or increasing taxes.

In the 1970s everything was thrown into chaos. Unemployment and inflation started to rise simultaneously; any policy that improved employment made inflation worse and *vice versa*. The accepted policies no longer seemed to work, and not only policies but also economic theory were thrown into disarray. This chapter will begin with a discussion of the measurement of inflation and unemployment, continue with an explanation of the current theories of inflation and unemployment, and end with a look at alternative policies.

Measurement of Inflation

Inflation is usually defined as an increase in the consumer price index (CPI), and indeed every change in the CPI gets attention from both labour and the press. An increase in the CPI will now lead to an increased basic exemption for income-tax payers, Canada Pension Plan payments for

239

those over 65, disability pensions, family allowance payments, family incomes eligible for child tax credit, alimony payments, labour and business contracts, rental agreements, war veterans' allowance, guaranteed income supplements, old-age security allowance payments, and annuity payments to retired members of the public service, the armed forces and the RCMP (McCracken and Ruddick 1980:1). For this reason it is important to know precisely what the CPI measures.

The CPI is designed to measure over time the cost of a representative basket of goods and services to the average Canadian family. It should therefore contain goods and services that the average family buys. In Canada, this basket of goods is determined by family spending surveys, the latest of which took place in 1974. According to Table 26, in 1974 the average family spent 34.1 percent of income on housing, followed by 21.5 percent on food, compared with 1967 when the average family spent 24.8 percent on food and 31.4 percent on housing. Each major group of commodities also contains subgroups; for example the food group contains meat, which is further broken down into beef, pork and poultry. Each group and subgroup is given a weight based on the proportion of the consumer budget the item represents. Each month federal government surveyors take 110,000 price quotations across Canada on 375 items. Retail and property taxes are included in the prices but income taxes are not as they do not constitute spending. The price increases are then weighted according to their assigned weights and summed. This sum is then compared to the sum in the base year and expressed as a proportion of the base year. An index calculated in this fashion is called *Laspeyeres'* index. There are many other forms an index can take; for example, Paasche's index is weighted on the basis of the current year's expenditures and various types of chain indices in which the weights are changed every year.

Table 27 lists the CPI since 1961. Note that a CPI of 191.2 means that prices have increased by 91.2 percent since the base period; that is, today's prices are 191.2 percent of those in 1971. Similarly, if the CPI shows an increase from 175.1 to 191.2 (1978 and 1979, respectively), this does not mean that prices have increased by 16.1 percent; rather the increase is $\underline{191.2 - 175.1} = 9.2$ percent.

$$175.1$$

There are several problems in using the CPI as an indicator of inflationary trends and of the movement of prices. When a shock to the system, such as a large OPEC increase in the price of oil or a world-wide crop failure, forces the price of energy and grain up, this will show up as increases in the CPI, and could be interpreted by some as a sign of an overheated economy. It is therefore important to look at the disaggregated indices as well. Statistics Canada includes these in its monthly publication, *The Consumer Price Index*. Table 26 shows the disaggregated index for January 1981. It also shows that by far the largest increases occurred in food prices, followed by transportation costs; *The Consumer Price Index* points to beef prices as being one of the major determinants of the food price increase, which has risen by 206 percent since 1971.

A second potential problem in interpreting CPI changes is that the weights are fixed so that the current index is based on expenditure patterns in 1974. Expenditure patterns change constantly. For example, in response to higher beef and fish prices, it is likely that consumers have shifted to pork and poultry, thus cushioning the effects of higher beef or fish prices on consumer welfare. Indeed a recent newspaper report says that Canadians have decreased their consumption of beef by 30 percent (*Globe and Mail*, 14 April, 1981). What this means is that if the elasticity of demand for beef or fish is high, the importance of these items in the budget has decreased, and therefore the CPI overstates the importance of some price increases.

Other problems arise from quality changes. If, for example, a refrigerator sold in 1981 contains more insulation than one sold in 1974, there has been a quality change, and part of the price increase reflects this change. Is a car sold in 1981 the same as a car sold in 1974? Quite likely not. It is obviously extremely difficult for a compiler of a consumer index to judge what part of a price increase is due to a quality change, and what part is not. How to assign accurate prices to the cost of shelter is also extremely difficult and surrounded by contro-

TABLE 26
Basket of Goods Used in Calculating the CPI (1967 and 1974)

Goods	Weight (1967)	Weight (1974)	CPI 1981 (Jan.)
Food	24.8	21.5	278.5
Housing	31.4	34.1	213.1
Clothing	11.3	10.1	184.1
Transportation	15.2	15.8	221.4
Health and personal care	4.5	4.0	207.9
Recreation, reading and education	6.9	8.3	183.1
Tobacco and alcoholic beverages	6.0	6.2	194.4
Total	100	100	224.1

Source: Statistics Canada, *The Consumer Price Index*, 1981 (Cat. 62.001).

TABLE 27
The Consumer Price Index, 1961–81

Year	CPI	Changes in CPI	Food
1961	74.9	0.9	1.5
1962	75.8	1.2	1.9
1963	77.2	1.8	3.2
1964	78.6	1.8	1.6
1965	80.5	2.4	2.6
1966	83.5	3.7	6.4
1967	86.5	3.6	1.4
1968	90.0	4.0	3.2
1969	94.1	4.6	4.2
1970	97.2	3.3	2.3
1971	100.0	2.9	1.0
1972	104.8	4.8	7.6
1973	112.8	7.6	14.6
1974	125.0	10.9	16.3
1975	138.5	10.8	12.9
1976	148.9	7.5	2.7
1977	160.8	8.0	8.3
1978	175.1	8.9	15.5
1979	191.2	9.2	13.2
1980	210.6	10.2	10.7
1981	236.9	12.5	11.4

Source: Statistics Canada. *The Consumer Price Index,* 1982, (Cat. 62.001).

versy. Obviously not just house prices should be included, since only a small proportion of the population are in the house-buying market. Shelter costs should also include rent, as well as property taxes, interest charges and maintenance costs. ·

In addition to the CPI, there are two other price indices published in Canada: the GNE price deflator and the wholesale price index. The GNE price deflator is used to calculate changes in real GNE and measures price trends of goods and services actually produced in the Canadian economy as well as changes in the amount consumed. It is not a base-weighted index, but rather the base shifts from year to year. It would therefore be expected to show more moderate changes than the CPI as it allows for changes in the consumption pattern. It is also more comprehensive in measuring price changes since it includes not only consumption goods, but also the other components of aggregate demand. This index is published on a quarterly basis.

The third index is the monthly industrial selling price index, which is an index of selling prices of goods leaving the factory gate (wholesale prices). It excludes sales and excise taxes, transport costs and distributors' margins. This index tends to lead the CPI: increases in industrial selling prices later show up as increases in the CPI.

Unemployment and Its Measurement

In the same way as there is much ignorance about what the CPI is and what it measures, there is also ignorance about the unemployment rate and other measures pertaining to the labour force. Information on employment and unemployment is compiled by Statistics Canada from a monthly survey and published in *The Labour Force*. The labour force survey is based on a sample of 56,000 households representing residents of Canada over 15 years of age, except for persons living in the NWT and the Yukon, persons living on Indian reservations, institutionalized people, and members of the armed forces. The labour force is composed of that proportion of the population 15 years or over who, during the sampling week, (a) did any work at all; (b) had work, but could not work that week because of illness or disability, personal or family responsibilities, bad weather, strike or a lock-out, vacation or other reasons; (c) were without work, had actively looked for work in the past four weeks and were available for work; (d) had not actively looked for work in the past four weeks, but had a new job which would begin in four weeks or less from the reference week, and were available for work.

People in categories (a) and (b) are counted as employed, and those in categories (c) and (d) as unemployed. The total labour force is therefore made up of the number of employed people plus the number of unemployed. Given this definition, students are not included in the labour force, nor are most pensioners, the reason being that if a person does not actively look for work, the person is not in the labour force (unless the person has been laid off within the last six months). Many people who live in areas of high unemployment become so discouraged that they give up hope of finding a job, and therefore are no longer included in the labour force. For this reason unemployment statistics probably underestimate the number of unemployed in depressed areas.

During the 1970s the labour force grew considerably.[1] The average growth rate between 1970 and 1979 was 3.9 percent compared with 2.2 percent for the previous decade. Some of this increase was obviously caused by population growth, but a large part was caused by increased participation of women and youths. The participation rate for women during the '70s climbed to an average of 39.4 percent from 29.4 percent a decade earlier, and by 1979 reached 44.8 percent. The participation rate for youth increased from 55.8 to 61.3 percent. Job availability did not keep up with these increases in the labour force. The employment growth averaged 2.8 percent compared with a 3.9 percent growth in the labour force, implying a rise in the unemployment rate. The average unemployment rate during the '70s was 6.7 percent compared with 4.6 percent in the previous decade. In 1979 the rate was 7.5 percent. In the same year (1979), the unemployment rate for adult men was only 4.6 percent, a rate which did not show large variations over the decade. In contrast, the unemployment rate for adult women showed a steady increase over the '70s, reaching 7.0 percent in 1979. The rate for youth was 11.8 percent. It is clear that unemployment affected these two groups disproportionately.

Unemployment is sometimes categorized into cyclical, seasonal, frictional, and structural unemployment. Cyclical unemployment is unemployment caused by a deficient demand for labour, which in turn is due to a deficient demand for goods and services. If most of the unemployment is diagnosed as cyclical, the obvious cure is to increase aggregate demand through measures that would increase (1) consumption, (2) investment, (3) government expenditures (4) exports, or (5) decrease imports. Seasonal unemployment occurs because some industries require only seasonal labour (for example, agriculture and construction). Accordingly, Statistics Canada publishes a seasonally adjusted unemployment rate. Frictional unemployment occurs because the labour market cannot operate perfectly, in that a job cannot be matched without delay to the person looking for work. When a young person enters the labour force, it is likely that he or she will have to spend some time looking for a suitable job even though there are plenty of job vacancies. Frictional unemployment can actually increase during periods of buoyant demand. People may spend a longer time looking for the ideal job when there are plenty of jobs around. Frictional unemployment can be defined as the amount of unemployment matched by vacancies.

Structural unemployment occurs when there are structural changes in the economy caused by technological change or a long-term decline in the demand for some products. Workers and vacancies are mismatched either in terms of geography or in terms of qualifications. Examples are the coal-mining industry in Cape Breton or the likely layoff of a substantial number of typists because of the introduction of word-processors. Solutions to structural unemployment include job-retraining programs and manpower mobility programs.

It is believed that the current unemployment rate can to a large degree be attributed to frictional and structural factors in the economy. Many of the new entrants to the labour force do not have the required skills to get a job. This could mean a real shortage of people in some occupations and surpluses in other areas. It takes the market considerable time to adjust to shortages, since it takes time for workers to acquire the necessary skills. At the time of writing there is a shortage of people with computer-oriented skills, and several studies forecast an imminent shortage of technically trained workers. Another factor which may work against the employment of young people is minimum wage legislation. Economic theory predicts that raising wages above the equilibrium level will decrease the quantity of work demanded of persons and therefore throw some persons out of work. It will also induce more workers to enter the labour force. Both these factors will increase the unemployment rate. A large number of studies have indicated that a minimum wage adversely affects the unemployment rate, particularly among young people (West and McKee 1980).

There are other explanations for the high unemployment rate in Canada. In the first place, because the unemployment rate is higher for women and young people, it may be assumed that the attachment of these groups to their job may be less firm than it is for adult males (or less firm than it used to be), partly because of changing priorities and attitudes regarding work. Women, for example, may give priority to family responsibilities.

Secondly, there is evidence that the introduction of unemployment insurance has increased unemployment. In theory, it is usually assumed that a person will trade off income for leisure, the amount depending on the opportunity cost of leisure, his or her lifestyle, and on how much leisure has already been obtained. The introduction of unemployment insurance basically decreased the opportunity cost (the price) of leisure and therefore encouraged people to consume more leisure: they stay unemployed longer than necessary, or quit their job for no good reason. Grubel, Maki and Sax (1975) studied the effects of the liberalization of unemployment insurance benefits in 1971. At that time people became eligible for unemployment insurance after working for eight weeks during the preceding year as compared with the previous regulation of thirty weeks during the two previous years. The new regulation allowed those who had quit their jobs to claim insurance, whereas before only those who had been laid off qualified. This liberalization in the law is estimated to have increased the unemployment rate by 0.8 percent.

The total contribution of unemployment insurance to the unemployment rate was estimated to be 1.4 percentage point or 22 percent of the number of unemployed (1972). Later studies have yielded even higher estimates. Bodkin and Cournoyer (1978) estimate the effects of liberalization to be 1.3 percent, Lazar (1978) 1.5 percent and Reid and Meltz (1979) 1.9 percent. Lazar also disaggregated his study according to men, women and youth. Unemployment insurance appeared to have the largest effect on the unemployment rate for youth.[2]

It should be noted, however, that even if the studies confirm that the liberalization of unemployment insurance has raised the unemployment rate, they have not necessarily proved that it is the workers who are taking advantage of the scheme; employers, too, may be taking advantage of the system and laying off workers at any downturn instead of keeping them on. An American study has shown that some of the effect, indeed a large part of the effect, of unemployment insurance is caused by employers laying off workers (Feldstein 1978).

Because unemployment has so many facets, it would be useful to know what a non-inflationary unemployment rate (the unemployment rate adjusted for cyclical unemployment) would be. Only cyclical unemployment is amenable to traditional monetary and fiscal policies. Estimates of the non-inflationary unemployment rate vary between 5.5 and 7.5 percent. In 1979, the Economic Council of Canada (1979:14) estimated the rate to be 6 percent. An unemployment rate of nearly 6 percent is considered a Keynesian full employment situation, and therefore any attempt to drive the rate below 6 percent would only lead to inflation.

Recent Theories of Unemployment and Inflation

Until recently, inflation theories were usually divided into the two major areas of demand-pull and cost-push. Demand-pull theory was basically a Keynesian theory, stating that inflation would occur if aggregate demand were pushed beyond the full employment level. If aggregate demand expanded when there was less than full employment, employment would expand to its highest level with little effect on prices. Any further expansion in aggregate demand could only result in inflation as no more output could be produced. The only way to eliminate this inflationary gap is to run a budgetary surplus to reduce aggregate demand through a cut in government expenditures, an increase in taxes, or an increase in interest rates designed to reduce investments.

The cost-push theory put the blame of inflation on either big business or unions. Inflation is started when unions attempt to gain a larger share of the pie by pushing for higher wages. These wages are paid by the consumer in the form of higher prices; the process continues if the unions continue demanding higher wages. Alternatively, inflation starts when corporations attempt to get higher profits by raising prices and unions respond by increasing wages.

The demand-pull theory stood up well during the immediate postwar period when inflation and unemployment appeared to be mutually exclusive. The cost-push theory was always popular, particularly the 'blame-the-unions' version, despite its many flaws. The theory rests on the assumption that unions or big business have some monopoly power; otherwise they could not raise prices. However, monopoly power explains why wages and prices are higher in the monopolized sectors but not why prices keep increasing. Neither does the theory explain why inflation suddenly starts—why unions or big corporations suddenly become greedy.

During the 1960s the monetarist theory, which saw inflation as a purely monetary phenomenon, gained supporters. The inflation rate was seen to be approximately equal to the rate of growth in money supply minus the rate of growth in output. The theory rested on the resurrected quantity theory of money: $MV = PT$, where M is the stock of money in circulation, V is the velocity of circulation, P is the price level, and T is the volume of transactions. The quantity theory was reformulated by Friedman into a theory of demand for money balances: $M_d = kPT$; that is, the demand for money balances is a function that varies directly with money income. The proportion of income that people wish to hold in the form of money (k) is determined by the opportunity cost of holding money and structural factors in the economy such as population growth, productivity and thrift. If the money supply in the economy is expanded beyond its expected rate, this means that people will have larger money balances than they want. It is assumed that these balances will be spent on goods and services. If the growth in the money supply is greater than the growth rate in goods and services, prices will be bid up and inflation will ensue.

Of course, a Keynesian would not quibble with the idea that money can cause inflation, but in the '60s and early '70s there was considerable disagreement between the two groups, particularly regarding the effects of the money rate of interest on investment and consumption: the Keynesians maintained that most spending is interest inelastic whereas the monetarists claimed that it is interest elastic. The monetarists even went so far as to claim that for this reason fiscal policy was useless. If a budgetary deficit were financed by borrowing from the central bank (that is, by printing money), this measure would only lead to inflation; if the deficit were financed by borrowing from the public, the net effect would be zero because public expenditures would crowd out private expenditures. The selling of bonds would drive up interest rates and therefore lead to a cut in private spending (consumption or investment). Even monetary policy was regarded as too rough a tool to be effective in the sense that the lag between implementation and result would be too long and too unpredictable. Monetarists concluded that both active fiscal and monetary policies should be rejected and the only course of action was for the monetary authorities to expand the money supply at a rate equal to the rate of growth of real output.

Since the 1970s, the debate has abated and there is at present more agreement on some issues.[3] Friedman has backed down somewhat on his contention that fiscal policy cannot have an effect on the economy, and Keynesians have agreed that it is essential for stabilization policy to limit the growth in the supply of money.

Recent models of inflation and unemployment can be divided into the Phillips curve approach, the monetarist approach and the structural theories.[4] In many cases the monetarist and Phillips curve approaches— the latter is sometimes described as neo-Keynesian—are merged.

The Phillips Curve

The Phillips curve (illustrated below) grew out of an equation, computed by A.W. Phillips, relating wage changes to the unemployment rate. Specifically, Phillips found an inverse relationship between the unemployment rate and the rate of change in wages, as did a number of other researchers. However, it was Richard Lipsey who worked out the theory behind this empirical relationship. Lipsey (1960) argued that the Phillips curve derived from two underlying relationships: (1) a positive relation between wage change and excess demand for labour (the larger the excess demand for labour, the larger the wage change); and (2) an inverse relation between the excess demand for labour and unemployment, as well as the rate of change in the unemployment rate. The relation between the unemployment rate and wage changes is straightforward. Any employer knows that unions can achieve higher wages in periods of booming business than in periods of slack demand. The relation between the rate of change in unemployment and excess demand is more complex. The rate of change in unemployment depends on the difference between the quit rate and the hiring rate. The quit rate is assumed to be constant, whereas the hiring rate varies directly with the unemployment rate and the level of excess demand. Therefore the rate of change in unemployment must vary inversely with unemployment and excess demand. A combination of these effects leads to the conclusion that the rate of wage change depends on the unemployment rate and its rate of change. This explains the typically downward sloping Phillips curve.

Friedman and other monetarists argued that the Phillips curve is an incomplete specification: since real wages and not money wages respond to excess demand, then the money-wage change is a function of not only excess demand and unemployment, but also of the expected inflation rate (Friedman 1968 and Phelps 1968). This means that the trade-off would become unstable over time and could explain the periods in the '70s of high unemployment *and* inflation. The process would be as follows: any rate of inflation that persists for a long period of time will be anticipated by labour and management, and therefore a wage settlement will be made on the basis of excess demand and inflation on the assumption that workers negotiate real wages and not money wages. Let us assume that the economy is at point A in the Phillips curve, and that government finds the unemployment rate of 6 percent too high. It attempts to bring unemployment down by means of monetary and fiscal policy to 2 percent (to B). At B, however, is a new unemployment rate and a new, higher inflation rate that is 4 percent higher than the anticipated rate.

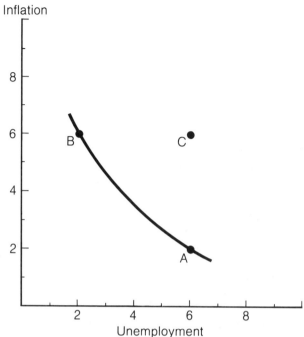

FIGURE 4
The Phillips Curve

Workers realize that their raise in money wages of 6 percent does not correspond to the same increase in real wages. They will therefore quit their jobs, and the unemployment rate will bounce back to 6 percent, by which time the inflation rate is higher. Any attempt to keep the unemployment rate at 2 percent would lead to accelerating inflation. The only possible rate is this 'natural' rate of 6 percent, and for this reason, the long-run Phillips curve becomes a vertical line at the natural rate.

Empirical testing has indeed confirmed the short-term Phillips curve and the near vertical long-run Phillips curve.[5] The position of the vertical curve is determined by frictional, structural and insurance-induced unemployment. Therefore the disappearance of the trade-off in the long run does not mean that economic policy is fruitless, but rather that policy should be geared toward decreasing structural, frictional and insurance-induced unemployment.

Monetarism and Rational Expectations

Monetarists, however, have developed the idea of the uselessness of all stabilization policy, except the policy of expanding the money supply in step with the rate of growth of GNP—if this can be called policy. This idea is based on the theory of rational expectations. The Phillips curve, at least in its early development, rested on the principle of adaptive expectations. For example, if policy-makers tried to reduce the unemployment rate below 6 percent by expansionary policies, the economy would move along the short-run Phillips curve to point B with 6 percent inflation and 2 percent unemployment. The workers would then realize that real wages had dropped, adjust their expectations accordingly and quit their jobs. It is possible, however, that initially they would not adjust their expectations upward by the full amount but err on the downward side—to 4 percent, rather than 6 percent. The theory of adaptive expectations assumes that expectations will be adjusted by a constant fraction of the difference between the most recently recorded actual inflation and previous expectations.

The rational expectations theory was developed by Muth and Lucas.[6] Muth argued that adaptive expectations are irrational in the sense that if people consistently underestimated inflation, surely they would revise their expectations upwards. Economic agents are assumed to be rational in their expectations in that they form their expectations according to economic theory; if predictions of economists were consistently better than expectations of firms (or individuals) then economists would be able to earn profits either by selling their information to firms or by setting up firms themselves. Good economic theory would therefore imply good economic practice.

This view of economic theory is consistent with the monetarist view that conventional stabilization policy does not work. Adherents of rational expectations theory even argue that there is no trade-off between inflation and unemployment in the short run. If stabilization policy is going to work, economic agents have to be taken by surprise—it has to be unpredictable. If stabilization policy had any regularity, then economic agents would predict the effects and act accordingly, nullifying the policy action. For example, if the government increased the money supply, the unemployment rate would not decrease because people would expect inflation and therefore no increase in real wages. Rational expectations are unbiased estimates of the inflation rate, given all information possible.

Structural Models

Structural models of inflation have achieved more prominence in Europe. They attempt to explain long-term tendencies of inflation in western economies. The economy is divided into a high-productivity sector (such as manufacturing and resources) and a low-productivity sector (such as the service sector). Wages in both sectors will tend to be equal because of union pressures for parity. The idea of two sectors with different productivities dates to Baumol (1967). Let us assume that there is a 4 percent increase in productivity in manufacturing and that the unions demand wage increases of 4 percent. This should have no effect on prices as the cost advantage to the firms of higher productivity outweighs the cost disadvantages of higher wage costs. The unions in the other sector will attempt to get the same increase. If there is zero productivity in this sector, however, prices have to increase or this industry will not be able to survive. Such analysis assumes that the industry is sheltered from competition; that is, it has a low price elasticity of demand (and high income elasticity)—otherwise prices could not be increased. The service sector is an example of an industry that is characterized by low productivity and protection, and the wages follow wages in the high productivity sector.

Another version of the structuralist model was developed in Scandinavia (the EFO model).[7] It expands on the basic structural relation between high- and low-productivity sectors to include open and closed sectors. The open sector is subject to competition on the world market since it produces tradable goods (both export and import competing goods), whereas the protected sector produces goods only for domestic consumption. The open sector, assuming exchange rates are fixed, is exposed to world inflation and is basically a price-taker. If prices of export-competing goods on the world market go up and the country has no inflation, there will be increased demand for the country's exports, which in turn will mean higher export prices for the goods produced. If prices of imported goods increase, the country's consumers will shift their demand to home-produced goods, which will increase their prices. Therefore prices in the exposed sector are linked directly to the rate of inflation abroad. According to standard marginal productivity theory, money wages in the exposed sector will be related to the marginal product of labour and product prices.

Firms in the sheltered sector are not price-takers but they practise mark-up pricing; that is, a constant profit mark-up is added to the per unit labour costs, and the rate of price increases in this sector are wage increases minus productivity increases. The rate of inflation in the economy is then equal to the weighted average of the inflation rate in the two sectors, with the weights determined by the relative importance of the two sectors in the economy. The inflation rate can be expressed as

$$\Pi = \Pi_w + L_s (P_E - P_s)$$

$$\begin{aligned}
\text{where } \Pi &= \text{ rate of inflation in the country} \\
\Pi_w &= \text{ rate of world inflation} \\
L_s &= \text{ share of sheltered sector} \\
P_E &= \text{ productivity in exposed sector} \\
P_s &= \text{ productivity in sheltered sector}
\end{aligned}$$

This equation says that the rate of inflation in a country is determined by world inflation, as well as by the difference in productivity between the two sectors and the importance of the sheltered sector. The larger the productivity gap, the higher the inflation rate. The more important the sheltered sector, the larger the inflation rate. Such a model explains rather well inflation in a small, open economy such as Sweden's.

The idea that inflation is a world-wide phenomenon and that it cannot be explained by models that treat each country as an island onto itself has been adopted in the monetary approach to the Balance of Payments pioneered by Harry Johnson (1972). This approach is basically an application of the monetarist approach to the international scene. According to this approach, the money supply that determines the rate of inflation is not just the domestic money supply, but the sum of all domestic money supplies. If this is correct, each country faces a level (and structure) of interest rates that is determined in world capital markets and an inflation rate determined by world conditions. Any attempt by a small country to change its inflation rate by monetary policy will therefore be doomed to failure. Domestic monetary policy can affect only the Balance of Payments. This model is perhaps one explanation of why inflation rates in various countries are fairly equal. However, it does not explain why some countries consistently have less inflation than others.

Neither the monetary approach to the Balance of Payments nor the Scandinavian model takes into consideration the fact that most exchange rates are not fixed, but operate under a managed float. A freely floating rate would of course insulate a country completely from the rate of world inflation, but it would not necessarily make the country's inflation rate less severe. If, under a floating rate, a country experienced severe inflation caused by excess demand, this inflation could not spill over into other countries, because the exchange rate would depreciate. This would mean that inflation would be bottled in. Indeed, some observers have argued that the introduction of flexible exchange rates has removed a major check (the Balance of Payments) on the monetary authorities, making them more inclined to be reckless.

What conclusions can be drawn from this brief survey? More specifically, what are the causes of the 'Great Inflation' of the 1970s and 1980s? What went wrong? In the first place, early policies and inflation theory neglected inflationary expectations. Given inflationary expectations, a fiscal or monetary policy aimed at reducing unemployment is doomed to failure. Inflationary expectations have become so embedded in the economy that people have reacted in such a way that they have a vested interest in continuing inflation. A good example is the housing market. To some it seems a puzzle that the housing market recently went through another boom period, given the fact that mortgage rates climbed to previously unheard of levels (16 to 18 percent). People were willing to pay from $150,000 to $200,000 for homes involving mortgage payments of $1,500 to $2,000 a month. They were prepared to take the risk, knowing that continuing inflation would reduce these payments over time to a manageable level, in that their income would increase whereas their mortgage payment would not.

Other factors that have increased the inflationary bias in the economy are likely the structural factors referred to above and perhaps more humane employers. In all western economies, more resources have shifted into the service sector, which is characterized by low productivity, and if wage gains in manufacturing are transferred to services, costs will spiral. Regarding employers, Okun (1980) has commented on the phenomenon of the invisible handshake. He pointed out that it is currently common for employers (even when they may be dealing with a non-unionized labour force) to grant general pay increases even when the labour market is slack—when they have plenty of applicants, no vacancies and low quit rates. Why? Because the firm is attempting to keep a well-qualified labour force over a longer time horizon. If the firm did not grant general wage increases even in a recession, it can expect dissatisfied workers to quit when labour market conditions are better. In tight labour markets, firms may induce workers to accept a job with them by implying that the workers' position will improve over time. If wage increases are not granted during a recession, workers may feel that the employer has reneged on his promise.

There is some evidence to support Okun's theory. A recent study confirms the findings of several economists that workers are less likely to leave jobs that offer better than average pay and regular pay increases (Leckie *et al.* 1980). The same type of behaviour can also be observed in product markets. For the majority of firms, customer relations are of crucial importance. In boom periods with excess demand, firms are reluctant to take advantage of the conditions and raise prices to market-clearing levels for fear of being accused of gouging, thereby losing customers. Instead, they engage in rationing by lengthening the backlog of unfilled orders. Firms want to make clear that they increase prices only when cost increases occur and they therefore adjust their prices upward even during a recession. This means that all prices will follow an upward trend, decelerating slightly during a recession and accelerating during inflation. This is in sharp contrast to auction markets where prices are fixed on exchanges (metals, grains and food products). For these commodities, prices fall during a recession. Given the small proportion of commodities subject to auction markets today, it is not surprising that prices follow an upward trend.

Much of recent inflation has been generated by shocks to the pricing system, such as the mammoth increases in the price of oil and the crop failures in the mid-seventies which pushed up food prices. If, under these circumstances, the government had taken no action and if most markets had been auction markets, the price of other commodities would have fallen, and so would have wages. People would have found that a greater proportion of their money income had to be spent on energy and hence a smaller proportion on other goods. The price of these goods would have fallen and inflation would not have occurred. Given that, in reality, most prices do not fall, unemployment would have resulted. However, massive unemployment would have been unacceptable and therefore the authorities in most countries opted for stimulative action, by holding interest rates down through monetary expansion. Therein lies much of the explanation for present-day inflation. Society is not prepared to accept the high cost of fighting it. The prospects for lower inflation are dim, particularly as more supply shocks can be expected in view of the world energy situation and the world food situation. In this context, perhaps one should question whether widespread publicity of the consumer price index benefits inflation. If people did not pay as much attention to this magic indicator, would inflation be as bad today? Most people know when prices are rising, but probably have little idea of the actual numbers involved. It is quite common for people to be happy about a wage settlement until the monthly CPI figures are made public.

Policies to Combat Inflation and Unemployment

There are basically two solutions to the inflation problem: one is to learn to live with it and the other to try to get rid of it. Given that imperfectly anticipated inflation has mainly distributional effects, these adverse effects could be eliminated by indexation. Inflation redistributes incomes from debtors to creditors, from people on fixed incomes to others, from individuals and corporations to governments. Indexation of taxes, incomes, interest rates, and other forms of income and payments would remove some of the undesirable effects of inflation.

Some economists argue that full indexation would make inflation worse as it would build inflation into the system. A supply-induced shock in agricultural prices for example, would, under indexation, spread rapidly to other sectors of the economy, probably more rapidly than at present. Others have argued that inflation would come down since wage earners would not need to include the risk of increased inflation in their negotiations. The unions might also be prepared to sign longer-term contracts, a factor which could also help alleviate inflation. No country has attempted full indexation (Israel has probably gone furthest). The consensus among economists seems to be that full indexation would not be desirable.

Monetarist Policies

As must be apparent from the previous section, the traditional textbook solution to the unemployment-inflation dilemma no longer works. Any policy to improve unemployment accelerates inflation and vice versa. There also seems to be considerable agreement and evidence that no trade-off exists in the long run. If this is true, no fiscal stimulus can lead to an improvement in the unemployment rate in the long run. The monetarists claim that the only policy rule to follow is for the monetary authorities to reduce the rate of growth in the money supply to the rate of growth in real income. If this were done there would be no inflation. However, even monetarists recognize that if such a measure were carried out too abruptly, substantial unemployment would result. Therefore, it is usually recommended that the money supply be gradually reduced (the policy of gradualism).

Yet there are problems with the monetarist approach to policy. One of the main problems is to decide which monetary aggregate to control. M_1 (currency and chequable demand deposits) is the narrow definition of money, and is usually the target for control. However, given that in inflationary times people switch their money holdings towards interest-bearing deposits such as savings accounts, a better measure of the money supply is M_2 (the monetary base), but is apparently far more difficult to control (see Chapter 14).

Monetarist policies have so far been met with limited success. The economic policies of the Thatcher government in Britain are regarded as monetarist. So far Thatcher's monetarism has had only moderate effects on inflation but the cost in terms of unemployment has been severe. However, some monetarists argue that "Thatcherism" is not proper monetarism and should therefore not be judged as such.

Wage and Price Controls

In order to cushion the effects of the decrease in the money supply on unemployment, it is sometimes suggested that wage and price controls should be implemented. Wage and price controls, if properly enforced, would moderate wage and price increases and would therefore lead to less unemployment in a period of severe monetary contraction. Controls could also reduce inflationary expectations. A minority of economists also maintain that inflation is essentially a cost-push phenomenon, for which some form of controls is always necessary.

Wage and price controls have been criticized on many grounds. There is little evidence that wage and price controls by themselves lower inflationary expectations (more than temporarily).[8] Indeed, the theory of rational expectations predicts that wage and price controls could not lower inflationary expectations, since people would expect prices to bounce straight back after the restraint—unless monetary restraint were exercised at the same time. Other critics argue that, at best, wage and price controls have little effect on the long-term inflation rate; at worst they do a lot of harm.

Price controls necessarily mean that distortions in the economy will arise. In a dynamic economy some prices will rise more quickly than others. Price controls will therefore create shortages of some commodities, with the possibility of resulting black markets, as well as future underinvestment, as prices are not allowed to rise sufficiently to give producers an incentive to invest. Firms may also attempt to avoid price controls by changing the quality of the product: restaurants can change recipes if they cannot increase prices, and producers of manufactured products can substitute cheaper materials. The implications can become serious if controls are maintained for any length of time, particularly in the case of rent control which is difficult to remove once it has been implemented. Indeed, a Swedish economist has been quoted as saying that apart from bombing, rent control is the most effective way of destroying a city. In most cities, it has usually led to a substantial shortage of rental accommodation and deterioration of the existing housing stock, as well as underinvestment in rental housing.

It is also possible that price controls would increase the concentration of industry in the sense that smaller, less profitable firms may be squeezed out of business through loss of profit, and in that large firms start to co-operate to find new ways of meeting government objectives. Both factors could lead to increased concentration.

Wage controls can also have many undesirable effects. Wage controls attempt to put a limit on people's incomes, on both wage incomes and incomes from profits. Faced with controls, individuals will naturally try to evade them. (Workers may be asked to have a part of their wages paid in fringe benefits such as increased vacation time, stock options, or a shorter work week.) Wage controls usually allow for higher wages through promotions and can therefore be avoided by the firm's placing people in different job categories.

Lipsey (1977) argues that wage and price controls can destroy our social fabric. When wage and price controls were first introduced in Britain it was against the wishes of the unions. In order to buy union support, the government had to agree to some union demands—the universal closed-shop legislation. Lipsey maintains that because of British wage and price controls, unions were given a degree of power they could otherwise not have had. Wage and price controls can also lead to a great deal of discontent in the sense that (as experience often shows) the individuals who create a lot of noise are the individuals who get the largest concessions. These types of inequities, caused by the granting of too much discretionary power, are likely to lead to social unrest.

For these reasons, peace-time wage and price controls are out of favour with most economists. However, there is still a hard-core group that feels that wage and profit increases are the cause of all inflation and therefore wages, and to a lesser extent, profits have to be controlled—but not with direct controls. Instead, the system could be made more flexible through a variant of tax-based incomes policies (TIP) developed by Weintraub and Wallich (1971). They argue that wage increases could be limited by imposing a financial penalty on all increases above a guideline figure. The larger the excess, the larger the penalty. This means that the system would have some flexibility, since the penalties would be applied only if average wages within the firm exceeded the guideline. The firm could pay some workers more than the guideline increases, as long as others got less. Further, a firm that was in desperate need to attract workers could exceed the guideline—if it was prepared to pay the penalty.

Another version of tax-based incomes policies would be the 'carrot' approach, that is, giving the workers who complied with the guidelines a tax reduction. This would mean that their net income would be as large as it would be in the absence of guidelines. A third means would be to make increases above a certain guideline subject to a super-tax.

These types of policies would indeed be more flexible than conventional wage controls. However, there is little evidence that inflation is caused by unions and workers. Unions may aggravate inflation once it has started because of inflationary expectations, but they do not cause inflation.

It is also difficult to see that the tax-based incomes policies would be more socially acceptable than wage and price controls. These policies usually impose penalties only on wages, not on profits, because it is assumed that profits would be controlled if wages were controlled (in the sense that the control of wages controls aggregate demand, which in turn will control prices). John Crispo (*Financial Post,* 1 Dec. 1979) feels that such policies do not solve the structural problems in the economy, as they would not tax professional guilds, marketing boards and the excessive profits that could be earned by some large corporations such as oil companies. Therefore the solution to the problem of some groups' receiving more than their fair share is a crackdown on the misuse of economic power through a more active competition policy, not tax-based incomes policies.

Downward Price Shocks

Another policy that has been suggested to shake out the inflationary psychology of the system is one involving a price shock. John Hotson of the University of Waterloo has suggested a radical percentage cut to all wage and non-wage personal incomes, and price cuts equal to income cuts plus average annual productivity gain (Bellan 1981:363–66). Apart from the difficulty that this would create in asset markets, it is difficult to see why this would be more advantageous than a currency reform. A currency reform is a time-honoured method of curing inflationary expectations. German hyperinflation in the early '20s was stopped by currency reform (and the introduction of conservative monetary and fiscal policies). The French imposed a currency reform in the '50s, when one new franc was equal to 100 old francs. The recent Israeli currency reform (1 new Scheckel = 100 old Israeli pounds) has not solved the Israeli inflation problem.

Supply-Side Economics

The last and currently the most popular approach to inflation is what has become known as supply-side economics. Its popularity probably stems from the fact that it promises to lick inflation by methods which, rather than hurt most individuals, would benefit them. The basic tenet of supply-side economics is that present economic policies have paid too little attention to supply, that is to the economy's capacity to produce. A high demand for goods and services does not cause inflation if the economy expands to keep up with demand. This argument is obviously correct in periods of high demand and shortages of capacity. However, increases in productivity do not guarantee a reduction in the inflation rate. An example is France,[9] where between 1974 and 1979, productivity in manufacturing rose at a faster rate than in other major industrial countries. However, the rate of inflation was also higher, the reason being that the productivity gains are not necessarily translated into lower prices, but may go into higher profits and wage gains considerably larger than the productivity increases.

If one believes that supply shortages have aggravated inflation, the obvious solution is to attempt to increase productivity and to encourage new investment in general. This is thought to be most efficiently achieved through tax reductions on (a) earned income, (b) business income and (c) investment income. Tax reductions on earned income are thought to increase productivity since this would give people an incentive to work hard—a concept that has been popularized by the so-called Laffer-curve, which hypothesizes that there is a level of taxation beyond which tax yield will decline because people will work less; therefore, a cut in taxes could actually increase the tax yield.

The crucial issue here is whether there is a link between productivity (or work effort) and the rate of taxation. Contrary to the beliefs of supply-side economists, it is possible that higher after-tax incomes would decrease the amount of labour supplied, since beyond a certain take-home pay, people would rather have more leisure than pay. Also, people work for reasons other than monetary rewards, and work hours are set as much by unions and governments as by individuals. Many studies have been done on this issue, but they are inconclusive. Summarizing the evidence, a U.S. Congressional Budget Office investigation concluded that a 10 percent cut in taxes would at the most increase labour supply by

1 to 3 percent. So the effect on aggregate supply may not be large (Gramley 1981).

A tax cut would also affect aggregate demand, because it is unlikely that all of the tax cut would be saved. Indeed, it is likely that increases in aggregate demand would outstrip increases in aggregate supply, and therefore personal tax cuts would fuel inflation instead of alleviating it.

A cut in business taxes is perhaps a more promising avenue of increasing productivity, particularly if these tax cuts took the form of increased depreciation allowance or investment tax credits. This would encourage business to reinvest profits in a new plant and machinery. In the United States it is estimated that if corporate tax payments were reduced by 17 percent, productivity growth would increase by 0.4 percent.

Another component of a supply-side tax package is a cut in taxes on investment incomes. The rationale is essentially Keynesian: increased investments must be financed by increased savings, otherwise inflation will ensue. In order to provide the necessary savings, taxes should be reduced on investment income. Again, the empirical evidence on whether a tax cut would increase the total amount of savings is conflicting. Of the three measures suggested, a cut in corporate taxes is probably the most efficient way of improving productivity.

Unemployment Policies

Let us turn our attention away from inflation to unemployment. It could be argued that our 'natural' unemployment rate of 6 percent is too high. The evidence presented above indicates that this rate cannot be reduced by monetary or fiscal policies, but this does not mean that the 'natural' unemployment rate cannot be reduced by other means. 'Natural' unemployment consists of frictional, structural and insurance-induced unemployment, and there are policies, at least in theory, geared to reducing these. Frictional unemployment could be decreased by more efficient dissemination of job information; structural unemployment could be alleviated by labour market policies aimed at retraining or relocating workers. The federal government implemented policies to combat both, but neither appears to be particularly effective. As mentioned in Chapter 10, relocation grants are claimed only by a minute portion of the people who move. Gunderson (1977) found little evidence that manpower training programs have had any effect on structural unemployment.

In view of the fact that unemployment is particularly high for women and young people, a special effort should be made to increase employment for these groups. Indeed, the federal government's employment programs appear to favour these groups. The Opportunities for Youth program was introduced in 1971 and was later replaced by the Local Initiatives Program and the Young Canada Works program. With regard to women, a program is underway to attract women into nontraditional jobs. There is little data available on the effectiveness of these programs.

The question of unemployment insurance is a difficult one. The system has been tightened considerably since 1971, and any further changes would probably have a major impact on poor families, who, as it is, receive a small share of benefits (Osberg 1979). If employers take advantage of unemployment insurance by increasing the frequency of layoffs, as has been suggested by Feldstein (1978), it becomes essential to discourage this practice. Reid (1980) has proposed that this practice could be eliminated through a system of experience-rating of contributions. A firm's contributions would be directly related to the number of layoffs it imposed in the past; that is, a firm which consistently laid off workers in periods of slack demand would be faced with higher unemployment insurance contributions than one who did not. The present system taxes firms with a steady employment picture and subsidizes those that have frequent layoffs.

Summary and Conclusions

This chapter described recent inflation and unemployment trends in Canada, and surveyed current theories: the monetarist, the neo-Keynesian and the structuralist theories. The monetarist and neo-Keynesian theories are no longer radically opposed. Most economists agree that the trade-off between unemployment and inflation occurs only in the short run and that therefore the long-run Phillips curve is vertical or near vertical because of inflationary expectations. The structuralist theories explain how inflation is transmitted to small open economies operating under fixed exchange rates. The chapter looks at other factors that have contributed to the inflation in most western economies. It was concluded that inflation is a monetary phenomenon in the sense that inflation must be fuelled by monetary expansion in order to continue (unless there are large expansions in output). However, this statement is almost a truism and does not answer the question of why inflationary pressure arises in the first place. Supply shocks, which resulted in higher food and energy prices, can obviously explain much of today's inflation. Additional explanations are the deeply embedded inflationary expectations, structural changes in most economies in favour of the low productivity service sector, and perhaps humane labour relations. Unless these pressures and price increases are accommodated by expansion in money supply, unemployment will ensue, a price that most politicians are reluctant to pay.

Anti-inflationary policies were surveyed with particular emphasis on monetarist policies, wage and price controls and the currently popular supply-side policies. We do not yet know how effective supply-side policies are in increasing productivity because the evidence on their efficiency is conflicting. It is unlikely, however, that supply-side policies— even if they are effective—will cure inflation because of the role of inflationary expectations. Given that inflation is a monetary phenomenon, a more effective policy would be to reduce monetary expansion. However, in order to minimize the effect of monetary expansion on unemployment, the underlying causes of inflationary pressure must be attacked as far as this is possible. Short-term wage and price controls, or some form of tax-based income policy can be useful in reducing inflationary expectations and in cushioning the impact on unemployment. Policies explicitly designed to reduce the 'natural' unemployment rate can also be helpful.

NOTES

1. The following account is based on Department of Finance 1980:17–20.
2. Not everyone agrees with the methodology and findings of these studies. For a review, see Osberg 1979.
3. For a useful survey, see Purvis 1980.
4. For good and exhaustive treatments, see Laidler and Parkin 1975; Frisch 1977; and Santomero and Seater 1978.
5. See Laidler and Parkin 1975; and Reid 1980.
6. The development of the theory is outlined in Kantor 1979.
7. See Edgren *et al.* 1973.
8. For a somewhat slanted survey, see Carr *et al.* 1976. However, the wage and price controls between 1975 and 1978 are credited with reducing wage rates by 4.5 percent (Reid 1979).
9. See Gramley 1981.

BIBLIOGRAPHY

Baumol, W.J. "Macroeconomics of Unbalanced Growth: The Anatomy of Urban Crisis." *American Economic Review* (57), 1967, pp. 415–26.

Bechterman, Gordon. *Skills and Shortages: A Summary Guide to the Findings of the Human Resources Survey.* Economic Council of Canada, Ottawa: Supply and Services, 1980.

Bellan R.C. "Alternative Stabilization Strategies." In R.C. Bellan and

W.H. Pope (eds.), pp. 359–73, *The Canadian Economy: Problems and Options.* Toronto: McGraw-Hill Ryerson 1981.

Bodkin, R.G. and M. Cournoyer. "Legislation and the Labour Market: A Selective Review of Canadian Studies." In H. Grubel and M. Walker (eds.), pp. 62–89, *Unemployment Insurance: Global Evidence of its Effects on Unemployment.* Vancouver: The Fraser Institute, 1978.

Carr, Jack, *et al. The Illusion of Wage and Price Controls.* Vancouver: The Fraser Institute, 1976.

Department of Finance. *Economic Review: A Perspective on a Decade.* Ottawa: Supply and Services, 1980.

Economic Council of Canada. *Two Cheers for the Eighties.* Sixteenth Annual Review. Hull: Supply and Services, 1979.

Edgren, Gosta, Karl-Olof Faxen and Clas-Erik Ohdner. *Wage Formation and the Economy.* London: Allen and Unwin, 1973.

Feldstein, Martin. "The Effect of Unemployment Insurance on Temporary Layoff Unemployment." *American Economic Review* (68), 1978, pp. 834–46.

Friedman, M. "The Role of Monetary Policy." *American Economic Review,* (58), 1968, pp. 1–17.

Frisch, H. "Inflation Theory 1963–1975: A Second Generation Survey." *Journal of Economic Literature* (XV) 1977, pp. 1289–1318.

Gramley, Lyle. "The Role of Supply-Side Economics in Fighting Inflation." *Challenge* (23), 1981, pp. 14–19.

Grubel, H.G., D. Maki and S. Sax. "Real and Insurance-Induced Unemployment in Canada." *Canadian Journal of Economics* (VIII), 1975, pp. 174–92.

Gunderson, M. "Training in Canada: Progress and Problems" *International Journal of Social Economics* (4), 1977, pp. 2–24.

Johnson, Harry. *Further Essays in Monetary Economics.* London: Allen and Unwin, 1972.

Kantor, Brian. "Rational Expectations and Economic Thought." *Journal of Economic Literature* (XVII), 1979, pp. 1422–76.

Laidler, D. and M. Parkin. "Inflation: A Survey." *Economic Journal* (85), 1975, pp. 741–809.

Lazar, Fred. "The Impact of the 1971 Unemployment Insurance Revisions on Unemployment Rates: Another Look." *Canadian Journal of Economics* (XI), 1978, pp. 559–70.

Leckie, N., G. Betcherman and K. Norton. *An Analysis of Turnover in Ontario Industrial Establishments.* Economic Council of Canada. Ottawa: Supply and Services, 1980.

Lipsey, Richard. "The Relationship Between Unemployment and the Rate of Change of Money Wage Rates in the U.K., 1862–1957: A Further Analysis." *Economica* (27), 1960, pp. 1–31.

―――― "Wage Price Controls: How to do a lot of harm by trying to do a little good." *Canadian Public Policy* (III), 1977, pp. 1–14.

McCracken, M.C. and E. Ruddick. *Towards a Better Understanding of the Consumer Price Index.* Occasional Paper, Economic Council of Canada. Ottawa: Supply and Services, 1980.

Okun, A. "The Invisible Handshake and the Inflationary Process." *Challenge* (22), 1980, pp. 5–13.

Osberg, L. "Unemployment Insurance in Canada: A Review of the Recent Amendments." *Canadian Public Policy* (V), 1979, pp. 223–36.

Phelps, E.S. "Money Wage Dynamics and Labour Market Equilibrium." *Journal of Political Economy* (76), 1968, pp. 678–711.

Purvis, Douglas D. "Monetarism: a review." *Canadian Journal of Economics* (XIII), 1980, pp. 96–123.

Reid, F. "The Effect of Controls on the Rate of Wage Change in Canada." *Canadian Journal of Economics* (12), 1979, pp. 214–222.

_____ "Unemployment and Inflation: An Assessment of Canadian Macroeconomic Policy." *Canadian Public Policy* (VI), 1980, pp. 283–300.

_____ and N.M. Meltz. "Causes of Shifts in the Unemployment-Vacancy Relationship: An Empirical Analysis for Canada." *Review of Economics and Statistics* (61), 1979, pp. 470–73.

Santomero, Anthony M., and John J. Seater. "The Inflation-Unemployment Trade-off: A Critique of the Literature." *Journal of Economic Literature* (XVI), 1978, pp. 499–545.

Wallich, H. and S. Weintraub. "A Tax-Based Incomes Policy." *Journal of Economic Issues* (V), 1971, pp. 1–19.

West, Edwin G. and Michael McKee. *Minimum Wages: The New Issues in Theory, Evidence, Policy and Politics.* Economic Council and the Institute for Research on Public Policy. Ottawa: Supply and Services, 1980.

CHAPTER 13

The Balance of Payments and the Canadian Dollar

It is frequently claimed that the Bank of Canada cannot pursue an independent monetary policy, but must match U.S. interest rates out of concern for the Balance of Payments and the external value of the Canadian dollar. It is also claimed that interest rates have to be sufficiently high to attract the foreign capital needed to finance the deficit on the current account. Others argue that this is a gross misrepresentation of reality, as it is the surplus on the capital account that has caused the deficit on the current account; the surplus on the capital account drove up the value of the Canadian dollar which hurt the export trade and encouraged imports, and therefore caused the deficit on the current account. For this reason the Balance of Payments is not a problem area at all. If the Bank of Canada lowers the interest rates, the argument goes, the capital inflow (foreign investment) will cease, the dollar will drop and the current account will balance.

In this chapter, the Balance of Payments will be reviewed as well as monetary and fiscal policies under fixed and fluctuating exchange rates. These topics form a necessary background to the discussion in Chapter 14. A summary of the controversial foreign investment issue ends Chapter 13.

The Balance of Payments

The Balance of Payments is a record of all transactions between residents of Canada and residents of other countries. A receipt in the Balance of Payments is any transaction which gives rise to an international monetary claim for Canada, and similarly a payment is a transaction which gives rise to the payment of an international monetary claim. The Balance of Payments can be divided into three accounts: the current account, the capital account and the exchange-fund account. The current account records transactions involving the purchase and sale of commodities; the capital account records the purchase and sale of securities as well as changes in short-term assets such as bank balances. The exchange-fund account is a balancing account and records the change in official reserves. ·

The current account is divided into the merchandise trade account, recording purchases and sale of goods, and the service account, recording purchases and sale of services. The service account is divided into the travel account, the interest and divided account, the freight and shipping account, other services, and transfers including official contributions. The travel account records as a receipt what foreigners spend in Canada as tourists, and the payments are what Canadians spend abroad as tourists. The interest and dividend account records service payments on Canada's debt held abroad, both to shareholders and to foreign holders of Canadian bonds; it also records what Canadians receive from their investments abroad. The freight and shipping account records such items as the amount Canadian ships on the Great Lakes receive from U.S. customers for transporting cargo, and also what Canadians have to pay to foreign shipping lines for transport of cargo in the deep-sea trades. "Other" services contain receipts and payments for consulting services and patent rights; for example, some of the engineering contracts for energy developments have been given to foreign engineering firms. Transfers consist of Canada's contributions to international agencies such as the United Nations and the World Bank, bilateral aid to developing countries, money that new immigrants bring into the country, as well as money that is sent out of the country to support relatives in foreign countries.

The capital account is more complex. It is divided into a long-term capital account and a short-term capital account. The long-term capital account is subdivided into a direct investment and portfolio investment account. Direct investment involves ownership and control, whereas portfolio investment is acquisition of stocks or bonds with no control. A capital inflow means that foreigners are investing in Canada by buying Canadian securities (i.e., Canada is exporting securities) and is recorded as a receipt. Similarly, if a Canadian province or public utility borrows money by issuing bonds for sale in the New York money markets, the buyers are also investing in Canada, so our borrowing also shows up as a receipt in the Balance of Payments. When foreigners invest in Canada, it is the same transaction as when Canadians borrow abroad.

The short-term capital account is basically a balancing account, but also records speculative movements of short-term capital between countries. The balancing aspect stems from the fact that the Balance of Payments, like most accounts, is kept on a double-entry basis. For example, an export sale has to be financed. The export sale will obviously be recorded as a receipt on the merchandise trade account, but there will

TABLE 28
Balance of International Payments, Current Account, 1960–80

Year	Merchandise trade	Freight and shipping	Travel	Interest and dividends	Other	Current account balance
1960	−148	−91	207	−485	−259	−1233
1961	173	−82	−160	−551	−282	−929
1962	184	−86	−43	−581	−315	−830
1963	503	−85	24	−630	−332	−521
1964	701	−35	−50	−678	−353	−−424
1965	118	−93	−49	−764	−342	−1130
1966	224	−65	−60	−822	−414	−1162
1967	566	−31	423	−916	−507	−499
1968	1471	−40	−29	−906	−601	−97
1969	964	−61	−214	−910	−600	−917
1970	3052	20	−216	−1022	−612	1106
1971	2563	−12	−202	−1141	−765	431
1972	1857	−74	−234	−1048	−884	−386
1973	2735	−66	−296	−1260	−1027	108
1974	1689	−224	−284	−1553	−1215	−1460
1975	−451	−433	−727	−1953	−1108	−4757
1976	1388	−148	−1191	−2498	−1336	−3842
1977	2730	−26	−1641	−3658	−2119	−4301
1978	3601	−218	−1706	−4499	−2615	−5046
1979	3972	+290	−1068	−5299	−3655	−5098
1980	7953	+433	−1138	−5561	−4471	−1538

Source: Department of Finance, *Annual Review,* 1981, Reference Table 74.
Note: The table is incomplete as it does not include transfers and net official contributions.

also be an entry on the short-term capital account, depending on how the transaction is financed. The buyer can pay for the good by drawing on his or her Canadian dollar account at Canadian banks. In this case the short-term capital account will record a reduction in the Canadian dollar deposits held by foreign residents. Other items in the short-term capital account include treasury bills, commercial paper and finance company paper.

The exchange-fund account records any change in Canada's official reserves. Official reserves consist of foreign currencies (U.S. dollars and other foreign exchange), gold—valued at $32 per ounce!, Special Drawing Rights, and Canada's reserve position with the International Monetary Fund. Special Drawing Rights are an international reserve currency

TABLE 29
Balance of International Payments,
Selected Items in Capital Account, 1960–80

Year	Direct in Canada	Direct abroad	New issues of Canadian securities	Balance on long-term capital account	Balance on short-term capital account	Changes in official reserves
1960	670	−50	448	929	265	−39
1961	560	−80	548	930	290	292
1962	505	−105	729	688	296	154
1963	280	−135	984	637	29	145
1964	270	−95	1100	750	38	364
1965	535	−125	1240	833	455	158
1966	790	−5	1465	1228	−425	−359
1967	691	−125	1307	1415	−896	20
1968	590	−225	1917	1669	−1223	349
1969	720	−370	2089	2337	−1355	65
1970	905	−315	1230	1007	−583	1663
1971	925	−230	1191	664	−318	896
1972	620	−400	1722	1688	−983	336
1973	830	−770	1323	628	−1203	−467
1974	845	−810	2423	1041	443	24
1975	725	−915	5038	3935	417	−405
1976	−300	−590	9026	7923	−3559	522
1977	475	−740	5889	4265	−1385	−1421
1978	85	−2010	6522	3362	−1615	−3299
1979	675	−1945	5273	2838	3949	1908
1980	535	−2675	5372	1374	−1334	−1281

Source: Department of Finance. *Annual Review,* 1981, Reference Table 77.

created in the early '70s to provide the international monetary system with more liquidity. The reserve position with the International Monetary Fund is the amount of credit Canada has outstanding in the fund, which is made up of Canada's contribution to the fund minus the fund's holdings of Canadian dollars plus any additional money Canada has lent to the fund through the General Agreements to Borrow or the newly created oil facility.[1]

Obviously, if there is a deficit on the current account (that is, if we spend more on goods and services than we receive), it has to be financed. This can be done by borrowing—encouraging long-term capital inflow—or by running down reserves, which can of course only be done for a limited time period. Tables 28 and 29 indicate that in most years Canada has had its current account deficit financed by borrowing.[2] Until the early '60s it was not unusual for half the foreign capital entering the country to take the form of direct investment. This situation has been radically altered. Indeed, in the last few years Canadians invested more abroad than foreigners invested in Canada. In 1976, the repatriation of foreign capital actually exceeded the inflow of new investment. However, the Balance of Payments statistics ignored the effect of earnings retained by foreign corporations. Retained earnings increase the book value of foreign direct investment in Canada without affecting the capital account. This source of foreign investment is at present greater than the direct inflow (Wilkinson 1980:48–50).

The current account deficit is made up of a surplus in the merchandise trade account and substantial deficits in the travel, interest and dividend account, and in the "other services" account. Politicians and laymen alike have been particularly concerned about the mounting deficit in the interest and dividend account. However, as in everything else in economics the absolute size of the deficit does not mean much; one has to ask, in relation to what? As a person becomes better off, the size of the person's interest payments to the bank may increase without necessarily meaning that the person has become less solvent. The most common measure of the debt burden or the solvency of a country is the debt-service ratio. The debt-service ratio is the ratio between the country's payment of service charges (interest and dividends) and the earnings from the export of goods and services. Another measure is debt-service charges in relation to the economy's total capacity to produce (GNP). Table 30 shows that the debt-service ratio declined steadily until 1974, reached a peak in 1978 and has since declined. The changes have not been great. As a comparison, many Third World countries have debt-service ratios in excess of 20 percent and Poland is reputed to have reached 90 percent. Service payments in relation to GNP declined until 1972 and have increased since then.

According to Wilkinson (1980:110–18), figures of this type can be grossly misleading as they do not take account of retained earnings. Retained earnings can be regarded as a debt service as well. If one includes retained earnings, the total deficit on the interest and dividend account in 1978 was $7,305 million instead of $4,499 million. The debt-service ratio based on interest, dividends and retained earnings for 1960 was 10.06 percent and for 1978 11.35 percent, again only a small increase.

Our reliance on foreign borrowing in the form of portfolio investment has increased. Table 30 shows that new issues of Canadian securities abroad as a proportion of GNE has fluctuated between 1.0 and 3.0 percent. Between 1975 and 1976 this figure rose to 4.72 percent. If the money borrowed were used for productive investments which increased exports, the effects on the current account deficit would not be serious. If, however, the money were used for current consumption, that is, to

TABLE 30
Selected Statistics Relating to the Balance of Payments, 1960–80

Year	New issues of Canadian securities as a proportion of GNE	Net interest and dividend payments as a proportion of GNP	Debt-service ratio
1960	1.17	1.26	6.72
1961	1.38	1.39	6.97
1962	1.70	1.35	6.79
1963	2.14	1.37	6.69
1964	2.19	1.35	6.22
1965	2.24	1.38	6.56
1966	2.37	1.33	6.04
1967	1.97	1.38	6.00
1968	2.64	1.25	5.19
1969	2.62	1.14	4.68
1970	1.44	1.19	4.66
1971	1.26	1.21	4.95
1972	1.64	1.00	4.11
1973	1.07	1.02	3.97
1974	1.64	1.05	3.85
1975	3.05	1.18	4.66
1976	4.72	1.29	5.30
1977	2.83	1.66	6.76
1978	2.86	1.87	6.99
1979	1.96	1.96	6.74
1980	1.86	2.03	6.03

Source: Calculated from Department of Finance, *Annual Review*, various issues.
Note: The debt-service ratio is the ratio of net interest and dividend payments and total earnings on the current account.

cover government deficits, then the debt-service ratio might become less favourable in the future.

Fixed and Flexible Exchange Rates: An Overview

An exchange rate, such as the price of Canadian dollars in terms of U.S. dollars, is determined by supply and demand. The demand for Canadian dollars is determined by the people who want to buy Canadian dollars. American residents may need Canadian dollars to travel in Canada, to buy Canadian goods or to invest in Canada. In the process of acquiring the necessary Canadian dollars, they supply U.S. dollars to the foreign exchange markets. They buy Canadian dollars, using U.S. dollars as payments. Similarly, Canadians need to acquire U.S. dollars to go to Florida, to import U.S. goods or to pay U.S. shareholders. In doing so, they demand U.S. dollars and supply Canadian dollars. The intersection of the demand and supply curves then fixes the price of Canadian dollars.

If interest rates in Canada are increased according to U.S. rates, then it becomes more profitable for foreigners to place some of their capital in Canada (or for Canadians to borrow abroad). This will increase the demand for Canadian dollars (shift the demand curve to the right) and therefore push up the value of the Canadian dollar. If, however, Canadians decide that Florida is not where they want to go, the demand for U.S. dollars will decrease, which means that the supply of Canadian dollars will decrease (shift to the left) and the value of the Canadian dollar will increase. The exchange rate is a mirror of the Balance of Payments. Deficits in the overall balance means necessarily that we do not earn as much foreign exchange as we need, which in turn means that the supply of Canadian dollars is greater than the demand and the external value of the dollar will drop. A Balance of Payments surplus means that we earn more foreign exchange than we use, rendering the demand for Canadian dollars greater than the supply and pushing the dollar up in value.

When the external value of the dollar increases, exports become more expensive and imports cheaper, movements which correct the imbalance. Similarly, Balance of Payments deficits will lead to a depreciation in the exchange rate, which will make exports cheaper on world markets and imports more expensive.

Politically, a depreciation in the exchange rate may be very unpopular. A lower value of a currency hurts people's pride—and it also increases the cost of going to Florida. A depreciation in the exchange rate can also be inflationary if traded goods account for a large proportion of GNE. To stop an exchange rate from falling, the central bank has to go against the prevailing market forces. A falling exchange rate indicates an excess supply of Canadian dollars. The Bank of Canada has to enter the market to mop up the excess by buying Canadian dollars (and selling foreign exchange). If the bank tries to go against the market for some time, it usually has to supplement reserves by borrowing from the International Monetary Fund, or by making exchange arrangements with other central banks. It can also attract foreign funds by raising interest rates. The government can interfere to stop a currency from appreciating if it is worried that the export sector will be adversely affected by an appreciation.

Before 1971, most countries except Canada were trying to maintain fixed exchange rates—rates that varied little around a fixed rate. This meant that the central bank had to interfere frequently to stop the currency from deviating from its fixed value. This system turned out to be untenable in accommodating the adjustments that had to be made because of the oil crisis. Instead, the new system that emerged came to be known as a managed float. It was recognized that currencies must be allowed to fluctuate in value, but that large short-term fluctuations should be avoided as they would be too destabilizing for trade. It was therefore felt that the central bank should intervene to smooth out the large day-to-day fluctuations in exchange rates.

In theory, domestic policy, particularly monetary policy, is far more effective under a flexible rather than a fixed rate. Under a fixed rate, inflation among trading partners is immediately transmitted to the domestic economy. Let us assume that the external value of the Canadian dollar is fixed. A high inflation rate abroad would mean higher import prices and increased demand for Canadian exports and therefore higher export prices as well. A Balance of Payments surplus would ensue. In order to stop the currency from appreciating, the monetary authorities would have to sell Canadian dollars and acquire foreign exchange from the chartered banks. Such a measure would increase the reserves of the chartered banks, and unless the monetary authorities sterilized this increase by selling bonds, monetary expansion and domestic inflation would result. Monetary policy would be tied to the Balance of Payments situation.

Under a fully flexible rate, the economy would be isolated from world inflation. The Balance of Payments surplus would lead to currency appreciation and therefore a neutralizing of inflationary pressures. Under flexible exchange rates, movements in the exchange rate can reinforce domestic policies. If, for example, the government pursued a restrictive monetary policy to reduce the inflation rate, this would lead to a higher interest rate in Canada, which in turn would force up the value of the Canadian dollar and dampen demand for Canadian exports, making imports cheaper. Higher interest rates also lead to lower aggregate demand, which in turn reduces imports and reinforces the upward pressure on the dollar. Indeed, simulations on econometric models of the Canadian economy have confirmed that this is the case (Helliwell and Lester 1976).

Fiscal policy may not be as effective as monetary policy. If fiscal policy were used to stimulate the economy, the financing of the budgetary deficit would put an upward pressure on interest rates, which would attract foreign capital flows and therefore put an upward pressure on the exchange rate. Such results could adversely affect employment in the export sectors, as well as in sectors subject to competition from imports, and would therefore be counterproductive. However, this analysis ignores any effects on the current account. A fiscal stimulus can increase demand for imports and result in a deficit on the current account and in a downward pressure on the exchange rate. Therefore, the effectiveness of fiscal policy under flexible rates depends on which effect is the strongest: the effect on the current account or the effect on the capital account. Recent studies have shown that the current-account effect is the most significant, indicating that even fiscal policy operates well under a flexible rate (Carr *et al.* 1976).

In order to protect the economy from foreign inflation, the rate must be truly flexible.[3] Monetary policy should be used to pursue domestic objectives only, not to control the exchange rate. The policy-makers should accept any exchange rate that would clear the foreign exchange market. However, a flexible exchange rate is not without problems. It cannot protect an economy from external shocks, such as the oil price shock, nor from the actions of other countries. The Reagan administration's anti-inflationary policies have led to very high interest rates in the United States and a resulting upward pressure on the U.S. dollar (which is equivalent to a downward pressure on the Canadian dollar).[4] This helps the American authorities in their battle against inflation, but creates problems in Canadian anti-inflationary policy.

There are three policy options open to the Canadian authorities.[5] The first is to ignore the depreciation and pursue existing monetary targets. Higher prices with no accommodating increases in the money supply would mean more unemployment. The second option is to accommodate the depreciation by expanding the money supply so that unemployment could be avoided. Both options imply an increase in the inflation rate. A third possibility would be to stabilize the exchange rate by reducing monetary expansion to push up interest rates even further and thereby create even more unemployment. The choice for the policy-maker is difficult. An added complication is that there is considerable debate about the pros and cons of stabilizing the exchange rate by encouraging even more capital inflow into Canada.

Foreign Investment and the Canadian Economy

The need, the costs and the benefits of foreign investment in Canada are hotly debated and are surrounded by controversy. The first issue that needs to be settled is the presumed need for foreign capital to finance the current account. At the beginning of this chapter, it was stated that a deficit on the current account must be financed by a surplus on the capital account (by borrowing). This and similar statements really belong to an earlier era of fixed exchange rates. Under flexible rates, a deficit does not need to be financed. An unfinanced deficit would lead to a sufficiently large drop in the exchange rate to make the accounts balance. Therefore one could argue, with some justification, that it is not the deficit in the current account that has caused the surplus on the capital account, but rather that the encouragement of foreign investment (the capital account surplus) necessarily causes a deficit in the current account. This deficit would disappear if long-term capital inflows were stopped.[6] Any attempt to maintain or increase the inflow of capital would maintain or increase the deficit.

The question is, then, why does capital move from the United States to Canada? Is it a conscious policy on the part of the federal government to attract capital to finance the deficit, or does capital flow automatically from the United States to Canada because its yield is higher in Canada than in the United States? Traditional trade theory explains capital flows in terms of capital-labour ratios or capital-land ratios. If the ratio of capital to labour (or to land) is high in one country compared to another— showing that one country is capital-rich and the other capital-poor—the country with the high capital-labour ratio would have a low yield on capital, as well as high wages, in comparison with the other country. Canada is blessed with a vast land (natural resource) mass, compared to the amount of capital available, and therefore payments to capital should be high in relation to land.

This view ties in with a 'stages' theory of international capital flow. In the first stage of industrial development, a country usually has little capital in relation to land and labour and so the return to capital must be high. The reason why a relatively poor country has little capital is that in general an undeveloped country consumes most of incomes earned; few savings are generated, savings that could be channelled into productive investments. For a country to develop, the necessary savings must come from outside through foreign investment. As the country achieves growth through this infusion of foreign savings, the capital-labour ratio will increase (as will the capital-land ratio), wages will increase and the return to capital will decrease. With higher returns to labour, domestic savings can be generated and foreign investment declines as the yield differentials narrow. When a country reaches maturity, the process reverses itself: a large amount of domestic savings are generated, and the yield on capital falls to such a low level that the country then becomes a net exporter of capital. The United States went through these stages. Canada is apparently still in the first stage, despite the fact that Canada is a developed country.

Dunn (1978:11−14) argues that there are three reasons why a rich country may still need to import capital. First, a resource-rich country with a vast land mass requires a higher than average capital-labour or capital-land ratio, the reason being that resource extraction is extremely capital-intensive, and a vast land mass requires large investments in transportation and energy development. Therefore it takes a long time for the return to capital to fall sufficiently low for the funds to stop coming in. Second, if, through immigration, the labour force outgrows the additions to capital, the return to capital may not fall and more capital will be attracted. Third, the basic national income-accounting identity, expressed in the equation,

$$S + T + M = X + I + G$$
or
$$(S - I) + (M - X) = (G - T)$$

where S = savings
T = taxes
M = imports
X = exports
I = investment
G = government expenditures

indicates that if there is a budgetary deficit, it must be financed by an excess of savings over investments, or by an excess of imports over exports (through foreign capital imports). Put another way, if the effect of the financing of a budgetary deficit crowds out sufficient domestic investment, foreign borrowing is necessary.

However, this explanation of foreign investment is probably rather simplistic. The flow of existing capital is more complex than merely going from the United States to Canada; indeed, at present capital flow is moving in both directions. An example is that Canadians invest more in the United States in the form of new direct investment than Americans invest in Canada, and Americans buy more Canadian bonds than Canadians buy American bonds. This presumably means that the U.S. yield is higher on stocks, and Canada's yield is higher on bonds.

Traditionally Canada has had a larger spread between the yields of short- and long-term securities than has the United States. The interest rate on a security usually increases with the maturity of the debt. In Canada, long-term interest rates are higher and short-term interest rates are lower than those in the United States. This has meant that long-term capital flows from the United States to Canada, whereas short-term capital flows in the opposite direction. The U.S. capital markets therefore act as a financial intermediary for Canada by borrowing short and lending long; that is, the U.S. market is serving the same function as a commercial bank. There could be several reasons for this. Dunn (1978:21–7) argues that one country, in this case Canada, may have a stronger liquidity preference than another country—the lender prefers short-term assets. Such a preference would result in little demand for long-term assets—and therefore low prices (equals high yields)—and substantial demand for short-term assets—and therefore higher prices and low yields. Another explanation could be that Canadians are more risk-averse than Americans. A risk-averse individual would prefer short-term assets to long-term assets. A third explanation is that one country may have a larger need for long-term capital than another country, in the sense that it needs to finance resource and transportation developments. Other factors, such as transactions costs and capital market regulations, could also affect the structure of interest rates. An immature, nonliquid ("thin") capital market would also produce the same effect, and so would lack of competition in the capital markets.

Dunn provides data to show that the spread between long-term and short-term interest rates is larger in Canada than in the United States. In a survey of people knowledgeable of both markets, seven out of sixteen respondents mentioned the high liquidity preference and conservatism of Canadian investors as being important in explaining yield differentials. Six respondents stressed the need for long-term capital in Canada and five mentioned thin (underdeveloped) capital markets in Canada. The respondents also commented on the importance of the relative size of the two capital markets. Many borrowers have to go to New York because they need more money than can be raised in a single offering in Canada. Canada has developed firms and institutions that are large by any standards, such as Ontario and Quebec Hydro. Canadian investors may not be sufficiently large and plentiful to absorb the large bond issues necessary to finance expansion of these utilities. After all, a prudent investor, be it a bank, an individual or any financial institution will want to diversify its assets. The limit of a borrower in the Canadian capital market—with the exception of the government of Canada—would be $150 million, whereas in New York offerings of $500 million or more are not unusual. One of Dunn's respondents pointed out that in the financing of the Churchill Falls Hydro project, $50 million were raised in Canadian capital markets and $500 million in New York.

According to Dunn, between 1950 and 1977 foreign savings provided 21 percent of the increase in the total Canadian capital stock and 31 percent of the capital stock in the private sector.[7] During the '50s and '60s the dependence on foreign savings actually decreased and in the mid-'70s it increased again. It is possible that this decrease was a temporary aberration, as it was largely caused by massive borrowing on the part of the federal government, borrowing that was necessitated by large new expenditures on social welfare, large investment projects for Ontario and Quebec Hydro and an expansionary fiscal policy.

In evaluating the effect of foreign investment on the Canadian economy, the question usually asked is how Canada would have fared if it had not gained access to foreign capital. What would our growth rate and living standards have been if foreign capital had not been available? The difficulties of measuring the impact of foreign investment on the

Canadian growth rate are immense. For example, it is possible that foreign investment drives out Canadian investment, making the impact very small. It is possible that the presence of foreign investment improves the productivity of Canadian firms by providing competition, and it is possible that the new investment is technologically advanced. It is also possible that foreign investment and ensuing higher wages attract many more immigrants, causing the population growth rate to outstrip the GNP growth rate and thereby lowering living standards.

In general, the effect of foreign investment on economic growth depends on how easily capital is substitutable for labour. If the labour force is growing, and if capital and labour must be used in fixed proportion (the elasticity of substitution is zero), then foreign capital can explain a large proportion of Canadian economic growth. If 20 to 30 percent of total capital has come from abroad, then it may be assumed that 20 to 30 percent of the increase in GNP would have been lost if it had not been for foreign capital. If, however, labour and capital were perfectly substitutable (the elasticity of substitution is infinite), only the marginal product of this capital would be lost, and capital would have no effect on the productivity of labour and land—in which case, Canada would have lost little if there had been no foreign investment. Given that most studies have shown that the elasticity of substitution is less than one, it is likely that the effect of foreign investment on growth has been quite substantial (Dunn 1978).

The studies that have been done in the area give divergent results, partly reflecting the different assumptions used. Powrie (1972), on the assumption of infinite elasticity of substitution, argued that only 0.1 to 0.3 percent of annual growth would have been lost without foreign investment. He revised his study (1977), using an elasticity of substitution equal to one, and again came to the conclusion that foreign capital had contributed only a modest amount to growth (equivalent to 6 months' growth in GNP). An earlier study by Penner (1966) concluded that Canadian GNP would have been reduced by 3.25 percent over the sample period without foreign capital, a loss of $56 per capita. Helliwell and Broadbent (1972) show that if foreign investment had not occurred, real wages would have been 17 percent lower than they were in the early 1970s. Most of these studies perhaps err on the low side as they assume that the foreign technology imported with the foreign investment is no better than Canadian technology.

The effect of foreign investment on domestic investment could be positive if an accelerator mechanism were used: more foreign investment leads to a higher GNP, which in turn leads to more investment (assuming that investment is a function of the change in sales or output in the economy). Van Loo (1977) estimated that the effect of one dollars' worth of direct investment led to $1.40 in total new investment—meaning that the foreign investment had a beneficial effect on domestic investment. However, van Loo's study also shows that foreign direct investment decreased exports (by pushing up Canadian prices), increased imports and decreased Canadian consumption, all of which have additional effects on domestic investment through the accelerator. The total effect of a dollars' increase in foreign investment is therefore reduced to \$.54 — \$.99; that is, some Canadian investment is crowded out.

Other studies in the positive vein show that the presence of foreign ownership in an industry improves the productivity performance of existing firms in the industry (Globerman 1979), and that the tax revenue gained from foreign corporations is between \$2.2 to 3.4 billion annually (Jenkins 1979).

There is some support to the hypothesis that foreign investment attracted more immigrants, reducing the per capita income gains. Helliwell (1974) has shown that immigration is influenced by fiscal policy in the sense that fiscal policy improves economic conditions and immigration responds to the state of the economy. Up to 80 percent of the effects of fiscal policy on unemployment has been offset by immigration. Inflow of immigrants raises the marginal product of capital, which in turn attracts more foreign capital. More capital means a higher marginal product of labour and therefore even more immigrants. Since 1956, 37 percent of the increase in the labour force has come from new immigrants, but the total amount of capital attracted has been less. This means that the capital labour ratio is lower than it would otherwise have been and therefore productivity and wages are lower.

Summary and Conclusions

This chapter provided a review of the Balance of Payments, exchange rates and the conduct of monetary and fiscal policy in an open economy. It also addressed the issue of the "need" for foreign capital to finance the deficit on the current account. The available evidence indicates that the spread between long-term and short-term interest rates is wider in Canada than in the United States. The reasons for this spread·are unclear. One explanation is that Canadians are risk-averse, preferring short-term assets; another is that there is a tremendous demand for long-term capital to finance resource and transportation investments, the result of which is a large supply of long-term assets with resulting low prices and high yields. A third explanation is that Canadian capital markets are not sufficiently large to supply the huge capital requirements for the transportation and energy investments.

There are many divergent views on the costs and benefits of the large amount of foreign capital that has been attracted to Canada. The lack of uniformity of opinion is due to the different assumptions employed in the analysis. The only conclusion that can be drawn is that most studies show that foreign investment has been of some benefit to Canada.

NOTES

1. For an account of the development of the und and the various facilities available, see Tew 1977.
2. This is a traditional argument. Strictly speaking, under a flexible exchange rate, there is no need to finance a deficit. Instead, the exchange rate will drop until the account is in balance.
3. Some economists have argued that the introduction of flexible exchange rates has led to more inflation. Under fixed-exchange rates, monetary authorities had to show restraint out of concern for the Balance of Payments. Under flexible rates, restraint is removed, encouraging the authorities to overexpand the money supply. For a discussion, see Purvis 1977.
4. Carr (*The Financial Post*, 17 Jan. 1981) argues that this is not necessarily true. Capital does not move in response to changes in nominal interest rates, but in response to changes in real interest rates. The real rate is the nominal rate adjusted for inflation.
5. This discussion is from Laidler 1981.
6. For an exposition of this view, see McConnell and Pope 1981, Ch. 43.
7. Dunn (1978:42) arrives at this figure by arguing that the deficit in the current account equals foreign savings. This analysis ignores the effect of retained earnings by foreign corporations. These are usually counted as domestic savings (see Wilkinson 1980:102–23).

BIBLIOGRAPHY

Carr, J.L., G.V. Jump and J.A. Sawyer. "The Operation of the Canadian Economy under Fixed and Flexible Exchange Rates. Simulation Results from the Trade Model." *Canadian Journal of Economics* (IX), 1976, pp. 102–20.
Dunn, Robert M. *The Canada-U.S. Capital Market*. Montreal: C.D. Howe Research Institute, 1978.
Economic Council of Canada. *A Climate of Uncertainty*. Seventeenth Annual Review. Ottawa: Supply and Services, 1980.

Globerman, Steven. *U.S. Ownership of Firms in Canada*. Montreal: C.D. Howe Research Institute, 1979.

Helliwell, John. "Trade, Capital Flows, and Immigration As Channels for the Transmission of Stabilization Policies." In Albert Ando, Richard Herring and Richard Marston (eds.), pp. 241–78, *International Aspects of Stabilization Policies*. Boston: Boston Federal Reserve Bank, 1974.

_____ and Jillian Broadbent. "How Much Does Foreign Capital Matter?" *B.C. Studies*, Spring 1972, pp. 38–42.

Helliwell, John and John V. Lester. "External Linkages of the Canadian Monetary System." *Canadian Journal of Economics* (IX), 1976, pp. 646–67.

Jenkins, Glenn. "Taxes, Tariffs and the Evaluation of the Benefits from Foreign Investment." *The Canadian Journal of Economics* (XII), 1979, pp. 410–26.

Laidler, D. "Inflation and Unemployment in an Open Economy." *Canadian Public Policy* (VII), Special Supplement, 1981, pp. 179–89.

McConnell, C.R. and W.H. Pope. *Economics—Principles, Problems and Policies*. Toronto: McGraw-Hill Ryerson, 1981.

Penner, R. "The Benefits of Foreign Investment in Canada." *Canadian Journal of Economics and Political Science* (XXXII), 1966, pp. 172–83.

Powrie, T.L. "What Does Foreign Capital Add?" *The Canadian Forum*, Jan.–Feb. 1972, pp. 34-7.

_____*The Contribution of Foreign Capital to Canadian Economic Growth*. Edmonton: Hurtig, 1977.

Purvis, Douglas D. "The Exchange Rate Regime and Economic Policy in Theory and in Practice." *Canadian Public Policy* (III), 1977, pp. 205–19.

Tew, Brian. *The Evolution of the International Monetary System 1945–77*. London: Hutchinson, 1977.

Van Loo, Frances. "The Effect of Foreign Direct Investment on Investment in Canada." *The Review of Economics and Statistics* (LIX), 1977, pp. 474–81.

Wilkinson, B.W. *Canada in the Changing World Economy*. Montreal: C.D. Howe Research Institute, 1980.

CHAPTER 14

Canadian Stabilization Policies: Past and Present

The last two chapters reviewed the tools available for stabilization policies in an open economy, operating under either a fixed or flexible exchange rate regime. In this chapter stabilization policies from 1950 to the present are surveyed and assessed. (Table 31, below, shows the movements of the main economic indicators in the postwar period; the statistics indicate that the main objectives of price stability and full employment were seldom achieved.) Particular emphasis is put on the events in the mid−'70s that led to wage and price controls and the adoption of the "gradualist" policy of the Bank of Canada.

The Freeing of the Dollar, 1950−62

Canada had been on a floating exchange rate during much of the interwar period, but like all other countries she reverted to a fixed exchange rate and exchange control during the war.[1] As one of the signatories of the Bretton Woods Agreement, which set out new arrangements for the international monetary system, Canada agreed to keep a fixed rate after the war was over. In 1939, the rate was $0.90 U.S. = $1 Canadian. After the war, after various controls had been lifted, there was a tremendous demand for consumer goods, a demand that had been built up over the war years. In order to contain the inflationary pressure, the currency was appreciated to equal that of the U.S. dollar. The appreciation went too far, with the result that the currency was overvalued. In 1949, following the depreciation of the pound sterling, Canada also depreciated its currency to $0.905 U.S. = $1 Canadian. However, it appears that the authorities again went too far, this time in the opposite direction, for soon after the news spread, capital began flowing into Canada. If a speculator expects a currency to appreciate in value, it is obviously advantageous to shift funds to this currency. This capital inflow created problems for Canadian policy-makers. To stop the rate from appreciating,

TABLE 31
Selected Indicators of the State of the Economy, 1956−80

Year	Change in CPI (%)	Unemployment rate (%)	Growth in GNP (1971 dollars) (%)	Wage increases* (%)	Price of Can. $ in U.S. $
1956	1.4	4.6	8.4	—	1.02
57	3.2	7.0	2.4	—	1.04
58	2.6	6.0	2.3	—	1.03
59	1.1	7.0	3.8	—	1.04
1960	1.2	7.1	2.9	—	1.03
61	0.9	7.1	2.8	—	0.99
62	1.2	5.9	6.8	—	0.94
63	1.8	5.5	5.2	—	0.93
64	1.8	4.7	6.7	—	0.93
65	2.4	3.9	6.7	—	0.93
66	3.7	3.6	6.9	—	0.93
67	3.6	4.1	3.3	8.3	0.93
68	4.0	4.8	5.8	7.9	0.93
69	4.6	4.7	5.3	7.7	0.93
1970	3.3	5.7	2.5	8.6	0.96
71	2.9	6.2	6.9	7.8	0.99
72	4.8	6.2	6.1	8.8	1.01
73	7.6	5.6	7.5	10.9	1.00
74	10.8	5.4	3.6	14.7	1.02
75	10.8	6.9	1.2	19.2	0.98
76	7.5	7.1	5.4	10.9	1.01
77	8.0	8.1	2.4	7.9	0.94
78	8.9	8.4	3.4	7.1	0.88
79	9.1	7.5	2.7	8.7	0.85
80	10.2	7.5	0.1	11.1	0.86

Source: Department of Finance, *Annual Review,* various issues.
* Wage increases include increases in all industries provided by collective agreements. Figures unavailable for years 1956−66.

the Bank of Canada had to sell Canadian dollars (buy foreign exchange). This led to a build-up of cash reserves in the chartered banks, a build-up which was difficult for the Bank of Canada to neutralize by open-market operations because of the limited size of the market. Open-market operations designed to mop up the excess cash reserves would have driven bond prices down by a wide margin, sending interest rates up, increasing capital inflow and exacerbating the upward pressure on the Canadian dollar. It was decided to float the dollar.

This was a startling decision in view of Canada's commitment to the Bretton Woods Agreement and the newly established International Monetary Fund (IMF). To qualify for membership in the IMF, the member country had to maintain a fixed value on its currency *vis-à-vis* the U.S. dollar. In view of Canada's earlier failure to find the "correct" rate, the decision had been a logical one, but it was met with considerable suspicion among members of the IMF. The issue was whether a floating rate would lead to instability. The experience with floating rates during the turbulent '30s suggested that they would fluctuate greatly. However, sympathetic to Canada's difficulties, the IMF allowed Canada to try a fluctuating rate for a limited time period (Plumptree 1977:137–52).

The experience with the floating rate during the 1950s turned out to be favourable; the rate fluctuated smoothly. The Bank of Canada had three guidelines to follow (Plumptree, p. 146): the exchange rate was to be determined by market demand and supply; the exchange fund should stand ready to buy or sell foreign exchange to maintain an orderly market—with the proviso that intervention should not be directed towards the establishment of a particular rate; the amount of foreign exchange or Canadian dollars which could be used to stabilize the rate was clearly specified. These guidelines were adhered to. The rate appreciated gradually to above par with the U.S. dollar, and on the whole the float was clean.[2]

The latter part of the 1950s was marred by two events: the conversion loan and the Coyne episode. Like other countries, Canada had to finance its war effort by borrowing. In Canada, the bonds sold to the public became known as Victory Bonds. By 1958 half of the country's 12 billion-dollar debt had been retired and the remainder was to mature between 1959 and 1966. This was a problem of great concern to the government, one reason being the need to finance a budgetary deficit of close to $1 billion (Christofides *et al.* 1976:427). The government decided to try to convert all of the outstanding issues at once instead of doing it as each issue matured. Between July and September 1958, in an all-out effort, the government converted 45 percent of the outstanding war debt with an average maturity of eight years to a debt with an average maturity of almost fifteen years. This was a remarkable effort. People were induced to convert their old bonds into new bonds through pure patriotism, through an increase in yields and through cash bonuses amounting to $93,862,500. Bond prices were supported at least during 1958, but declined subsequently (Christofides *et al.* 1976:427–28).

The effects of the conversion loan were many. It decreased the liquidity of the public by changing the debt balance from long-term to short-term securities, and drove down bond prices which led to higher interest rates.[3] Higher interest rates and reduced liquidity in a period of high unemployment and little inflation imposed a severe cost on the economy. Christofides *et al.* (1976) estimated the cost to the economy at 1 percent of GNP, caused mainly by the adverse effects of high interest rates on investments. In retrospect, it would probably have been better if the government had adopted a step-by-step approach and issued bonds, the revenue from which could have been used to finance budgetary deficits and the retirement of the debt as it matured.

Also problematic to the government and the economy were the actions of the governor of the Bank of Canada, Mr. J. Coyne. Coyne felt strongly that the main problems facing the economy were inflation and the deficit on the current account.[4] Again, in retrospect, it is usually contended that the problem was one of unemployment, not inflation. With Coyne's diagnosis of the problem, a tight money policy (high interest rate policy) was followed, adding to the problems caused by the conversion loan. Of course, a tight money policy under a fluctuating exchange rate can by itself create a current-account deficit, as it tends to appreciate the exchange rate. Coyne made speech after speech during the years 1959–61 about the dangers of inflation and the need for a tight money policy. He also lambasted the government for being spendthrift, statements which did not endear him to government officials.

Pressures were building up on the government to ease monetary policies and thereby to force the value of the dollar down. Minister of Finance Donald Fleming maintained that he could do nothing, since the governor of the Bank of Canada was independent of the government. In the end, however, Coyne was forced to resign. The new governor, Louis Rasminsky, laid down two principles to clarify once and for all the relationships between the government and the Bank of Canada: (1) in the ordinary course of events, the bank has the responsibility for monetary policy, and (2) if the government disapproves of the monetary policy being carried out by the bank, it has the right and the responsibility to direct the bank regarding the policy which the bank is to carry out.

The Period of a Fixed Rate, 1962–70

Unemployment had by this time increased to an intolerable level—the rate was 7.5 percent in the first months of 1961. The reason for the high rate was seen to lie in the high value of the dollar. There were pressures for increased protection and support for Canadian industries. In 1961, Fleming announced that the government would intervene by using the exchange fund to drive the value of the dollar down to a more appropriate level (Officer and Smith 1974:17–20). The government therefore abandoned its policy of a "clean" float. The announcement led to an immediate drop in the dollar, as speculators withdrew their funds from the Canadian markets in expectation of a depreciation. By February 1962 the rate had moved to a discount of 5 percent to the dollar (so far with no interference by the Bank of Canada), and the market was relatively calm. In April a general election was called and when the bounteous promises of large new public spending programs led to a run on the dollar of crisis proportions, the government decided that the only course of action to restore stability was to peg the rate at $0.925 U.S. = $1 Canadian. This was low, considering that the common rate during the early part of the year was 95 cents U.S. to the dollar.

The government was hoping that it had gone far enough to restore confidence in the exchange markets. This was not the case. The return of a minority Conservative government did not bolster confidence in the exchange markets. Then the new government introduced an emergency package containing tariff surcharges to reduce imports, measures to bolster currency reserves through borrowing from the IMF, swap arrangements with the United States and England, and measures by the Bank of Canada to bolster interest rates. These support measures allayed the fears of the international community, and stability returned.

The remaining years of the 1960s were characterized by rapid growth, high employment and relatively mild inflation. They were the golden years. Between 1961 and 1965, real GNP grew at an average yearly rate of 6.4 percent, the consumer price index rose at an average rate of 1.8 percent and unemployment decreased to 4 percent in 1964. Monetary and fiscal policies were coordinated and became mildly expansionary.

While expansion continued throughout the '60s, inflationary pressures increased towards the end of the decade, with the consumer price index increasing at an average annual rate of 4.6 percent. The Bank of Canada became concerned with inflationary pressures and tried to tighten monetary policies. However, the bank had difficulty in implementing a strict policy, partly because of the fixed exchange-rate regime, and partly because of developments in the United States.

In the early 1960s the United States faced an increasingly severe Balance of Payments problem, with a resultant weakening in the state of the U.S. dollar (Officer and Smith 1974:20–22). As part of a package of measures to correct the situation, the U.S. government imposed an Interest Equalization Tax in 1963 to discourage capital outflows from the United States. As explained in the previous chapter, a capital outflow is recorded as a payment on the capital account, and an inflow as a receipt. When a Canadian province borrows money in New York, it is a capital outflow for the United States and a capital inflow for Canada. Interests on long-term capital are usually lower in the United States than in Canada (see Chapter 13), making it cheaper—assuming there are no exchange risks—to borrow in the United States than in Canada. The Interest Equalization Tax was designed to obliterate any interest differentials and therefore to discourage foreign borrowing in the United States.

The stability of the Canadian dollar and, to some extent, the stability of the Canadian capital markets depended on the U.S. bond markets. This measure was therefore thought to have considerable impact on Canada—as indeed it did. The share prices plunged and outflow of dollars from Canada reached massive proportions as speculators expected a devaluation in the dollar. Canada therefore tried to get an exemption from the tax. This was granted, but the exemption had conditions attached to it, the main one being that Canada would not permit its foreign exchange reserves to rise above the existing level at that time. This meant that Canada faced severe restrictions on monetary policy: it could not accumulate large Balance of Payments deficits because currency reserves would then be rapidly depleted; nor could the exchange-fund account accumulate large surpluses because of this commitment. Both restrictions meant that when inflationary pressures were building up during the late '60s, the Bank of Canada was powerless. If the bank tightened up the money supply, interest rates in Canada would rise, which would encourage capital inflow into Canada and put pressure on the exchange rate to appreciate. To stop the exchange rate from appreciating, the bank would have to buy U.S. dollars (and sell Canadian) and this would mean that its reserves of U.S. dollars would increase.

The problems with monetary policy were exacerbated by fiscal policy. The 1965 budget included a reduction in federal taxes, even though there were few signs of an impending recession. By 1967 it was clear that a recession was not forthcoming and inflation was getting worse. Further attempts were made to tighten monetary policy while fiscal policy was essentially neutral. In 1968, the United States agreed to remove the reserve ceiling, and this meant that Canadian monetary policy could become more restrictive. The Canadian government, following the election of 1968, introduced voluntary wage and price restraint and established the Prices and Incomes Commission a year later. Fiscal policy was tightened by means of a budgetary surplus. However, by this time the government had a recession on its hands, and unemployment had risen to 6 percent.

The Floating of the Dollar in 1970

In 1970, pressures were building up on the Canadian dollar, not because its value was too high, but rather because its value was too low. The Balance of Payments was in surplus to the tune of over $1 billion (see Table 28). There were several reasons for this surplus.

The agreement under the autopact (discussed in Chapter 6) was extremely favourable for Canada at this time, because the car models made in Canada under the agreement were in great demand. In addition, the anti-inflationary policies of the Bank of Canada led to high interest rates and therefore a substantial capital inflow. During the first few months of 1970, Canadian reserves had increased by $1.2 billion U.S. (Plumptree 1976:220). The Bank of Canada had to stop the dollar from rising by buying foreign exchange. This was an inflationary measure, forcing the cash reserves of the chartered banks to increase, resulting in monetary expansion. On 31 May the government announced it was no longer prepared to defend the Canadian dollar, and the dollar was returned to a float. (Compare the course of events to those of 1950.) By year's end the currency had risen from 92.5 cents to 99 cents U.S.

The appreciation of the exchange rate alleviated some of the inflationary pressures. Inflation actually decreased in 1970 and 1971. However, unemployment was increasing and there were real fears that further increases in the value of the exchange rate would make this situation worse. For this reason, the dollar was not given a clean float. The Bank of Canada intervened actively to stop the dollar from rising and kept interest rates low to discourage capital inflows. Between 31 May 1970 and July 1972, net purchases of foreign exchange reached $2 billion. In short, monetary policy was excessively expansive. Courchene maintained that the change from a tight policy to an easy money policy was very abrupt (1976:166–67).

Intervention to stabilize the dollar increased the cash requirements of the federal government, resulting in an increase in the federal deficit. This deficit had to be financed either by borrowing from the general public or from the chartered banks. Selling bonds was out of the question, as such a measure would have led to low bond prices, higher interest rates and capital inflows, and further pressure on the dollar to appreciate. The government therefore opted for borrowing from the chartered banks, which increased the liquid asset ratio of the chartered banks to a potentially inflationary level (liquid assets above the required reserve ratios could be sold, resulting in higher cash reserves and therefore increased monetary expansion). Monetary expansion in 1971 was excessive by any measure (see figures on M1 and M2 in Table 32, below), and 1972 continued in the same vein, but with increasing unemployment and increasing inflation. The increasing unemployment rate provided the necessary justification for continuing high monetary expansion and a stimulative fiscal policy in the form of a cut in corporate taxes.

There are several reasons why the unemployment rate started to climb. First, the labour force had expanded greatly, with adult products of the "baby boom" years becoming of working age, along with increased participation rates for women. Second, there was the introduction of more liberalized unemployment insurance in 1971, which, as studies have shown, had a measurable impact on the unemployment rate (see Chapter 12).

The year 1973 witnessed the beginning of the energy crisis, escalating food costs, and other events. The unemployment rate dropped and real GNP grew rapidly. Inflation was accelerating—not a surprising feat in view of the excessive monetary expansion in previous years. The federal government was still concerned about the high unemployment rate. It cut personal taxes by 5 percent to stimulate spending and indexed personal income taxes—a measure the government has since regretted. The Bank of Canada realized that monetary policy had been excessively lax and announced its intention of tightening up the reins gradually. Short-term interest rates rose, but not sufficiently in view of the escalation in the inflation rate. The real cost of credit actually fell (Courchene 1976:201).

In 1974 everything came to a head. Unemployment dropped, but inflation soared to record-high levels. The economy started to slow down, with growth in real GNP down to 3.6 percent from a high of 7.5 percent in 1973. The world economy and the Canadian economy were bracing themselves for a downturn. In order to protect the Canadian economy from the impact of the expected recession, the government again made fiscal policy stimulative with further tax cuts. The earlier tax cut of 5 percent was increased to 8 percent, and interest income was made deductible up to a maximum of $1,000. The latter was a move to encourage people to invest in Canada Savings Bonds. Sales taxes were eliminated on clothing, footwear, transportation, construction and water distribution equipment, and were reduced on building materials.

The stated policy of the Bank of Canada was again restraint, but the data show differently. During 1974, the money supply recorded its highest quarterly growth rate since 1970. Towards the end of 1974, when it became certain that the economy was headed for a serious recession, the bank decided to ease monetary policy. The housing sector went wild, with Canadians scrambling to find a hedge against inflation. Wages started to escalate. Labour contracts were negotiated for a shorter time period (the average duration was 22 months, compared with 26 months between 1970 and 1973) (Courchene 1976), and the proportion of contracts containing cost-of-living clauses increased significantly.

In 1975, Canada entered a recession—from which the expansionary policies had cushioned her previously. If the inflation of 1973 and 1974 had not been accommodated by increases in the money supply, an increase in unemployment would have occurred sooner. Higher prices mean that more money is needed. If more money is not forthcoming, then business and households will have difficulty financing purchases and economic activity will suffer.

Wage and Price Controls, 1975–78

The Department of Finance believed that inflation was going to be short-lived, and that it was caused by the increased price of oil, raw materials and food. The government was therefore vehemently opposed to the imposition of wage and price controls in its election campaign of 1974 and mocked the Conservatives for introducing such a preposterous idea into the campaign. However, once re-elected, the government tried to develop a voluntary restraint program among major business leaders and the Canadian Labour Congress. As with most efforts in voluntarism, this one failed miserably.

In the summer of 1975 the government became concerned about wage settlements, which in some areas had become spectacular as unions tried to catch up with inflation, particularly in the public sector. B.C. supermarket employees demanded an increase of 76 percent, letter carriers 47 percent and teachers in Metropolitan Toronto 44 percent (Maslove and Swimmer 1980:8). The government felt that these gains might jeopardize economic recovery and a decrease in inflation rates, both of which were thought to be just around the corner. The government also believed that traditional fiscal restraint policies were no longer adequate because the lags were seen to be too long and because expensive new social programs had left little room for expenditure cuts. In addition, the major automatic stabilizer—progressive income taxes—had been taken out of commission because of indexation. Restrictive anti-inflationary policies were not popular with the political strategists. They felt that the anti-inflationary policies of 1969−71, which resulted in substantial increases in the unemployment rate, had been partly to blame for the Liberal government's near defeat in the 1972 election.

The government came under strong pressure to do something about inflation. The resignation of John Turner as Minister of Finance made the public feel that the government was helpless. At a cabinet meeting in September 1975, the following options were considered: (a) to do nothing, since it seemed likely that the worst was over; (b) to impose excess profits taxes or excess income taxes; or (c) to impose wage and price controls (Maslove and Swimmer 1980:12). The first option was rejected on political grounds, the second on administrative grounds. The Department of Finance felt that it would be next to impossible to identify what constituted excess income.

On Thanksgiving Monday, Prime Minister Trudeau appeared on television to announce a new package of anti-inflationary measures.[5] The package contained 4 major thrusts:
1. Fiscal and monetary policies designed to increase total demand and production at a rate consistent with a declining rate of inflation;
2. Government expenditure policies designed to limit the growth in public expenditures and the rate of increase in public service employment;
3. Structural policies designed to deal with particular sectors (agricul-

ture, energy and housing), including policies to increase the supply of housing and to protect farmers;
4. A prices and incomes policy.

The first two sets of policies included substantial restraints on the expansion of the public service and a previously announced new approach to monetary policy wherein the Bank of Canada would attempt to control the money supply and allow it to expand at a rate consistent with the real rate of growth in the economy.

The government's main concern was with wages in the public sector, but obviously other wages had to be controlled as well. Price controls were thrown in as a gesture to placate the unions (Maslove and Swimmer 1980:32). The basic thrust of the program was voluntary compliance, but there was statutory enforcement for certain key groups: firms that employed more than 500 employees; firms whose workers bargained jointly with workers in other firms; federal, provincial and municipal governments. Included were employees of all these groups, as well as all professionals.

The controls were intended for a three-year period. The wage guidelines had three components: (a) a basic protection factor set at 8 percent for the first year of the program, 6 percent the second year and 4 percent for the third year; (b) a productivity allowance of 2 percent; and (c) a catching-up allowance of plus or minus two percent. If a union had in previous years achieved a salary gain of less than the national average, it could get an additional 2 percent; if the salary increase was more than the national average, it would get a reduction. Therefore, in the first year of controls, employees could get an 8 to 12 percent increase depending on how they had fared in previous years. The maximum was set at $2,400.

Price increases were limited to cost increases, except for prices on farm and fish products which were exempt. For firms that could not allocate costs directly, the pre-tax net profit margin was not to exceed 95 percent of its average pre-tax net profit margin in the last five fiscal years. Some exceptions were allowed. These included cases where an employer was unable to attract or keep workers at existing rates, or where a longstanding relationship had existed between wages in closely related groups. An increase could also exceed the guidelines if a cost increase had been incurred because of an increase in the cost of improved health and safety conditions, elimination of restrictive practices and discrimination, and anomalies in pension funds.

The controls were to be administered by three agencies: the Anti-Inflation Board, which was to monitor adherence to the guidelines; the administrator, who was to investigate and enforce compliance; and the tribunal, which was to hear appeals from the rulings.

The interesting aspect of the Canadian controls program, compared with similar programs in other countries, was that it did not contain an immediate wage freeze, nor did it include all sectors of the economy. An additional feature was that the controls were very flexible—exemptions could be granted. Apparently, the Department of Finance wanted both a freeze and a policy of no exemptions, but any policy of comprehensive, inflexible controls was strongly opposed by the prime minister (Maslove and Swimmer 1980:29−30). The prime minister wanted minimum coercion. An additional explanation was that several officials subscribed to the Galbraithian view that the economy contained two sectors: one monopolistic, dominated by large corporations and large unions, and one competitive. As long as the monopolistic sector was controlled, the competitive sector would control itself.

The decision not to include a freeze was made partly on political grounds, partly on administrative grounds. The political reasons included a desire to differentiate the program from that proposed by the Conservatives in the election campaign. The administrative reasons included the difficulty of imposing a freeze in view of the fact that many collective agreements included automatic increases during the period of the proposed freeze; any attempt to stop these increases were thought to be unacceptable by organized labour. A comprehensive wage and price freeze was thought to be inconsistent with a selective program and would require a vast bureaucracy.

In retrospect, it seems as if the government panicked or was forced into a controls program by political pressure, for inflation seemed to be abating at the time. In addition, constitutionally, the government was allowed to impose controls only in the event of a national emergency.[6] The state of the economy was not a national emergency.

In 1976, inflation did abate, largely because of the decline in food prices. Between October 1975 and October 1976, they declined by 0.9 percent (Reid 1980:295). However, food prices were exempt from controls and were not therefore an indicator of how well the controls were working. In 1977 and 1978, inflation increased again, but did not reach double-digit levels. Wage settlements became more moderate. Unemployment, however, rose. A cursory examination of Table 31, above, indicates that controls had a moderating effect on wages, and also on prices, facts which are borne out by econometric studies. Reid (1979) estimated that wage increases in manufacturing were 4.5 percent lower during the control period than they would have been in the absence of controls. Auld, et al. (1979) found that prior to any rollback of wages by the Anti-Inflation Board, at the end of the three-year period, wage increases were 3.2 percent lower in the private and 4.6 percent lower in the public sector than they would have been otherwise. The profit controls had no discernible effect on prices, but the wage controls did, in the sense that most firms use costs plus a markup type of pricing scheme.

This means that if costs are restrained, so are prices. It is also noteworthy that wages did not skyrocket following the dismantling of controls.

Monetarism and the Bank of Canada

In September 1975, about a month before wage and price controls were announced, the Bank of Canada adopted new targets for monetary policy. No longer would the prime target for monetary policy be credit conditions, but rather the rate of monetary growth. Bank of Canada policy had traditionally attempted to control the cost of credit and the availability of credit. The cost of credit was monitored through interest rates and the availability of credit through an indicator called the Canadian Liquid Asset Ratio, which should not be confused with the Secondary Reserve Ratio. The Secondary Reserve Ratio is a legal requirement the banks have to meet involving the ratio of liquid assets (treasury bills, day loans to investment dealers and cash reserves above the required primary reserve ratio) to total deposit liabilities. The Canadian Liquid Asset Ratio is the ratio of liquid assets (including total cash reserves) to total assets (total assets are the sum of liquid assets, less liquid assets such as loans, mortgages and non-government securities). The higher the Canadian Liquid Asset Ratio, the larger the potential for expanding credit. If the ratio is very low, the banks have to ration credit regardless of interest rates. The market was regarded as sufficiently imperfect for interest rates to be a less-than-adequate indicator of credit conditions.

The new policy, the strategy of gradualism, called for a gradual decrease in the money supply to combat inflation, that is, monitoring the actual money supply rather than credit conditions. The new policy included a target range set for each year for the expansion of the money supply. In November 1975, the target range was set at 10 to 14 percent, in August 1976 at 8 to 12 percent, in October 1977 at 7 to 11 percent, and in September 1978 at 6 to 10 percent. The Bank of Canada's new policy gave the impression that the bank had adopted pure Friedmanesque policy—to increase the money supply at a yearly rate consistent with the real growth rate of the economy, and to abandon any real attempts at interventionist monetary policy.

However, there is considerable controversy about the way the Bank of Canada has chosen to implement monetarism.[7] One argument centres on the choice of monetary aggregates. The policy-maker must choose between M1, M1B, M2, or M3, where M1 consists of currency outside banks and demand deposits, where M1B is M1 plus chequable personal savings and chequable nonpersonal notice deposits, where M2 equals M1B plus nonchequable savings and notice deposits and fixed-term personal savings deposits, and where M3 is M2 with the addition of nonpersonal term deposits and foreign currency deposits of Canadian residents. The Bank of Canada chose M1 because in its view, M1 was the most easily controllable monetary aggregate. Critics feel that a broader measure should have been adopted (Courchene 1977, 1979).

The other aspect of the Bank of Canada's new policy which has come under severe criticism is the choice of instrument. The bank has chosen to control M1 via short-term interest rates. If M1 grows at a rate higher than the target range, then interest rates will be raised; if it grows below, interest rates will be lowered. The choice of interest rates as the instrument really precludes any other target than M1. Interest rates cannot be used to control M2, as the bank cannot control the relevant rates in this area. Given that interest rates are the instrument, one could perhaps question if the bank has turned monetarist at all, particularly since the bank takes monetary growth as an indicator of nominal income growth—therefore not a target in itself. Monetarists, such as Tom Courchene, argue that instead of trying to regulate the demand for money through interest rates, the bank should control the supply of money which, in their opinion, is far more stable. Supply control could be achieved through monetary base control, that is, through some variation of control of the growth of cash reserves (Courchene 1977, 1979).

Table 32 (below) shows that the Bank of Canada has been successful in bringing down the growth rate of M1 (the figure for 1978 is distorted by a postal strike, which increased the demand for money). The important question, however, is whether the policy was effective in bringing down inflation.

The Post-Control Period

Inflation during the post-control period has become gradually worse (see Table 31, above). There are several factors behind this. The drop in inflation after controls were set was largely caused by levelling off in food prices. But in 1977 and 1978, food prices started to escalate again, and the Canadian dollar depreciated in value, making imports more expensive. The economy also moved closer to capacity. Canadian energy prices gradually increased toward world levels. Canada had benefitted greatly from the world commodity boom during the early '70s, but commodity markets weakened in the mid-'70s and there was less oil and gas available for export than expected. Productivity also slowed down, some of which can be attributed to lagging investments.

In 1980, the economy experienced substantial growth, partly because of a good trade performance and strong investments in plant and machinery. Inflation was, however, accelerating, again partly because of higher food prices, to which poor harvests were a contributing factor. Higher energy prices also led to increases in the consumer price index. Productivity growth lagged even further, resulting in a GNP growth rate of only 0.1 percent.

TABLE 32
Growth Rates of Monetary Aggregates, 1969–80

Year	M_1	M_2
1968	4.4	—
1969	7.2	10.4
1970	2.2	6.8
1971	12.7	12.4
1972	14.3	10.6
1973	14.5	14.2
1974	9.6	20.1
1975	13.6	15.0
1976	8.1	12.6
1977	8.3	14.0
1978	10.1	10.7
1979	7.3	15.8
1980	6.4	18.1

Source: Department of Finance, *Annual Review*, 1981.

During 1978 and 1979 fiscal policy was stimulative: investment tax credits were given and reductions in the federal sales tax were made. Given that there appears to have been capacity constraints in some sectors, these measures were probably a mistake.

Late in 1979, interest rates were being pushed up in the United States because of inflation and a more restrictive monetary policy. The Bank of Canada followed suit and Canadian interest rates climbed to record-high levels. The bank felt that Canadian rates had to follow U.S. rates to prevent further depreciation of the dollar, which result was regarded as highly inflationary. In 1980, the monetarist policies of the Federal Reserve Board in the United States led to extremely volatile interest rates.[8] The prime lending rate in the United States moved from 15.25 percent at the beginning of the year to 20 percent in April, to 11 percent in August and 21.5 percent in December (Bank of Canada, 1981). This volatility led to difficulties for the Bank of Canada. In trying to moderate these trends, the Bank had to allow the exchange rate to drop to a low of 0.8249 in December, and interest rates followed in a dampened fashion. In order to make interest rate adjustments easier, the Bank of Canada introduced a floating bank rate in March 1980 by which the bank rate each week was set at ¼ percent above the average established in the weekly tender for 91-day treasury bills issued by the Government of Canada.

The immediate prospects for curing inflation seem dim. The gradualism introduced by the Bank of Canada appears to have been too gradual to wind down the inflation rate. Any gains have probably been swamped by price shocks in the food and energy sectors. An additional factor is ineffetive fiscal policy. Lipsey[9] contends that the Bank of Canada has had to shoulder an unfair burden, as the bank alone has had to conduct the fight against inflation. Indeed, fiscal policy in the last few years has been stimulative on a cyclically adjusted basis. Of course, given the large proportion of transfers in federal government expenditures, fiscal restraint has been a difficult route to rollow. The National Energy Policy and the new energy accord with Alberta will make it possible for the federal government to reduce its deficit and retire some of the debt. This in turn should increase bond prices and therefore reduce interest rates. Whether the government will use revenue for this purpose is perhaps open to doubt.

Summary and Conclusions

This chapter surveyed stabilization policies since the 1950s. Apart from a brief period in the 1960s, the economy seldom achieved internal and external balance. Fiscal and monetary policies were uncoordinated in many instances, and monetary policy was mostly aimed at maintaining stability in the exchange rate. One could question if Canada has maintained a flexible exchange rate at all in recent years. If this monetary policy continues, the Canadian inflation rate will remain tied to the U.S. inflation rate.

The immediate prospects of reducing inflation and unemployment seem dim. The high interest rates and restrictive monetary policies may well have moderated inflation, but the cost in terms of unemployment appears very high. Perhaps the current monetary restraint should be combined with more active supply-side policies. Appropriate supply-side policies do not necessarily include tax cuts, but may include policies to remove rigidities in labour and capital markets; policies to improve manpower training in areas where there are skill shortages; and policies to reduce restrictive business practices, promote competition and improve productivity in industry. Indeed, the first part of the book pointed out many of the areas where considerable improvements in efficiency could be made.

NOTES

1. The events of the '40s and the '50s are surveyed in Officer and Smith 1970:8−40.
2. For an account, see Wonnacott 1965.
3. Whether it led to higher interest rates is a contentious issue (see

Pesando 1975 and Christofides *et al*. 1976). However, simulations on the RDX econometric model seem to indicate that it did (Christofides *et al*. 1976).

4. For the events which finally led to the resignation of Mr. Coyne, see Plumptree 1977:162−65.
5. For a summary of the package, see Government of Canada (1975).
6. The constitutionality was actually challenged in the Supreme Court of Canada. (See Maslove and Swimmer, pp. 42−4 and Lipsey's brief to the Supreme Court, an abridged version of which is reprinted in Reuber 1980).
7. For a critical analysis, see Courchene 1977, 1979, and Fortin 1979.
8. This is to be expected under a monetarist policy. Either interest rates are controlled, with the amount of money being variable, or the amount of money is controlled, in which case interest rates must be allowed to fluctuate.
9. "Bouey needs help, not disarming." In *The Financial Post*, 20 June 1981.

BIBLIOGRAPHY

Auld, D.A.L., L.N. Christofides, R. Swidinsky, and D.A. Wilton. "The Impact of the Anti-Inflation Board on Negotiated Wage Settlements." *Canadian Journal of Economics* (XII), 1979, pp. 195−214.

Bank of Canada, *Annual Report, 1980*, 1981.

Christofides, L.N., J.H. Helliwell and J.M. Lester. "The Conversion Loan of 1958: a Simulation Study of its Macroeconomic Consequences." *Canadian Journal of Economics* (IX), 1976, pp. 425−42

Courchene, T.J. *The Strategy of Gradualism. An Analysis of Bank of Canada Policy from Mid-1975 to Mid-1977*. Montreal: C.D. Howe Research Institute, 1977.

―――― *Money, Inflation and the Bank of Canada. An Analysis of Canadian Monetary Policy from 1970 to Early 1975*. Montreal: C.D. Howe Research Institute, 1976.

―――― "On Defining and Controlling Money." *Canadian Journal of Economics* (XII), 1979, pp. 604−15.

Fortin, Pierre. "Monetary Targets and Monetary Policy in Canada." *Canadian Journal of Economics* (XII), 1979, pp. 625−47.

Government of Canada. *Highlights of the Government of Canada's Anti-Inflation Program*. 1975.

Maslove, Allan M. and Gene Swimmer. *Wage Controls in Canada 1975−78: A Study of Public Decision Making*. Montreal: The Institute for Research on Public Policy, 1980.

Officer, L.H. and L.B. Smith. *Canadian Economic Problems and Policies.* Toronto: McGraw-Hill Ryerson, 1970.

_____ *Issues in Canadian Economics.* Toronto: McGraw-Hill Ryerson, 1974.

Pesando, J.E. "The Impact of the Conversion Loan on the Term Structure of Interest Rates in Canada: Some Additional Evidence." *Canadian Journal of Economics* (XIII), 1975, pp. 281–8.

Plumptree, A.F.W. *Three Decades of Decision: Canada and the World Monetary System.* Toronto: McClelland and Stewart, 1977.

Reid, Frank. "The Effect of Controls on the Rate of Wage Change in Canada." *Canadian Journal of Economics* (XII), 1979, pp. 214–28.

_____ "Unemployment and Inflation: An Assessment of Canadian Macroeconomic Policy." *Canadian Public Policy* (VI), 1980, pp. 283–300.

Reuber, G.L. *Canada's Political Economy.* Toronto: McGraw-Hill Ryerson, 1980.

Wonnacott, Paul. *The Canadian Dollar 1948–62.* Toronto: University of Toronto Press, 1965.

Author Index

Subject Index

Thatcherism, 255
Third Law of the Sea Conference, *see*
 industry, fishing
Thomson Newspapers Ltd., *see*
 mergers, cases of
tidal power, 73
Tokyo round, *see* tariffs, negotiations
 of
Toronto city-gate price, *see* natural
 gas prices
trade
 barriers to, 112
 policy, 123–28
Trading with the Enemy Act, *see*
 Legislation
transportation
 Bill C-33, on, 157
 costs and productivity, 111
 costs and regional income, 205
 cross-subsidization in, 156
 investment policies, 157–58, 161
 modes of, 153, 162
 policies, 153
 problems, 158–60, 161–66
 railway, 30, 31, 38. *See also*
  passenger trains.
 regulation of, 153–57
  urban, 160–61
 subsidies, 156, 161–63
 water, 166, 168–74. *See also*
  shipping.
travel
 mode, selection of, 159, 161, 162
 time cost of, 158, 159
trucking, 156, 166, 167
 regulation of, 166, 167
Trudeau, Pierre Elliott, 288, 290
truncation of firms, 118, 131

unemployment
 cyclical, 244
 definition of, 243
 effects of, 3–4
 frictional, 244, 259

insurance, 195, 245, 286
insurance induced, 245, 260
international comparisons of, 4
 measures, 242–46
natural rate of, 249, 259
of women, 259, 260, 286
policies, 259–60
rate, 244
regional disparities in, 203
seasonal, 244
structural, 244, 259
United Nations
 Universal Declaration of Human
  Rights, 184
uranium, 69, 88
 breeder reactor extraction of
  energy from, 69
urban size, 205
user charges
 in medicine, 140, 143
 in transport, 160

voluntary restraint program, 288

wages, minimum, 194, 245
Water Transport Committee, 166,
 173
Watkins Report, 130
wave power, 73
wealth
 distribution of, 188
Western Grain Stabilization Act, *see*
 Legislation
Western Economic Opportunities
 Conference, 157, 167
windmills, *see* energy, wind
working poor, 194
World Energy Conference, 75
World Food Conference, 29
World Food Emergency Fund, 29
Young Canada Works Program, *see*
 employment, programs

Zero-Sum Growth, 12